# Healthy Living Made Easy

**FOREWORD**

We created this cookbook—our first—just for you. These are the dishes that nourish us and inspire us ... the ones we cook again and again. The best part? Every delicious recipe can be cooked in 30 minutes or less using simple, wholesome ingredients, almost all of which you can find at member-only prices right on Thrive Market.

At Thrive Market, our mission is simple: make healthy living easy and affordable for everyone. Think of this cookbook as an extension of that vision. It's tangible proof you don't have to spend a lot of time or money to cook a delicious meal for your family that's also mindful of your diet and values.

The recipes in this book are also a reflection of our community. Some come from our team, but many were shared with us by members like you and others contributed by our longtime friends and partners, thought leaders like Amanda Chantal Bacon (Moon Juice), Mark Sisson (Primal Kitchen), and Melissa Urban (Whole30®).

A heartfelt thank-you to each of them—and to you, too. Thank you for taking your health and that of our planet into your own hands, for choosing to be part of our community, and for supporting Thrive Market's mission to make healthy living accessible to all.

I hope these healthy recipes quickly become as beloved in your home as they have been in ours.

Happy cooking!

*–Nick Green, Thrive Market Co-Founder & CEO*

We dedicate this cookbook to
our incredible member community.

Thank you for supporting our mission of
making healthy living accessible to all.

We wouldn't be here without you.

# Table of Contents

## Partners
Page 06

## Breakfast
Page 14

Granola Jam Bars, pg. 18
Southwest Chorizo Scramble, pg. 20
Superfood Breakfast Cookies, pg. 22
Quinoa Pancakes, pg. 24
Blueberry & Macadamia Smoothie, pg. 26
**Coffee Grown for Good, pg. 28**
Homemade Coconut Granola, pg. 32
Beet-Ginger Smoothie Bowl, pg. 34
Gluten-Free Strawberry Oatmeal Cakes, pg. 36
Peanut Butter Protein Bars, pg. 38

## Lunch
Page 42

Gluten-Free Fish Sticks, pg. 44
Gluten-Free Bánh Mì With Seared Ahi Tuna, pg. 46
Paleo Chicken Nuggets, pg. 48
Chickpea Falafel, pg. 50
Kale Caesar Salad, pg. 52
**Grecian Gold, pg. 54**
Salmon Cakes, pg. 58
Grain-Free Flautas, pg. 60
Green Shakshuka, pg. 62
Buffalo Chicken Salad, pg. 64

## Dinner
Page 68

Paleo Hazelnut-Crusted Halibut, pg. 72
Seafood Scallop Chowder, pg. 74
Chipotle Tofu Tacos, pg. 76
Shrimp & Cauliflower "Grits," pg. 78
Lamb Burgers With Pistachio Pesto, pg. 80
**Returning to Bordeaux, pg. 82**
Roasted Spice-Rubbed Chicken Thighs, pg. 86
Ginger Cod in Lemongrass Coconut Broth, pg. 88
Rainbow Bowl With Sautéed Chicken, pg. 90
Stir-Fry Beef Salad, pg. 91
Pork Chops With Creamy Mushroom Sauce, pg. 92
**Meat Matters, pg. 94**
Baked Meatballs With Fresh Mozzarella, pg. 98
Herbed Sweet & Spicy Salmon, pg. 100
Vegan Roasted Red Pepper Pasta, pg. 102
One-Pot Chile-Ginger Chicken & Rice, pg. 104

## Snacks & Sides
Page 108

Veggie Tots, pg. 110
Grilled Corn With Chipotle-Lime Mayonnaise, pg. 112
4-Ingredient Vegan Coconut Bacon, pg. 114
Creamed Collard Greens, pg. 116
Cumin-Spiced Sweet Potato Chips, pg. 118
Avocado Dip With a Kick, pg. 120
Jicama, Apple & Pear Slaw, pg. 122
Grilled Romaine Salad With Avocado-Lime Dressing, pg. 124
Salt & Vinegar Brussels Sprouts Chips, pg. 126
Cauliflower Mash, pg. 128

## Dessert
Page 132

Grilled Peaches With Yogurt & Granola, pg. 134
Vegan Olive Oil Skillet Brownies, pg. 136
Very Berry Cobbler, pg. 138
Chocolate, Almond Butter & Jam Cracker Sandwiches, pg. 140
Sea Salt Caramel Brittle, pg. 142
Keto Pumpkin Spice Donuts, pg. 144
Boozy Toasted Marshmallow Milkshake, pg. 146
Keto Collagen Brownie Bombs, pg. 148
Hazelnut Chocolate Chunk Cookies, pg. 150
Peppermint Chocolate Macaroons, pg. 152

## Drinks
Page 154

Superfood Vanilla Latte, pg. 158
Vegan Lemon Moringa Latte, pg. 159
Golden Milk Latte, pg. 159
Grapefruit & Sage Sparkling Cocktail, pg. 160
Elderberry Fizz, pg. 160
Blood Orange Spritz, pg. 161
Moon Juice Morning Tonic, pg. 163
Wellness Shot, pg. 163
Triple Citrus Whiskey Cocktail, pg. 164
Superfood Sunrise, pg. 165
Crimson Spritz, pg. 165

## Index
Page 168

**Gluten-free? Have a nut allergy?
Use these icons to find recipes that fit your lifestyle.**

Visit ThriveMarket.com to explore 90+ values and shop the healthy products that work for you.

 Gluten-Free
 Grain-Free
 Dairy-Free
 Vegan
 Egg-Free
 Nut-Free

# Our Partners in Healthy Living

**Amanda Chantal Bacon (@amandachantalbacon)** is the Founder of Moon Juice, a wellness brand rooted in adaptogens and the wisdom of alternative medicine. Over 10 years, the brand's supplements and clean beauty products have attracted a cult following.

**Thomas & Amber DeLauer (@thomasdelauer & @amberdelauer)** are authors and keto influencers who reside in the central coast of California. Thomas runs a nutrition and business-performance coaching business; Amber is a blogger and mom.

**Rachael DeVaux (@rachaelsgoodeats)** is a registered dietitian, personal trainer, and food blogger with a passion for travel. She is based in Seattle.

**Dr. Mark Hyman (@drmarkhyman)** is a physician and advocate for using food as medicine. A 14-time *New York Times* bestselling author, he focuses on cooking with real food and regenerative farming.

**Dr. Mikhail Varshavski D.O. (@doctor.mike)**, also known as Doctor Mike, is a board-certified family medicine physician, media personality, educator, and dog dad. Through his TV appearances and successful YouTube channel, he combats misinformation and promotes balanced nutrition.

**Chris Kresser (@chriskresser)** is a functional medicine clinician, an educator, and the bestselling author of *The Paleo Cure*. Having overcome chronic illness with ancestral nutrition, he now helps others optimize their health by eating right.

**Megan Mitchell (@chefmeganmitch)** is an LA-based chef and food stylist focusing on healthy, approachable, and delicious cooking. She's also the host of Thrive Market's *Prep School* series.

**Jeannette Ogden (@shutthekaleup)** is the influencer behind shutthekaleup, a food and lifestyle blog. A proud California native, she advocates for balanced, real-food eating and body positivity.

**Bobby Parrish (@flavcity)** is the host of the popular YouTube channel and blog FlavCity. His daily recipes include lots of keto-friendly and gluten-free options.

**Pamela Salzman (@pamelasalzman)** is a SoCal-based cooking instructor and cookbook author. Her recipes feature comfort foods made from minimally processed ingredients and meals that come together in minutes.

**Caitlin Shoemaker (@frommybowl)** is a Washington-based yoga instructor and the blogger behind From My Bowl. She creates plant-based recipes with easy-to-find, affordable ingredients that pack a flavorful punch.

**Wes Shoemaker (@highfalutinlowcarb)** is the host behind the YouTube series Highfalutin' Low Carb, where he tests different keto-friendly recipes on the internet to find the best ones. Based in San Diego, he is also a proud dog dad.

**Mark Sisson (@marksdailyapple)** is the paleo expert, former endurance athlete, and founder of the Primal Blueprint lifestyle behind the popular paleo blog Mark's Daily Apple. He also founded Primal Kitchen, a line of real-food condiments, sauces, dressings, and more.

**Shawn Stevenson (@shawnmodel)** is a nutritionist and author of the *USA TODAY* bestselling book *Eat Smarter*. After being diagnosed with a spinal condition at age 20, he embraced the power of food to transform his mind and body.

**Melissa Urban (@melissau)** is a bestselling author and the Co-Founder and CEO of Whole30®. In 2009, she began a 30-day self-experiment based on real-food eating, and has since touted its energy-boosting, sleep-improving, craving-busting benefits.

**JJ Virgin (@jj.virgin)** is a *New York Times* bestselling author, a triple board-certified health expert, and a mom of two. She's helped over a million people look and feel their best by eating and exercising smarter.

**Danielle Walker (@daniellewalker)** is a *New York Times* bestselling cookbook author (*Against All Grain, Meals Made Simple, Celebrations*, and *Eat What You Love*), health advocate, wellness expert, and self-trained chef.

**Katie Wells (@wellnessmama)** is the founder of Wellness Mama, a blog and podcast focused on parenting and healthy living. She shares natural health remedies and recipes for meals with simple, minimally processed ingredients.

**Robb Wolf (@dasrobbwolf)** is a bestselling author and former research biochemist. On a mission to help others fight inflammation, he shares tips on paleo, keto, and gluten-free eating.

"You shouldn't have to make a hard decision between the healthy option and the affordable one. Or between the healthy option and the convenient one. Or even the healthy option and the tastiest one! Making the best choice for yourself, your family, and the planet should be easy."

**NICK GREEN**
BUSY FATHER OF TWO,
THRIVE MARKET CO-FOUNDER & CEO

Thrive Market was born and bred in Los Angeles, a city known for healthy living. We want to make it possible for everyone to live their healthiest, happiest life—and to help build a better world in the process, with the highest-quality organic and sustainable products.

From our home to yours, we're so grateful to be able to help you save time, save money, and live your healthiest life.

# Breakfast

**PAGE 18**
Granola Jam Bars

**PAGE 20**
Southwest
Chorizo Scramble

**PAGE 22**
Superfood
Breakfast Cookies

**PAGE 24**
Quinoa Pancakes

**PAGE 26**
Blueberry &
Macadamia Smoothie

**PAGE 32**
Homemade
Coconut Granola

**PAGE 34**
Beet-Ginger
Smoothie Bowl

**PAGE 36**
Gluten-Free Strawberry
Oatmeal Cakes

**PAGE 38**
Peanut Butter
Protein Bars

YIELD 8-10 SERVINGS    ACTIVE TIME 5 MINUTES    TOTAL TIME 30 MINUTES

Good old-fashioned rolled oats are one of the most versatile pantry staples, whether in a hot bowl of morning oatmeal, whizzed in the food processor until they become oat flour, or blended into a smoothie. Now, meet your new favorite way to eat them: these chewy, fruity granola jam bars.

BREAKFAST

# Granola Jam Bars

Dairy-Free    Vegan    Egg-Free

**INGREDIENTS**

Cooking Spray

1 3/4 cups Thrive Market Organic All-Purpose Flour

1 3/4 cups Thrive Market Organic Gluten-Free Rolled Oats

1 cup Thrive Market Organic Walnuts, coarsely chopped

1 cup Thrive Market Organic Coconut Sugar

1/2 teaspoon Thrive Market Organic Ground Nutmeg

1/2 teaspoon kosher salt

1 teaspoon Thrive Market Baking Soda

3/4 cup melted Thrive Market Organic Virgin Coconut Oil

1 1/4 cups Thrive Market Organic Fruit Spread (any flavor you like)

**INSTRUCTIONS**

Preheat oven to 350°F. Spray a 9-inch by 13-inch baking dish with cooking spray. Line the bottom with parchment paper. Spray the parchment paper with cooking spray and set aside.

Whisk flour, oats, walnuts, sugar, nutmeg, salt, and baking soda in a large bowl. Pour in the oil and stir until mixture is coated with all the oil.

Press 3/4 cup of the oat mixture onto the bottom of the baking dish. Spread an even layer of jam on the oat mixture. Sprinkle the remaining crust on top. Bake for 25 to 30 minutes, until the crust is golden brown.

Let cool completely before cutting. Store in an airtight container in the refrigerator for up to 2 weeks.

Scan here to shop the recipe

**YIELD** 2 SERVINGS   **TOTAL TIME** 15 MINUTES

If you've got a few eggs, some tasty toppings, and a single pan, you've got brunch. Give your breakfast a lively southwestern kick from savory chorizo, creamy avocado, and tangy salsa. This simple scramble is courtesy of **Shawn Stevenson**, author and host of The Model Health Show.

**BREAKFAST**

# Southwest Chorizo Scramble

Gluten-Free   Grain-Free   Dairy-Free   Nut-Free

### INGREDIENTS

1/4 pound ground chorizo

4 large eggs, whisked

1/4 teaspoon Thrive Market Organic Turmeric Powder

Sea salt and black pepper, to taste

1/4 cup Thrive Market Organic Salsa

1 large avocado, peeled, pitted, and sliced

### INSTRUCTIONS

Heat a sauté pan over medium heat. Add the chorizo and cook until lightly browned, about 5 minutes.

Add the eggs and turmeric and season lightly with salt and pepper. Scramble the eggs, stirring with a spatula, for about 3 minutes.

Transfer the scramble to plates and top with salsa and avocado slices.

Scan here to shop the recipe

YIELD 18-20 COOKIES    ACTIVE TIME 15 MINUTES    TOTAL TIME 25 MINUTES

Here's a breakfast that will please kids and adults alike. A combination of nuts, seeds, dried fruit, and maple syrup makes these cookies both crunchy and chewy—while packing a nutritional punch that'll last until lunch. Plus, they're just plain fun to eat.

BREAKFAST

# Superfood Breakfast Cookies

Gluten-Free    Grain-Free    Dairy-Free    Vegan    Egg-Free

## INGREDIENTS

1/4 cup Thrive Market Organic Pumpkin Seeds

1/2 cup Thrive Market Organic Walnuts

1/2 cup Thrive Market Organic Raw Cashews

1/4 cup Thrive Market Organic Shredded Coconut, unsweetened

1 cup Thrive Market Organic Coconut Chips

1/2 teaspoon Thrive Market Organic Ground Ginger

1 tablespoon Thrive Market Organic Ground Flaxseed

1/2 teaspoon salt

3/4 cup Thrive Market Organic Raw Almonds, coarsely chopped

3/4 cup mixed dried berries (try Thrive Market Organic Goji Berries, Organic Mulberries, and Organic Seedless Raisins)

3 ripe bananas, mashed

1/4 cup Thrive Market Organic Virgin Coconut Oil, melted

1 tablespoon Thrive Market Organic Maple Syrup

1 teaspoon Thrive Market Organic Vanilla Extract

## INSTRUCTIONS

Preheat oven to 350°F and line a baking sheet with parchment paper. In a blender or food processor, coarsely grind together pumpkin seeds, walnuts, cashews, and shredded coconut.

Pour mixture into a large bowl and mix with coconut chips, ground ginger, ground flaxseed, salt, almonds, and mixed dried berries.

In a small bowl, whisk together the mashed bananas, coconut oil, maple syrup, and vanilla extract. Pour wet ingredients into nut and seed mixture and mix to thoroughly combine.

With a 1 1/2-inch to 2-inch scoop, scoop out batter and place 1 inch apart on baking sheet. Bake for 10 to 15 minutes, rotating the sheet halfway through the baking time.

When cookies are golden brown, remove from oven and let cool before serving.

Scan here to shop the recipe

YIELD 2 SERVINGS    ACTIVE TIME 10 MINUTES    TOTAL TIME 15 MINUTES

A classic diner stack made extra wholesome—that's what this recipe promises. New to quinoa flour? It has a similar look and feel to all-purpose wheat flour, but is naturally gluten-free, and provides both protein and fiber. In this recipe, quinoa flour transforms your go-to morning feast into something unique.

BREAKFAST

# Quinoa Pancakes

Gluten-Free    Dairy-Free

### INGREDIENTS

1/2 cup Thrive Market Organic Quinoa Flour

2 teaspoons Thrive Market Baking Powder

1/2 teaspoon Thrive Market Organic Ground Cinnamon

1/4 teaspoon Thrive Market Organic Ground Nutmeg

1/2 teaspoon sea salt

1 egg

1/4 cup water

2 tablespoons Thrive Market Organic Apple Sauce

2 tablespoons Thrive Market Organic Maple Syrup, plus more for serving

Thrive Market Organic Virgin Coconut Oil, for cooking

1 cup blueberries

### INSTRUCTIONS

In a large bowl, whisk quinoa flour, baking powder, cinnamon, nutmeg, and salt.

In a small bowl, whisk egg, water, apple sauce, and maple syrup.
Fold wet ingredients into dry and stir until just combined. Let the batter sit for 3 to 5 minutes, until it expands slightly.

In a nonstick skillet, melt coconut oil (enough to coat the pan) over medium heat. When the oil is shimmering, add a 1/4-cup scoop of batter and use the bottom of the measuring cup to flatten it. Cook until golden, about 3 to 4 minutes. Flip and cook for another 1 to 2 minutes. Repeat with remaining batter.

In the same skillet, add blueberries and let them blister, about 2 minutes. Serve pancakes stacked on a plate with blueberries spooned on top, plus extra maple syrup as desired.

Scan here to shop the recipe

**YIELD** 1 SERVING    **ACTIVE TIME** 5 MINUTES    **TOTAL TIME** 5 MINUTES

Yes, this smoothie recipe, from author and nutrition expert **Chris Kresser**, contains egg yolk—but don't be alarmed. It imparts supremely creamy texture along with protein and vitamins. Rich coconut milk, juicy blueberries, and buttery macadamia nuts (either soaked in water overnight or in boiling water for 10–20 minutes right before using) are the flavors that really sing.

BREAKFAST

# Blueberry & Macadamia Smoothie

Gluten-Free   Grain-Free   Dairy-Free

**INGREDIENTS**

1 cup blueberries, fresh or frozen

1/2 cup Thrive Market Organic Raw Macadamia Nuts, soaked

1 cup Thrive Market Organic Almond Beverage

1/2 cup Thrive Market Organic Coconut Milk

1 egg yolk

**INSTRUCTIONS**

Place all of the ingredients in a high-speed blender and blend until smooth. If the smoothie is thicker than desired, add an additional splash of almond or coconut milk.

Scan here to shop the recipe

THRIVE MARKET ORGANIC COFFEE
PERU

# Coffee Grown for Good

*Thrive Market sourcing guru (and Chief Merchandising Officer) Jeremiah McElwee tells us about the Peruvian families that grow and harvest Thrive Market Organic Coffee Beans.*

**Tell us about this special coffee program in Peru.** We buy all of our beans directly from a small-scale coffee farming cooperative that grows its beans using sustainable, regenerative agriculture techniques. For example, they grow the coffee plants on the side of a mountain interspersed with all kinds of fruit plants (this is known as intercropping). Additionally, the co-op recaptures its own water to use for farming and uses compost to improve soil quality. The group's regenerative efforts help to pull carbon out of the atmosphere and into the soil, which helps to reverse the effects of climate change.

The farmers, who are second- and third-generation coffee growers, were worried that their children would leave the farming community to seek a better life in big cities like Lima. They didn't believe that there were enough people out there who cared about regenerative agriculture and were willing to pay fair trade prices. When I told them how much our members care about sustainably and ethically sourced products, they were thrilled to be able to work with us. I think it's amazing that our members get to truly make a big difference for this community every time they enjoy Thrive Market Coffee.

**So there's no middle man?** Correct. Typically, big industry players will buy large amounts of coffee beans on the open market. But they won't know exactly where the beans are coming from or how they're grown. They may have a vague idea of the region where the coffee was sourced, but it's typically not from a fair trade cooperative where the crops are organic and regeneratively grown. In such a transaction, there's no transparency and minimal traceability, and there's no way of knowing whether the workers and farmers were paid fairly.

The difference with our coffee is that it's all coming from one source. That way we're able to spend time with the growers in their community. We can see that the quality of the beans is closely monitored. The farmers in the cooperative are experts at growing coffee and they have an amazing facility where they test every single batch for quality and consistency. They reject certain batches if they don't meet the quality standards required to be shipped to America. Our beans go through the same rigorous process at our master roaster, which is also a high-quality, accredited facility.

**How does Thrive Market support the local community in Peru?** Whenever you get involved in single-origin partnerships and you're moving from fair trade to direct trade—meaning you're agreeing to a price based on a fair market value for that region plus a premium so there's a living wage being provided—you're making a huge impact on your partners' lives. We wanted to find a way to partner with the Peruvian coffee co-op that wasn't just transactional and made them feel like they're part of the Thrive Market family.

Our Thrive Gives Mission Leader and I traveled to Peru as a team so we could spend time in the community and better understand their needs. We didn't want to guess what would be most helpful to them; instead, we wanted to spend several days there to have a dialogue and better understand their biggest challenges. We kept hearing from the farmers that they needed more drying modules so that they could process the beans more quickly and could include more local growers in the cooperative.

For us, it was a no-brainer. We helped fund the materials and labor needed to build out 20 more drying modules dispersed throughout the region. By doing this, we knew we'd be helping the community and enabling the cooperative to produce more high-quality beans, which will better serve our members.

Our organic, whole-bean Breakfast Blend is a medium-roast coffee with flavors of dark chocolate, toffee, and caramel. We ethically source the highest quality, single-origin Arabica beans directly from a farming co-op in Peru, then roast them in small batches to ensure maximum flavor.

**YIELD** 2 SERVINGS    **TOTAL TIME** 30 MINUTES

This grain-free and gluten-free take on granola—from nutrition coach, mom of six, and Wellness Mama Founder **Katie Wells**—gets its chewy, crunchy texture from a mix of coconut chips, nuts, and raisins. Bake in the morning and serve warm or let it cool and store in an airtight container so you always have the ultimate yogurt topping on hand.

**BREAKFAST**

# Homemade Coconut Granola

Gluten-Free    Grain-Free    Dairy-Free    Vegan    Egg-Free

**INGREDIENTS**

1/4 cup Thrive Market Organic Virgin Coconut Oil

1/4 cup Thrive Market Organic Maple Syrup or Honey

1 teaspoon Thrive Market Organic Vanilla Extract

2 cups Thrive Market Organic Coconut Chips

1 cup nuts and/or seeds of choice (try a mix of Thrive Market Organic Cashews, Sunflower Seeds, Pumpkin Seeds, and/or Pecans)

Pinch of Thrive Market Organic Ground Cinnamon

1/2 cup mix of dried fruit of choice (try Thrive Market Organic Dried Cranberries and Apricots)

2 tablespoons Thrive Market Organic Black Chia Seeds (optional)

**INSTRUCTIONS**

Preheat oven to 350°F. Melt coconut oil and honey/maple syrup in a small saucepan until it starts to bubble. Swirl in the vanilla.

In a large bowl, mix together the coconut chips, nuts, cinnamon, dried fruit, and chia seeds.

Pour the coconut oil mixture over the dry ingredients and mix well. The consistency will vary some depending on the honey, coconut chips, and coconut oil you use. If there is not enough of the honey mixture to lightly coat all of the ingredients, add slightly more melted coconut oil and honey in equal parts.

Spread mixture on a parchment paper-lined baking dish. Bake for 15 to 20 minutes, until it starts to brown. Remove and let cool, then crumble into pieces. Store in an airtight jar and use within 2 weeks.

*Scan here to shop the recipe*

YIELD 1 SERVING    TOTAL TIME 5 MINUTES

No one will blame you for posting a photo of this meal before eating it. Beets lend their crimson hue to this smoothie bowl, which is then topped with antioxidant-rich raspberries, pomegranate seeds, and cacao nibs to make it the ultimate superfood breakfast.

BREAKFAST

# Beet-Ginger Smoothie Bowl

Gluten-Free    Grain-Free    Dairy-Free    Egg-Free

## INGREDIENTS

**For the Smoothie Bowl**

1 raw or cooked beet, peeled and roughly chopped

1 tablespoon grated ginger

1/4 cup frozen pineapple, cubed

1/4 cup blueberries

1 cup Thrive Market Organic Coconut Water

**For the Topping**

Small handful of raspberries (fresh or frozen)

1/4 cup pomegranate seeds

1 teaspoon bee pollen

2 teaspoons Thrive Market Organic Cacao Nibs

2 teaspoons Thrive Market Organic Black Chia Seeds

## INSTRUCTIONS

Place all of the smoothie ingredients in a high-speed blender and blend until smooth.

Pour smoothie into a bowl and top with raspberries, pomegranate seeds, bee pollen, cacao nibs, and chia seeds.

Scan here to shop the recipe

**YIELD** 6–8 SERVINGS    **ACTIVE TIME** 15 MINUTES    **TOTAL TIME** 25 MINUTES

Cake for breakfast? Yes, please! This kid-friendly recipe is a delightfully gluten-free and vegan start to any morning. Apple sauce, bananas, and maple syrup provide just enough all-natural sweetness. Serve with a schmear of nut butter for a boost of protein and healthy fats.

BREAKFAST

# Gluten-Free Strawberry Oatmeal Cakes

Gluten-Free · Dairy-Free · Vegan · Egg-Free

### INGREDIENTS

**For the Cakes**

3 cups Thrive Market Organic Gluten-Free Rolled Oats

1 tablespoon Thrive Market Baking Powder

1/2 teaspoon sea salt

2 teaspoons Thrive Market Organic Ground Cinnamon

2 flax eggs (see below)

1/4 cup Thrive Market Organic Maple Syrup

2 teaspoons Thrive Market Organic Vanilla Extract

1/2 cup Thrive Market Organic Apple Sauce (unsweetened)

2 ripe bananas

1/2 cup chopped strawberries

**For 1 Flax Egg**

1 tablespoon Thrive Market Organic Ground Flaxseed

3 tablespoons water

### INSTRUCTIONS

First, make 2 flax eggs: In a small bowl, mix together flaxseed meal and water until combined. Let sit for 5 minutes to come together.

While the flax eggs sit, make the cakes: Preheat oven to 375°F.

In a medium bowl, stir together dry ingredients. Add wet ingredients and stir until just combined.

Distribute batter evenly into muffin tin cups and bake for 10 minutes, or until set.

*Scan here to shop the recipe*

**YIELD** 12 BARS   **ACTIVE TIME** 5 MINUTES   **TOTAL TIME** 30 MINUTES

Few ingredients get along as well as peanut butter and chocolate. These DIY protein bars—from **Rachael DeVaux**, registered dietitian and creator of the blog Rachael's Good Eats—taste like cookie dough, but rely on wholesome ingredients like honey and PB to achieve that craveable flavor and texture.

BREAKFAST

# Peanut Butter Protein Bars

Gluten-Free   Grain-Free   Dairy-Free   Egg-Free

## INGREDIENTS

1 1/2 cups Thrive Market Almond Flour

1/2 cup vanilla or unflavored protein powder of choice (try Thrive Market Organic Plant Protein in Vanilla)

3/4 cup Thrive Market Organic Peanut Butter, Creamy

5 tablespoons Thrive Market Organic Honey

3 tablespoons Thrive Market Organic Almond Beverage

1/3 cup Thrive Market Organic Dark Chocolate Chips, plus extra for topping

Pinch sea salt

## INSTRUCTIONS

Line an 8x8 inch baking dish with parchment paper.

Combine almond flour and protein powder in a large bowl. Stir in the peanut butter, honey, and almond milk. Mix in the chocolate chips and sea salt.

Pour batter into the prepared baking dish and flatten with a spatula. Sprinkle with additional chocolate chips.

Transfer baking dish to the freezer for 25 minutes. Once set, remove from the freezer and slice into 12 bars. Store bars in the refrigerator in an airtight container.

*Scan here to shop the recipe*

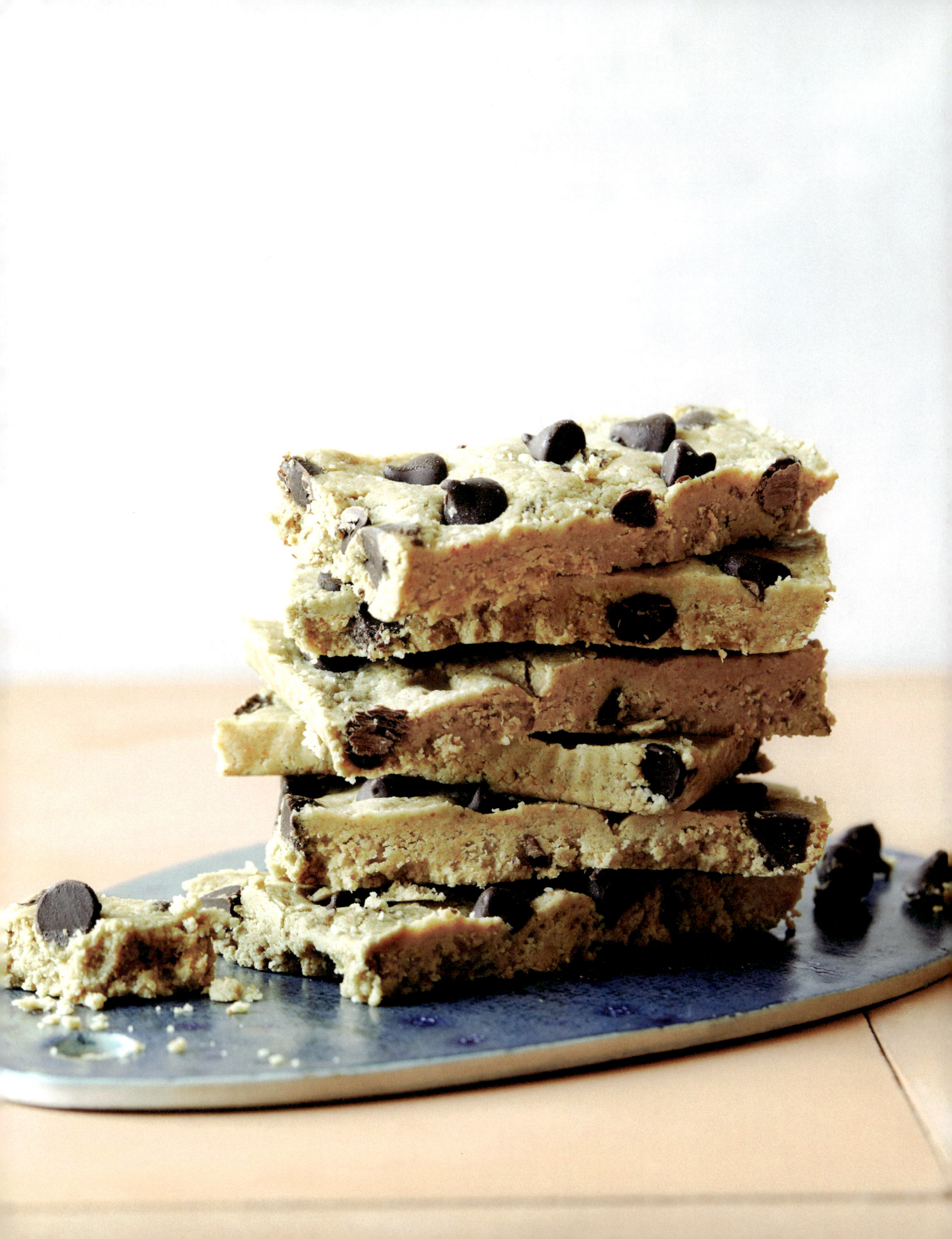

The coconuts we use to make our Organic Regeneratively Grown Coconut Oil are farmed in Sri Lanka, using techniques that benefit both the planet and local communities.

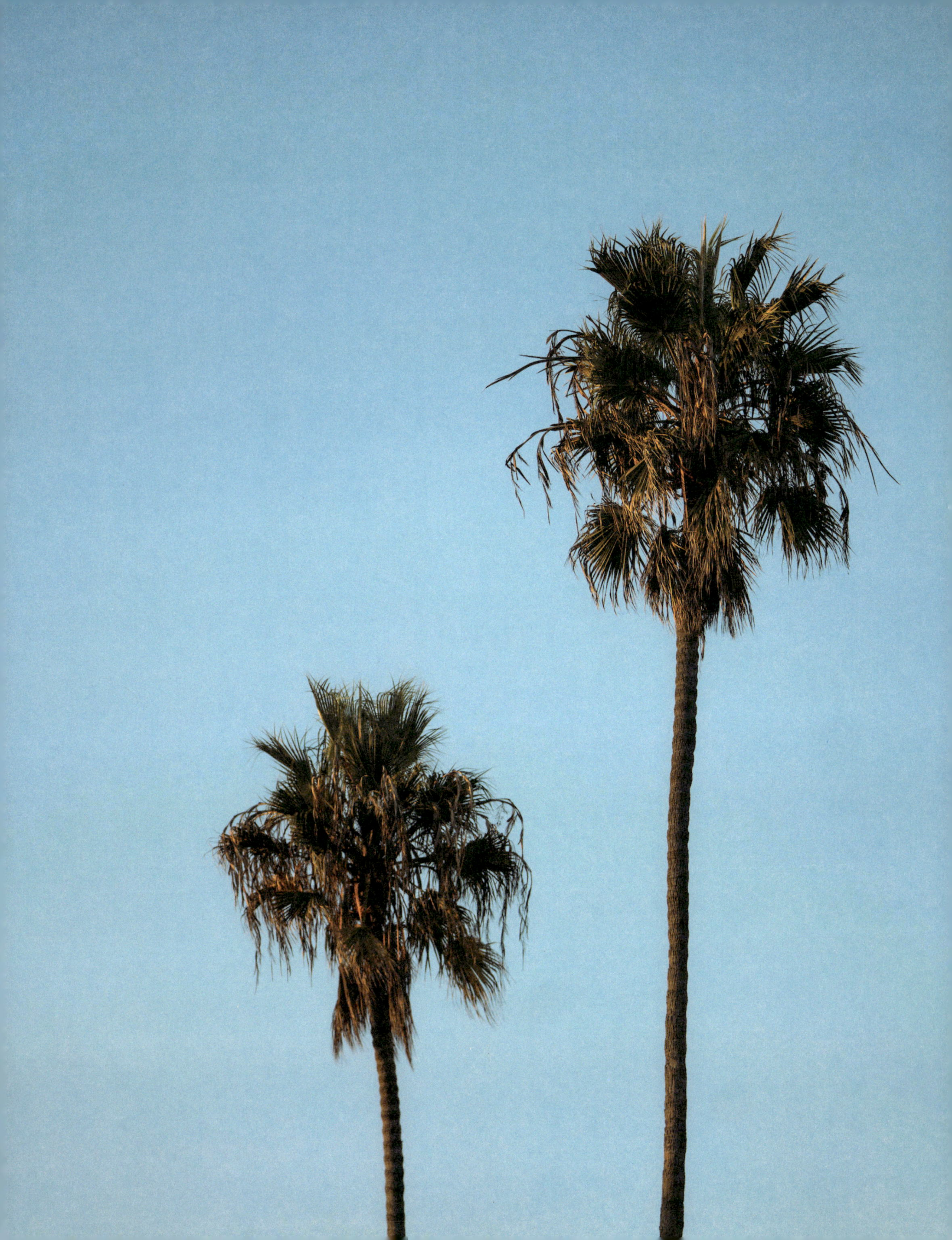

# Lunch

**44**
Gluten-Free Fish Sticks

**46**
Gluten-Free Bánh Mì With Seared Ahi Tuna

**48**
Paleo Chicken Nuggets

**50**
Chickpea Falafel

**52**
Kale Caesar Salad

**58**
Salmon Cakes

**60**
Grain-Free Flautas

**62**
Green Shakshuka

**64**
Buffalo Chicken Salad

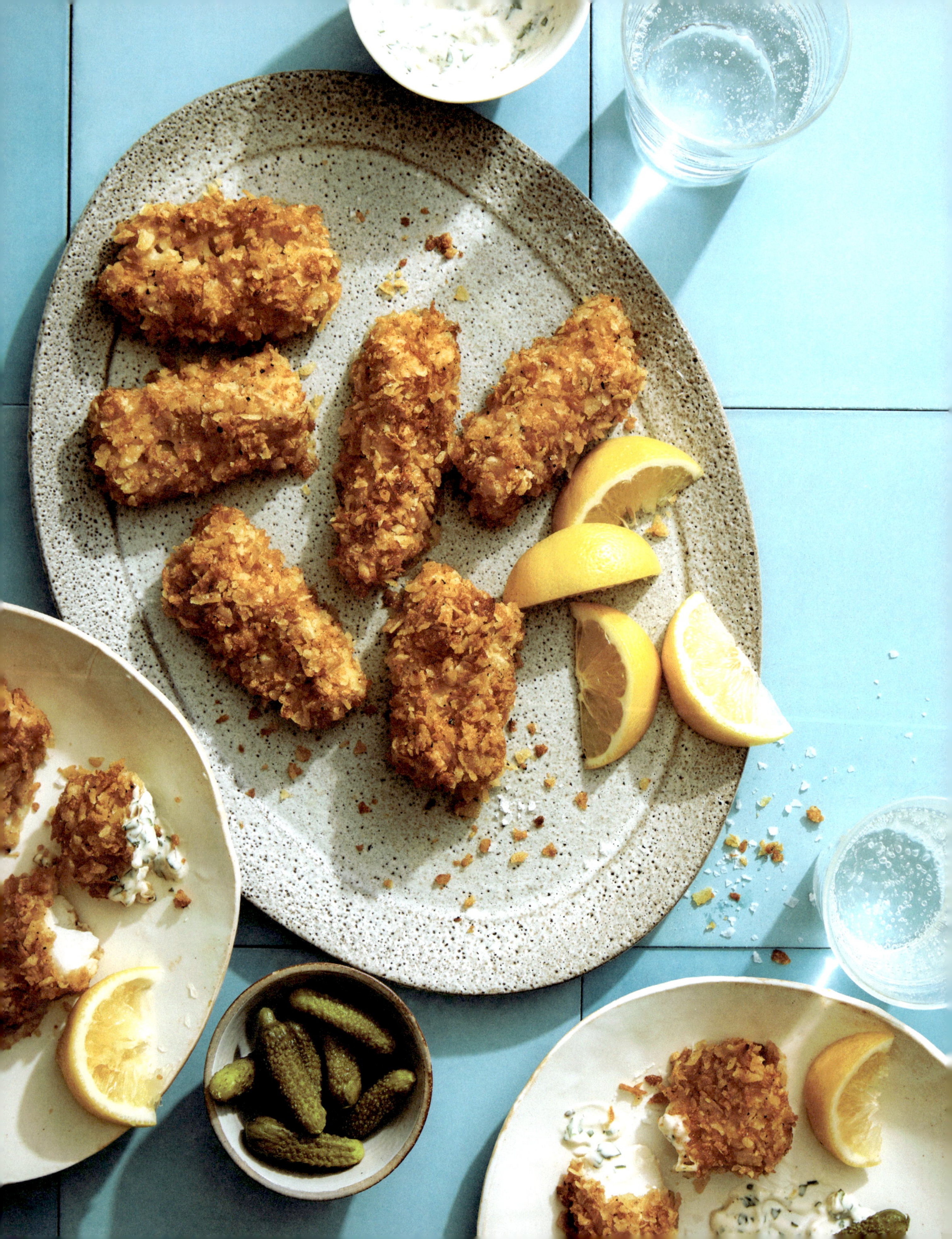

YIELD 4-6 SERVINGS    ACTIVE TIME 10 MINUTES    TOTAL TIME 25 MINUTES

Mild, delicately flaky cod is a great way to sneak seafood past picky eaters of all ages. These fish sticks are baked in a crispy, salty, buttery crust made from gluten-free chips and cornflakes.

LUNCH

# Gluten-Free Fish Sticks

Gluten-Free    Egg-Free

### INGREDIENTS

3 cups Thrive Market Coconut Oil or Avocado Oil Potato Chips, crushed

2 cups gluten-free cornflakes, crushed

5 tablespoons Thrive Market Organic Ghee, melted

2 pounds skinless Thrive Market Wild-Caught Atlantic Cod fillets, cut into 1-inch strips

Sea salt and pepper, to taste

Lemon slices and roughly chopped parsley, to garnish

### INSTRUCTIONS

Preheat oven to 400°F and line a baking sheet with parchment paper.

In a large bowl, combine the crushed chips and cornflakes with the melted ghee and stir.

Place the cod strips about an inch apart on the baking sheet. Season with salt and coat with chip-and-cornflake mixture, pressing it down to help the mixture adhere to the fish.

Bake for 15 minutes until the crust is golden, flaky, and crisp. Sprinkle with parsley and serve with lemon slices.

*Scan here to shop the recipe*

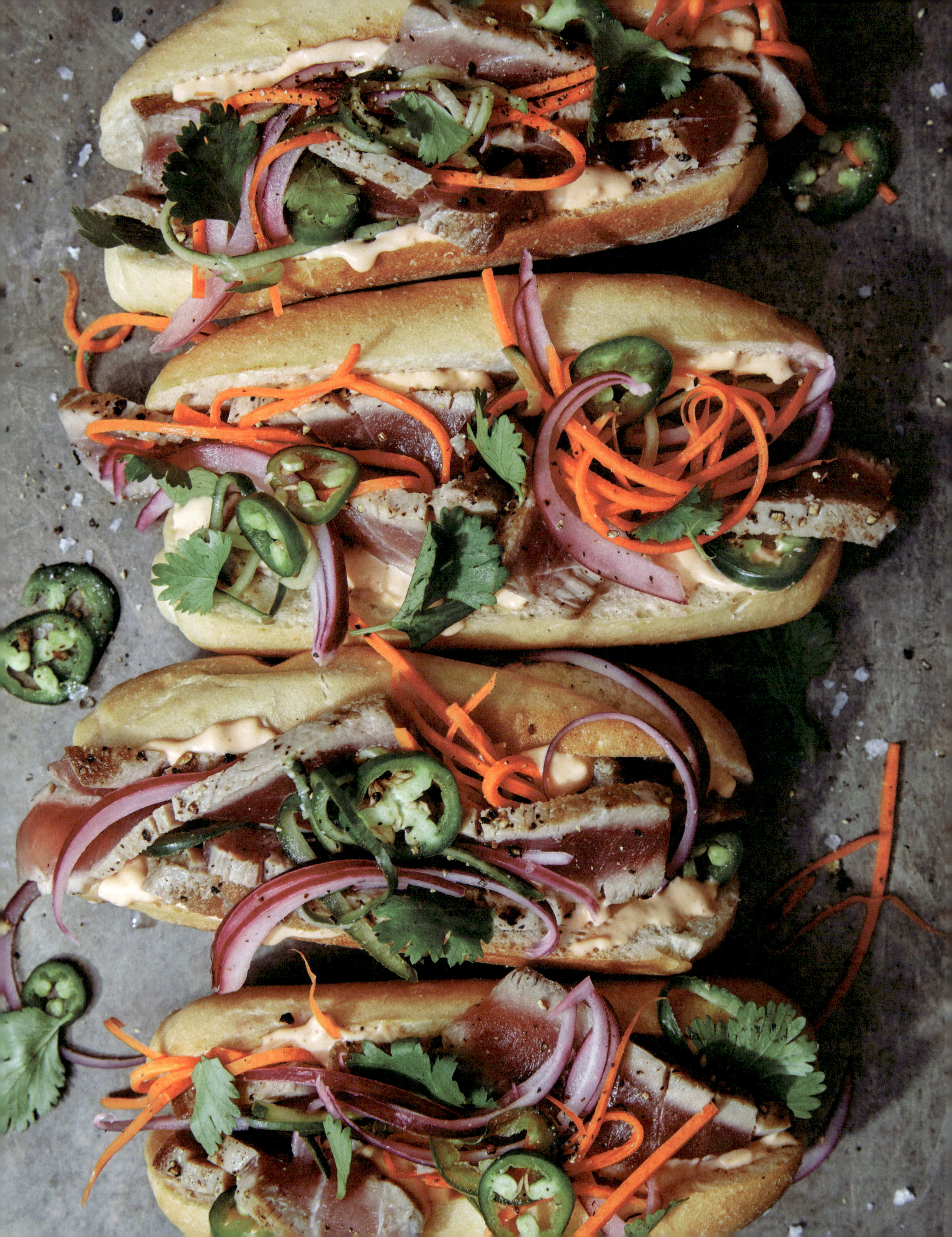

YIELD 2 SERVINGS     ACTIVE TIME 20 MINUTES     TOTAL TIME 30 MINUTES

In this twist on traditional bánh mì, seared ahi tuna takes the place of pork as the protein of choice. Tuck thinly sliced steaks into gluten-free baguettes and top with a generous helping of quick-pickled vegetables for bright, briny flavor in each bite.

LUNCH

# Gluten-Free Bánh Mì With Seared Ahi Tuna

*Gluten-Free, Egg-Free, Nut-Free*

## INGREDIENTS

**For the Pickled Vegetables**

3 tablespoons Thrive Market Organic Rice Vinegar

1 teaspoon Thrive Market Organic Honey

1/2 teaspoon Thrive Market Organic Garlic Powder

1/2 teaspoon sea salt

1 Persian cucumber, thinly sliced

1 large carrot, shredded

1/2 small red onion, thinly sliced

1 small jalapeño, thinly sliced

**For the Sauce**

1/2 cup Thrive Market Vegan Mayonnaise

1 teaspoon organic red sriracha

**For the Tuna**

2 (4-ounce) ahi tuna steaks; try Thrive Market Wild-Caught Ahi Tuna

Sea salt

Thrive Market Organic Ground Pepper, to taste

1 tablespoon Thrive Market Organic Extra Virgin Olive Oil

**For the Sandwiches**

1 gluten-free baguette (or roll of your choice), sliced lengthwise

Cilantro leaves, for serving

## INSTRUCTIONS

First, make the pickled vegetables: Whisk rice vinegar, honey, garlic powder, and salt in a medium bowl. Add cucumbers, carrots, onions, and jalapeño; toss to coat.

Make the sauce: Whisk mayonnaise and sriracha in a small bowl.

Make the tuna: Season tuna with salt and pepper on both sides. Heat a large nonstick skillet over high heat and add 1 tablespoon oil. Add tuna and sear on both sides; 1 to 2 minutes total for rare, or 3 to 4 minutes total for medium-well. Transfer tuna to a cutting board and slice against the grain into 1/2-inch pieces.

Make the sandwiches: Preheat broiler. Arrange bread on a sheet tray and toast for 2 minutes, or until slightly golden. Spread sauce on one half of the bread, then layer slices of tuna on top.

Top with pickled vegetables, cilantro leaves, and another drizzle of sauce. Top with the remaining half of bread; slice and serve.

*Scan here to shop the recipe*

**YIELD** 20 NUGGETS    **ACTIVE TIME** 15 MINUTES    **TOTAL TIME** 30 MINUTES

Skip the drive-thru and make chicken nuggets that kiddos and their health-conscious parents will enjoy. This healthy take skips the mystery meat in favor of ground chicken and uses wholesome ingredients like flaxseed and coconut flour to create that must-have crispy coating.

LUNCH

# Paleo Chicken Nuggets

Gluten-Free  Grain-Free  Dairy-Free

### INGREDIENTS

1/2 cup Thrive Market Organic Coconut Flour, divided

2 tablespoons Thrive Market Organic Ground Flaxseed

1 1/4 teaspoon sea salt, divided

1 pound ground chicken

1 large egg, beaten

1 teaspoon Thrive Market Organic Onion Powder

3/4 teaspoon minced garlic

1/2 teaspoon black pepper

1/4 cup Thrive Market Organic Extra Virgin Olive Oil or Thrive Market Organic Ghee, melted

### INSTRUCTIONS

Preheat oven to 375°F and line a baking sheet with parchment paper.

On a medium-sized plate, combine 1/4 cup coconut flour, ground flaxseed, and 1/4 teaspoon sea salt. Set aside.

Place ground chicken, egg, remaining 1/4 cup coconut flour, remaining 1 teaspoon sea salt, onion powder, minced garlic, and black pepper together in a large bowl and mix to combine (don't overmix).

Scoop out 1 1/2 tablespoon-sized balls. Flatten each ball into a small patty in the palm of your hand. Dip each nugget into the coconut flour mixture, coating each side, and place on baking sheet.

Bake for 15 minutes. Remove from the oven, brush each nugget with melted ghee or olive oil on both sides, and return to the oven to bake for 5 more minutes.

Serve warm with your choice of dip (try Thrive Market Ranch Dressing & Marinade).

*Scan here to shop the recipe*

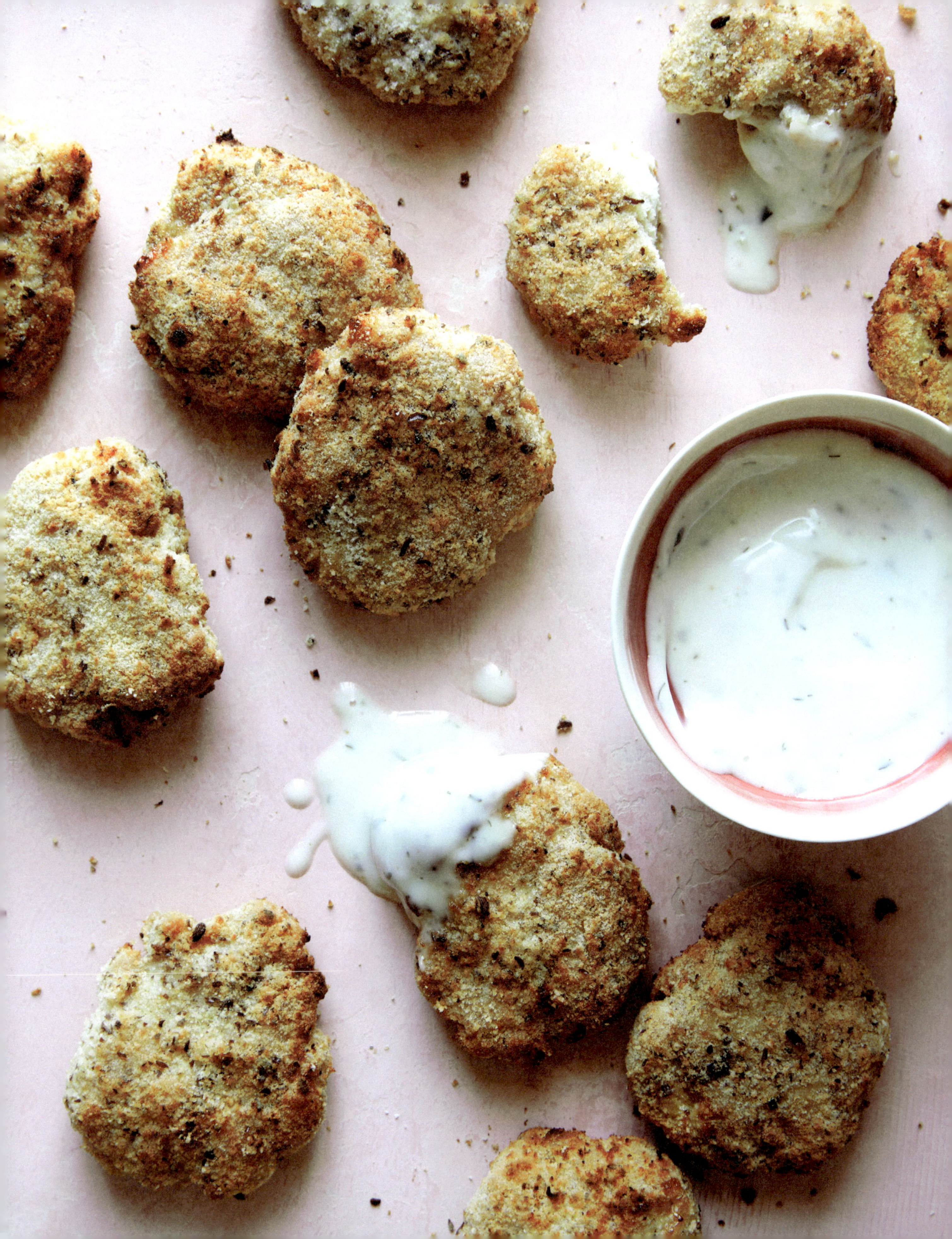

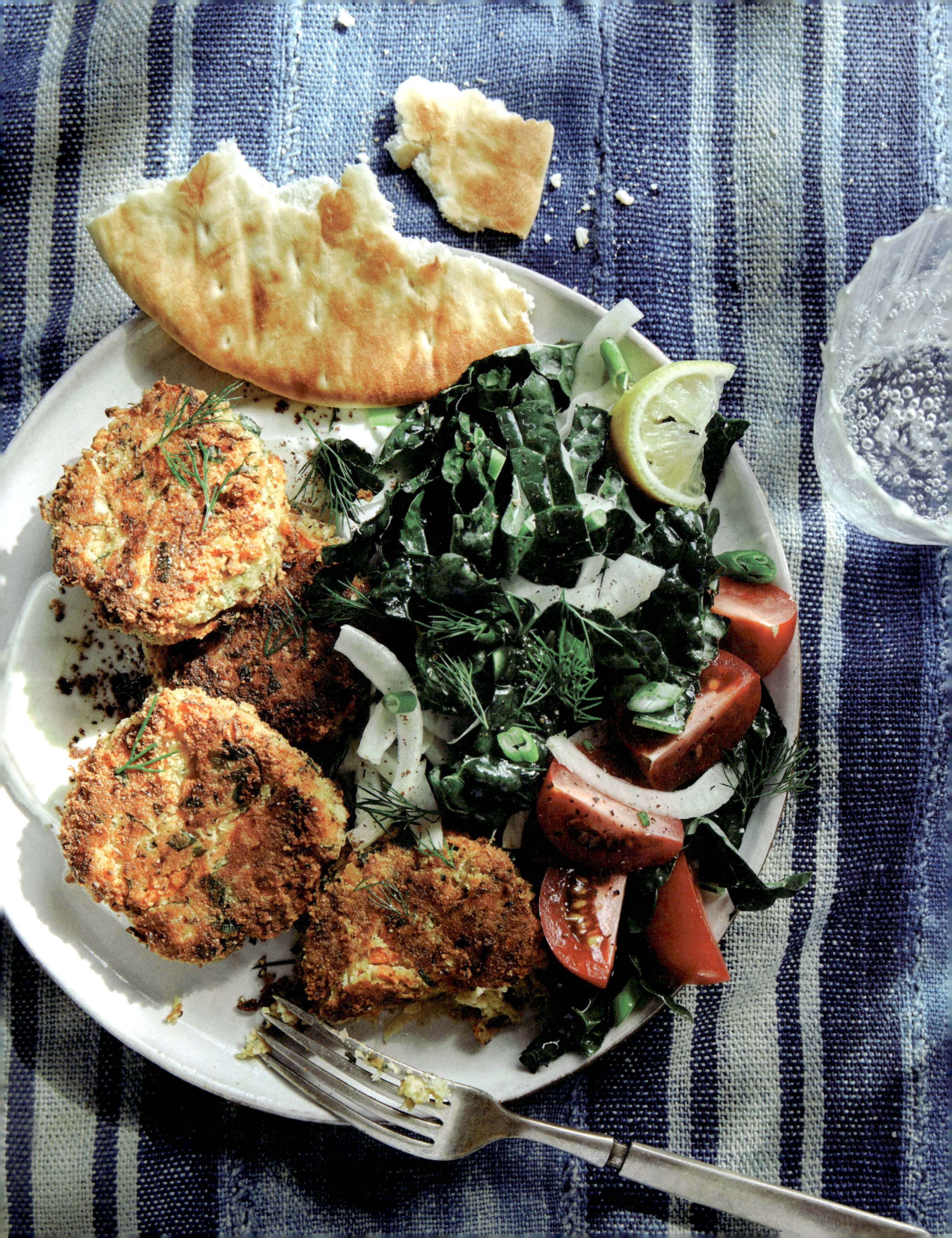

**YIELD** 24 PATTIES   **ACTIVE TIME** 15 MINUTES   **TOTAL TIME** 20 MINUTES

These lightened-up chickpea patties get started on the stovetop and finished in the oven, giving them the crunchy outer layer usually achieved with deep-frying, only with less mess. They're wonderfully addictive on their own or as the main component of a simple pita sandwich, with parsley, cucumbers, cabbage, and yogurt sauce.

LUNCH

# Chickpea Falafel

Gluten-Free   Dairy-Free   Vegan   Egg-Free

## INGREDIENTS

1 cup Thrive Market Almond Flour, packed

1 pouch Thrive Market Organic Chickpeas, mashed (or 1 14.5-ounce can)

1/3 cup plus 2 tablespoons Thrive Market Organic Tahini

3 tablespoons Thrive Market Organic Coconut Aminos (or soy sauce)

1 large onion, finely diced

2 carrots, peeled and finely diced

1 bunch parsley, chopped

Juice of 2 lemons

1/2 teaspoon lemon zest

1 teaspoon Thrive Market Organic Garlic Powder

1 teaspoon Thrive Market Organic Ground Cumin

1/4 teaspoon Thrive Market Organic Ground Cinnamon

1/4 teaspoon Thrive Market Organic Cayenne Pepper

1 tablespoon sumac (optional)

## INSTRUCTIONS

Preheat oven to 350°F and line a baking sheet with parchment paper.

Place all ingredients in a bowl and stir to combine. Form the mixture into patties about 2 inches wide.

Warm a drizzle of oil in a skillet over medium heat. Working in batches, cook patties for 2 minutes on each side, until browned and crispy. Transfer patties to the prepared baking sheet. Bake for 5 minutes until cooked through.

*Scan here to shop the recipe*

YIELD 3-4 SERVINGS    TOTAL TIME 10 MINUTES

The secret to truly tasty kale salads? Massage the leaves with a little oil and salt. The process tenderizes kale leaves by breaking down their tough cellulose structure. In this recipe, massaged kale forms a nutrient-packed base for a dairy-free take on the classic Caesar salad. Nutritional yeast mimics the umami flavor of Parmesan, and crispy bacon adds extra savoriness.

LUNCH

# Kale Caesar Salad

*Gluten-Free · Grain-Free · Dairy-Free · Egg-Free · Nut-Free*

## INGREDIENTS

**For the Salad**

2 bunches Tuscan kale, stalks removed and discarded, leaves sliced or torn into pieces

2 tablespoons Thrive Market Organic Extra Virgin Olive Oil

Large pinch sea salt

4 strips Thrive Market Non-GMO No Sugar Added Uncured Bacon, cooked until crispy

1 avocado, peeled, pitted, and sliced

1/2 small red onion, thinly sliced

1 tablespoon Thrive Market Nutritional Yeast

**For the Paleo Caesar Dressing**

1 (2-ounce) can or 7 to 8 fillets anchovies, drained

2 cloves garlic

3 tablespoons Thrive Market Nutritional Yeast

1/2 teaspoon Thrive Market Organic Dijon Mustard

Juice of 1 1/2 lemons

1/4 cup vegan mayonnaise

Thrive Market Organic Ground Pepper, to taste

## INSTRUCTIONS

First, massage the kale: Place the kale leaves in a large bowl. Drizzle with olive oil and a pinch of salt. Massage the kale for about 3 minutes. The leaves will shrink a little and appear darker in color.

Next, make the dressing: Place all the ingredients except the pepper in the bowl of a small food processor. Process until smooth and season to taste with pepper.

Assemble the salad: Drizzle the dressing over the kale and toss. Top the dressed salad with crumbled bacon, avocado, red onion, and nutritional yeast.

*Scan here to shop the recipe*

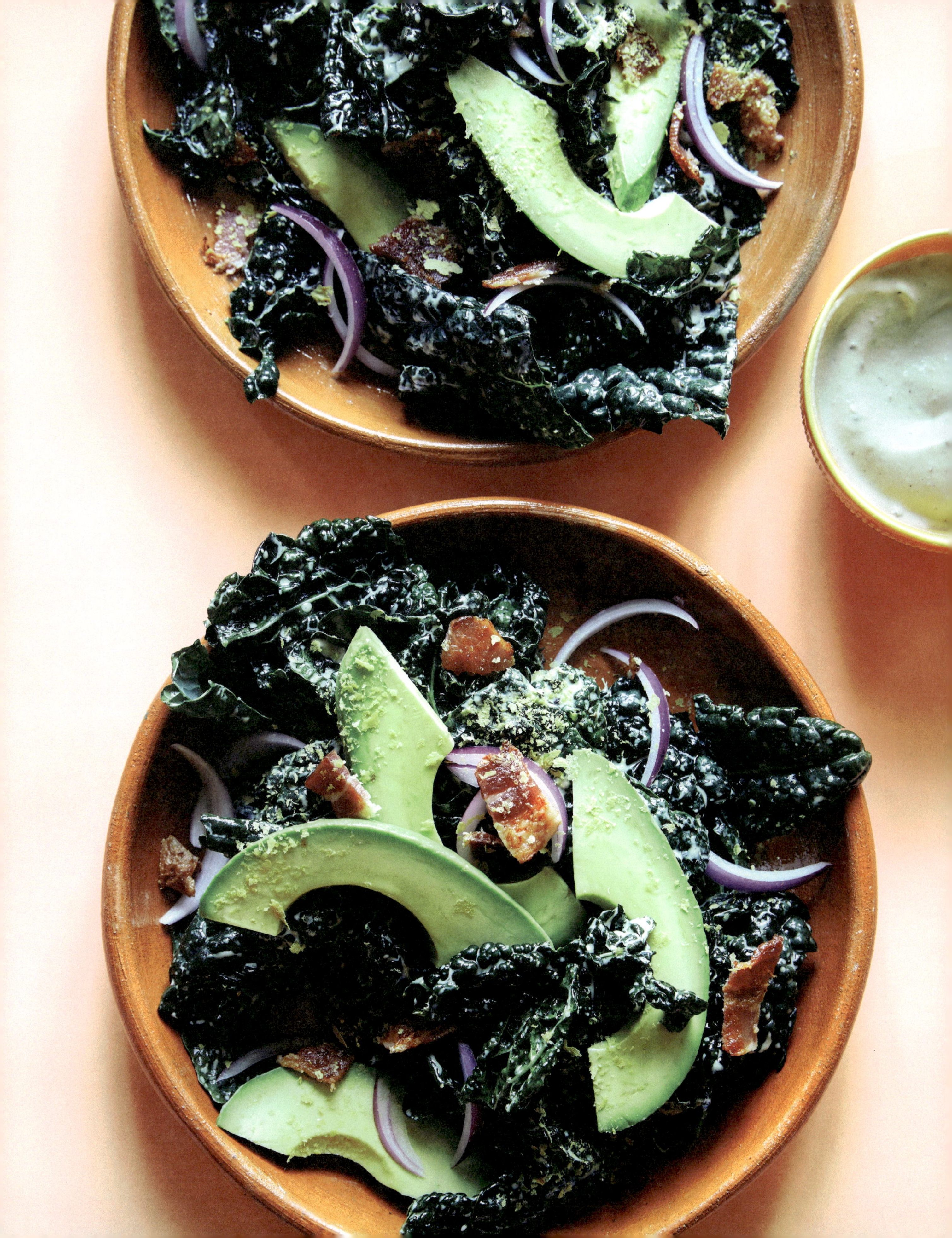

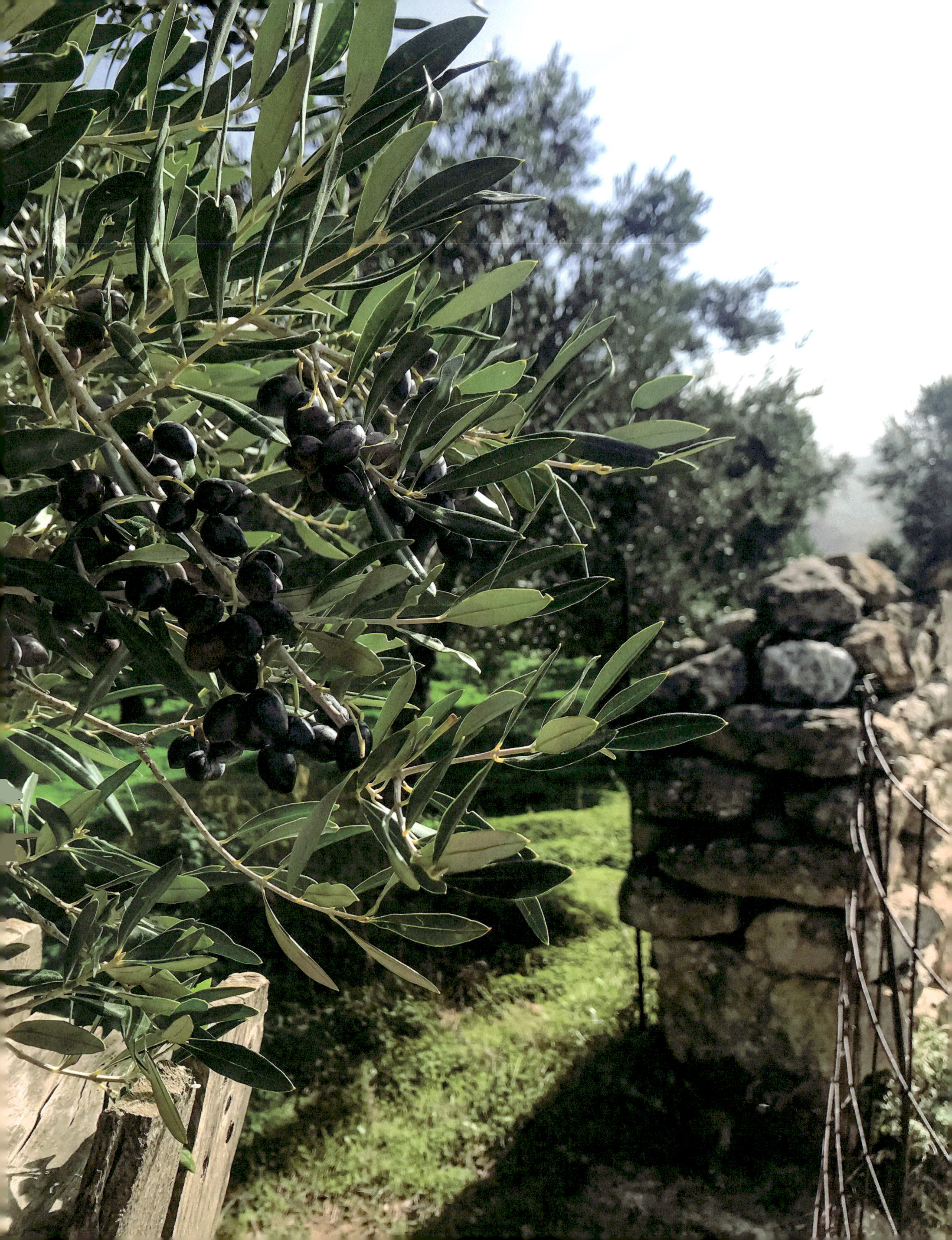

**THRIVE MARKET ORGANIC EXTRA VIRGIN OLIVE OIL**
**CRETE, GREECE**

# Grecian Gold

*When Jeremiah McElwee first tasted a sample of what would become Thrive Market's Organic Extra Virgin Olive Oil, he was pretty certain he'd discovered the best olive oil in the world. But flavor alone wasn't enough. If he was going to offer this olive oil to Thrive Market's members, he needed to get the whole story firsthand.*

**First of all, why olive oil?** When you see pictures of people's kitchens around the world, there's always an oil on the shelf. Oils are in every pantry in every household worldwide. Everyone uses fat to cook with, and olive oil is right at the top of the list.

When we were building out the Thrive Market line, I was very passionate. I told Thrive Market Co-Founder and CEO Nick Green, *We've got to have the olive oil that is the best our members have ever tasted.*

**Thrive Market has high standards for all the products it creates and carries. What were some of the most important factors when it came to olive oil?** Fraud is a big issue with olive oil, so knowing and having a connection to the source was important for us. That's how we approach everything at Thrive Market. We want to see the farms and verify that the product will be from the same place every time.

We wanted a single-origin olive oil, and to have transparency into the supply chain. You can just buy a certain grade of olive oil, but there's no way to know where it came from because it's mixed from a variety of sources. Olive oil is often refined and processed to get a consistent product. When that happens, you lose out on that natural variation. The average person might not notice the difference, but we love single-origin olive oil for the incredible, fresh, vibrant experience it provides.

**So you learned of this particular olive farm in Crete. What makes their olive oil so good?**
It's a family farm run by a father and his three sons, who are third-generation olive farmers. All their trees are organic, and they don't use any pesticides or GMOs. They do one harvest a year, and it's a giant celebration, a cultural tradition that brings the whole community together. They harvest the olives and press them right away, when they're fresh. Then they put the oil into these airtight, stainless steel drums and bring it to this incredible facility they've built over the years. The drums get plugged directly into a bottling line, so the oil never touches oxygen or plastic after it goes into the drums. This process results in a pristine, super-fresh product.

**You went to Crete to see for yourself how their olive oil is made. What were some personal highlights of the visit?** The trip was an amazing whirlwind. We went through the countryside and saw all the olive groves. Right down the road from the facility is this little seafood restaurant on the Mediterranean. I'm plant-based, and they made every traditional Greek dish vegan for me.

**What are some qualities of Thrive Market's Organic Extra Virgin Olive Oil that stand out?**
I remember when I first tried it. I poured some onto this little white plate, and it was this beautiful, bright, vibrant green. The smell was earthy and buttery. It was the freshest olive oil I'd ever seen or tasted.

**When did you know you'd found the perfect olive oil for Thrive Market's line?** At the end of my visit, the patriarch of the family said he wanted to take me to the airport. He doesn't speak any English, and I don't speak Greek. We get to the airport and he grabs me by the shoulders and starts going on and on in Greek. He was very serious—he almost seemed angry! I'm thinking, oh no, what did I do? He's probably upset that his wife had to make me vegan food. Then the translator said, the father says that having you here was a true delight, and that you have to come back and bring your whole family and stay with his family at their house. It was such a sweet moment. At that point we were all convinced. We were all in on this olive oil.

Made from 100% certified organic Koroneiki olives, our extra-virgin olive oil is grown, harvested, and bottled on a single, family-run estate in western Crete.

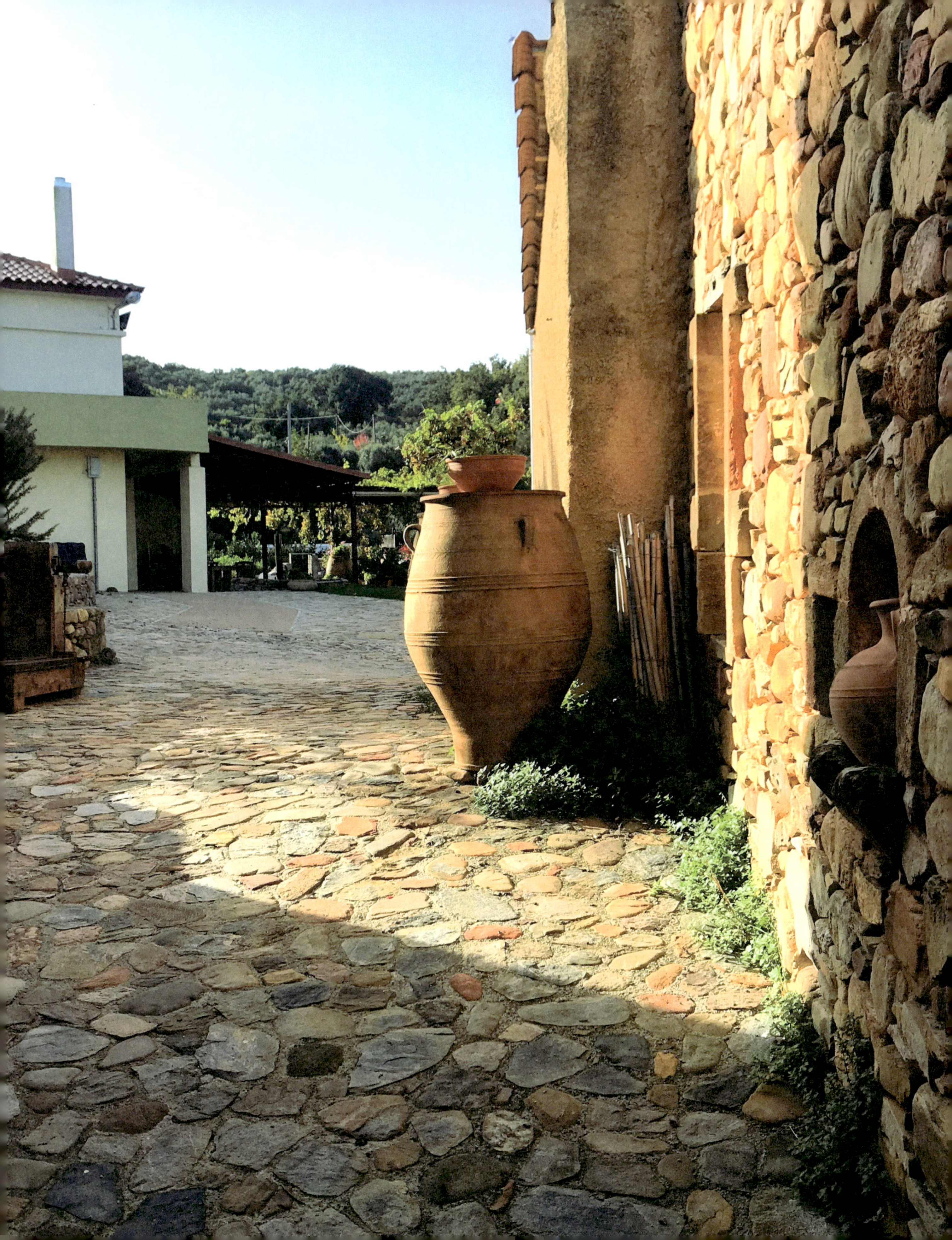

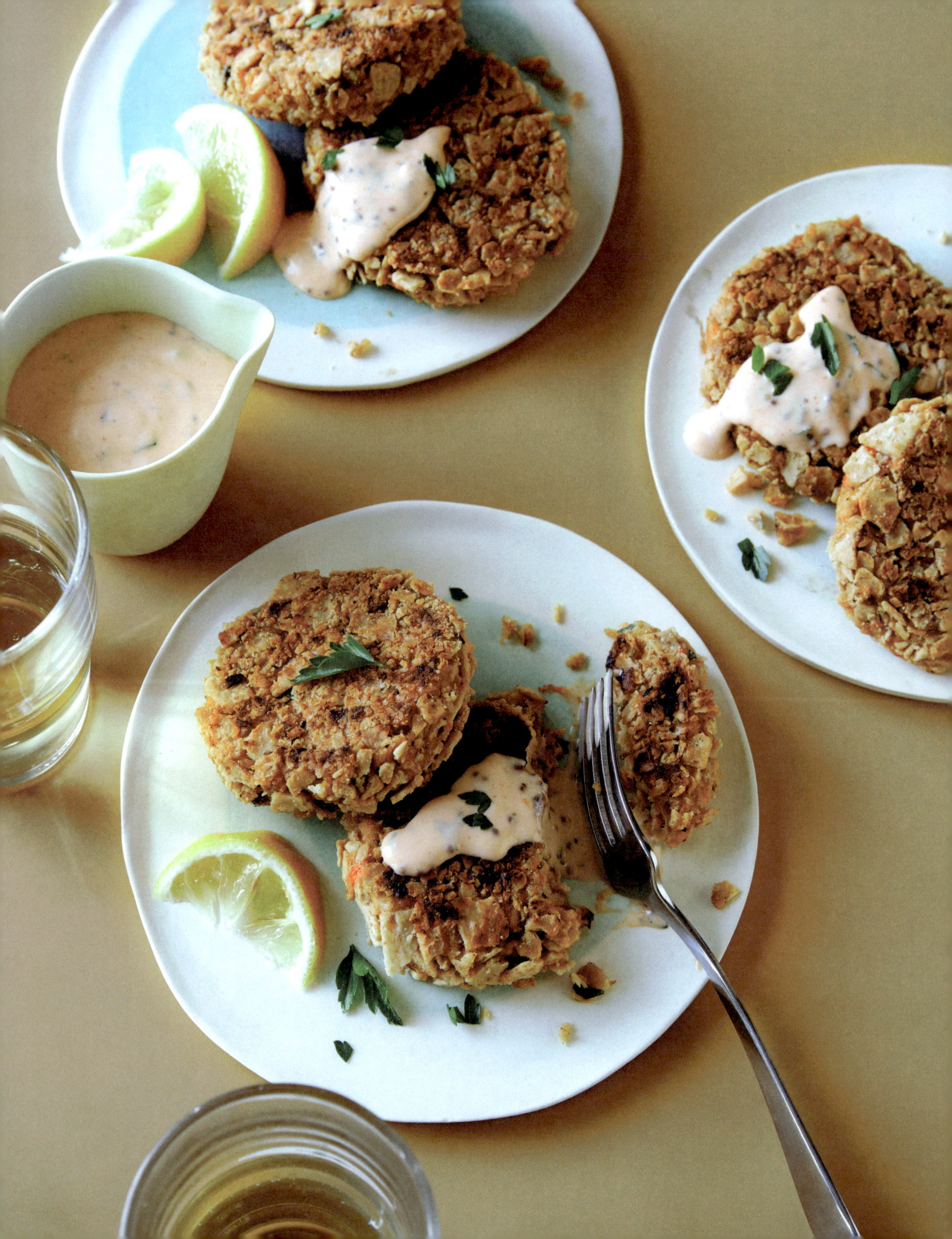

YIELD 6 CAKES    ACTIVE TIME 15 MINUTES    TOTAL TIME 30 MINUTES

With pantry staples like canned wild salmon and basic spices, this elegant dish is deceptively easy. Bell peppers, shallots, and fresh parsley add a bit of brightness, while a creamy spiced remoulade brings the flavor and flair. Serve with crackers or a leafy green salad for a light yet satisfying lunch.

LUNCH

# Salmon Cakes

Gluten-Free    Grain-Free

## INGREDIENTS

**For the Salmon Cakes**

1 (6-ounce) can wild-caught salmon, drained

1/2 medium shallot, minced

1/2 roasted red bell pepper, finely chopped

1 garlic clove, minced

1 egg

1 (4.25-ounce) box almond flour crackers, crushed and divided

1/3 cup mayonnaise

1 tablespoon parsley leaves, finely chopped

1 teaspoon Thrive Market Organic Capers, finely chopped

1/2 teaspoon sea salt

1/4 teaspoon Thrive Market Organic Ground Pepper

2 to 3 tablespoons Thrive Market Organic Ghee

**For the Remoulade**

1/2 cup mayonnaise

Juice of 1 lime

1 tablespoon Thrive Market Organic Stone Ground Mustard

1 tablespoon parsley, finely chopped

1/2 teaspoon sea salt

1/2 teaspoon Thrive Market Organic Ground Pepper

1/2 teaspoon organic red sriracha

## INSTRUCTIONS

First, make the salmon cakes: Add salmon to a large mixing bowl and break up large chunks with a fork. Add shallot, bell pepper, garlic, egg, 1/2 cup crushed crackers, mayonnaise, parsley, capers, salt, and pepper. Stir until well blended.

Pack salmon into a 1/4-cup measuring cup; tap it into your hand to form a patty, place the patty on sheet tray, and continue with the remaining mixture. Add remaining crackers to a plate and dredge each salmon cake on both sides.

Melt 2 tablespoons ghee in a large nonstick sauté pan over medium-high heat. Add patties and gently push down with the back of a spatula to flatten slightly. Cook for 2 to 3 minutes, or until bottom is golden; flip and reduce heat to medium. Cook on second side for another 3 to 4 minutes.

To make the remoulade, whisk all ingredients in a small bowl and serve alongside salmon cakes.

*Scan here to shop the recipe*

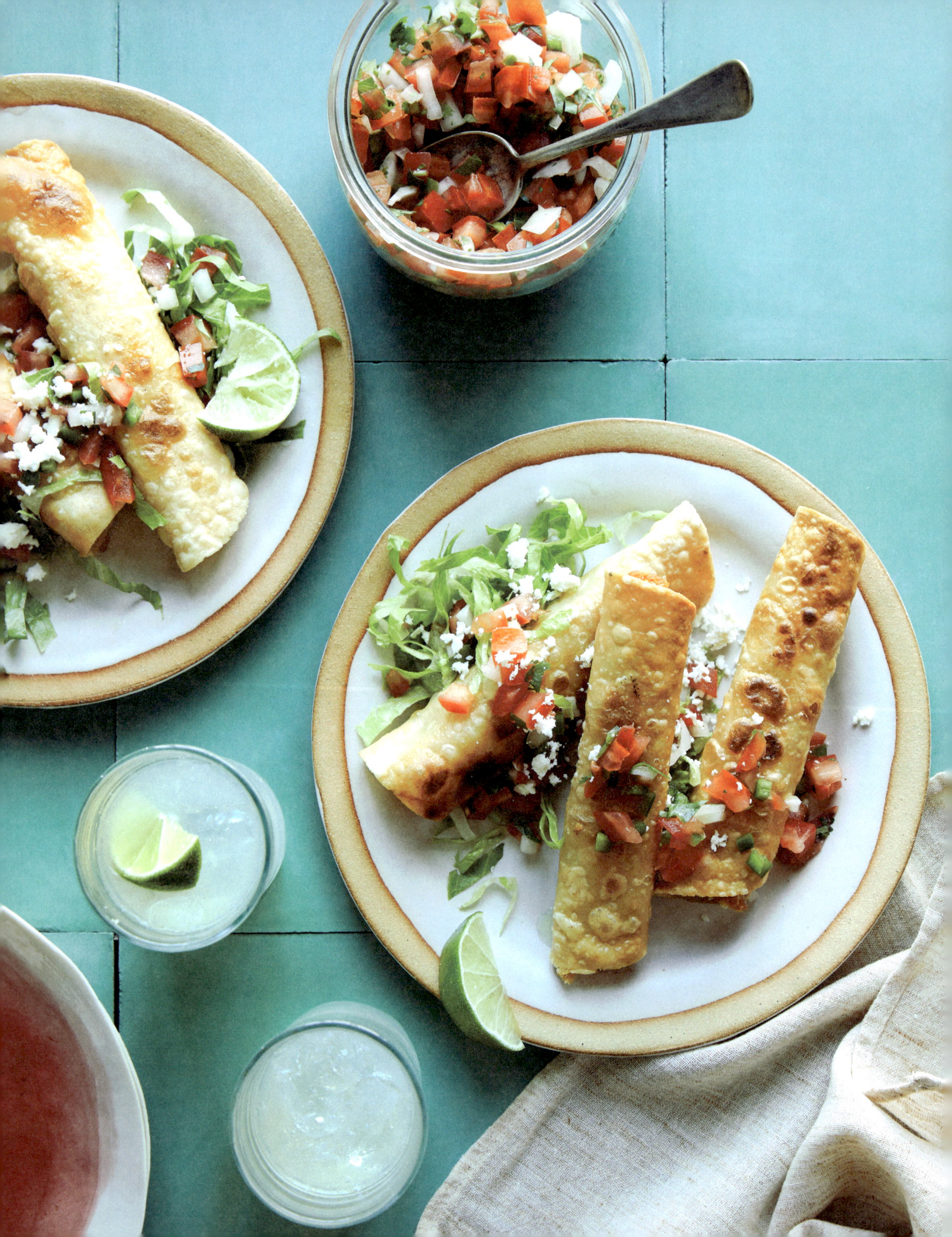

YIELD 6 SERVINGS (3 FLAUTAS PER SERVING)   TOTAL TIME 20 MINUTES

Got leftover chicken in the fridge? Give it new life by tucking it into hearty, flavorful flautas. **Jeannette Ogden**, aka *@shutthekaleup*, took her mother's recipe and tweaked it with grain-free tortillas and nut-based cheese. You can easily substitute these ingredients to suit your diet and tastes.

LUNCH

# Grain-Free Flautas

Gluten-Free · Grain-Free · Dairy-Free · Egg-Free · Nut-Free

## INGREDIENTS

1/3 cup Thrive Market Avocado Oil

18 grain-free tortillas of your choice

1 whole chicken (about 2 pounds), cooked and shredded

1/2 a head of romaine lettuce, shredded

2 cups cheese of your choice (can use dairy-free)

1 bunch fresh cilantro, de-stemmed

1 jar Thrive Market Organic Salsa

## INSTRUCTIONS

Lightly coat 1 skillet with oil over medium heat; you'll use this pan to warm up the tortillas before filling and rolling them. Meanwhile, add about 1/4 cup of avocado oil to another pan over medium heat; you'll use this pan to fry the flautas.

Warm the tortillas 2 at a time, 1 layered on top of the other. Be careful not to leave them in the pan too long; you want them to stay soft.

Remove the warmed tortillas from the pan and add a small handful of shredded chicken. Roll tightly and place into the frying skillet. Cook until golden and crispy, 3 to 4 minutes per side. Repeat with all the remaining tortillas.

To serve, top flautas with romaine lettuce, cheese, cilantro, and salsa as desired.

*Scan here to shop the recipe*

**YIELD** 4 SERVINGS     **TOTAL TIME** 30 MINUTES

In **Dr. Mark Hyman**'s verdant take on shakshuka, aromatic herbs and a garden of green vegetables stand in for the traditional tomato sauce. To maximize nutrients and support humane farming practices, Dr. Hyman recommends using pasture-raised eggs if you can.

LUNCH

# Green Shakshuka

*Gluten-Free   Grain-Free   Dairy-Free   Nut-Free*

## INGREDIENTS

- 2 tablespoons Thrive Market Organic Extra Virgin Olive Oil
- 1 large leek, finely chopped
- 2 large shallots, finely chopped
- 2 small fennel bulbs, finely chopped
- 1 bunch Swiss chard, de-stemmed and roughly chopped
- 1 bunch spinach, de-stemmed and roughly chopped
- 4 kale leaves, de-stemmed and roughly chopped
- 3 large garlic cloves, thinly sliced
- 1 large zucchini, finely diced
- Zest from 1 lemon
- 1/4 jalapeño (optional), thinly sliced
- 3/4 teaspoon sea salt
- 1/2 teaspoon Thrive Market Organic Whole Black Peppercorns, freshly ground
- 2 scallions, chopped
- 4 to 8 large eggs
- 1/4 cup filtered water
- 1/4 cup fresh dill

## INSTRUCTIONS

Place a large skillet over medium heat and add olive oil. Add leeks, shallots, and fennel to the skillet and cook, stirring occasionally, until softened and caramelized, about 5 minutes.

Add the Swiss chard, spinach, kale, and garlic to the skillet and stir. Cover and cook for 5 minutes. Stir in zucchini, cover, and cook for another 5 minutes, until zucchini is soft. Add the lemon zest, jalapeño (if using), salt, pepper, and chopped scallions; stir.

Create a well for each egg in the middle of the shakshuka base and carefully crack one egg into each well. Cook for 2 to 3 minutes.

Pour water around the edge of the skillet, cover, and cook until egg whites are set, about 2 more minutes. Remove lid and sprinkle with chopped dill before serving.

*Scan here to shop the recipe*

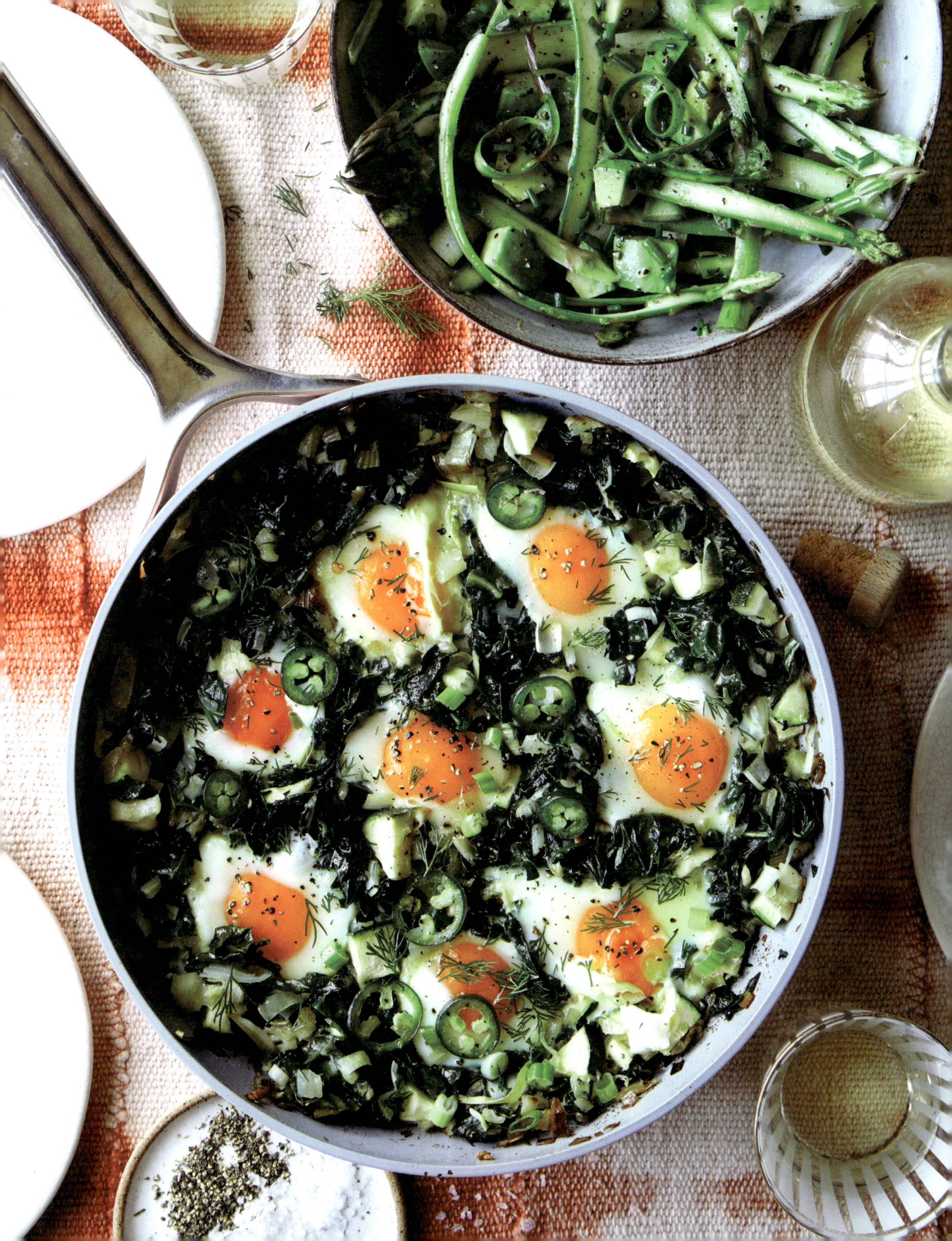

YIELD 4 SERVINGS    TOTAL TIME 30 MINUTES

If anyone knows how to keep it interesting (and delicious) on the Whole30® program, it's Co-Founder and CEO **Melissa Urban**. This satisfying salad uses bottled sauces as a shortcut to major flavor. No air fryer? We've included an oven method that works just as well.

LUNCH

# Buffalo Chicken Salad

Gluten-Free · Grain-Free · Dairy-Free · Nut-Free

## INGREDIENTS

1 pound boneless, skinless chicken breasts, thick sides pounded to make of even thickness

1/2 cup Whole30® Buffalo Vinaigrette

6 cups chopped romaine lettuce

1 cup thinly sliced celery

1/2 cup shredded carrot

3 to 4 tablespoons Whole30® House Ranch

1 small ripe avocado, peeled, pitted, and sliced

1 cup cherry tomatoes, halved

Freshly ground black pepper

2 teaspoons finely chopped chives

## INSTRUCTIONS

In a large resealable plastic bag, combine chicken and Whole30® Buffalo Vinaigrette. Massage to coat. Seal bag and marinate in the refrigerator for at least 2 hours and up to 4 hours.

Preheat air fryer to 375°F. Remove chicken from bag; discard marinade. Add the chicken to the air fryer. Cook until chicken is no longer pink and the internal temperature is 170°F, turning once, about 15 minutes. Let stand while making the salad.

In a large bowl, combine the romaine, celery, and carrots. Add the Whole30® House Ranch; toss to combine. Divide salad among 4 serving plates.

Slice the chicken. Top the salads with sliced chicken, avocado, and cherry tomatoes. Season to taste with black pepper. Sprinkle with chives.

Oven method: Preheat oven to 350°F. Heat an oven-safe skillet over high heat for 5 minutes or until it is very hot (cast iron works well). Place the chicken on the hot skillet and cook for 1 minute, then flip and cook for 1 minute more on the other side.

Transfer the skillet to the oven and bake until no longer pink in the center, the juices run clear, and the chicken reaches an internal temperature of 165°F, 8 to 10 minutes.

*Scan here to shop the recipe*

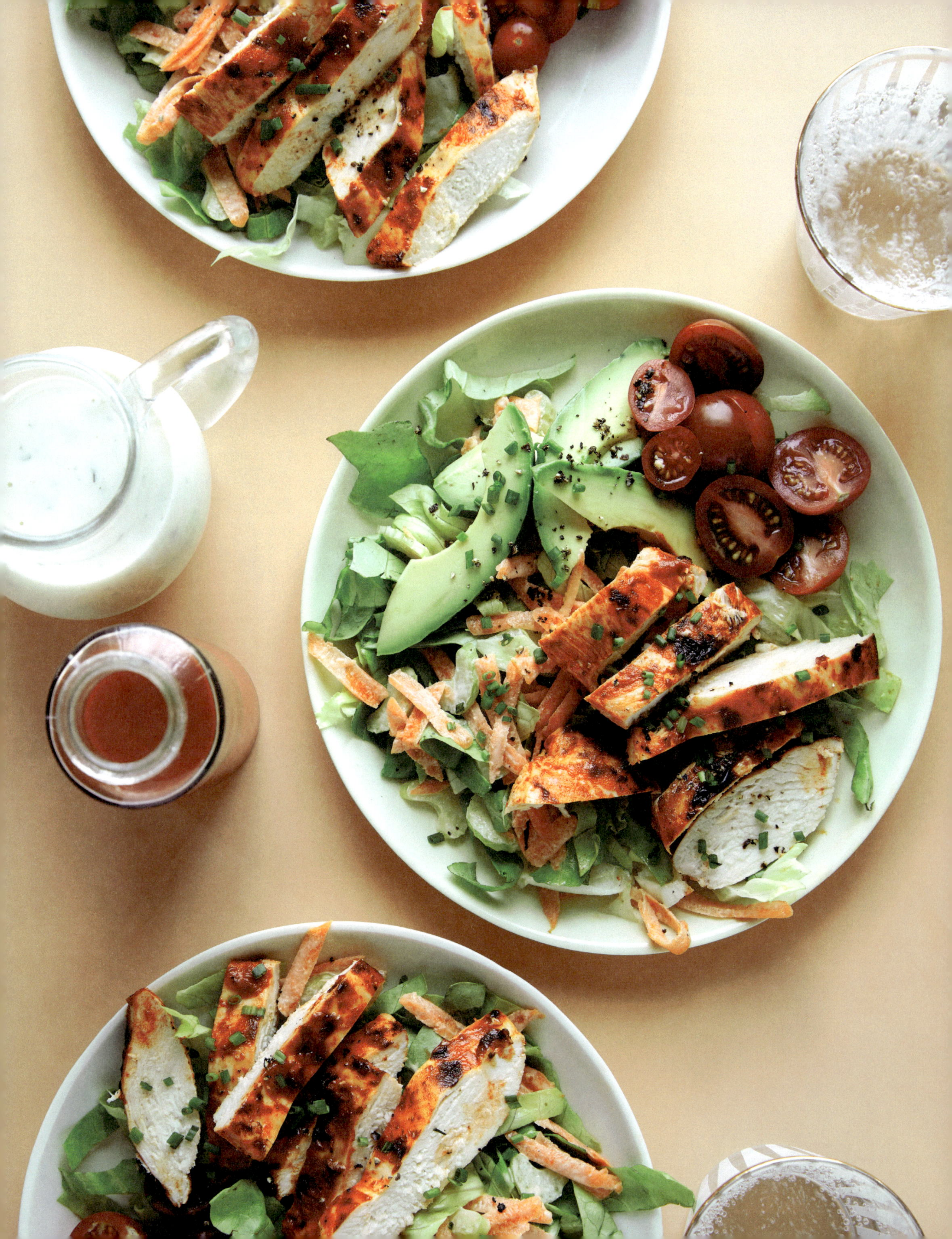

THRIVE
MARKET
REGENERATIVELY GROWN
ORGANIC
RAW
MACADAMIA
NUTS
NO ADDED SALT
THRIVE
MARKET
REGENERATIVELY GROWN
ORGANIC
DRY ROASTED & SALTED
MACADAMIA
NUTS
SALTED

Our Organic Macadamia Nuts are regeneratively grown by a co-op of small-scale farmers in Kenya who work to restore soil health and help heal the environment.

# Dinner

**PAGE 72**
Paleo Hazelnut-
Crusted Halibut

**PAGE 74**
Seafood Scallop
Chowder

**PAGE 76**
Chipotle Tofu Tacos

**PAGE 78**
Shrimp &
Cauliflower "Grits"

**PAGE 80**
Lamb Burgers With
Pistachio Pesto

**PAGE 86**
Roasted Spice-Rubbed
Chicken Thighs

**PAGE 88**
Ginger Cod in Lemongrass
Coconut Broth

**PAGE 90**
Rainbow Bowl With
Sautéed Chicken

**PAGE 91**
Stir-Fry Beef Salad

**PAGE 92**
Pork Chops With Creamy
Mushroom Sauce

**PAGE 98**
Baked Meatballs With
Fresh Mozzarella

**PAGE 100**
Herbed Sweet
& Spicy Salmon

**PAGE 102**
Vegan Roasted
Red Pepper Pasta

**PAGE 104**
One-Pot Chile-Ginger
Chicken & Rice

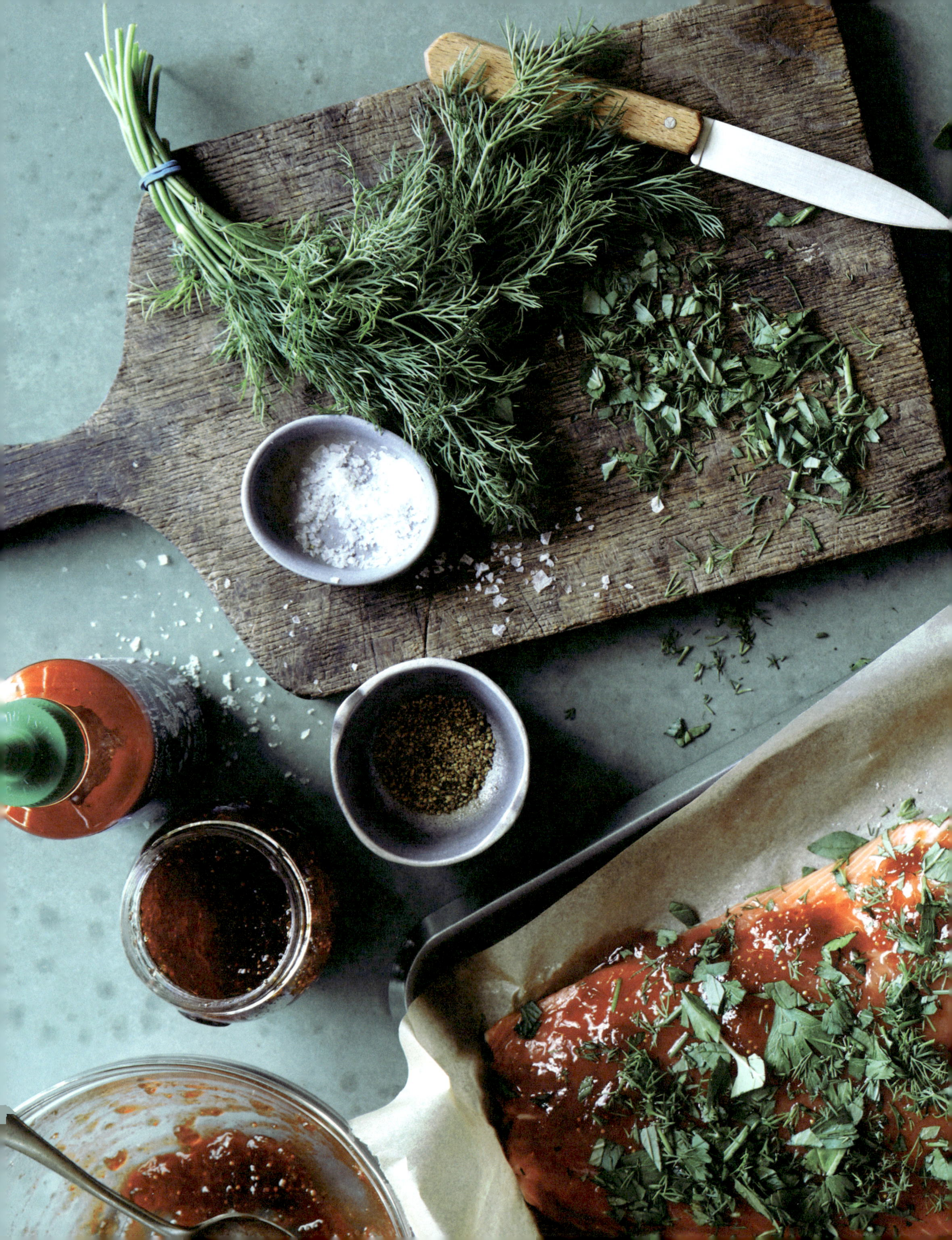

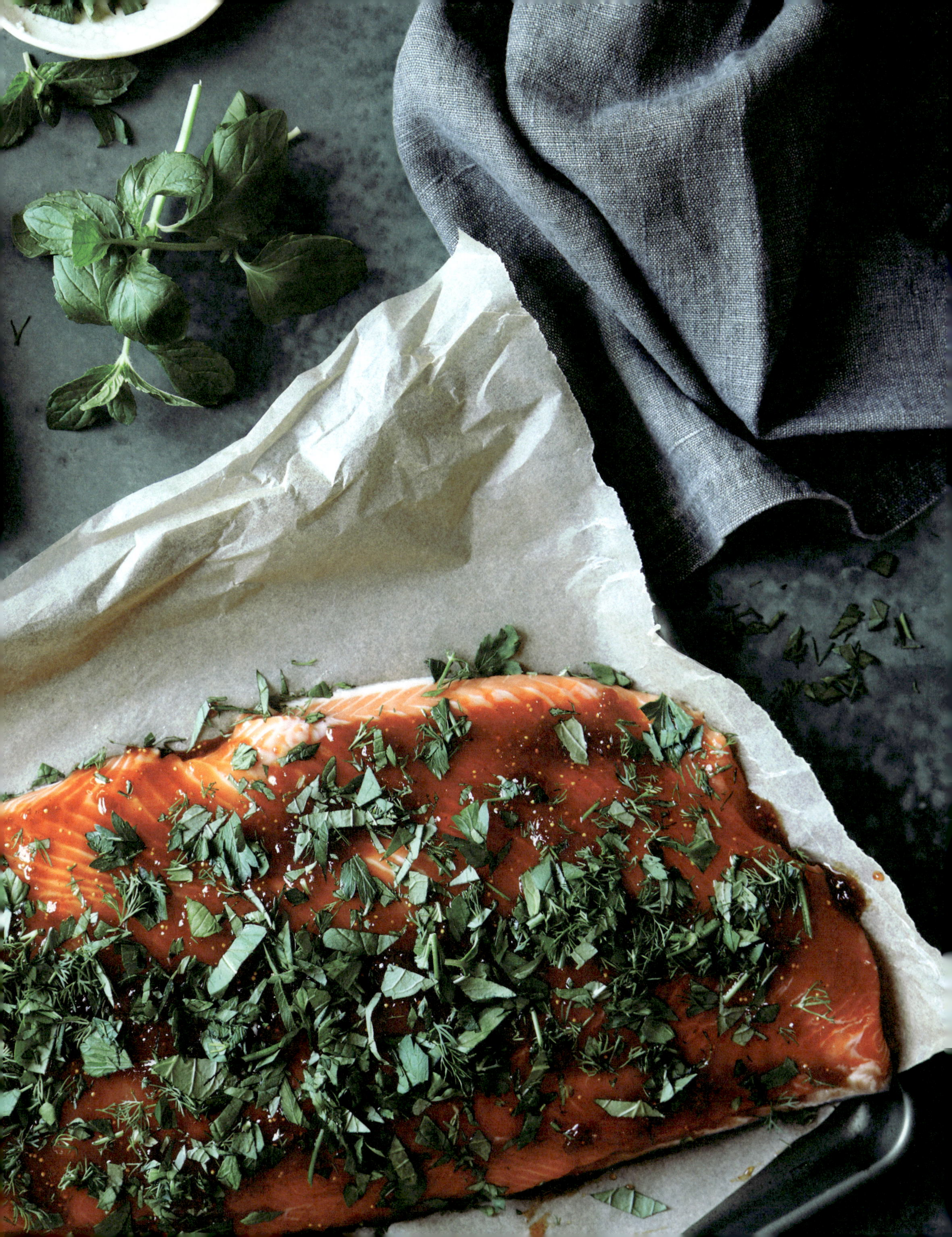

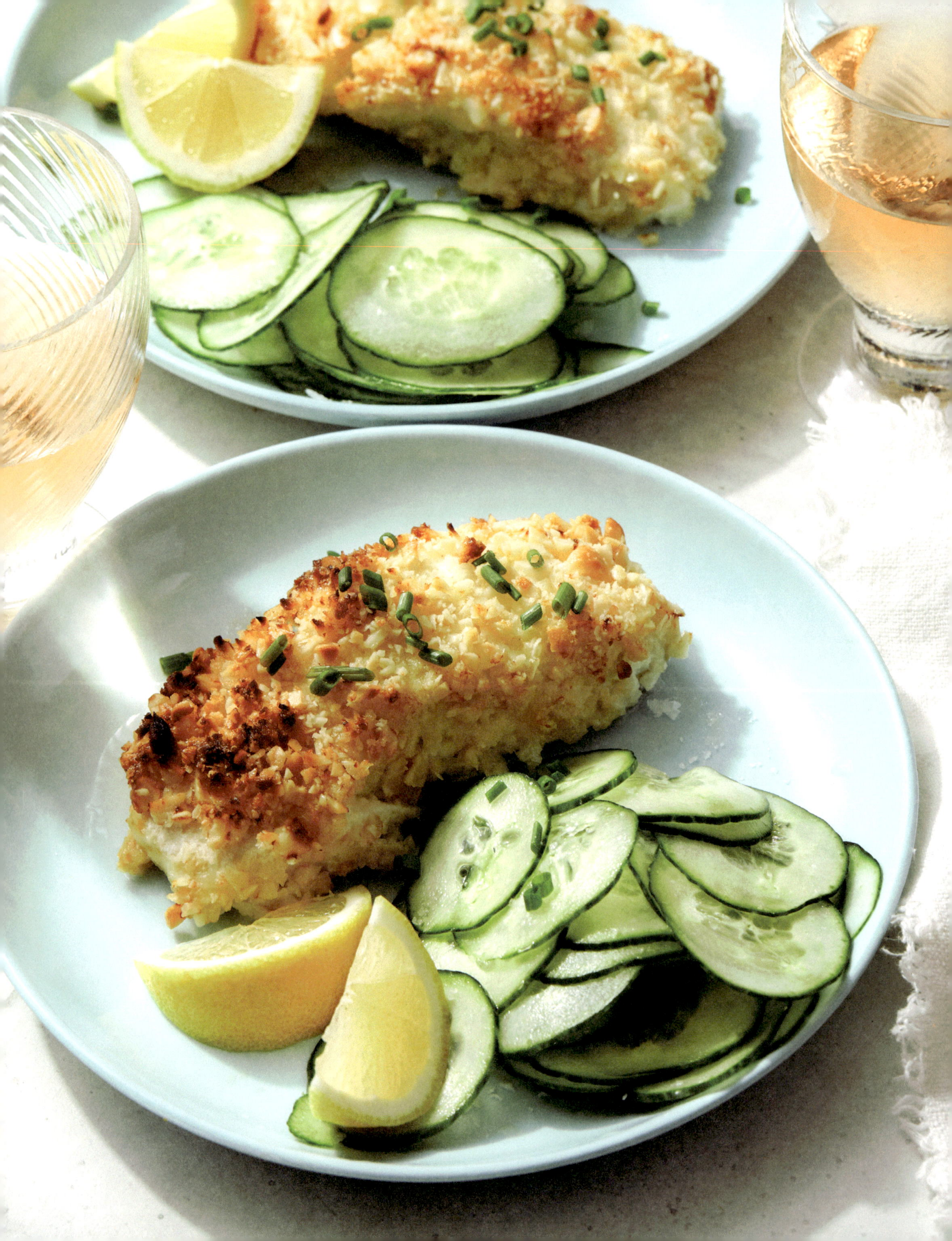

**YIELD** 2 SERVINGS    **ACTIVE TIME** 10 MINUTES    **TOTAL TIME** 25 MINUTES

The mild taste of halibut is the ideal blank slate for a lemony hazelnut crust in this energizing dish from functional medicine expert **Chris Kresser**. Refreshing cucumbers and chives complete this restaurant-worthy meal perfect for dining al fresco.

DINNER

# Paleo Hazelnut-Crusted Halibut

Gluten-Free · Grain-Free · Dairy-Free · Egg-Free

### INGREDIENTS

1 tablespoon Thrive Market Organic Virgin Coconut Oil

Sea salt and white pepper, to taste

2 8-ounce halibut fillets

1 cup Thrive Market Vegan Mayonnaise

1 1/2 cups hazelnuts, very finely chopped

Juice of 1 lemon

Fresh chives, chopped

1 large cucumber, very thinly sliced

### INSTRUCTIONS

Preheat oven to 375°F. Grease an ovenproof baking dish with coconut oil or ghee.

Salt and pepper the halibut and thoroughly coat with mayonnaise. Dredge the fillets in the chopped hazelnuts and place in the baking dish.

Bake for 15 minutes, or until the fish flakes easily with a fork. Keep a close eye while baking, as the hazelnuts can burn easily. If necessary, lower the temperature to 350°F.

Plate the cooked fillets, squeeze lemon over them, and garnish with chives. Arrange the sliced cucumber on the side.

*Scan here to shop the recipe*

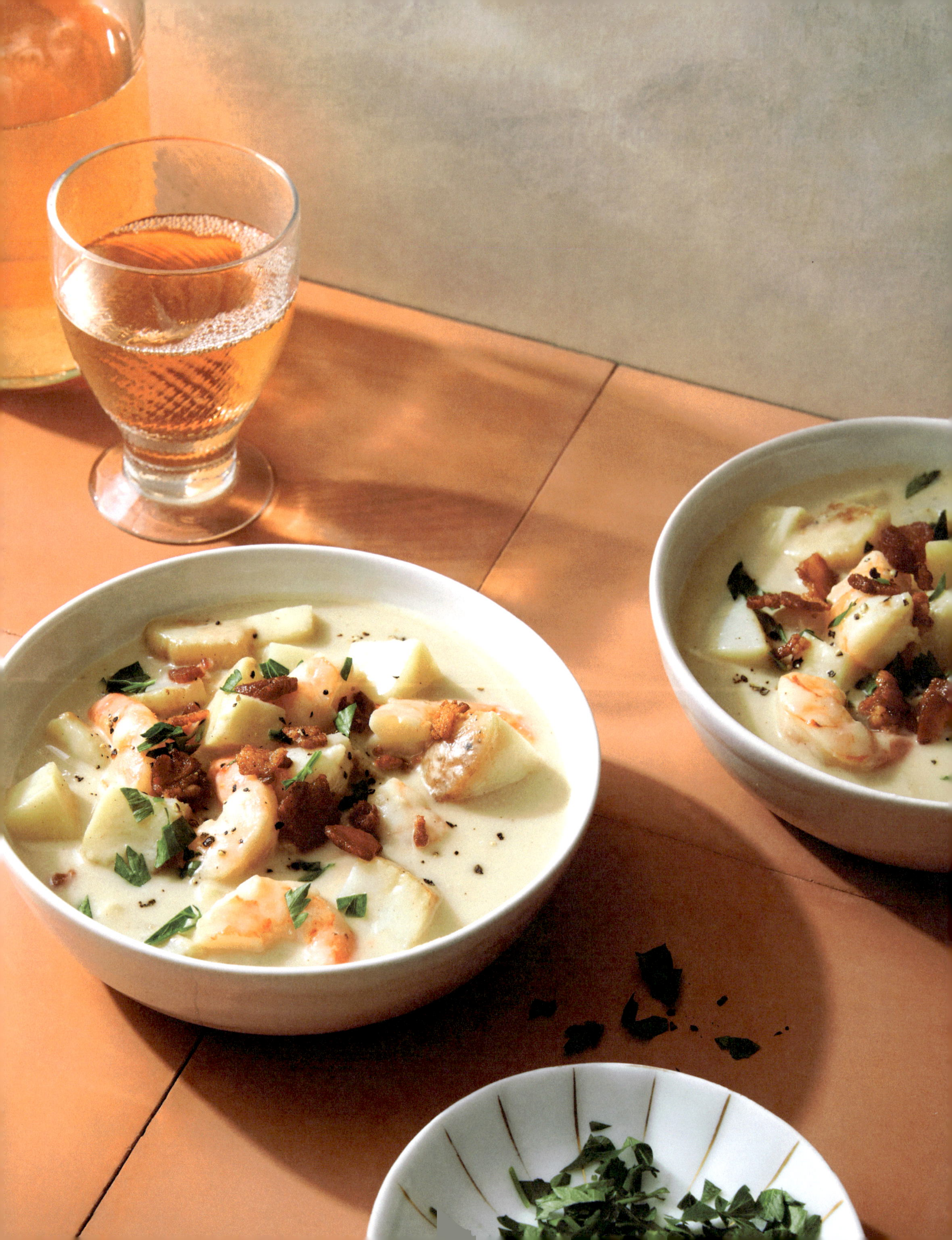

YIELD 4–5 SERVINGS    ACTIVE TIME 5 MINUTES    TOTAL TIME 30 MINUTES

Coconut milk brings creamy texture (sans dairy) to this spin on traditional seafood chowder. We recommend topping your bowls with crispy bacon immediately before serving for a hit of salt and smoke to balance it all out.

DINNER

# Seafood Scallop Chowder

Gluten-Free · Grain-Free · Dairy-Free · Egg-Free

## INGREDIENTS

1 pound scallops (try Thrive Market Wild-Caught Sea Scallops), patted dry

2 teaspoons sea salt, divided

2 teaspoons Thrive Market Organic Ground Pepper, divided

1 tablespoon Thrive Market Organic Virgin Coconut Oil

6 slices bacon, cut into cubes (try Thrive Market Non-GMO No Sugar Added Uncured Bacon)

1 medium onion, diced

2 cloves garlic, minced

1 small cauliflower, cut into small florets

1 (13.5-ounce) can Thrive Market Organic Coconut Milk, Regular

4 cups Thrive Market Organic Chicken Bone Broth

1 medium celery root, peeled and cut into 1/2-inch cubes

1 bag (30-40) shrimp, chopped (try Thrive Market Wild-Caught Peeled Shrimp)

Chopped parsley, for serving

## INSTRUCTIONS

Arrange scallops on a sheet tray. Blend 1 teaspoon salt and 1 teaspoon pepper and sprinkle the mixture on both sides.

Heat coconut oil in a large Dutch oven over medium-high heat. When hot, add bacon and cook until crisp, about 3 to 5 minutes; remove with a slotted spoon to drain on a paper towel-lined plate. Add scallops to bacon fat and sear on both sides, about 1 to 2 minutes. Transfer to a plate and cool.

Add onion and garlic to the Dutch oven; sauté until soft, about 5 to 7 minutes. Stir in cauliflower, coconut milk, chicken bone broth, remaining 1 teaspoon salt, and remaining 1 teaspoon pepper to taste. Bring to a boil. Reduce heat to simmer and let cauliflower cook until tender, about 10 minutes.

Using an immersion blender, purée until smooth. (Alternatively, you can purée the soup in batches in a high-speed blender.) Add celery root and simmer until pieces are easily pierced with a fork, about 5 minutes.

Cut scallops into smaller pieces, then return them (including any juices) to the pot. Add shrimp and stir. Cook for 3 to 4 minutes, until shrimp have turned pink and curled slightly.

Sprinkle parsley on soup before serving.

*Scan here to shop the recipe*

**YIELD** 4 SERVINGS     **TOTAL TIME** 30 MINUTES

A spicy-sweet marinade transforms tofu into a craveable taco filling in this lively dish from holistic health pro **Pamela Salzman**. Serve with a light and citrusy avocado crema—and maybe a margarita?

DINNER

# Chipotle Tofu Tacos

Gluten-Free · Grain-Free · Dairy-Free · Vegan · Egg-Free

## INGREDIENTS

1 block (12 to 15 ounces) extra-firm tofu, preferably organic/non-GMO and sprouted

### For the Marinade

1 tablespoon Thrive Market Organic Extra Virgin Olive Oil

1 tablespoon Thrive Market Organic Coconut Aminos

1 tablespoon fresh orange juice

2 teaspoons Thrive Market Organic Maple Syrup

1 tablespoon arrowroot starch or Thrive Market Organic Corn Starch

1/2 teaspoon chipotle powder

1/2 teaspoon Thrive Market Organic Chili Powder

1/2 teaspoon Thrive Market Organic Garlic Powder

1/2 teaspoon Thrive Market Organic Smoked Paprika

### For the Avocado-Lime Crema (optional)

1 large ripe avocado, peeled and pitted

1/2 cup Thrive Market Vegan Mayonnaise

1/2 cup cilantro leaves and tender stems

Juice of 1 lime, about 2 tablespoons

1/4 teaspoon of salt, plus more to taste

### For Serving

Warm grain-free tortillas or lettuce leaves

Pickled onions (optional)

Shredded cabbage (optional)

Radishes (optional)

Thrive Market Organic Salsa (optional)

## INSTRUCTIONS

Preheat oven to 400°F and line a large, rimmed baking sheet with parchment paper.

Slice the tofu in half lengthwise, wrap the blocks in paper towels, and place on a cutting board. Place something heavy (like a skillet filled with cans) on top of the tofu and allow to sit for 15 minutes or longer, if possible, to drain excess liquid. Once drained, cut tofu into 1-inch cubes.

In a medium bowl or a container that can hold the tofu in 1 layer, mix all the marinade ingredients until well combined. Add the tofu and gently coat each piece, trying not to break the cubes.

While the tofu marinates, make the crema: In a blender or the bowl of a food processor fitted with the metal S blade, combine all the crema ingredients and process until smooth, adding a tablespoon or 2 of water to thin it out if necessary.

Arrange the tofu in 1 layer on the prepared baking sheet and bake for 20 to 25 minutes, tossing halfway, until it is crispy and golden on the edges.

Fill tortillas or lettuce leaves with tofu along with crema and your choice of toppings.

*Scan here to shop the recipe*

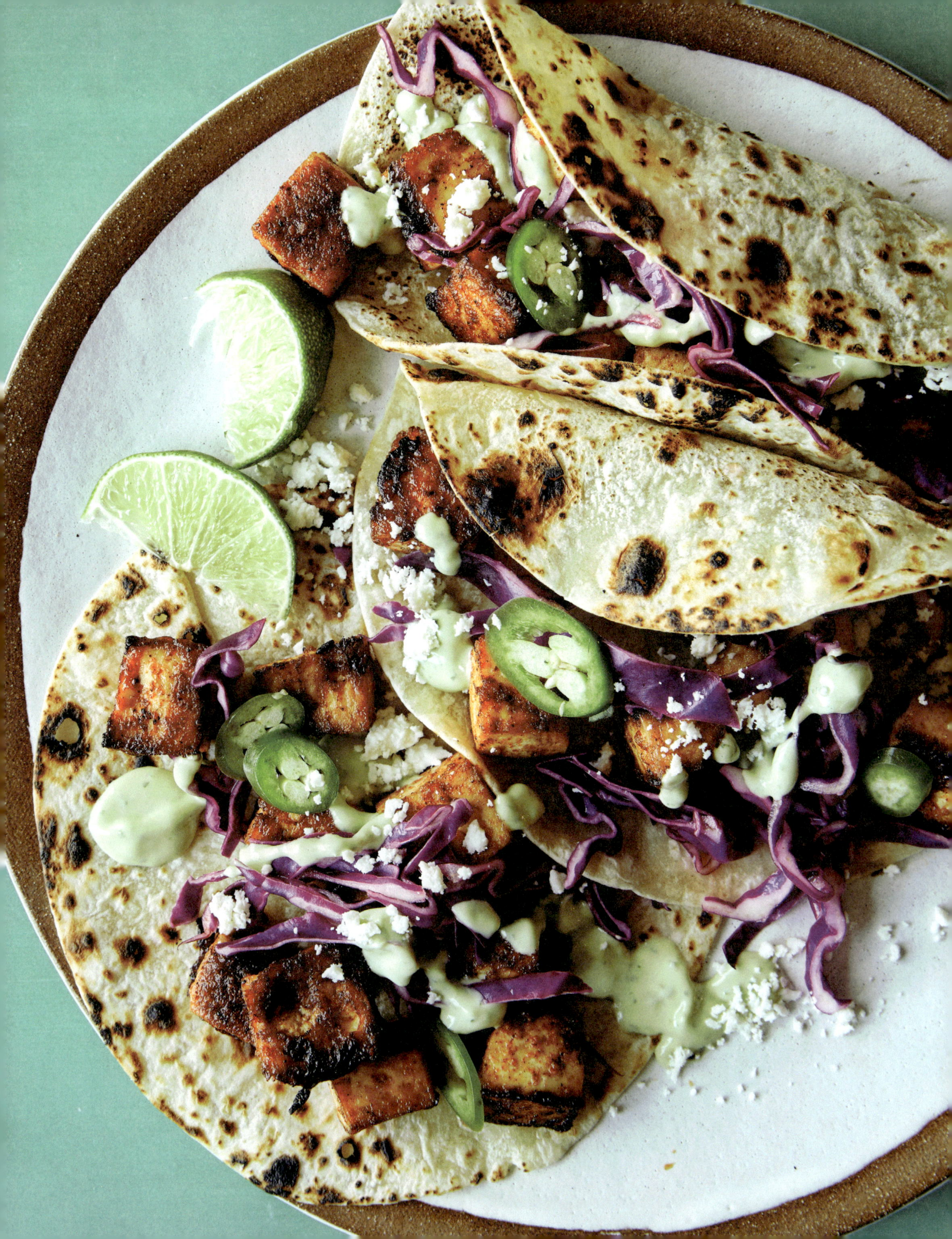

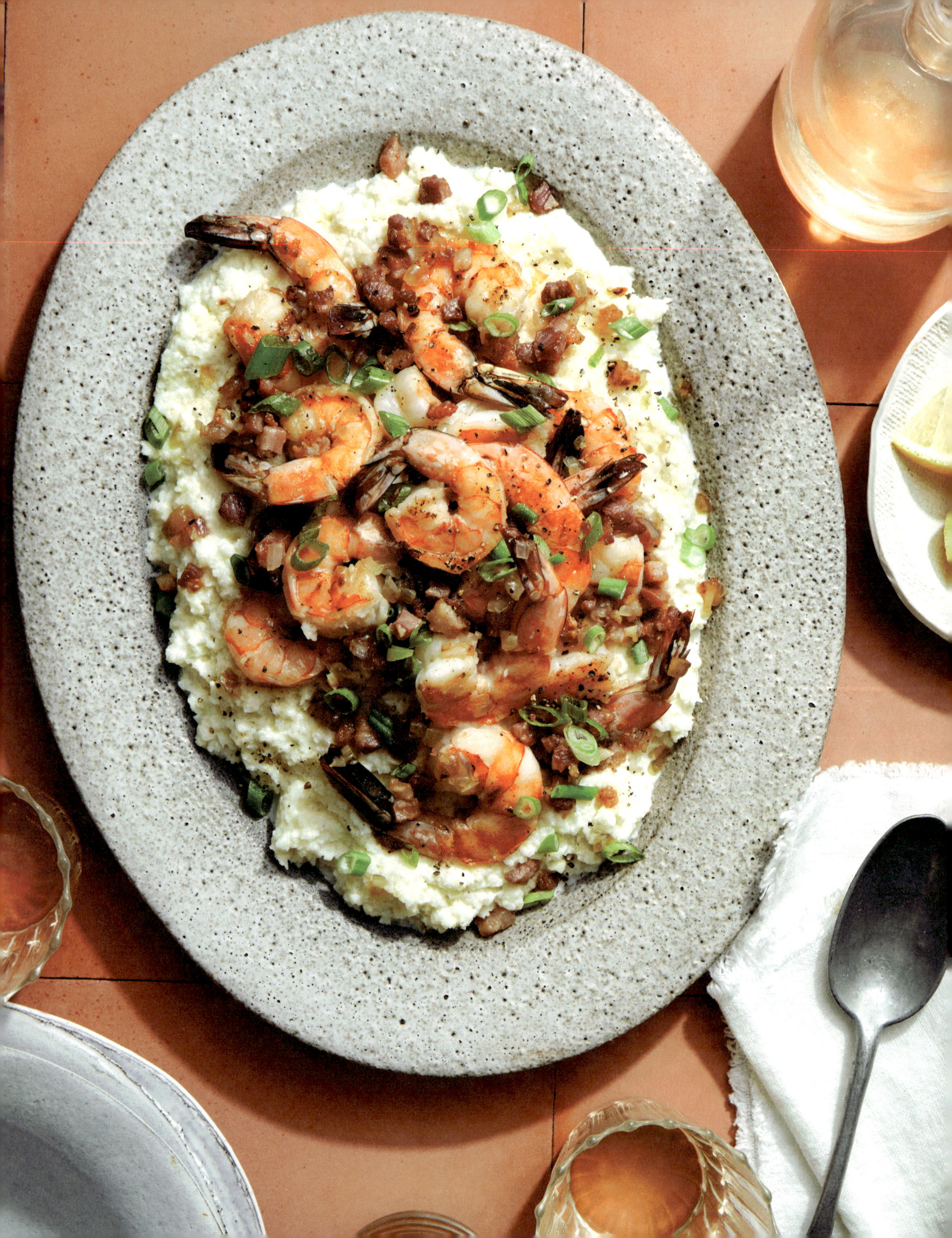

YIELD 6 SERVINGS   TOTAL TIME 30 MINUTES

Cauliflower stands in for grits in this carb-conscious version of a Southern comfort food classic, created by **Wes Shoemaker** of Highfalutin' Low Carb. With garlicky shrimp and salty bacon, this savory dish is sure to be a hit on the dinner table; it also makes an impressive brunch spread.

DINNER

# Shrimp & Cauliflower "Grits"

Gluten-Free   Grain-Free   Nut-Free

### INGREDIENTS

1 pound frozen cauliflower florets

3 tablespoons butter or Thrive Market Organic Ghee, divided

3 tablespoons heavy whipping cream

4 ounces gouda cheese, shredded

Salt & Thrive Market Organic Ground Pepper to taste

4 ounces diced pancetta or Thrive Market Non-GMO No Sugar Added Uncured Bacon

1 shallot, diced (or 2 tablespoons diced onion)

1 tablespoon minced garlic

1 pound Thrive Market Wild-Caught Peeled Shrimp

4–5 green onions, thinly sliced (green parts only)

Squeeze of lemon

### INSTRUCTIONS

Microwave the frozen cauliflower in a covered glass bowl for 10–12 minutes, stirring occasionally. Mash with a potato masher until it is the consistency of grits. Add 1 tablespoon of butter, the heavy whipping cream, and gouda cheese. Mix well and season with salt and pepper to taste. Keep warm.

Sauté the pancetta or bacon over medium-low heat until crispy. Remove and set aside. In the remaining bacon fat, add 2 tablespoons of butter and cook the shallots or onions until lightly browned. Add the garlic and stir until fragrant, about 30 seconds.

Add the shrimp. Cook for 8 to 10 minutes or until the shrimp are just cooked and still tender. Remove from heat and mix in the reserved bacon/pancetta and scallions.

Serve the cauliflower "grits" in a shallow bowl and top generously with the shrimp and sauce. Top with a squeeze of lemon and serve.

*Scan here to shop the recipe*

YIELD 4 SERVINGS    ACTIVE TIME 20 MINUTES    TOTAL TIME 30 MINUTES

In this rewarding departure from your average beef burger—shared by paleo expert and Primal Kitchen Founder **Mark Sisson**—vibrant pistachio pesto balances the savory flavor of lamb, while cooling mint gives each bite a fresh finish.

DINNER

# Lamb Burgers With Pistachio Pesto

Gluten-Free  Grain-Free  Dairy-Free  Egg-Free

## INGREDIENTS

**For the Burgers**

1 1/2 pounds ground lamb

1 teaspoon Thrive Market Organic Ground Cumin

1/4 teaspoon Thrive Market Organic Ground Cinnamon

1/4 teaspoon Thrive Market Organic Ground Allspice

1/2 teaspoon salt

1/4 teaspoon Thrive Market Organic Ground Pepper

1/4 cup mint leaves, finely chopped

1/4 cup parsley, chopped

**For the Pistachio Pesto**

1 garlic clove

1 cup Thrive Market Organic Roasted & Salted Pistachios

1/2 cup Thrive Market Avocado Oil

1 teaspoon lemon juice, or more to taste

1/4 cup mint leaves, loosely packed

Pinch of salt

## INSTRUCTIONS

First, make the burgers: Mix together the ground lamb, spices, chopped mint, and parsley. Form 4 patties and pan-fry or grill them, about 4 to 6 minutes per side.

Next, make the pistachio pesto: While the burgers are cooking, blend together garlic, pistachios, avocado oil, lemon juice, whole mint leaves, and salt in a food processor. Serve burgers with pesto on top.

*Scan here to shop the recipe*

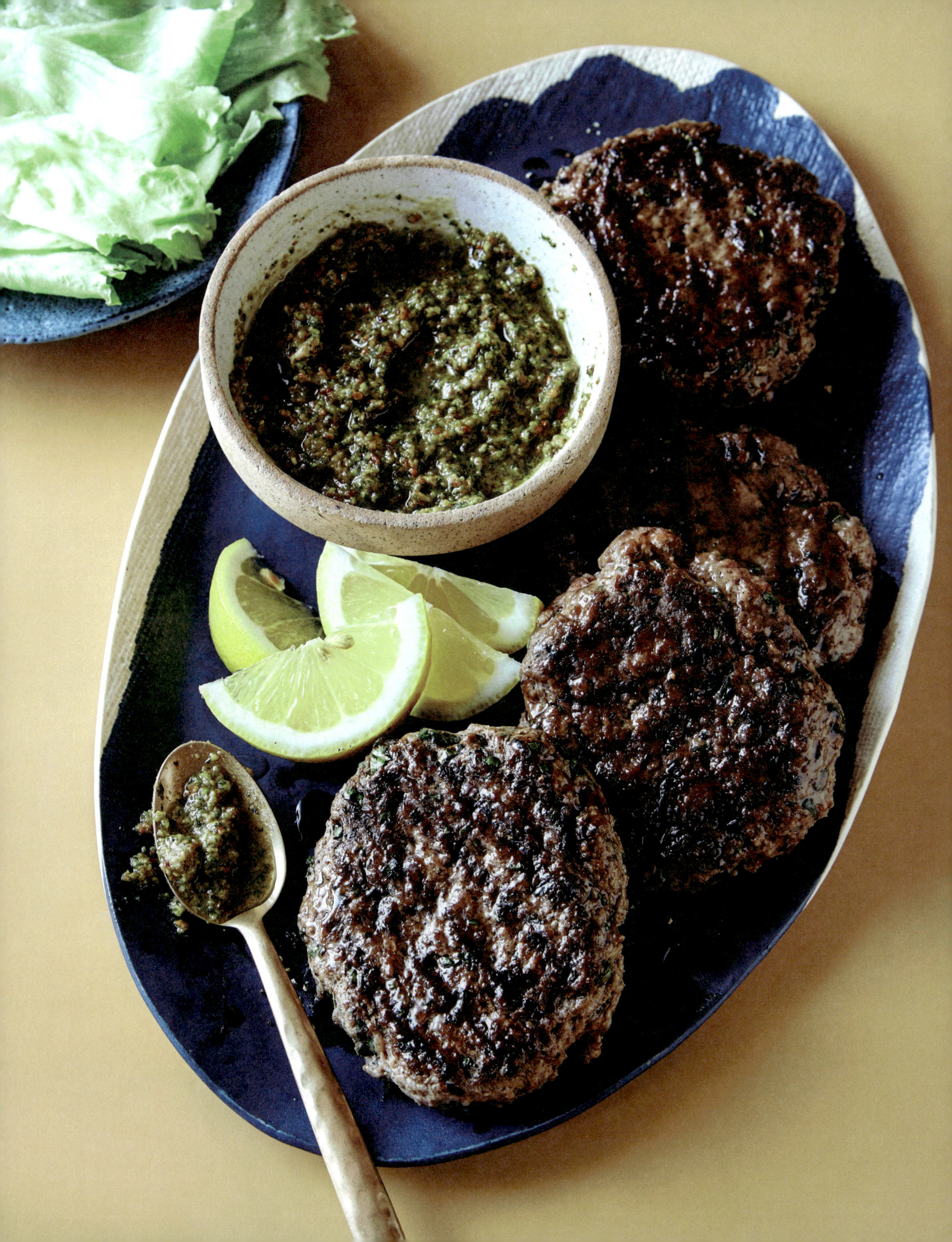

**LES VIGNES DE COULOUS**
**CADILLAC CÔTES DE BORDEAUX, FRANCE**

# Returning to Bordeaux

*Josh Nadel, Master Sommelier for Thrive Market's clean wine program, had the privilege of tasting winemaker Pauline Lapierre's first-ever vintage at a wine trade fair in Germany. He was drawn to her responsible practices and the beautiful expression of terroir in her wines, which he says "represent expertise, passion, and risk."*

*He hopes her approach ushers in a new guard of vintners doing things the old way. "She's paving the way for other winemakers who want to get back to the roots of winemaking and transition to organics," he says.*

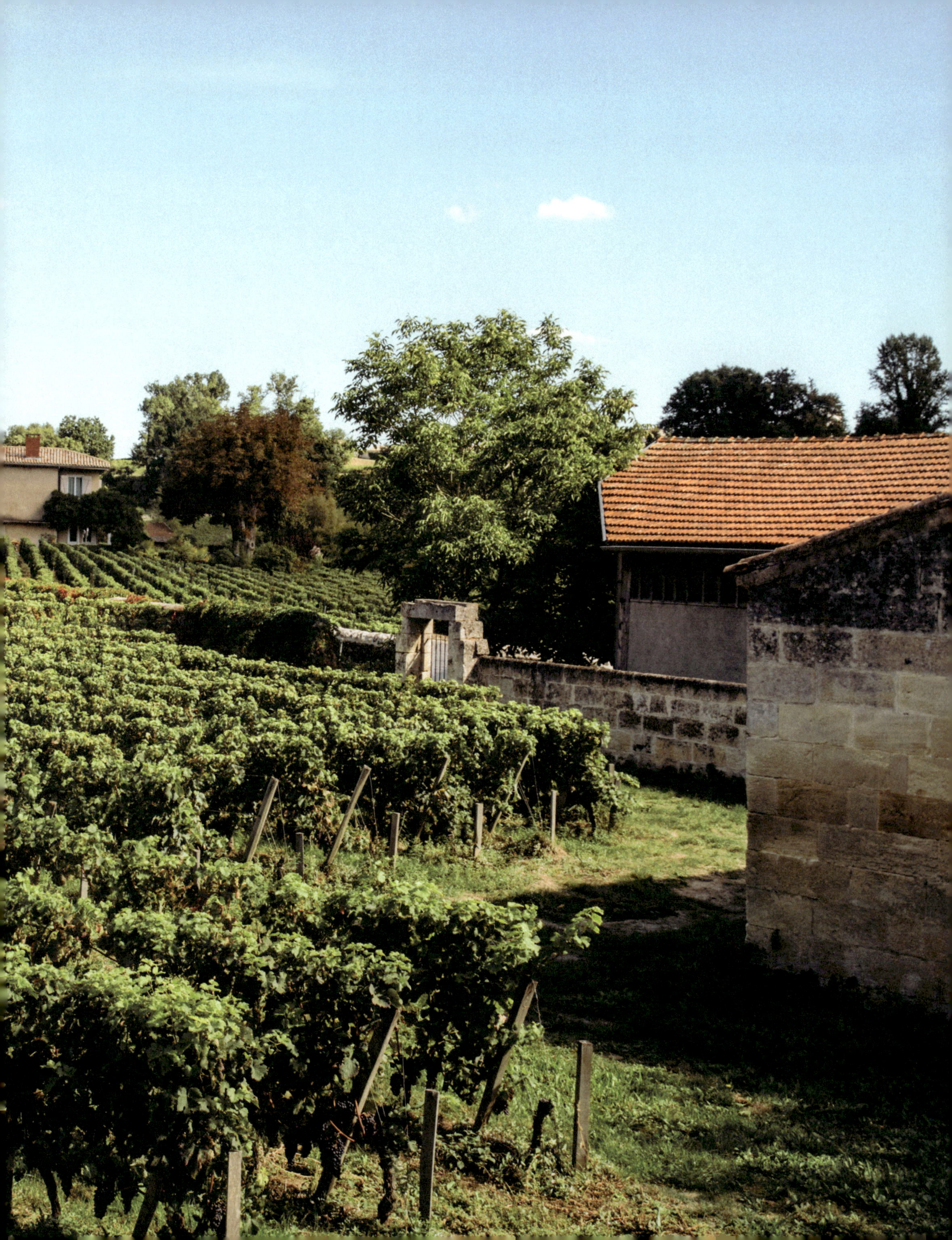

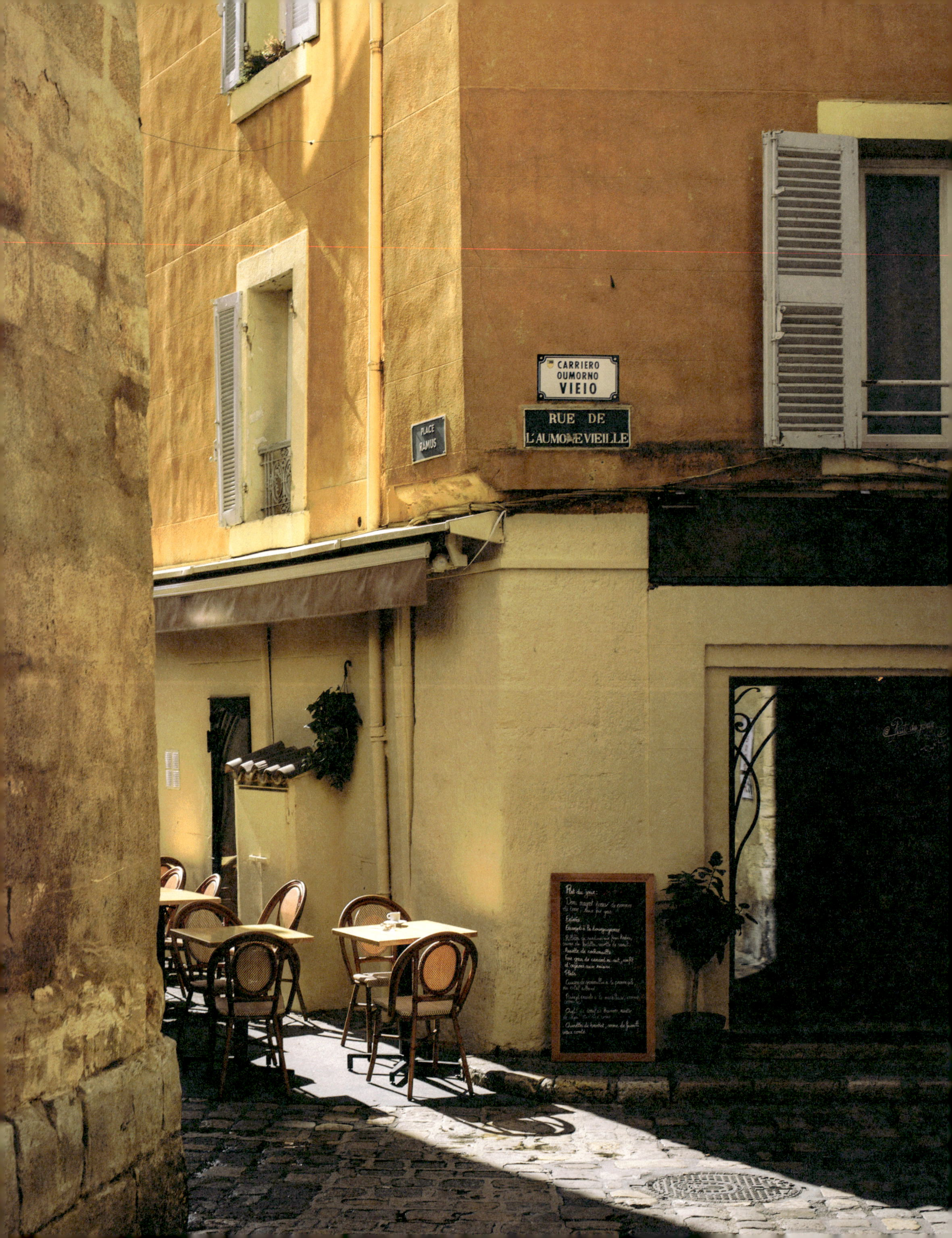
CARRIERO
OUMORNO
VIEIO
RUE DE
PLACE
RAMUS

*Here, Nadel and Lapierre talk about Pauline's journey back to Bordeaux in search of better wine and organic methods that help heal the earth.*

**Tell me about your connection to Bordeaux.** I spent my childhood on my family's winery, Château Haut-Rian, in Bordeaux. Years later, I bought my own small plot of land just a few miles from my parents' estate. I saw it as an opportunity to train in organic farming and do my own thing.

My small estate had been farmed organically for a decade by the previous owner. My number-one priority became growing healthy grapes in a healthy environment without relying on chemicals. This is, I think, the main task of my generation.

**Before starting your own winery, what were you doing with your life?** In my twenties, I spent two years in Singapore working as a financial controller. During that time, I couldn't find a delicious bottle of wine at a fair price. In Singapore, 6,700 miles from France, every bottle I came across was either absurdly expensive or super industrial.

When my parents came to visit me in Singapore, they brought wine from the family estate. It was pure and fresh. The taste immediately brought me back to my childhood. That's when I knew something was missing from my life.

I realized I was just doing a job. I didn't feel any fulfillment or accomplishment. So I left my career in finance and returned to France to study oenology, the science of wine and winemaking.

**What's different about your approach to wine and winemaking?** When my parents founded their vineyard over 30 years ago, most winemakers believed that technology would improve everything. In contrast, my approach to winemaking involves good land management and minimal intervention between the grapes I grow and the wine you drink.

My wines get their character from the air, the gravelly soil, and the way the sun hits my southeast-facing vineyard. My grape yields are relatively low, given that the vines are up to 50 years old and I let grass grow wild around them. I exclusively use my estate-grown organic grapes, and we do everything from fermentation to bottling at my winery, Les Vignes de Coulous.

```
We're constantly discovering new winemakers and grape varietals
to introduce to our members, which means our wine selection
is constantly changing. No matter which wine we feature on
ThriveMarket.com, know that they are produced using organic
and sustainable farming practices and clean winemaking methods.
```

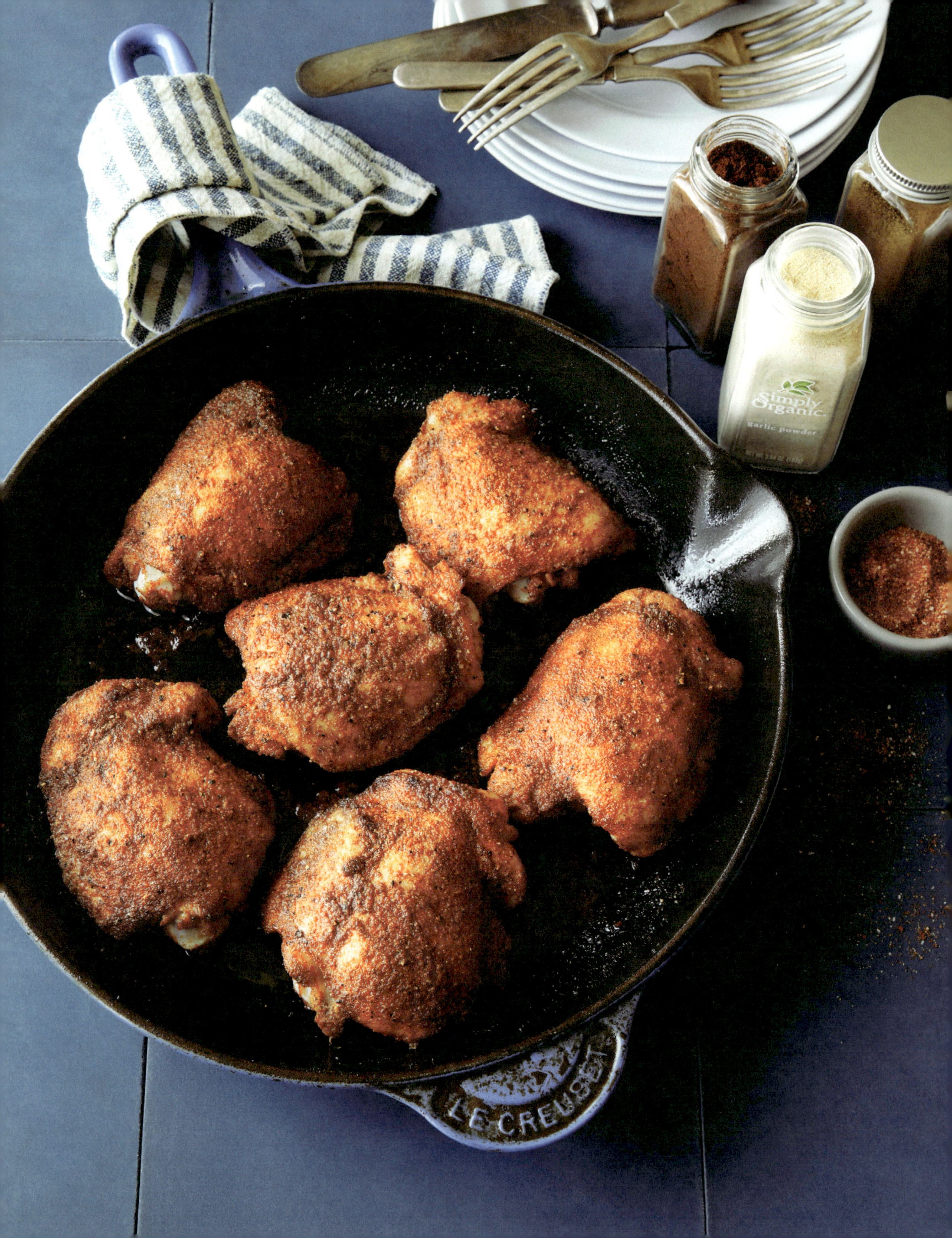
Simply Organic
garlic powder
LE CREUSET

YIELD 4 SERVINGS    ACTIVE TIME 5 MINUTES    TOTAL TIME 30 MINUTES

A lively medley of coriander, paprika, garlic, and cinnamon turn simple weeknight chicken into an aromatic treat for the taste buds in this recipe from **JJ Virgin**.

**DINNER**

# Roasted Spice-Rubbed Chicken Thighs

Gluten-Free | Grain-Free | Dairy-Free | Egg-Free | Nut-Free

### INGREDIENTS

1 teaspoon Thrive Market Organic Ground Coriander

1 teaspoon Thrive Market Organic Paprika

3/4 teaspoon Thrive Market Organic Garlic Powder

1/4 teaspoon Thrive Market Organic Ground Cinnamon

3/4 teaspoon sea salt

1/4 teaspoon Thrive Market Organic Ground Pepper

8 organic free range bone-in skinless chicken thighs, about 2 to 2 1/4 pounds, trimmed

1 tablespoon Thrive Market Avocado Oil or red palm fruit oil

### INSTRUCTIONS

Preheat oven to 400°F. Lightly oil a large, shallow roasting pan.

Combine the coriander, paprika, garlic powder, cinnamon, salt, and pepper in a small bowl.

Toss the chicken and oil in a separate bowl. Pour the spice mixture over the chicken and toss to coat. Place chicken on the prepared roasting pan.

Roast chicken in the center of the oven until a thermometer inserted into the thickest part of the thigh registers 165°F. It should take approximately 23 to 25 minutes. Let rest 5 minutes before serving.

*Scan here to shop the recipe*

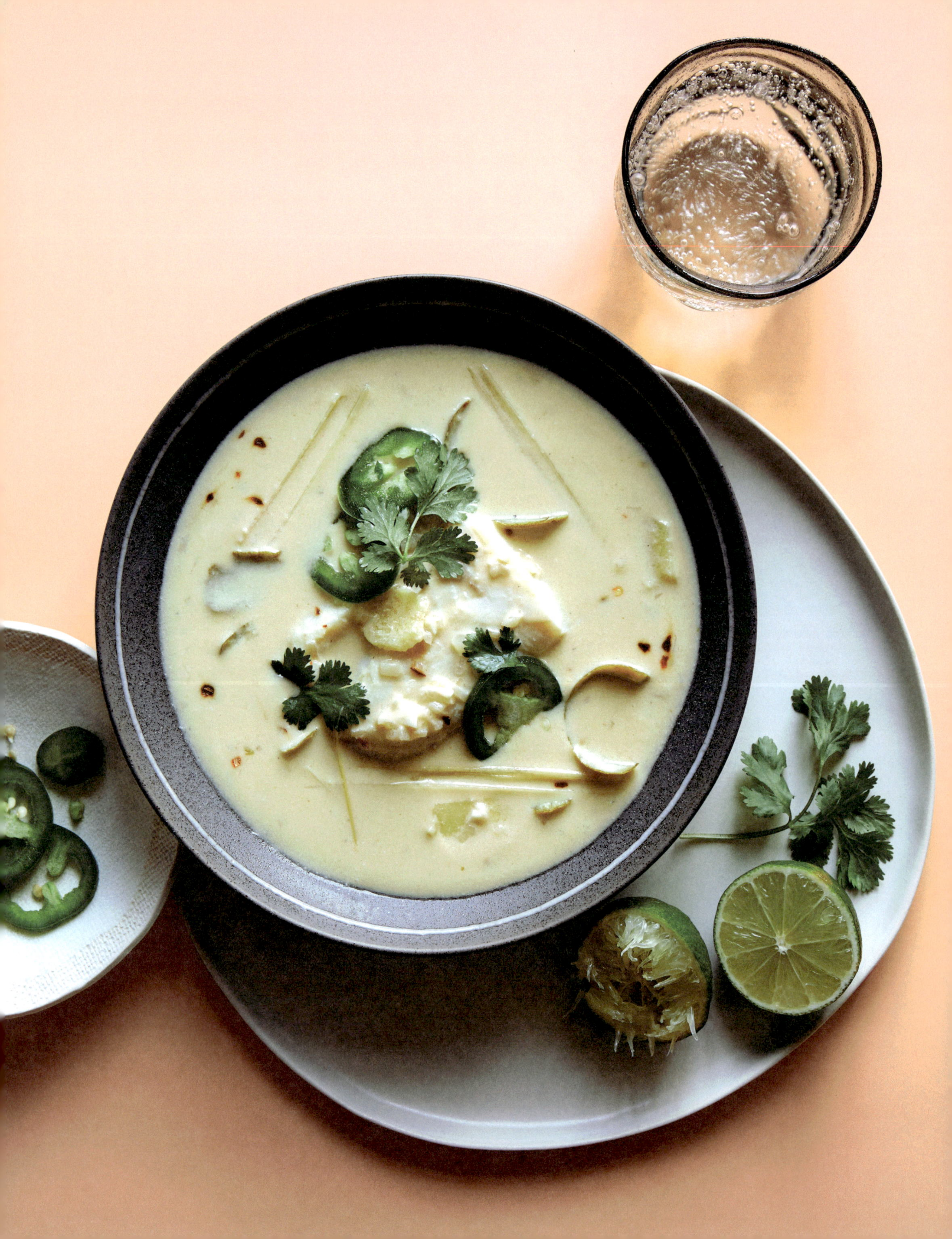

YIELD 4 SERVINGS    ACTIVE TIME 20 MINUTES    TOTAL TIME 30 MINUTES

Poaching infuses mild, flaky cod with the fresh flavors of lemongrass, lime, and ginger. Crushed red pepper flakes and jalapeño provide a kick, which you can adjust to suit your taste.

**DINNER**

# Ginger Cod in Lemongrass Coconut Broth

Gluten-Free | Grain-Free | Dairy-Free | Egg-Free

### INGREDIENTS

2 tablespoons Thrive Market Organic Virgin Coconut Oil

1 large shallot, minced

3 garlic cloves, roughly chopped

1/2 teaspoon Thrive Market Organic Crushed Red Pepper

1 (14.5-ounce) can Thrive Market Organic Coconut Milk

1 cup vegetable broth

2 (4-inch) stalks lemongrass, halved lengthwise and smashed

Peels and juice from 2 limes

1 (2-inch) piece ginger, peeled and thinly sliced

2 teaspoons fish sauce

2 sprigs fresh cilantro, plus more for garnish

4 (4-ounce) boneless, skinless Thrive Market Wild-Caught Atlantic Cod fillets

1 teaspoon sea salt

1/4 teaspoon Thrive Market Organic Ground Pepper

1 jalapeño, thinly sliced, for garnish

### INSTRUCTIONS

Add coconut oil to a large skillet and warm over medium heat. When melted, add shallot, garlic, and red pepper flakes; sauté until shallot is translucent, about 2 to 3 minutes.

Add coconut milk, vegetable broth, lemongrass, lime peels, ginger, fish sauce, and cilantro. Simmer, whisking occasionally, for 2 minutes.

Lightly place the fish into the sauce and bring sauce back to a simmer, then cover the pan and reduce heat to low. Cook about 5 to 6 minutes, or until cod is cooked through and flaky.

Transfer fish to a shallow bowl. Whisk lime juice, salt, and pepper into the sauce, then ladle it over the fish. Garnish with cilantro and jalapeño.

*Scan here to shop the recipe*

**YIELD** 1–2 SERVINGS    **TOTAL TIME** 20 MINUTES

To maximize the nutrients in your diet, the more colors on your plate, the better. Kids will love eating the rainbow with this many-hued, vegetable-forward bowl created by Dr. Mikhail Varshavski, better known as **Doctor Mike**.

DINNER

# Rainbow Bowl With Sautéed Chicken

Gluten-Free    Dairy-Free    Egg-Free

## INGREDIENTS

**For the Bowl**

1/2 cup Thrive Market Organic Sprouted Quinoa

1 cup chicken or vegetable stock

1 tablespoon Thrive Market Organic Extra Virgin Olive Oil

1 clove garlic, minced

1 chicken breast, cubed

1/4 teaspoon Thrive Market Organic Garlic Powder

Salt and pepper, to taste

1/4 cup diced onion

1/2 large carrot, shredded

1/2 cup sliced cherry tomatoes

1/2 cup shredded red cabbage

1/4 cup shelled edamame, steamed

1/2 avocado, peeled, pitted, and sliced

Fresh scallions

Sesame seeds

Cilantro

**For the Dressing**

2 tablespoons gluten-free soy sauce or Thrive Market Organic Coconut Aminos

1 teaspoon Thrive Market Organic Honey

1/4 teaspoon sesame oil

1 clove garlic, minced

## INSTRUCTIONS

Cook quinoa in chicken or vegetable stock according to package instructions and set aside.

In a saucepan over medium heat, add olive oil and sauté 1 clove of minced garlic. Once lightly browned, add cubed chicken, garlic powder, salt, and pepper to taste and sauté until fully cooked.

In a small bowl, make the dressing by whisking together soy sauce or coconut aminos, honey, sesame oil, and remaining garlic. Set aside.

Assemble the bowl(s): Start with a scoop of cooked quinoa, then add chicken, onion, carrots, cherry tomatoes, cabbage, and edamame. Top with sliced avocado, scallions, cilantro, and sesame seeds as desired. Drizzle with dressing and serve.

*Scan here to shop the recipe*

YIELD 4 SERVINGS    ACTIVE TIME 15 MINUTES    TOTAL TIME 15 MINUTES

Thinly sliced beef tip steak, diced bell peppers, and mixed greens form a primal trifecta in this warm salad created by **Robb Wolf**, author of *The Paleo Solution* and *Wired to Eat.* We recommend topping this hearty mix with a drizzle of balsamic vinegar.

DINNER

# Stir-Fry Beef Salad

Gluten-Free   Grain-Free   Dairy-Free   Egg-Free

### INGREDIENTS

2 teaspoons Thrive Market Organic Extra Virgin Olive Oil

3/4 cup sliced onion

1 pound beef tip steak, sliced into thin strips

1 tablespoon Thrive Market Organic Coconut Aminos

1 to 2 cups sliced bell peppers

1 bag of mixed greens

Balsamic vinegar, to serve

### INSTRUCTIONS

Add olive oil to a skillet over medium heat. Add sliced onions and sauté for about 5 minutes, until soft.

Add the beef and the coconut aminos and cook, tossing frequently, for about 5 minutes or until beef has browned.

Add the bell peppers and cook for a few minutes, until your desired texture is reached (longer for softer peppers, less time if you want more crunch).

Arrange mixed greens on plates, then top with the stir-fry mixture. Drizzle with balsamic vinegar and more olive oil to taste.

*Scan here to shop the recipe*

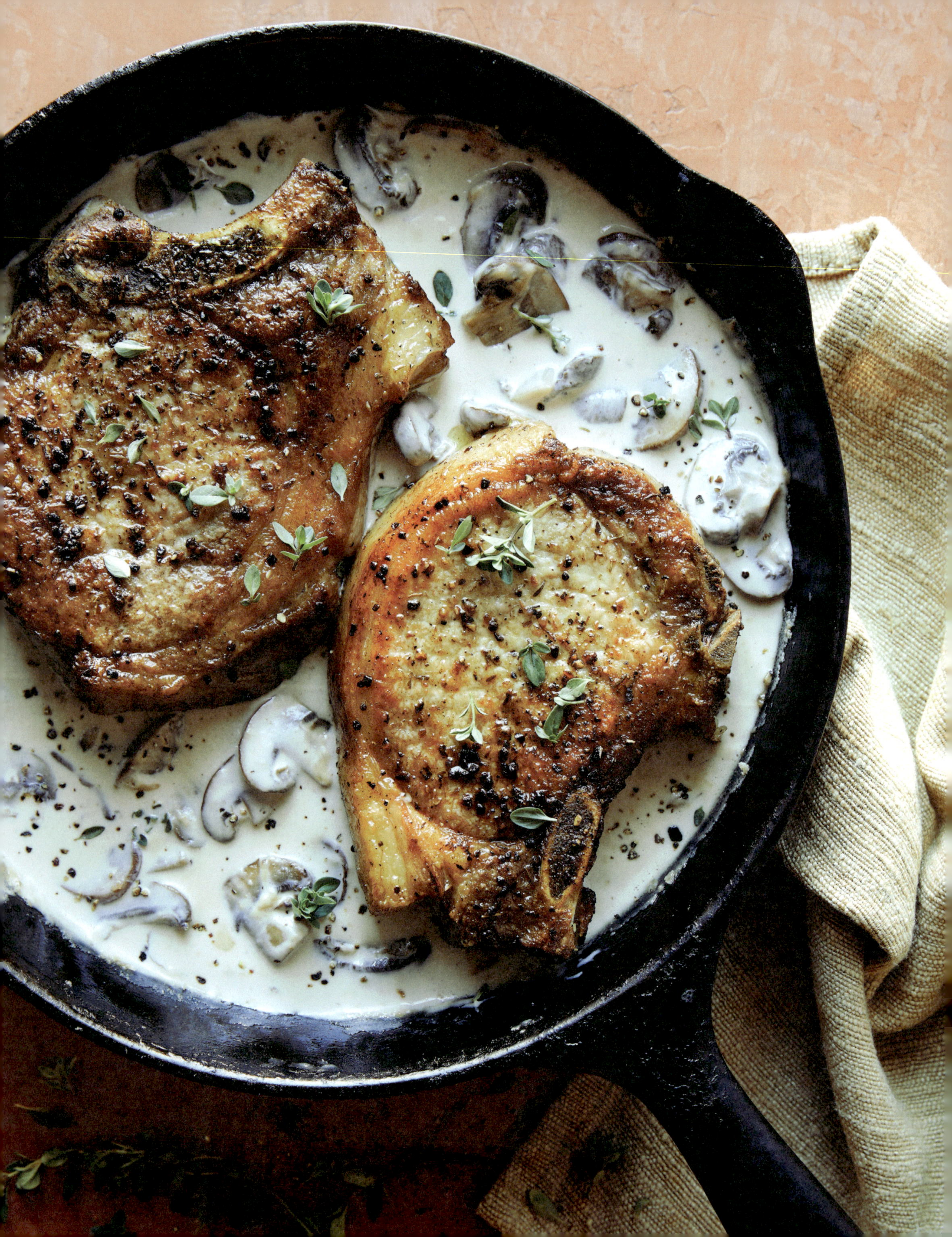

**YIELD** 2 SERVINGS  **TOTAL TIME** 30 MINUTES

This easy and impressive dinner for two feels celebratory, making it equally appropriate for date night or just a regular Tuesday. It calls for a splash of white wine, so grab a couple of glasses and enjoy a sip while you cook.

DINNER

# Pork Chops With Creamy Mushroom Sauce

Gluten-Free · Grain-Free · Egg-Free · Nut-Free

### INGREDIENTS

- 2 (1 1/4-inch thick) bone-in pork rib chops
- 1 1/2 teaspoons sea salt, divided
- 1/2 teaspoon Thrive Market Organic Garlic Powder
- 1/2 teaspoon Thrive Market Organic Thyme
- 1/4 teaspoon Thrive Market Organic Ground Pepper
- 3 tablespoons unsalted butter, divided
- 8 ounces cremini mushrooms, sliced
- 1/4 cup dry white wine
- 1/2 cup heavy cream
- 1/2 cup Thrive Market Organic Chicken Bone Broth
- 2 tablespoons cream cheese
- 2 tablespoons parsley, chopped

### INSTRUCTIONS

Preheat oven to 350°F and season pork chops with 1 teaspoon salt, garlic powder, thyme, and pepper. Add 1 tablespoon butter to a cast iron skillet set over medium-high heat. Sear pork chops for 4 minutes per side, until a golden crust forms. Transfer pork to a plate.

To the same pan, add remaining 2 tablespoons butter and mushrooms, arranging them in a single layer. Let mushrooms caramelize (resist the urge to stir at this stage), about 3 to 4 minutes. Add remaining 1/2 teaspoon salt, stir, and cook for 2 minutes more. Add wine and let it reduce for 2 to 3 minutes, then add the heavy cream and chicken broth.

Add cream cheese and whisk until incorporated. Simmer sauce until slightly thickened, about 3 to 5 minutes. Return chops to the pan and reduce heat to low. Baste the chops with sauce and simmer 2 to 3 minutes, then place the pan in the oven and cook for about 5 minutes, or until the internal temperature of the pork chops reaches 145 to 150°F. Let stand for 5 minutes before slicing. Sprinkle with parsley and serve.

*Scan here to shop the recipe*

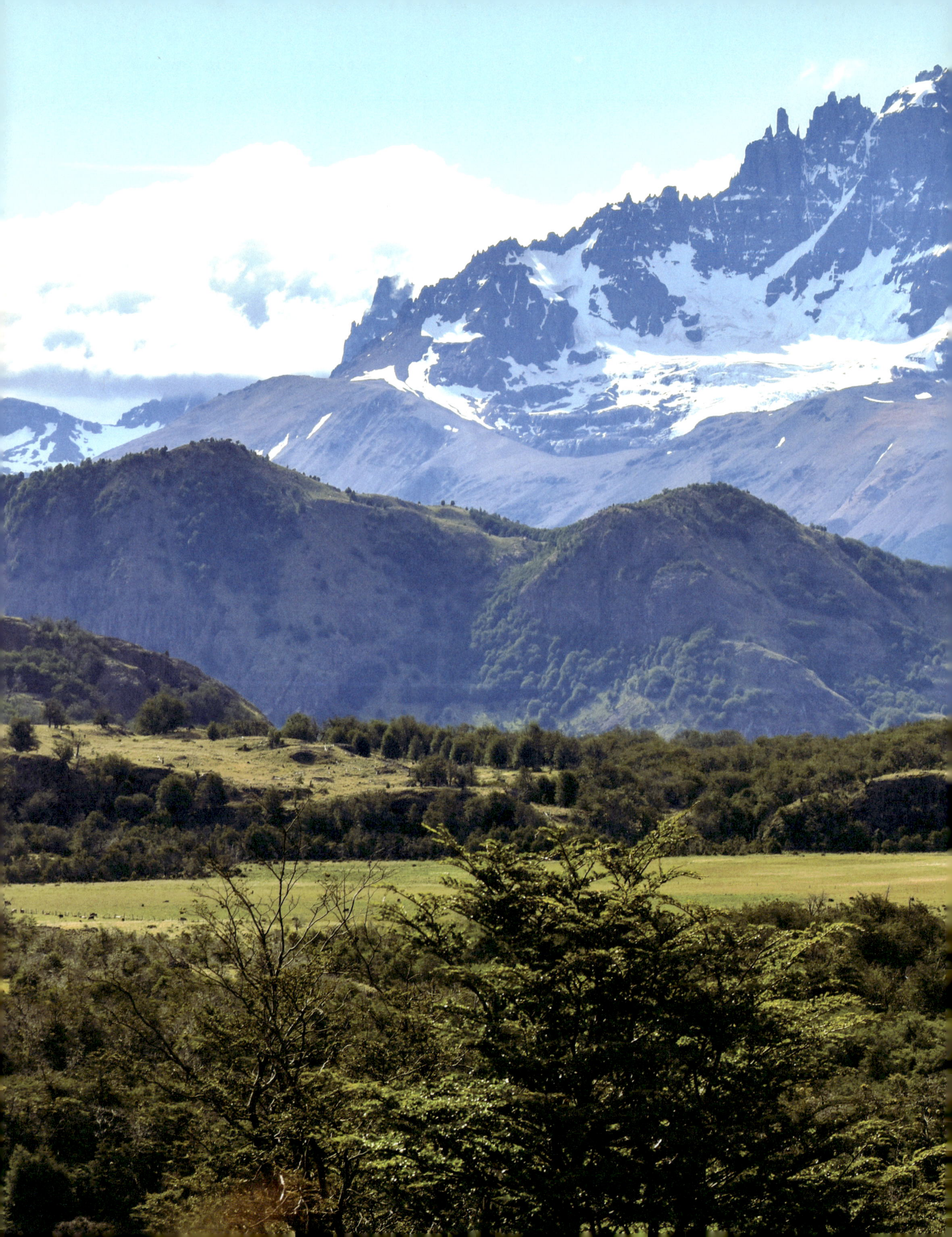

**THRIVE MARKET GRASS-FED BEEF
PATAGONIA, CHILE**

# Meat Matters

*Mike Hacaga is the Lead Product Innovator for Thrive Market Meat & Seafood. We spoke to him about his first (of many) trips to visit our grass-fed beef partner in Patagonia.*

**How are cattle raised differently in Chile as compared to the U.S.?** In Patagonia, the beef industry is connected to its roots. The land and cattle are tended by huasos, or Chilean cowboys, who favor a natural and humane approach. This is a far cry from the modern factory farming practiced worldwide.

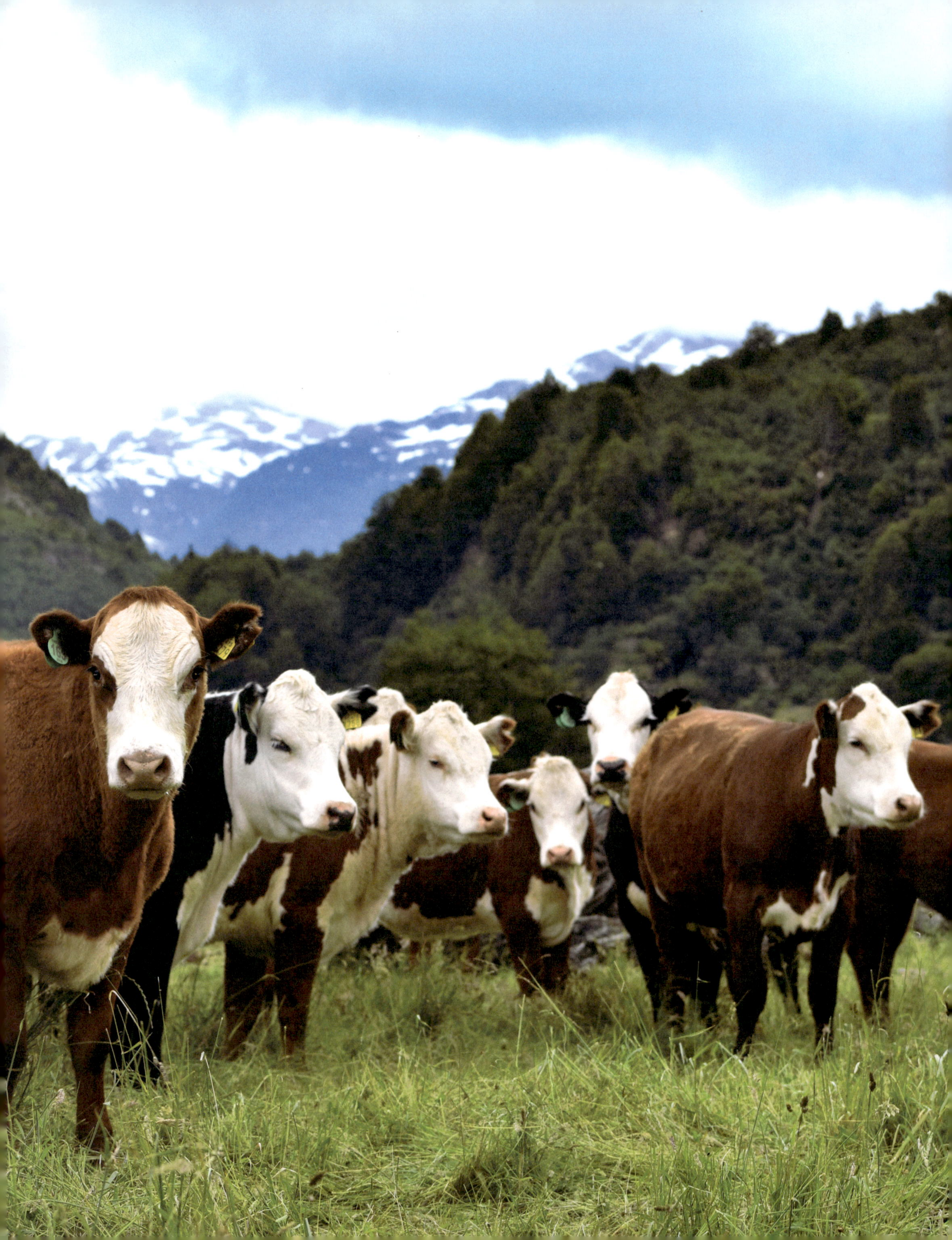

The huasos expertly move the cattle across the prairies, from one fresh parcel of green grass to another, using nothing more than a horse, a whistle, and a couple of herding dogs. In comparison, herders in the U.S. often use ATVs.

When you watch them herd the cattle, it's nothing less than poetry in motion. The dogs don't nip at the cattle's heels; instead, they wait patiently at the horse's front hoof, looking up at their huaso and awaiting a command. The dogs use their training and their natural herding instincts to move the animals in perfect synchrony.

Unlike cows in the U.S., these Chilean cows aren't fearful because they've never been mishandled or mistreated. The animals are curious and more than willing to approach a perfect stranger like myself.

Eating pasture-raised, grass-fed beef—instead of the industrially raised, grain-fed beef most of us in the U.S. have become accustomed to—is a crucial choice. It's not only better for your own nutrition and well-being; it's better for the future health of the ranchers, their animals, and the planet.

**Why do you want members to have access to grass-fed beef as opposed to grain-fed?** For the majority of my life, I admittedly wasn't a huge fan of the flavor and texture of grass-fed beef. But my opinion changed during my first visit to Chile. At night, the ranchers barbecued beef and lamb over a wood-burning fire in the pasture, overlooking a beautiful lake. I kid you not, this was unlike any other grass-fed beef I had tasted. It was tender and had a rich, deep, robust beef flavor.

But it's not just the flavor. The ranchers have successfully married old-world techniques with new learnings, resulting in a perfect balance between sustainability, animal welfare, and regenerative agriculture. Witnessing this harmony keeps me hopeful about the future.

**What is the future of sustainably raised and harvested beef?** That future includes setting a new benchmark for the beef Americans feed their families. By bringing this incredible product to Thrive Market members, I can give people access to beef that is of higher quality and better provenance than anything I've found in my 30 years in the industry.

Our G.A.P. Certified, 100% grass-fed beef comes from Patagonia, Chile, where ranchers prioritize animal welfare and sustainability. For every cow that's harvested, a native tree is planted.

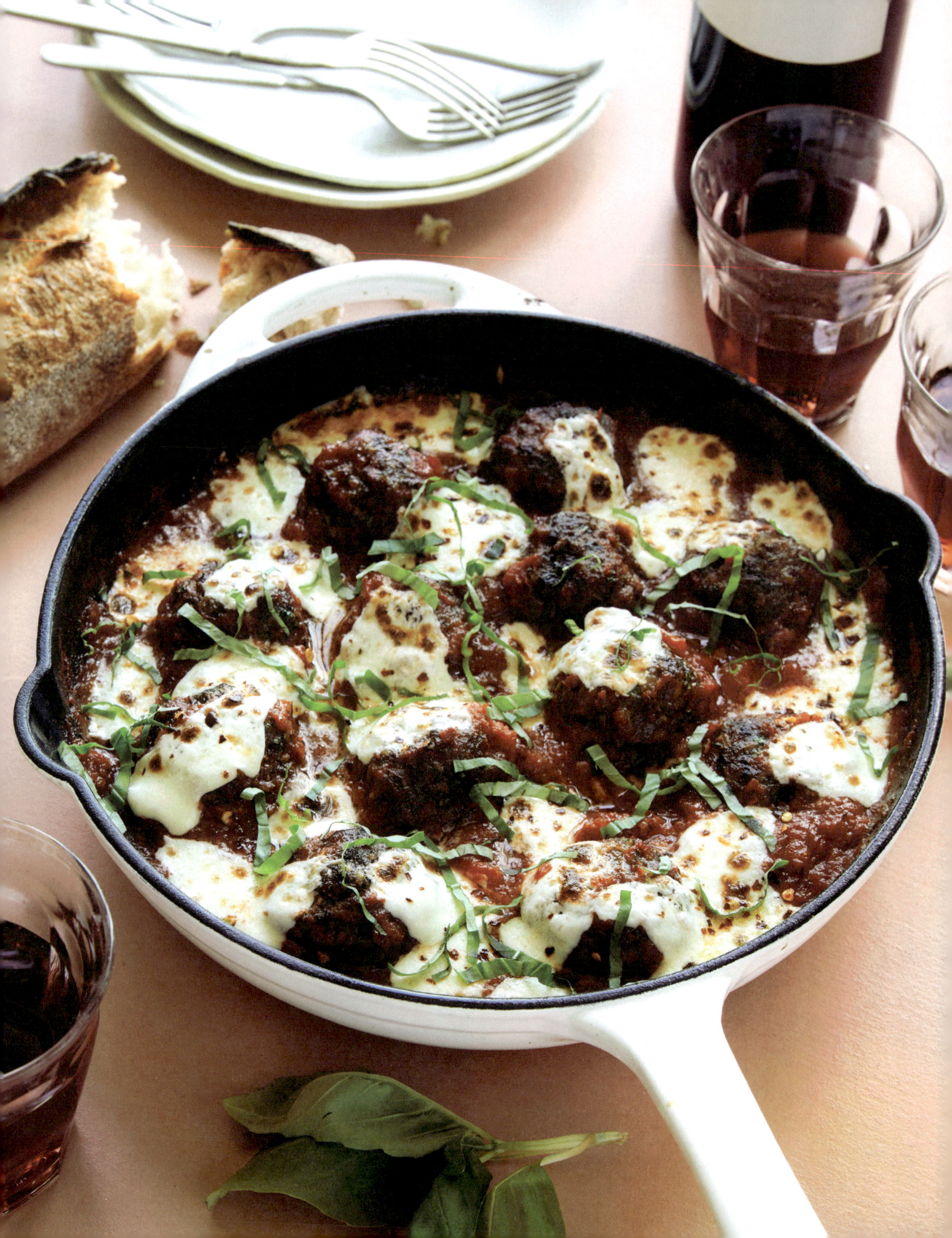

YIELD 6 SERVINGS    ACTIVE TIME 15 MINUTES    TOTAL TIME 15 MINUTES

In this hearty recipe, jarred tomato sauce is a shortcut that tastes anything but. Serve these juicy, flavorful meatballs with pasta, zucchini noodles, or however you wish—with fresh mozzarella and chopped basil, you really can't go wrong.

DINNER

# Baked Meatballs With Fresh Mozzarella

Gluten-Free · Grain-Free · Nut-Free

### INGREDIENTS

1 pound Thrive Market Grass-Fed Ground Beef

1 cup grated shallots, squeezed and drained of their juices

2 egg yolks

2 tablespoons chopped parsley

3 tablespoons chopped chives

1/4 teaspoon Thrive Market Organic Ground Allspice

1/2 teaspoon Thrive Market Organic Garlic Powder

1 teaspoon Thrive Market Organic Ground Cumin

2 teaspoons sea salt

Zest of 2 lemons

1 tablespoon Thrive Market Organic Extra Virgin Olive Oil

1 jar Thrive Market Organic Pasta Sauce, Tomato Basil

1 cup fresh mozzarella, sliced

1/4 cup fresh basil, for garnish

### INSTRUCTIONS

Preheat oven to 350°F.

Place beef, shallots, egg yolks, parsley, chives, allspice, garlic powder, cumin, salt, and lemon zest in a large bowl and mix together with a fork until just combined. Shape into 1-inch meatballs.

Heat olive oil in a large ovenproof skillet. Brown meatballs on all sides. Pour tomato sauce over meatballs. Place skillet in the oven and allow meatballs to cook through, about 8 minutes.

Remove the skillet from the oven and arrange sliced mozzarella over the top. Place under the broiler for 5 minutes until cheese is melted and bubbly.

Let cool slightly and top with fresh basil before serving.

*Scan here to shop the recipe*

YIELD 4–6 SERVINGS    TOTAL TIME 20 MINUTES

Fig preserves and sriracha sauce may strike you as an unlikely combination, but they pair beautifully in this simple salmon recipe from holistic health expert **Pamela Salzman**. No fig preserves on hand? Salzman says apricot also works.

DINNER

# Herbed Sweet & Spicy Salmon

Gluten-Free · Grain-Free · Dairy-Free · Egg-Free · Nut-Free

## INGREDIENTS

1 (24-ounce) Wild-Caught Salmon fillet (skin-on or skinless)

2 teaspoons Thrive Market Organic Extra Virgin Olive Oil

3/4 teaspoon sea salt

Thrive Market Organic Ground Pepper

3 tablespoons no-sugar-added fig preserves (or other fruit preserves; try Thrive Market Organic Apricot Fruit Spread)

3/4 teaspoon organic red sriracha

1 cup mixed fresh tender green herbs, finely chopped (try flat-leaf parsley, mint, dill, or any combination)

## INSTRUCTIONS

Preheat oven to 425°F. Line a rimmed baking sheet with parchment paper.

Place the salmon on the prepared baking sheet. Drizzle the salmon with olive oil and rub to coat evenly. Sprinkle with salt and pepper.

In a small bowl, combine the preserves and the sriracha. Spread a thin layer of the mixture on the salmon. Press the herb mixture on top of the salmon to cover evenly.

Roast the salmon for 10 to 12 minutes, or until fish flakes evenly when poked with the tip of a paring knife. You want the fish to be slightly rare in the center. Cut crosswise into pieces and serve immediately.

*Scan here to shop the recipe*

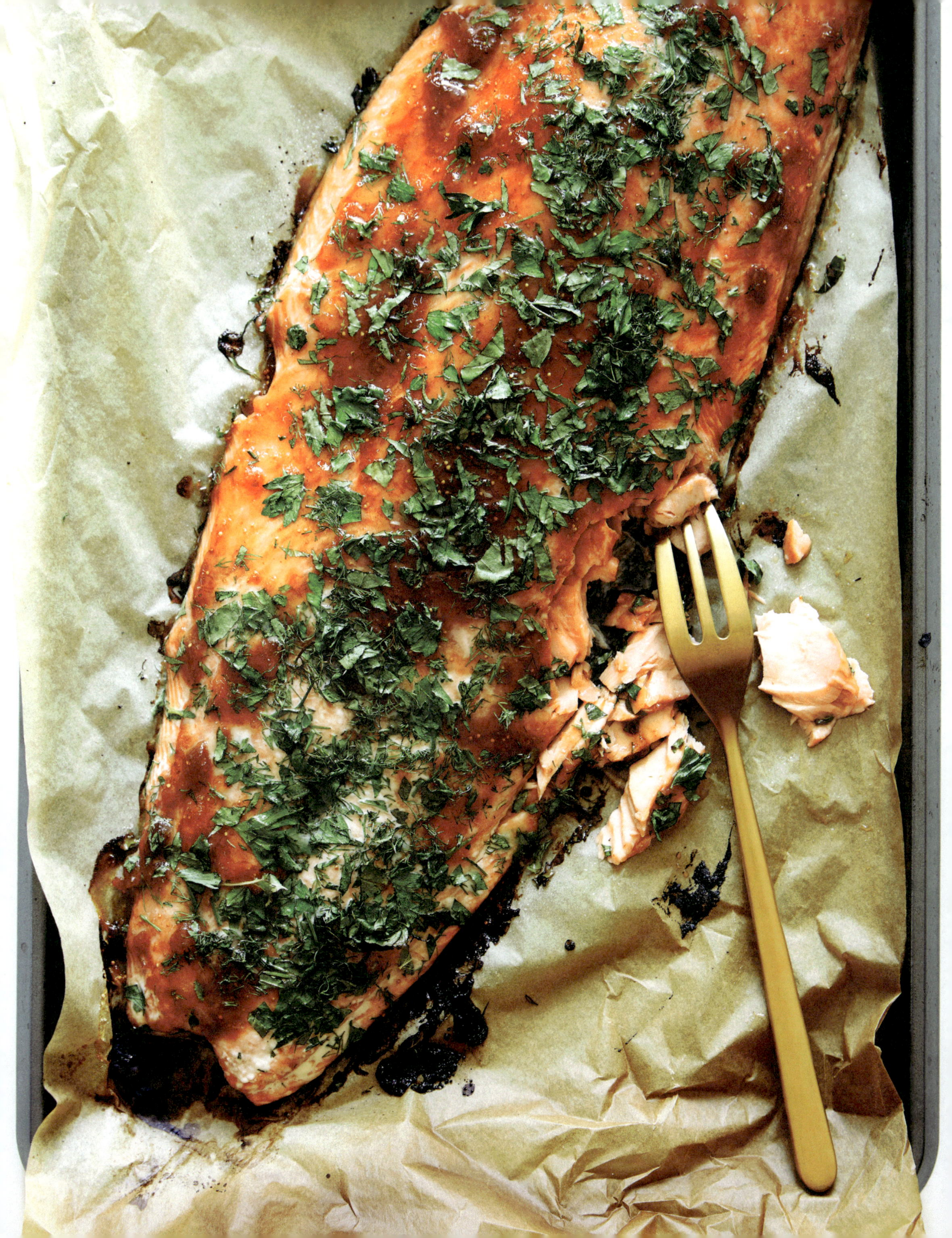

YIELD 2–4 SERVINGS    TOTAL TIME 20 MINUTES

Few things say "comfort food" like a bowl of pasta with sauce. This plant-rich version—from vegan chef **Caitlin Shoemaker**, aka *@frommybowl*—requires only five main ingredients, but you can also toss in some fresh greens or roasted vegetables to make it your own.

**DINNER**

# Vegan Roasted Red Pepper Pasta

Dairy-Free    Vegan    Egg-Free

## INGREDIENTS

Sea salt

8 ounces pasta of choice (try Thrive Market Organic Biodynamic Whole Wheat Spaghetti)

1 12-ounce jar or 14.5-ounce can roasted red peppers, drained and rinsed (can also use 8 ounces homemade)

2 cloves garlic

1 cup Thrive Market Organic Coconut Milk

1/2 cup vegetable broth

1/4 teaspoon Thrive Market Organic Crushed Red Pepper (optional)

## INSTRUCTIONS

Bring a large pot of salted water to a boil and cook the pasta according to the package instructions.

In the meantime, add the peppers, garlic, coconut milk, vegetable broth, and red chili flakes (optional) to a blender. Blend on high for 45 to 60 seconds, until the sauce is smooth and creamy. Season with salt and pepper to taste, if necessary.

Drain the pasta once cooked, but do not rinse. Return the empty pot to the stovetop and add the red pepper sauce. Bring the sauce to a simmer over medium-high heat and cook for 2 to 3 minutes, until bubbly and thickened.

Remove the pot from heat and add the cooked pasta. Toss pasta with sauce using tongs. If the sauce appears runny, allow the pasta to sit for an additional 3 to 5 minutes to absorb more of it.

Transfer the pasta into bowls and serve.

*Scan here to shop the recipe*

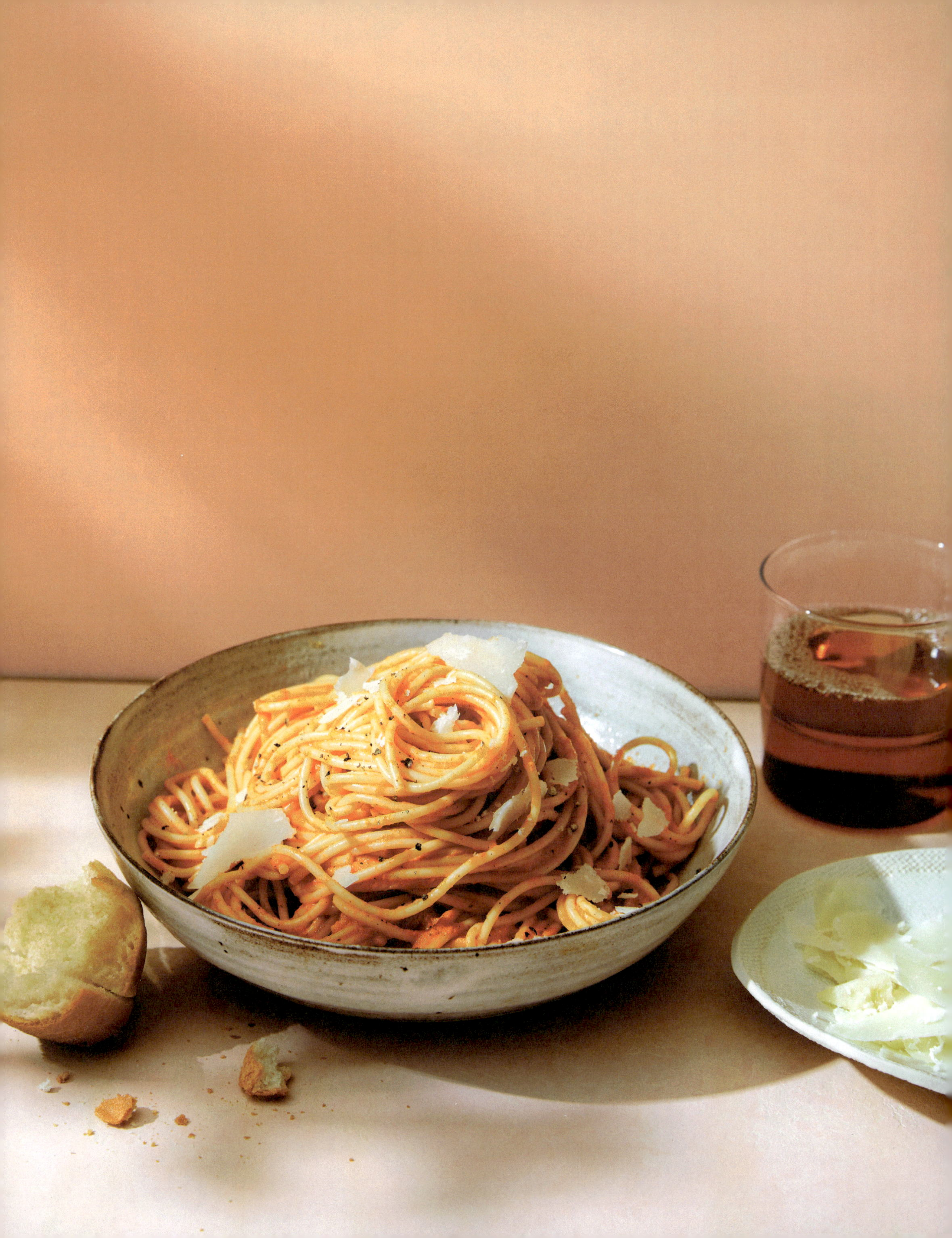

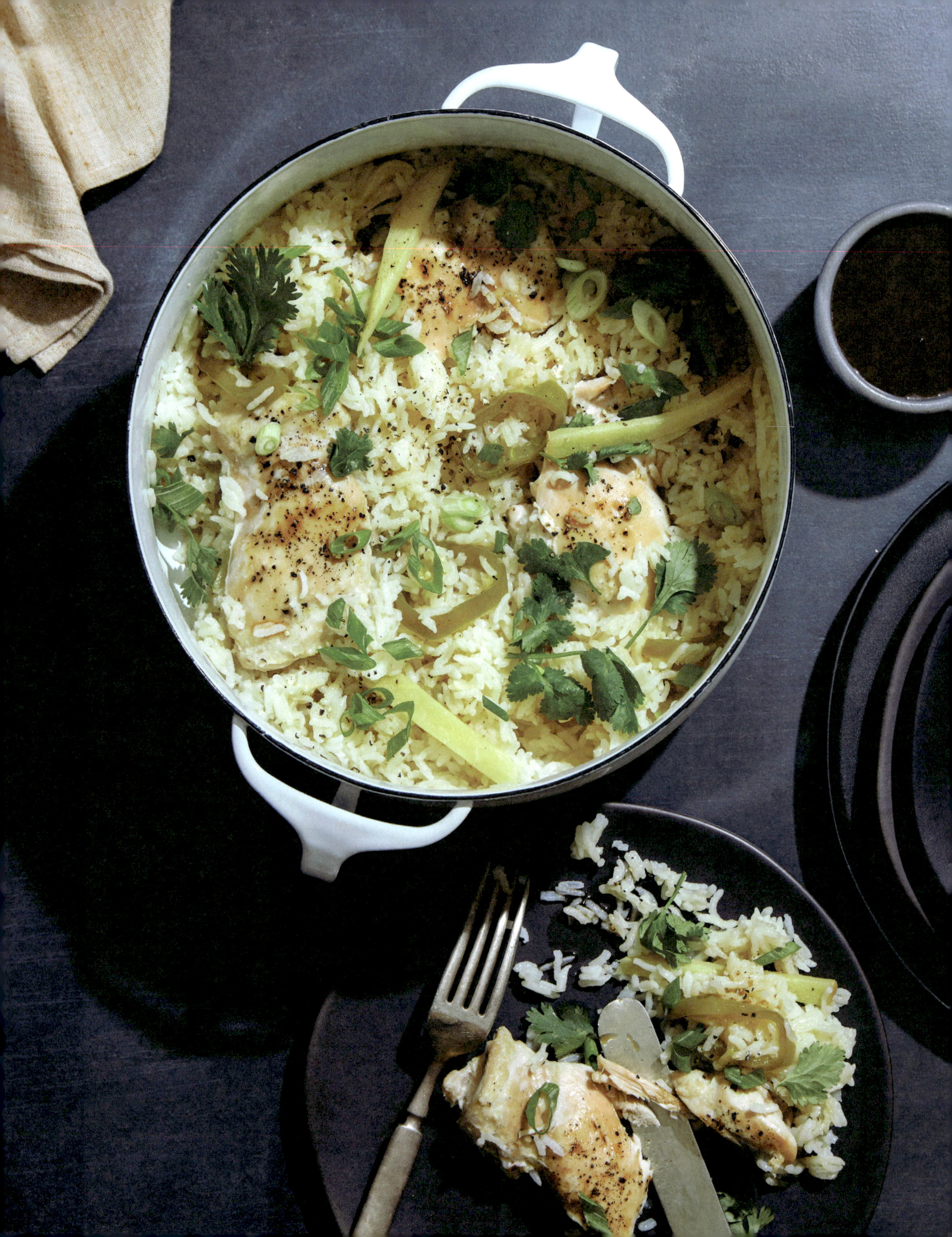

YIELD 4 SERVINGS    ACTIVE TIME 10 MINUTES    TOTAL TIME 30 MINUTES

In this recipe, steaming with bone broth keeps the chicken extraordinarily tender, while allowing the rice to soak up all the bold flavor that fresh ginger, garlic, and green chiles have to offer. Bonus: easy cleanup.

DINNER

# One-Pot Chile-Ginger Chicken & Rice

Gluten-Free  Dairy-Free  Egg-Free

### INGREDIENTS

3 cups Thrive Market Organic Chicken Bone Broth

6 large slices ginger, cut lengthwise

4 cloves garlic, peeled and halved

1 long green chile, such as Anaheim or Hatch, sliced

1 1/2 cups Thrive Market Organic White Jasmine Rice

4 small boneless skinless chicken thighs

1 teaspoon sea salt

Thrive Market Organic Ground Pepper

1 bunch scallions, sliced

1 cup cilantro, roughly chopped

### INSTRUCTIONS

Stir chicken broth, ginger, garlic, and chile together in a 3 1/2-quart Dutch oven or another deep pan with high sides. Bring to a boil over medium heat, then add rice and stir. Bring to a boil again, then add chicken and season with salt and pepper.

Cover, turn heat down to low, and cook for 20 minutes. At this point, the rice should have absorbed all liquid and chicken should be tender. Top with scallions and cilantro. Serve with coconut aminos on the side.

*Scan here to shop the recipe*

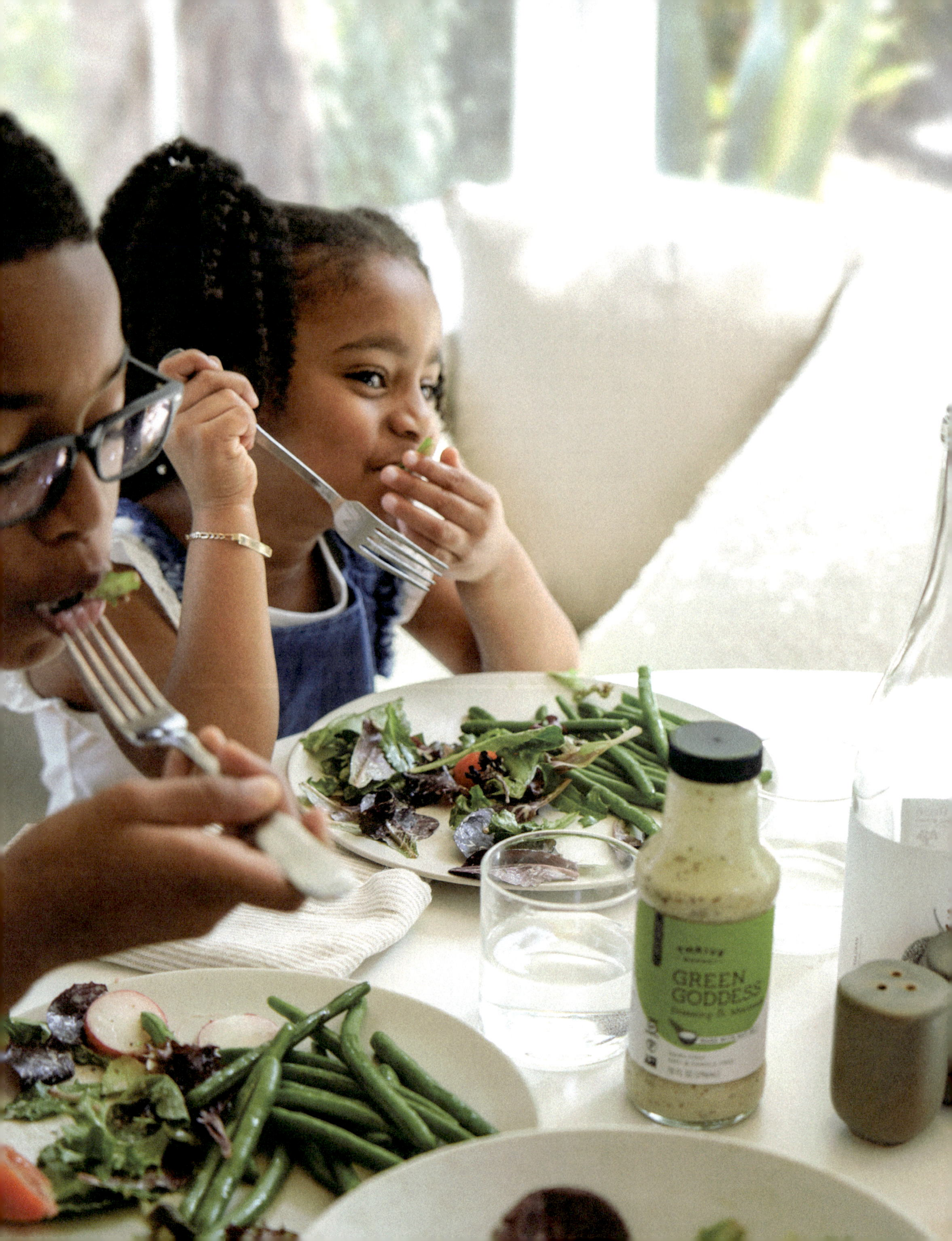
GREEN GODDESS

Zippy and herbaceous, our Green Goddess Dressing & Marinade is made with MCT oil for a dose of healthy fats.

# Snacks & Sides

**PAGE 110**
Veggie Tots

**PAGE 112**
Grilled Corn With
Chipotle-Lime Mayonnaise

**PAGE 114**
4-Ingredient Vegan
Coconut Bacon

**PAGE 116**
Creamed Collard Greens

**PAGE 118**
Cumin-Spiced
Sweet Potato Chips

**PAGE 120**
Avocado Dip
With a Kick

**PAGE 122**
Jicama, Apple
& Pear Slaw

**PAGE 124**
Grilled Romaine Salad With
Avocado-Lime Dressing

**PAGE 126**
Salt & Vinegar Brussels
Sprouts Chips

**PAGE 128**
Cauliflower Mash

**YIELD** 20 TOTS   **ACTIVE TIME** 15 MINUTES   **TOTAL TIME** 30 MINUTES

---

These are tots like you've never had them: baked, not fried, and bursting with nutritious broccoli and cauliflower. A flavorful blend of spices and a bright and citrusy mayo dipping sauce (that comes together in no time thanks to a few shortcuts) make them borderline addictive.

---

SNACKS & SIDES

# Veggie Tots

*Gluten-Free*   *Grain-Free*   *Dairy-Free*

### INGREDIENTS

**For the Veggie Tots**

Thrive Market Avocado Oil Spray (can also use coconut oil spray)

2 cups cauliflower florets

1 cup broccoli florets

1 egg white

1 tablespoon avocado oil mayo

1/2 cup Thrive Market Almond Flour

1/4 cup fresh parsley leaves

1 teaspoon sea salt

1/4 teaspoon Thrive Market Organic Garlic Powder

1/2 teaspoon Thrive Market Organic Onion Powder

1/4 teaspoon Thrive Market Organic Ground Pepper

**For the Dipping Sauce**

1/4 cup mayonnaise; try Thrive Market Vegan Mayonnaise or Coconut Oil Mayonnaise

2 tablespoons premade citrus vinaigrette of your choice (can also use homemade)

### INSTRUCTIONS

Preheat oven to 400°F. Line a baking sheet with parchment paper and mist with oil spray.

Place cauliflower and broccoli in a food processor and pulse until the mixture is the consistency of rice. Add egg white, mayonnaise, almond flour, parsley, salt, garlic powder, onion powder, and black pepper. Pulse until fully blended.

Scoop the mixture using a tablespoon and form into oval-shaped patties between your palms; place on the prepared baking sheet. Repeat with remaining mixture. Bake for 20 minutes in the top rack of the oven, rotating the sheet halfway through.

While the tots cook, whisk mayo and dressing in a small bowl. Serve alongside veggie tots.

*Scan here to shop the recipe*

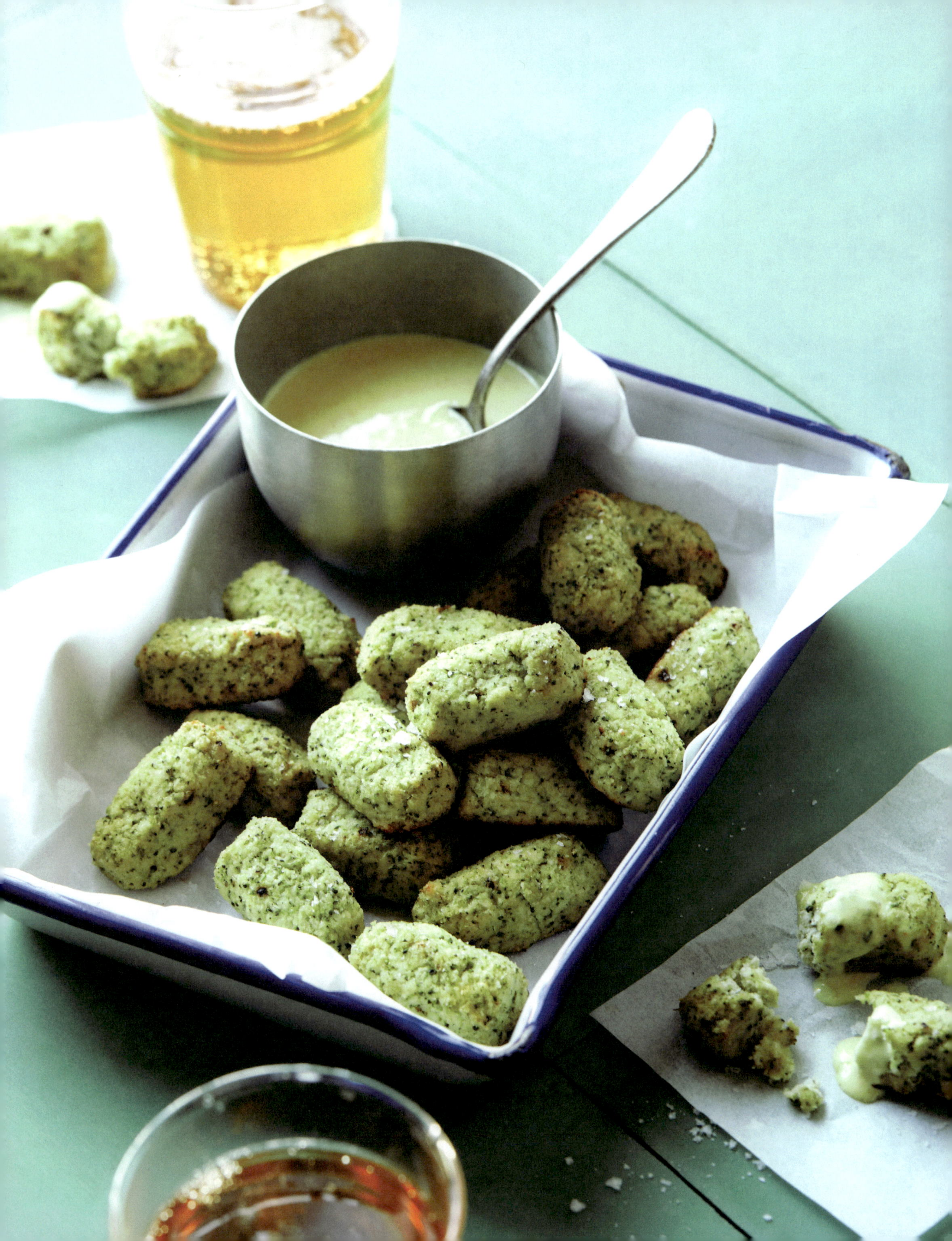

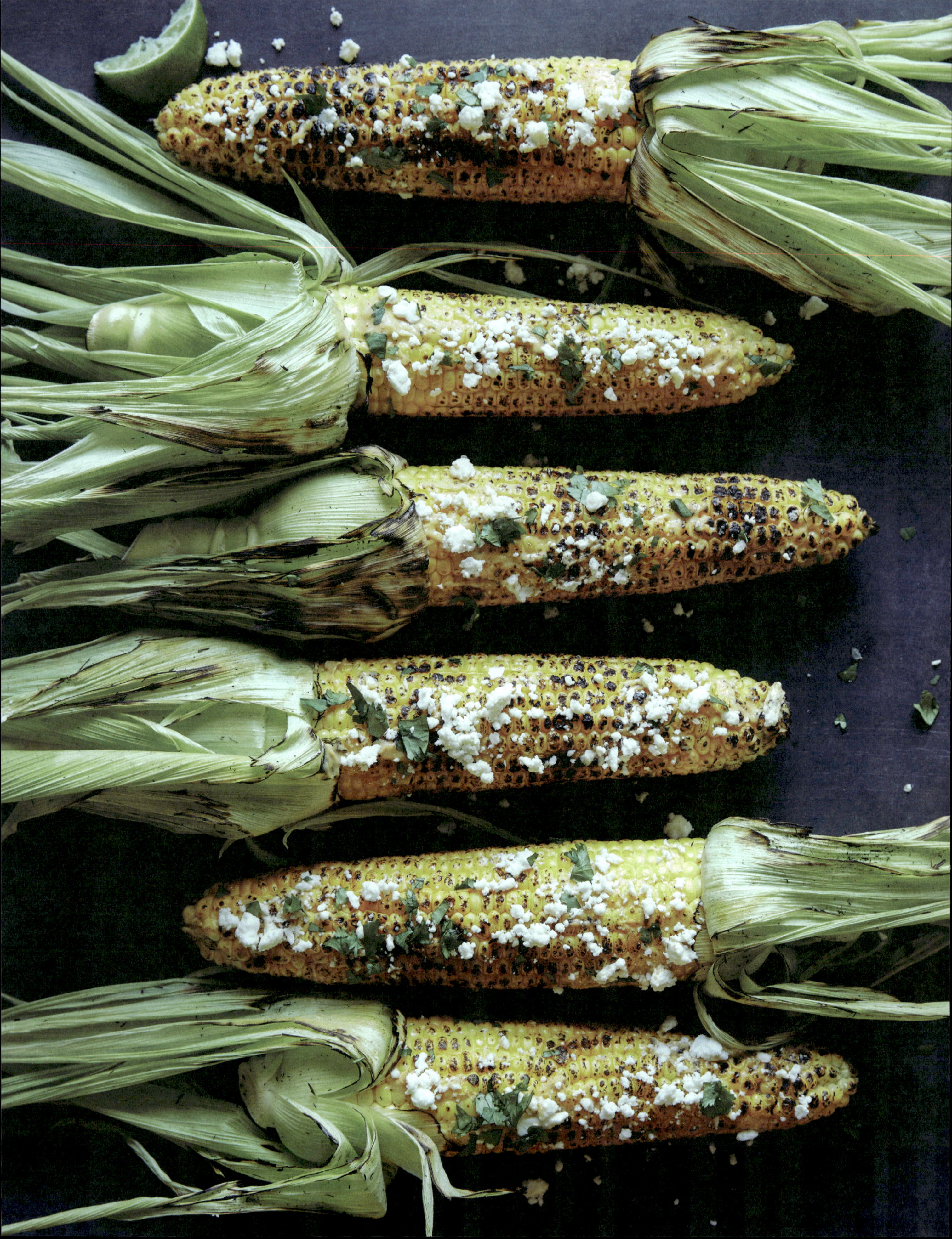

YIELD 6 SERVINGS    ACTIVE TIME 15 MINUTES    TOTAL TIME 20 MINUTES

Inspired by the Mexican street food staple, this flavorful (and delightfully messy) elote stars creamy mayonnaise, crumbly feta, and plenty of fresh lime.

SNACKS & SIDES

# Grilled Corn With Chipotle-Lime Mayonnaise

Gluten-Free    Grain-Free

### INGREDIENTS

6 ears of corn, husked

1 cup Thrive Market Coconut Oil Mayonnaise

1 cup crumbled feta cheese

Zest of 2 limes

1/3 cup chopped cilantro

2 limes, sliced, to serve

### INSTRUCTIONS

Heat grill to medium. Place corn on grill and cook until kernels begin to char, 3 to 5 minutes. Turn ears and repeat until cooked on all sides.

Remove corn from grill, slather with mayo, and roll in feta cheese to coat on all sides. Sprinkle with lime zest and cilantro. Serve with lime wedges.

*Scan here to shop the recipe*

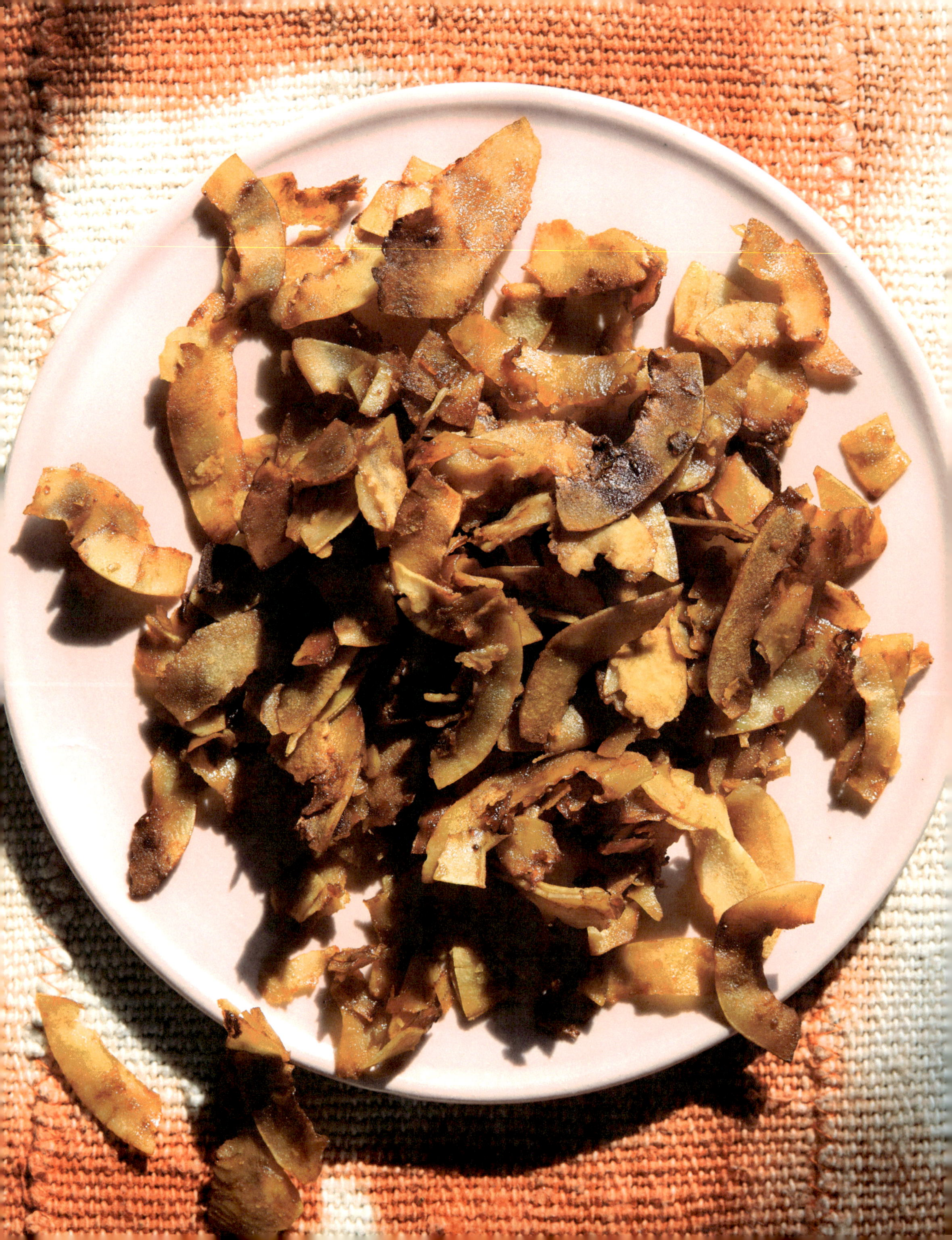

**YIELD** 2-3 CUPS    **TOTAL TIME** 20 MINUTES

If plant-based eating has you nostalgic for bacon, you're in luck. This recipe transforms coconut flakes into salty, smoky, bacon-like bits that are delicious sprinkled over a salad, tucked into a baked potato, or—why not?—on a maple-flavored donut. Make sure to use unsweetened coconut.

SNACKS & SIDES

# 4-Ingredient Vegan Coconut Bacon

Gluten-Free · Grain-Free · Dairy-Free · Vegan · Egg-Free

### INGREDIENTS

3 cups Thrive Market Organic Coconut Chips

4 tablespoons Thrive Market Organic Coconut Aminos

2 tablespoons liquid smoke

Drizzle of Thrive Market Organic Maple Syrup

### INSTRUCTIONS

Preheat oven to 350°F. Line a baking sheet with parchment paper.

In a bowl, combine all ingredients until coconut chips are completely coated. Transfer the coconut chips to the baking sheet in an even layer.

Bake for 12 to 14 minutes, tossing occasionally. Let cool, then store in the fridge for up to 7 days or in the freezer indefinitely.

*Scan here to shop the recipe*

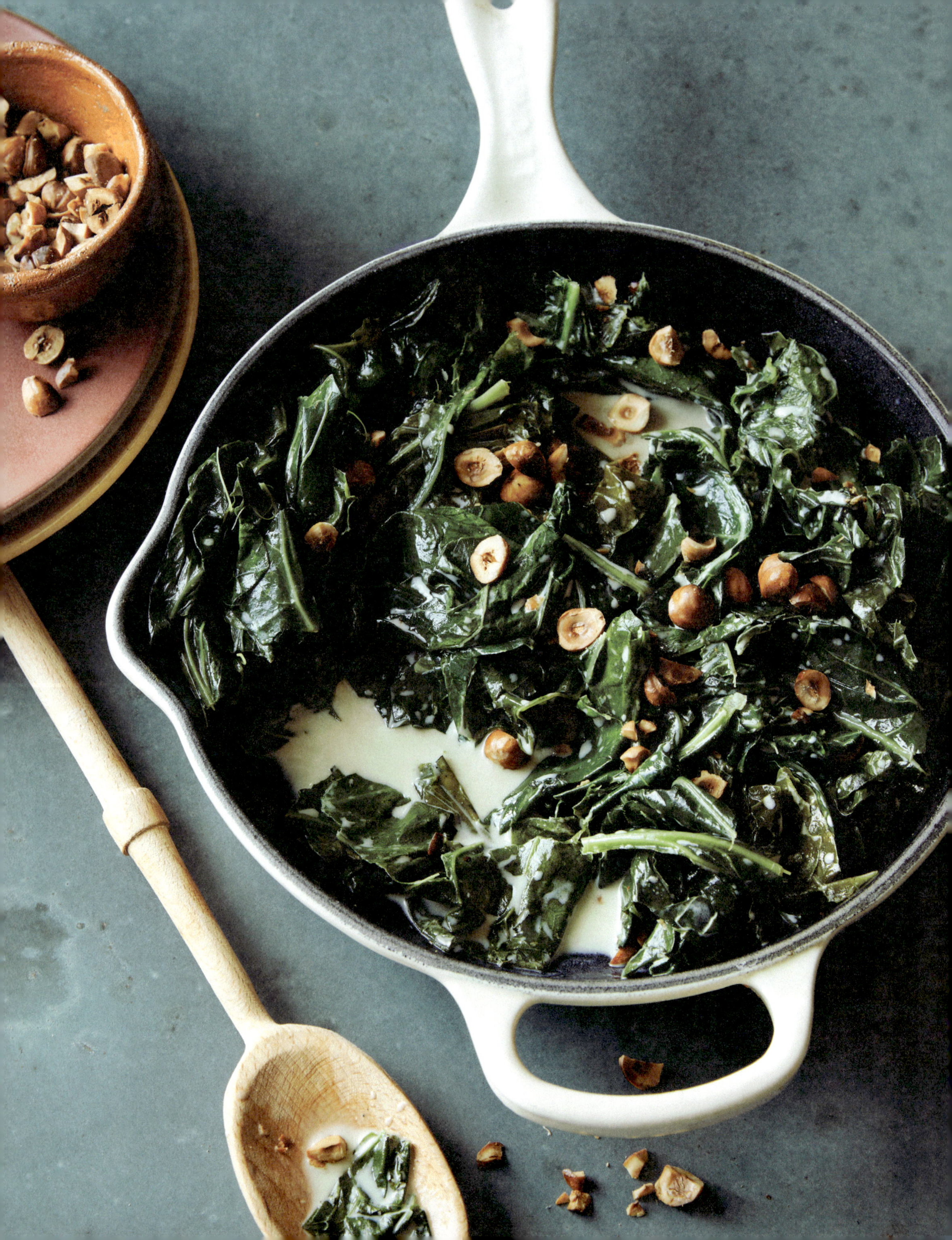

YIELD 2 SERVINGS    ACTIVE TIME 5 MINUTES    TOTAL TIME 15 MINUTES

In **Chris Kresser**'s lightened-up version of a classic steakhouse side, coconut milk takes the place of whole milk and heavy cream, while a pinch of nutmeg warms up each bite.

SNACKS & SIDES

# Creamed Collard Greens

Gluten-Free    Grain-Free    Dairy-Free    Egg-Free

### INGREDIENTS

1 tablespoon Thrive Market Regenerative Pork Fat

1 pound collard greens, washed and cut into large pieces

1 cup Thrive Market Organic Coconut Milk

1 tablespoon Thrive Market Organic Coconut Aminos

Pinch of Thrive Market Organic Ground Nutmeg

Sea salt and freshly ground pepper, to taste

Hazelnuts, roasted and chopped for garnish (optional)

### INSTRUCTIONS

Melt fat in a sauté pan and add all the ingredients except optional hazelnuts (if using). Cook at medium-high heat for 10 minutes or until the liquid has greatly reduced. Add salt to taste.

Garnish with chopped hazelnuts, if using, and serve.

*Scan here to shop the recipe*

YIELD 4 SERVINGS   ACTIVE TIME 5 MINUTES   TOTAL TIME 30 MINUTES

Warm, savory cumin and paprika balance out the naturally caramelized flavor of sweet potato in these crunchy baked chips—which are just as addictive as the bagged variety, but a lot more wholesome.

SNACKS & SIDES

# Cumin-Spiced Sweet Potato Chips

Gluten-Free · Grain-Free · Dairy-Free · Vegan · Egg-Free

## INGREDIENTS

1 large sweet potato, peeled

2 tablespoons Thrive Market Organic Virgin Coconut Oil, melted

2 teaspoons Thrive Market Organic Ground Cumin

Pinch Thrive Market Organic Paprika

1 1/2 teaspoons salt

## INSTRUCTIONS

Preheat oven to 400°F. Line a baking sheet with parchment paper.

Using a mandoline or sharp knife, slice sweet potato into very thin rounds. Place in a large bowl and toss with coconut oil, cumin, paprika, and salt.

Spread potato slices on baking sheet in a single, even layer. Bake for 20 to 25 minutes or until crisp and golden brown. Let cool fully before enjoying; chips will firm up slightly as they cool.

*Scan here to shop the recipe*

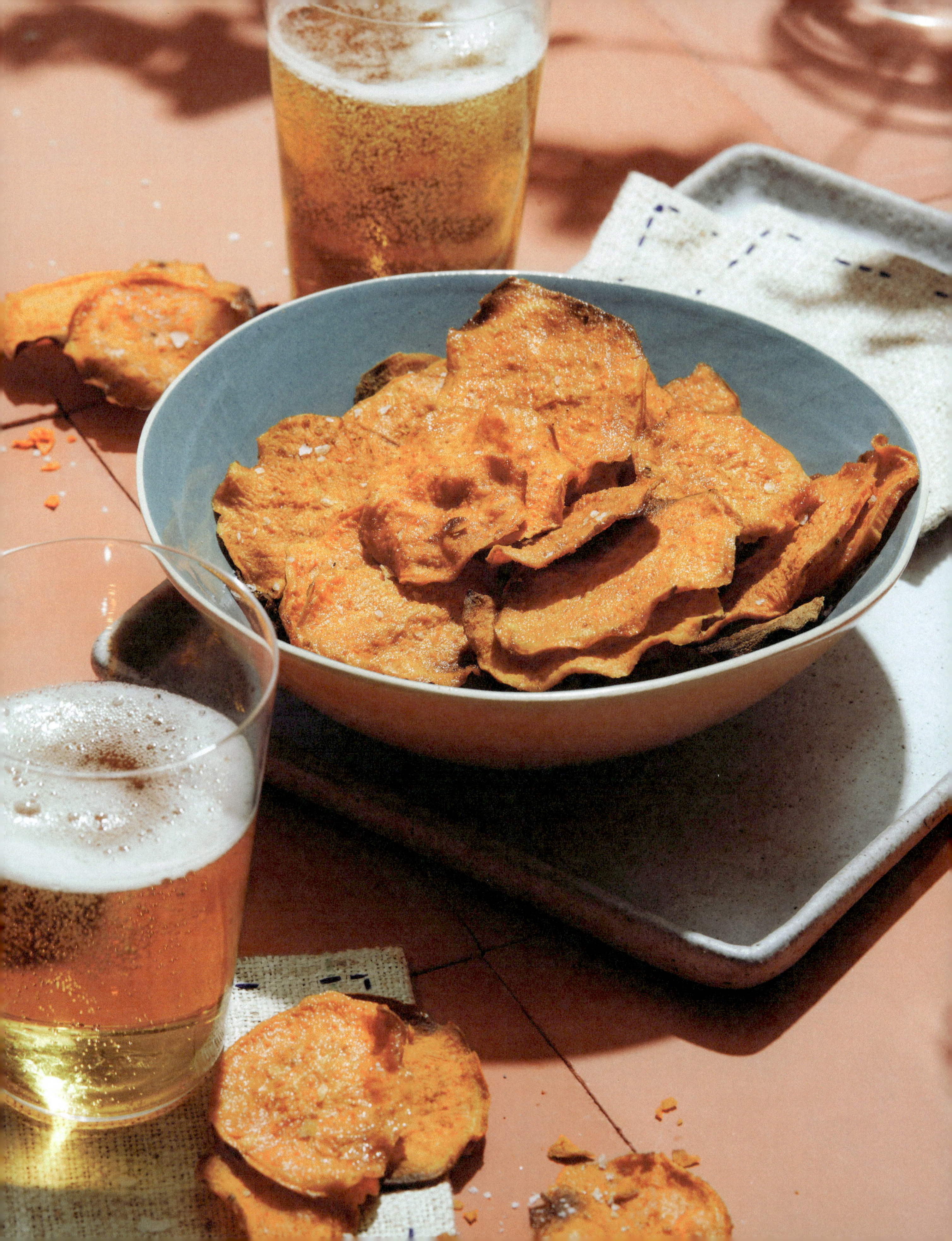

**YIELD** 1 1/2 CUPS   **ACTIVE TIME** 10 MINUTES   **TOTAL TIME** 10 MINUTES

Naturally creamy avocado plus a splash of almond milk give this dip its luscious texture, while a squeeze of lime adds brightness and fresh jalapeño turns up the heat. Pair with chips (try Thrive Market Non-GMO Grain-Free Lime Tortilla Chips) or carrot sticks for a casual but crowd-pleasing appetizer.

SNACKS & SIDES

# Avocado Dip With a Kick

Gluten-Free · Grain-Free · Dairy-Free · Vegan · Egg-Free

## INGREDIENTS

2 ripe avocados, peeled and pitted

Zest and juice of 1 lime

1/2 jalapeño, chopped (seeds removed for less heat)

1/4 cup Thrive Market Organic Almond Beverage

1 tablespoon chopped cilantro

1 teaspoon Thrive Market Organic Garlic Powder

1/2 teaspoon sea salt

1/4 teaspoon Thrive Market Organic Ground Pepper

## INSTRUCTIONS

Add all ingredients to a food processor; blend until smooth. Chill until ready to eat.

Store dip in an airtight container in the fridge for up to 5 days.

*Scan here to shop the recipe*

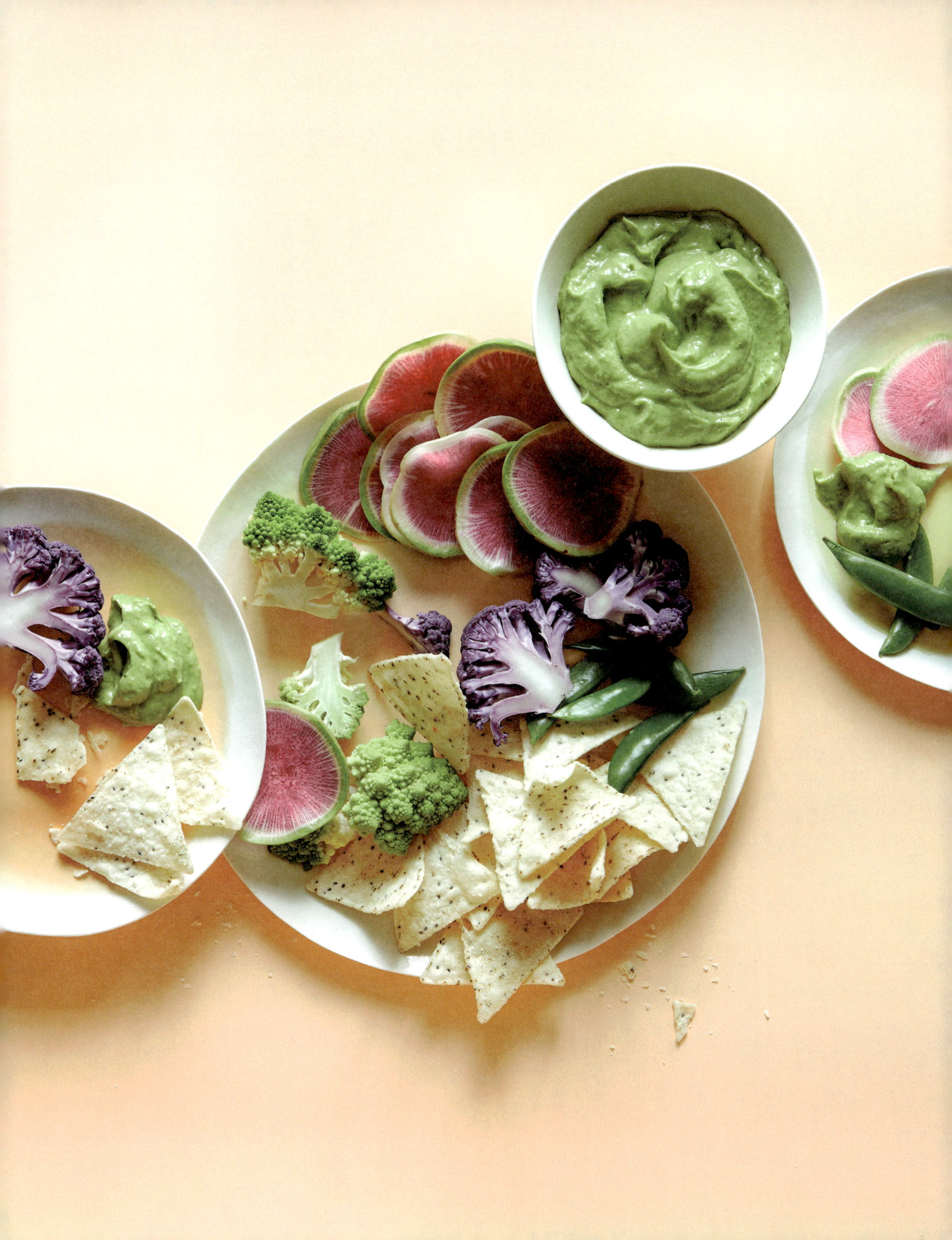

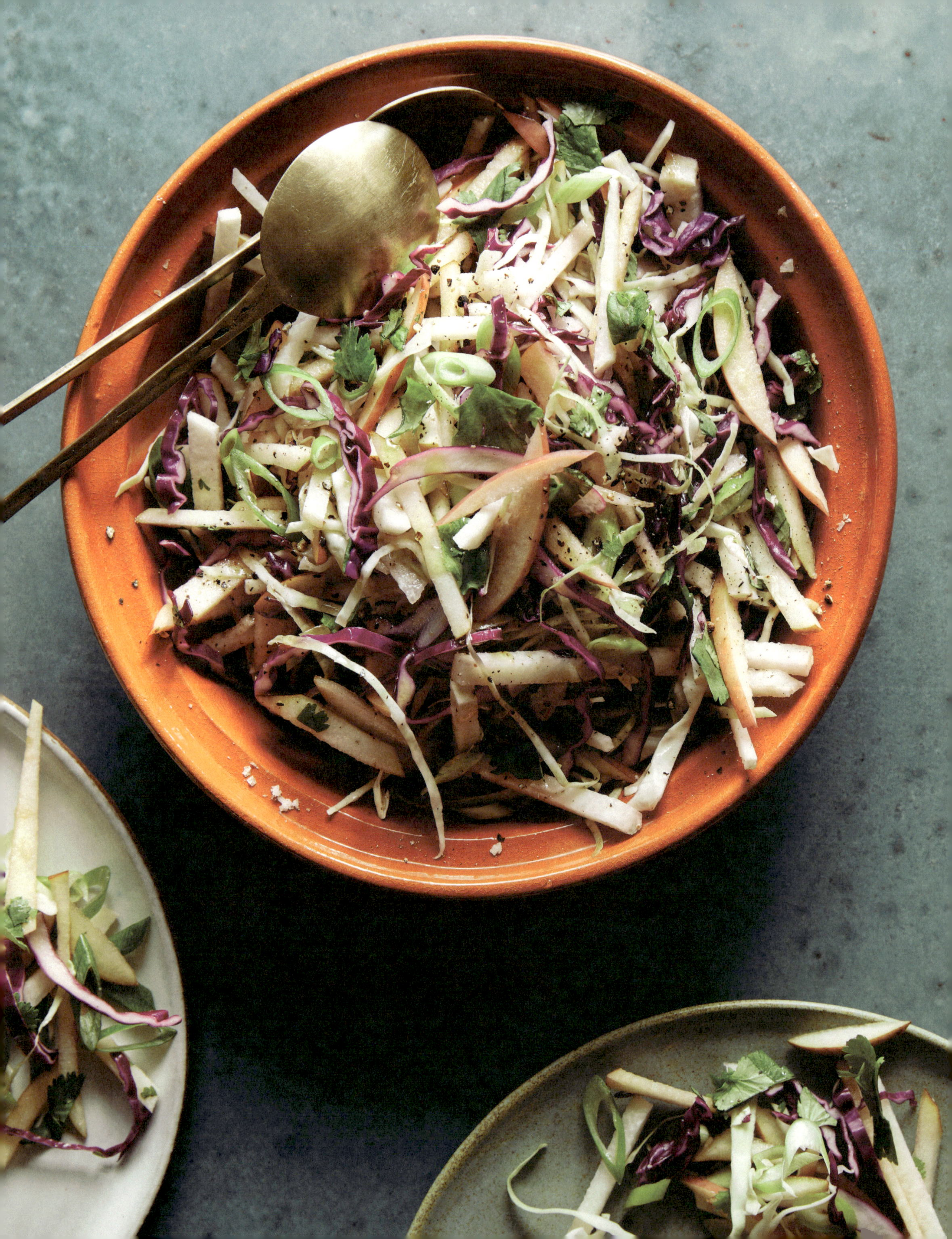

**YIELD** 4 SERVINGS    **ACTIVE TIME** 5 MINUTES    **TOTAL TIME** 35 MINUTES

Delightfully crisp and refreshing, **JJ Virgin**'s vegan slaw will brighten up any picnic spread. Chopping accounts for most of the work—then just let the mixture hang out in a tart, herbaceous vinaigrette and absorb its flavor.

**SNACKS & SIDES**

# Jicama, Apple & Pear Slaw

Gluten-Free · Grain-Free · Dairy-Free · Vegan · Egg-Free

**INGREDIENTS**

1 cup shredded red cabbage

1 cup shredded green cabbage

1 medium apple, cored and cut into matchsticks

1 medium ripe pear, cored and cut into matchsticks

1/2 small jicama, peeled and cut into matchsticks, about 1 cup

3 green onions, chopped

4 teaspoons Thrive Market Organic Apple Cider Vinegar

1 tablespoon macadamia nut oil

1 tablespoon chopped fresh cilantro

1/4 teaspoon sea salt

**INSTRUCTIONS**

Toss the cabbage, apple, pear, jicama, green onions, vinegar, oil, cilantro, and salt together in a large bowl. Let stand 30 minutes, tossing occasionally, to allow the flavors to develop.

*Scan here to shop the recipe*

**YIELD** 6 SERVINGS    **TOTAL TIME** 10 MINUTES

If you've never thought to throw your salad on the grill, give it a try—starting with romaine hearts. The outer leaves soften and char as they cook, while the core remains crunchy. Drizzle with an avocado-lime dressing and serve warm for a showstopping salad.

SNACKS & SIDES

# Grilled Romaine Salad With Avocado-Lime Dressing

Gluten-Free   Grain-Free   Nut-Free

## INGREDIENTS

**For the Avocado-Lime Dressing**

1 avocado, peeled and pitted

1/4 cup cilantro leaves

Juice of 3 limes

Large pinch sea salt

Freshly ground pepper

1 teaspoon Thrive Market Organic Onion Powder

Small pinch Thrive Market Organic Cayenne Pepper

1/4 to 1/3 cup Thrive Market Organic Extra Virgin Olive Oil

**For the Salad**

6 romaine hearts, sliced lengthwise into halves

Thrive Market Organic Extra Virgin Olive Oil, for grilling

2 to 4 hard-boiled eggs, halved (optional)

Grated Parmesan cheese (optional)

## INSTRUCTIONS

Heat grill to medium.

While the grill heats, make the dressing: Combine avocado, cilantro, lime juice, salt, pepper, onion powder, and cayenne in a blender or food processor and blend until smooth. Drizzle in olive oil and blend until creamy and pourable. If the dressing is too thick, add a few drops of water to thin.

Once the grill is hot, brush romaine hearts with olive oil and grill for 20 seconds on each side.

Serve warm romaine hearts drizzled with dressing and, if you like, topped with quartered eggs and grated Parmesan.

*Scan here to shop the recipe*

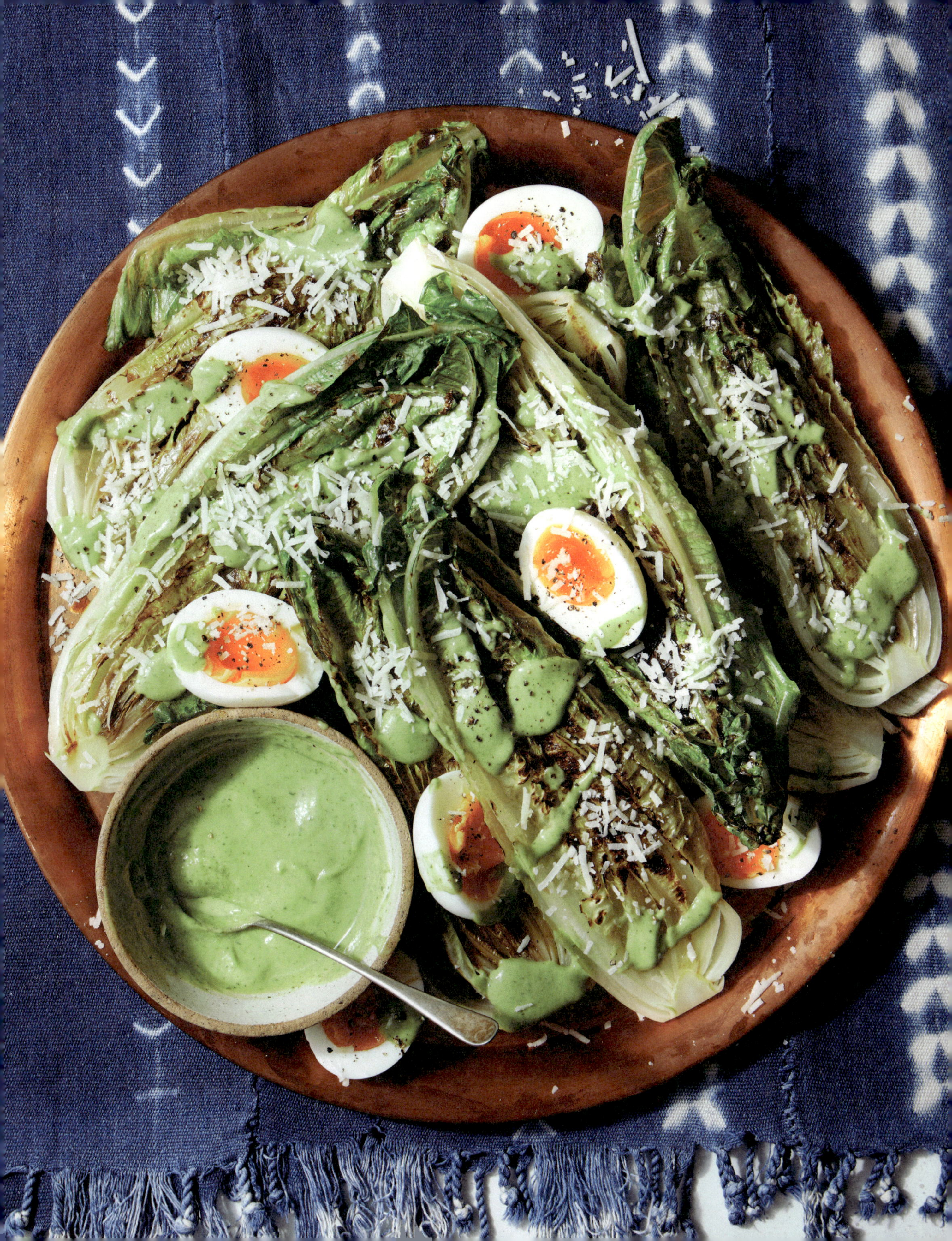

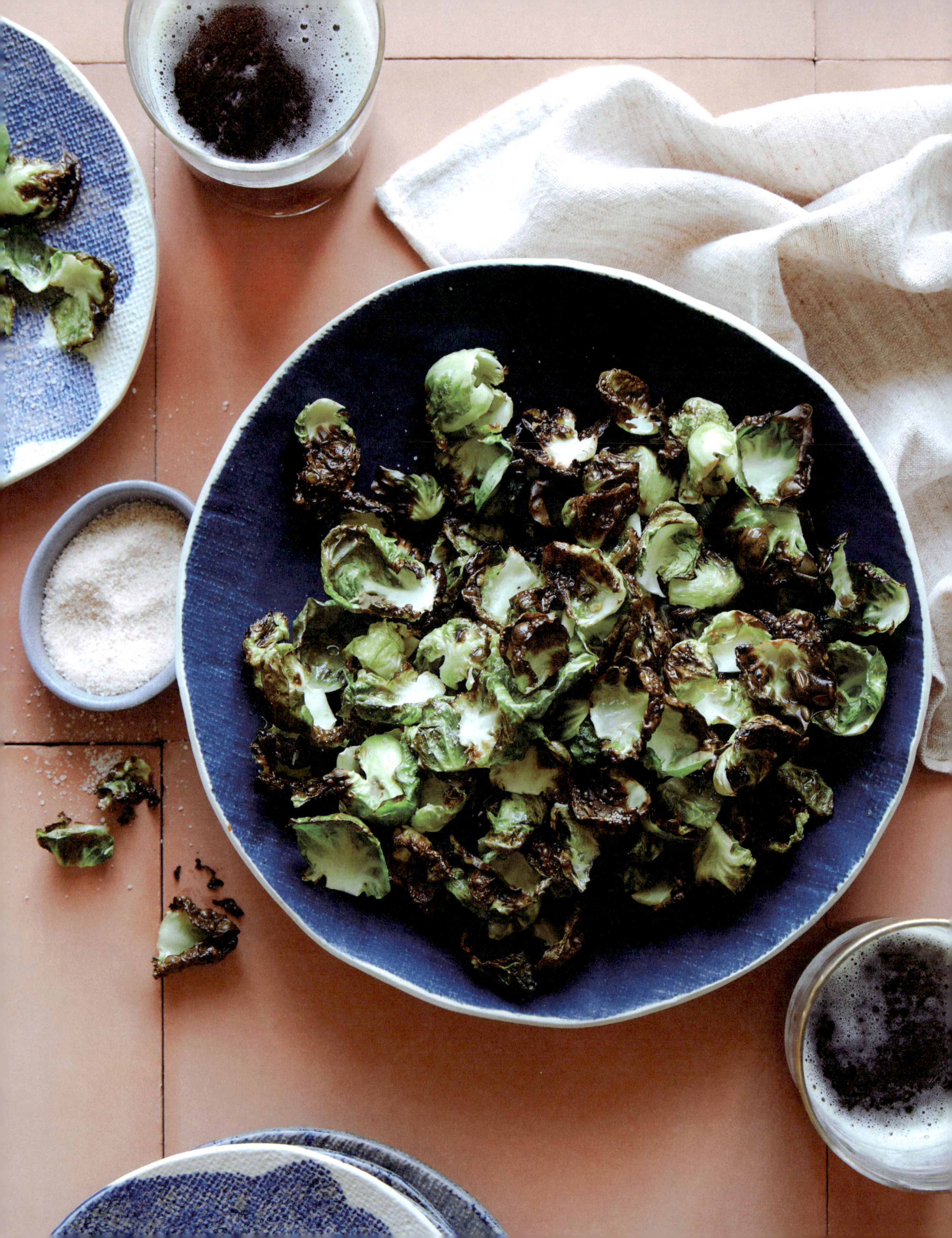

YIELD 4 SERVINGS    ACTIVE TIME 5 MINUTES    TOTAL TIME 15 MINUTES

Potato chips, hold the potato (and the deep-frying). Delicate Brussels sprouts leaves turn crispy and craveable when tossed with an acidic salt-and-vinegar combo and roasted for just a few minutes.

SNACKS & SIDES

# Salt & Vinegar Brussels Sprouts Chips

Gluten-Free · Grain-Free · Dairy-Free · Vegan · Egg-Free · Nut-Free

### INGREDIENTS

1 pound Brussels sprouts

2 tablespoons Thrive Market Organic Extra Virgin Olive Oil

1 tablespoon Thrive Market Organic Apple Cider Vinegar

1/2 teaspoon Thrive Market Pink Himalayan Salt

### INSTRUCTIONS

Preheat oven to 350°F. Line a baking sheet with parchment paper.

Cut off the bottom of each sprout to remove the outer leaves. Continue trimming the sprouts until all large leaves are removed. Reserve any leftover sprouts for another use (such as roasting or shredding for a salad).

Place sprout leaves in a bowl and toss with olive oil, vinegar, and salt. Transfer to the baking sheet in a single, even layer.

Roast for 7 to 10 minutes until crisp and slightly browned. Remove from oven and let cool completely on baking sheet before serving or storing.

*Scan here to shop the recipe*

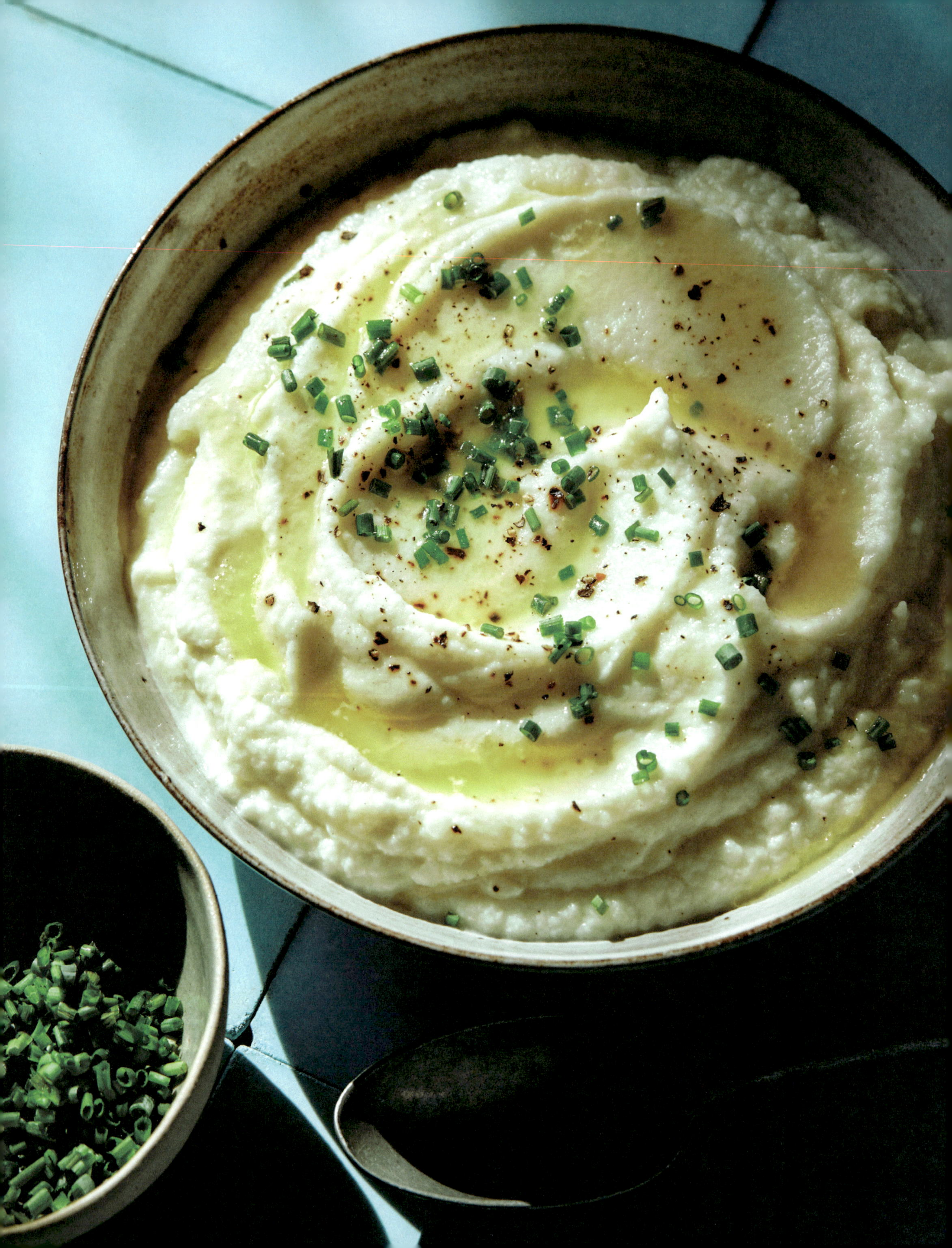

**YIELD** 4 SERVINGS    **TOTAL TIME** 15 MINUTES

What can't cauliflower do? In this recipe from keto meal prep maestro **Bobby Parrish**, aka **@flavcity**, it takes the place of potatoes—proving you can still enjoy a creamy, hearty mash while avoiding starchy foods. Garlic, butter, and cheese keep it rich and flavorful.

**SNACKS & SIDES**

# Cauliflower Mash

Gluten-Free · Grain-Free · Egg-Free

## INGREDIENTS

1 tablespoon plus 1/4 teaspoon salt, divided, plus more to taste

1 large head of cauliflower, cut into bite-sized florets

4 garlic cloves, peeled

1/4 cup grated Parmesan or Pecorino Romano cheese

1 tablespoon Thrive Market Organic Ghee

Thrive Market Organic Whole Black Peppercorns, freshly ground

## INSTRUCTIONS

Bring a large pot of water to a boil and add 1 tablespoon of salt. Add cauliflower florets and garlic; boil until cauliflower is just soft enough to mash with a fork, about 7 to 10 minutes. (Avoid overcooking or the mash will be too loose).

Drain the cauliflower and garlic, reserving 1 cup of water. Transfer cauliflower to a blender along with cheese, ghee, 1/4 teaspoon of salt, and a few cracks of pepper.

Blend until smooth and creamy, using a plunging stick (if your blender has 1) to help blend all of the cauliflower. Add reserved water 1 tablespoon at a time if the mash is too thick. Season to taste with additional salt and pepper if desired.

*Scan here to shop the recipe*

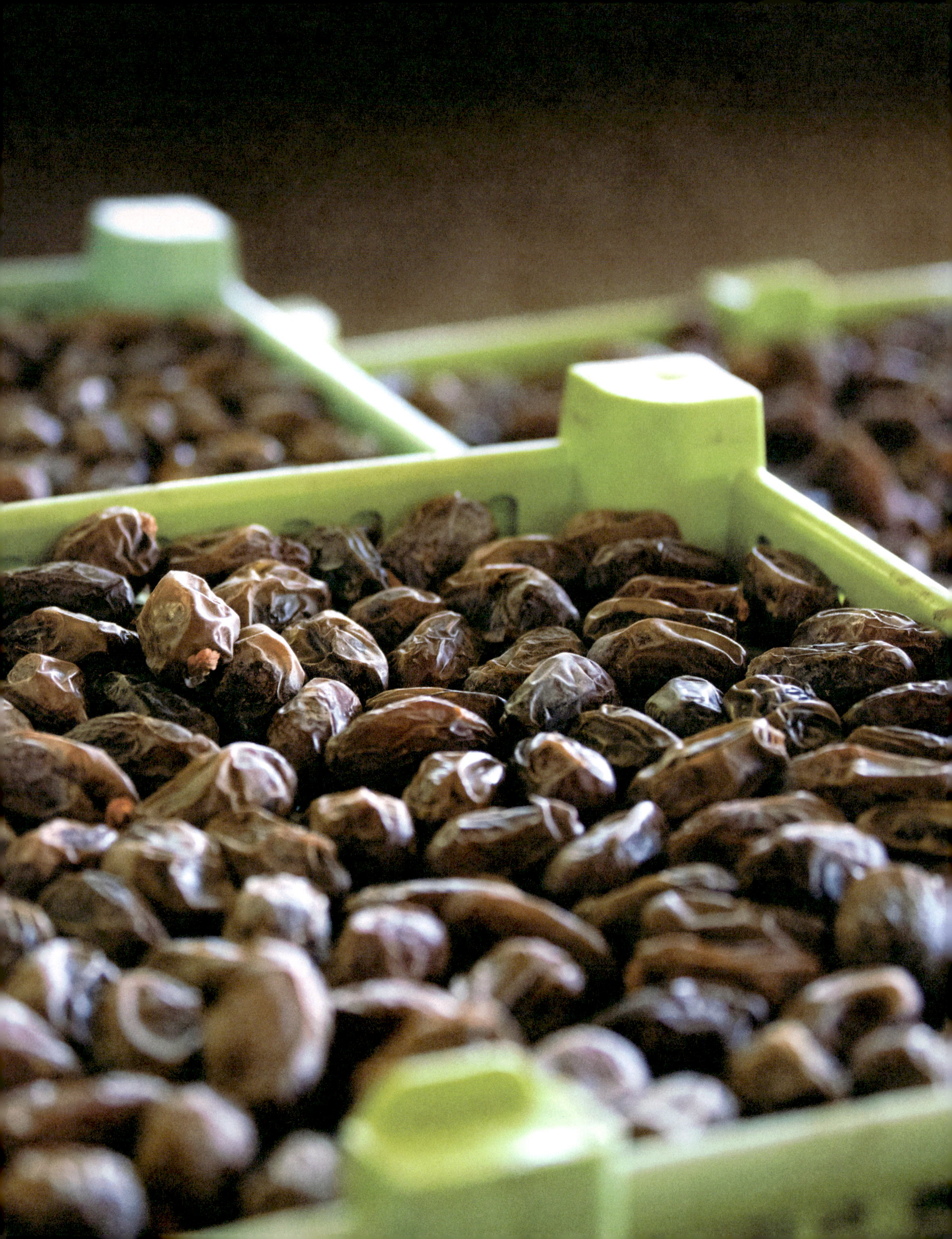

Our Organic Medjool Dates come from California's Coachella Valley, where they get natural sweetness from the desert sun.

# Dessert

**PAGE 134**
Grilled Peaches With
Yogurt & Granola

**PAGE 136**
Vegan Olive Oil
Skillet Brownies

**PAGE 138**
Very Berry Cobbler

**PAGE 140**
Chocolate, Almond
Butter & Jam Cracker
Sandwiches

**PAGE 142**
Sea Salt Caramel Brittle

**PAGE 144**
Keto Pumpkin
Spice Donuts

**PAGE 146**
Boozy Toasted
Marshmallow Milkshake

**PAGE 148**
Keto Collagen
Brownie Bombs

**PAGE 150**
Hazelnut Chocolate
Chunk Cookies

**PAGE 152**
Peppermint Chocolate
Macaroons

# Contents

Introduction ............................................. 3

The Ketogenic Diet and its Benefits ........... 3

Ketogenic Diet Health Benefits ................. 3

Foods Allowed and Disallowed in the Keto Diet ........................................................ 4

What is a "chaffle"? ................................... 5

How To Eat/Serve A Basic Chaffle ............ 5

Chaffle Making Tips, Frequently Asked Questions ................................................... 6

# RECIPES ............................................. 9

Basic Keto Chaffles .................................................. 9
Chocolate Chip Chaffle Keto Recipe ...................... 9
Keto Blueberry Chaffle ........................................... 10
Crispy Chaffles With Egg & Asparagus ................. 10
Cinnamon Roll Chaffles ......................................... 11
Yogurt Chaffles ....................................................... 11
Raspberry Chaffles ................................................. 12
Coconut Chaffles .................................................... 12
Garlic And Parsley Chaffles .................................... 12
Scrambled Eggs On A Spring Onion Chaffle ........ 13
Strawberry Shortcake Chaffles ............................... 14
Glazed Chaffles ....................................................... 14
Cream Mini-Chaffles .............................................. 15
Lemon Curd Chaffles .............................................. 15
Egg On A Cheddar Cheese Chaffle ........................ 16
Avocado Chaffle Toast ............................................ 16
Cajun & Feeta Chaffles ........................................... 17
Crispy Chaffles With Sausage ................................. 17
Chili Chaffle ............................................................ 18
Simple Savory Chaffle ............................................. 18
Pizza Chaffle ............................................................ 19
Bacon Chaffle .......................................................... 19
Chaffles Breakfast Bowl .......................................... 20
Morning Chaffles With Berries ............................... 20
Chocolate Vanilla Chaffles ...................................... 21
Keto Chaffle Breakfast Sandwich ........................... 21
Keto Chaffle Taco Shells ......................................... 21
Peanut Butter Chaffle .............................................. 22
Pumpkin Chocolate Chip Chaffles .......................... 22
Broccoli & Cheese Chaffle ...................................... 23
French Dip Keto Chaffle Sandwich ......................... 23
Fudgy Chocolate Chaffles ....................................... 24
Keto Cornbread Chaffle .......................................... 24
Keto Chaffle Stuffing Recipe .................................. 24
Banana Nut Chaffle Recipe ..................................... 25
Crispy Bagel Chaffle Chips ..................................... 25
Chaffle Churros ....................................................... 26
Peanut Butter Chaffle .............................................. 26
Cinnamon Pecan Chaffles ....................................... 27
Almond Flour Chaffles ............................................ 27
Oreo Keto Chaffles .................................................. 27
Chicken Bites With Chaffles ................................... 28
Crunchy Fish And Chaffle Bites ............................. 28
Grill Pork Chaffle Sandwich ................................... 29
Chaffle & Chicken Lunch Plate .............................. 29
Keto Blt Chaffle Sandwich ...................................... 30
Keto Lemon Chaffle Recipe .................................... 30
Bacon Cheddar Bay Biscuits Chaffle Recipe ......... 31
Lime Pie Chaffle Recipe ......................................... 31
Jicama Hash Brown Chaffle .................................... 32
Easy Corndog Chaffle Recipe ................................. 32
Sloppy Joe Chaffle Recipe ...................................... 33
Keto Smores Chaffle ............................................... 33
Pumpkin Chaffle With Cream Cheese Frosting ..... 34
Keto Vanilla Twinkie Copycat Chaffle Recipe ....... 34
Peppermint Mocha Chaffles With Buttercream Frosting ................................................................... 35
Cranberry Swirl Chaffles With Orange Cream Cheese Frosting ..................................................... 35
Zucchini Nut Bread Chaffle Recipe ........................ 36
Keto Apple Fritter Chaffles ..................................... 37

| Recipe | Page |
|---|---|
| Monte Cristo Chaffle Crepes Recipe | 38 |
| Easy Turkey Burger With Halloumi Cheese Chaffle Recipe | 38 |
| Rice Krispie Treat Chaffle Copycat Recipe | 38 |
| Biscuits & Gravy Chaffle Recipe | 39 |
| Bbq Chicken Chaffle | 39 |
| Cheddar Chicken And Broccoli Chaffle | 40 |
| Gingerbread Chaffle | 40 |
| Chocolate Peanut Butter Chaffle | 41 |
| Pumpkin Pecan Chaffles | 41 |
| Italian Cream Chaffle Sandwich-Cake | 41 |
| Chocolate Cherry Chaffles | 42 |
| Banana Nut Chaffle | 42 |
| Belgium Chaffles | 43 |
| Bacon Chaffles | 43 |
| Chaffle Egg Sandwich | 44 |
| Chaffle Minutesi Sandwich | 44 |
| Chaffle Cheese Sandwich | 44 |
| Chicken Zinger Chaffle | 45 |
| Double Chicken Chaffles | 45 |
| Chaffles With Topping | 46 |
| Chaffle With Cheese & Bacon | 46 |
| Grill Beefsteak And Chaffle | 47 |
| Cauliflower Chaffles And Tomatoes | 47 |
| Layered Cheese Chaffles | 48 |
| Chaffles With Keto Ice Cream | 48 |
| Vanilla Mozzarella Chaffles | 48 |
| Bruschetta Chaffle | 49 |
| Egg-Free Psyllium Husk Chaffles | 49 |
| Mozzarella & Almond Flour Chaffles | 50 |
| Pulled Pork Chaffle Sandwiches | 50 |
| Cheddar & Egg White Chaffles | 50 |
| Spinach & Artichoke Chicken Chaffle | 51 |
| Chickfila Copycat Chaffle Sandwich | 51 |
| Strawberry Shortcake Chaffle | 52 |
| Chocolate Chaffle Cake | 52 |
| Keto Birthday Cake Chaffle | 53 |
| Chocolate Chip Cookie Chaffle Cake | 54 |
| Cap'n Crunch Cereal Chaffle Cake | 54 |
| Jicama Loaded Baked Potato Chaffle | 55 |
| German Chocolate Chaffle Cake Recipe | 55 |
| Keto Peanut Butter Chaffle Cake | 56 |
| Keto Boston Cream Pie Chaffle Cake Recipe | 56 |
| Coconut Cream Cake Chaffle Recipe | 57 |
| Almond Joy Cake Chaffle Recipe | 58 |
| Pumpkin Chaffle Keto Sugar Cookies Recipe | 59 |
| Maple Iced Soft Gingerbread Cookies Chaffle | 59 |
| Spicy Shrimp And Chaffles | 60 |
| Creamy Chicken Chaffle Sandwich | 60 |
| Chaffle Cannoli | 61 |
| Strawberry Shortcake Chaffle Bowls | 61 |
| Chocolate Melt Chaffles | 62 |
| Pumpkin & Pecan Chaffle | 62 |
| Spicy Jalapeno & Bacon Chaffles | 63 |
| Zucchini Parmesan Chaffles | 63 |
| Cheddar & Almond Flour Chaffles | 63 |
| Simple & Beginner Chaffle | 64 |
| Asian Cauliflower Chaffles | 64 |
| Sharp Cheddar Chaffles | 65 |
| Egg-Free Almond Flour Chaffles | 65 |
| Mozzarellas & Psyllium Husk Chaffles | 65 |
| Pumpkin-Cinnamon Churro Sticks | 66 |
| Chicken Jalapeño Chaffles | 66 |
| Chocolate & Almond Chaffle | 67 |
| Keto Chocolate Fudge Chaffle | 67 |
| Broccoli & Cheese Chaffle | 67 |
| Chaffled Brownie Sundae | 68 |
| Cream Cheese Chaffle | 68 |
| Garlic Chaffles | 69 |
| Cinnamon Powder Chaffles | 69 |
| Chaffles With Raspberry Syrup | 70 |
| Crispy Bagel Chaffles | 70 |
| Bacon And Ham Chaffle Sandwich | 71 |
| Parmesan Garlic Chaffle | 71 |
| Buffalo Chicken Chaffles | 72 |
| Garlic Cheese Chaffle Bread Sticks | 72 |
| Egg-Free Coconut Flour Chaffles | 73 |
| Cheeseburger Chaffle | 73 |
| Buffalo Hummus Beef Chaffles | 73 |
| Basic Mozzarella Chaffles | 74 |
| Brie And Blackberry Chaffles | 74 |
| Turkey Chaffle Burger | 75 |
| Double Choco Chaffle | 75 |
| Guacamole Chaffle Bites | 76 |
| Mayonnaise & Cream Cheese Chaffles | 76 |
| Blue Cheese Chaffle Bites | 77 |
| Raspberries Chaffles | 77 |
| Simple Chaffle Toast | 77 |
| Savory Beef Chaffle | 78 |
| Chaffles With Almond Flour | 78 |
| Nutter Butter Chaffles | 79 |
| Hot Dog Chaffles | 79 |
| Keto Reuben Chaffles | 80 |
| Carrot Chaffle Cake | 80 |
| Colby Jack Slices Chaffles | 81 |
| Egg & Chives Chaffle Sandwich Roll | 81 |
| Basic Chaffles Recipe For Sandwiches | 81 |
| Cereal Chaffle Cake | 82 |
| Okonomiyaki Chaffles | 82 |
| Bacon & Chicken Ranch Chaffle | 83 |

| Recipe | Page |
|---|---|
| Keto Cocoa Chaffles | 83 |
| Barbecue Chaffle | 83 |
| Chicken And Chaffle Nachos | 84 |
| Ham, Cheese & Tomato Chaffle Sandwich | 84 |
| Pizza Chaffle | 85 |
| Eggs Benedict Chaffle | 85 |
| Breakfast Chaffle | 86 |
| Cheddar Jalapeño Chaffle | 86 |
| Broccoli And Cheese Chaffles | 87 |
| Hash Brown Chaffle | 87 |
| Chicken Parmesan Chaffle | 87 |
| Red Velvet Chaffles | 88 |
| Mayonnaise Chaffles | 88 |
| Layered Chaffles | 88 |
| Cream Mini-Chaffles | 89 |
| Pumpkin & Psyllium Husk Chaffles | 89 |
| Blackberry Chaffles | 90 |
| Pumpkin Cream Cheese Chaffles | 90 |
| Cinnamon Sugar Chaffles | 90 |
| Cream Cheese Chaffles | 91 |
| Mozzarella & Butter Chaffles | 91 |
| Pumpkin Pecan Chaffles | 92 |
| Taco Chaffle Shell | 92 |
| Pulled Pork Chaffle | 93 |
| Chicken Bacon Chaffle | 93 |
| Spiced Pumpkin Chaffles | 93 |
| Vanilla Chaffle | 94 |
| Whipping Cream Pumpkin Chaffles | 94 |
| Chocolate Vanilla Chaffles | 95 |
| Churro Waffles | 95 |
| Chocolate Chips Lemon Chaffles | 96 |
| Mocha Chaffles | 96 |
| Carrot Chaffles | 96 |
| Ube Chaffles With Ice Cream | 97 |
| Berries Chaffles | 97 |
| Cinnamon Swirl Chaffles | 98 |
| Colby Jack Chaffles | 98 |
| Acocado Chaffle Toast | 99 |
| Bacon And Ham Chaffle Sandwich | 99 |
| Ham And Jalapenos Chaffle | 100 |
| Burger Chaffle | 100 |
| Bbq Chicken Chaffles | 101 |
| Avocado Chaffle | 101 |
| Zucchini & Onion Chaffles | 101 |
| Chaffle Cuban Sandwich | 102 |
| Salmon Chaffles | 102 |
| 3 Cheeses Herbed Chaffles | 103 |
| Bagel Seasoning Chaffles | 103 |
| Grilled Cheese Chaffle | 104 |
| Pandan Asian Chaffles | 104 |
| Ham Chaffles | 104 |
| Chaffle Katsu Sandwich | 105 |
| Spinach & Cauliflower Chaffles | 106 |
| Rosemary Chaffles | 106 |
| Zucchini Chaffles With Peanut Butter | 106 |
| Pepperoni & Cauliflower Chaffles | 107 |
| Pulled Pork Chaffle | 107 |
| Buffalo Chicken Chaffles | 108 |
| Japanese Breakfast Chaffle | 108 |
| Garlic And Spinach Chaffles | 109 |
| Cauliflower Chaffle | 109 |
| Cauliflower & Italian Seasoning Chaffles | 110 |
| Chaffle Cuban Sandwich | 110 |
| Protein Chaffles | 111 |
| Garlic Powder & Oregano Chaffles | 111 |
| Tuna Chaffles | 111 |
| Sausage & Veggie Chaffles | 112 |
| Crispy Bagel Chaffles | 112 |
| Vegan Chaffle | 112 |
| Turkey Chaffle Sandwich | 113 |
| Sausage & Veggies Chaffles | 113 |
| Broccoli & Almond Flour Chaffles | 114 |
| Bacon & Serrano Pepper Chaffles | 114 |
| Bacon Chaffle Omelettes | 114 |
| Aioli Chicken Chaffle Sandwich | 115 |
| Sage & Coconut Milk Chaffles | 115 |
| Hot Ham Chaffles | 116 |
| Japanese Breakfast Chaffle | 116 |
| Scallion Cream Cheese Chaffle | 116 |
| Grilled Cheese Chaffle | 117 |
| Lemony Fresh Herbs Chaffles | 117 |
| Basil Chaffles | 118 |
| Scallion Cream Cheese Chaffle | 118 |
| Chicken Taco Chaffles | 118 |
| Crab Chaffles | 119 |
| Bacon & Egg Chaffles | 119 |
| Chicken & Bacon Chaffles | 120 |
| Belgium Chaffles | 120 |
| Chaffle Katsu Sandwich | 120 |
| Pork Rind Chaffles | 121 |
| Chicken & Ham Chaffles | 121 |
| Eggs Benedict Chaffle | 122 |
| Chicken & Veggies Chaffles | 122 |
| Turkey Chaffles | 123 |
| Pepperoni Chaffles | 123 |
| Hot Sauce Jalapeño Chaffles | 124 |
| Garlic Herb Blend Seasoning Chaffles | 124 |
| Protein Cheddar Chaffles | 124 |
| Cheese-Free Breakfast Chaffle | 125 |
| Savory Bagel Seasoning Chaffles | 125 |

| | |
|---|---|
| Dried Herbs Chaffles | 126 |
| Cookie Dough Chaffle | 126 |
| Thanksgiving Pumpkin Spice Chaffle | 126 |
| Pumpkin Spice Chaffles | 127 |
| Chaffle Fruit Snacks | 127 |
| Open-Faced Ham & Green Bell Pepper Chaffle Sandwich | 128 |
| Christmas Morning Choco Chaffle Cake | 128 |
| Lt Chaffle Sandwich | 128 |
| Mozzarella Peanut Butter Chaffle | 129 |
| Double Decker Chaffle | 129 |
| Cinnamon And Vanilla Chaffle | 129 |
| New Year Cinnamon Chaffle With Coconut Cream | 130 |
| Chaffles And Ice-Cream Platter | 130 |
| Choco Chip Pumpkin Chaffle | 131 |
| Sausage & Pepperoni Chaffle Sandwich | 131 |
| Maple Chaffle | 132 |
| Red Velvet Chaffle | 132 |
| Walnuts Lowcarb Chaffles | 132 |
| Beginner Brownies Chaffle | 133 |
| Holidays Chaffles | 133 |
| Cherry Chocolate Chaffle | 133 |
| Bacon, Egg & Avocado Chaffle Sandwich | 134 |
| Crunchy Coconut Chaffles Cake | 134 |
| Coffee Flavored Chaffle | 135 |
| Italian Sausage Chaffles | 135 |
| Chaffles With Strawberry Frosty | 136 |
| Hot Chocolate Breakfast Chaffle | 136 |
| Pecan Pumpkin Chaffle | 136 |
| Swiss Bacon Chaffle | 137 |
| Bacon, Olives & Cheddar Chaffle | 137 |
| Breakfast Spinach Ricotta Chaffles | 137 |
| Pumpkin Chaffle With Frosting | 138 |
| Thanksgiving Pumpkin Latte With Chaffles | 138 |
| Choco And Strawberries Chaffles | 139 |
| Lemon And Paprika Chaffles | 139 |
| Triple Chocolate Chaffle | 140 |
| Mixed Berry-Vanilla Chaffles | 140 |
| Nut Butter Chaffle | 141 |
| Keto Coffee Chaffles | 141 |
| Scrambled Egg Stuffed Chaffles | 141 |
| Peanut Butter Sandwich Chaffle | 142 |
| Easter Morning Simple Chaffles | 143 |
| Apple Cinnamon Chaffles | 143 |
| Churro Chaffle | 143 |
| Super Easy Chocolate Chaffles | 144 |
| Mini Keto Pizza | 144 |
| Keto Chaffle With Almond Flour | 145 |
| Chaffles With Caramelized Apples And Yogurt | 145 |
| Keto Chaffle With Ice-Cream | 145 |
| Chaffle Tortilla | |

| | |
|---|---|
| 146 Chicken Quesadilla Chaffle | 157 Cheddar Chicken And Broccoli Chaffle |
| 146 Chocolate Chip Chaffle | 158 Turkey Chaffle Sandwich |
| 147 Cheese Garlic Chaffle | 158 Bbq Sauce Pork Chaffle |
| 147 Lemon And Vanilla Chaffle | 159 Chicken Bacon Ranch Chaffle |
| 147 Christmas Smoothie With Chaffles | 159 Chicken Taco Chaffle |
| 148 Raspberry And Chocolate Chaffle | 160 Italian Chicken And Basil Chaffle |
| 148 Pumkpin Chaffle With Maple Syrup | 160 Beef Meatballs On A Chaffle |
| 149 Maple Syrup & Vanilla Chaffle | 161 Leftover Turkey Chaffle |
| 149 Garlic Mayo Vegan Chaffles | 162 Beef Meatza Chaffle |
| 150 Broccoli Chaffle | 162 Chicken Jalapeno Chaffle |
| 150 Celery And Cottage Cheese Chaffle | 163 Pork Tzatziki Chaffle |
| 151 Mushroom And Almond Chaffle | 163 Mediterranean Lamb Kebabs On Chaffle |
| 151 Spinach And Artichoke Chaffle | 164 Beef And Sour Cream Chaffle |
| 152 Avocado Croque Madam Chaffle | 164 Pork Loin Chaffle Sandwich |
| 152 Fruity Vegan Chaffles | 165 Beef Chaffle Tower |
| 152 Almonds And Flaxseeds Chaffles | 166 Turkey Bbq Sauce Chaffle |
| 153 Vegan Chocolate Chaffles | 166 Strawberry Cream Sandwich Chaffles |
| 153 Vegan Chaffles With Flaxseed | 167 Ham Sandwich Chaffles |
| 154 Asparagus Chaffle | 167 Chicken Sandwich Chaffles |
| 154 Rosemary Pork Chops On Chaffle | 168 Salmon & Cheese Sandwich Chaffles |
| 155 Classic Beef Chaffle | 168 Blueberry Peanut Butter Sandwich Chaffles |
| 155 Beef And Tomato Chaffle | 168 Berry Sauce Sandwich Chaffles |
| 156 Classic Ground Pork Chaffle | 169 Pork Sandwich Chaffles |
| 156 Spinach & Artichoke Chicken Chaffle | 169 Tomato Sandwich Chaffles |
| 157 Beef Chaffle Taco | 170 Cheesy Garlic Chaffle Bread Recipe 170 |

| | |
|---|---|
| Best Keto Pizza Chaffle | 171 |
| Easy Keto Chaffle Sausage Gravy Recipe | 172 |
| Fudgy Chocolate Chaffles | 172 |
| Mouthwatering Blueberry Chaffles | 173 |
| Open-Faced French Dip Keto Chaffle Sandwich | 173 |
| Maple Pumpkin Keto Chaffle Recipe | 174 |
| Basic Keto Low Carb Chaffle Recipe | 174 |
| Keto Protein Chaffle | 175 |
| Chaffle Tacos | 175 |
| Lettuce Chaffle Sandwich | 176 |
| Cocoa Chaffles With Coconut Cream | 177 |
| Shrimp Avocado Chaffle Sandwich | 177 |
| Cuban Pork Sandwich | 178 |
| Simple Heart Shape Chaffles | 179 |
| Cauliflower Turkey Chaffle | 179 |
| Pork Chaffles On Pan | 180 |
| Oven-Baked Chaffles | 180 |
| Pumpkin Pecan Chaffle | 180 |
| Sloppy Joe Chaffle | 181 |
| Choco Peanut Butter Chaffle | 182 |
| Lobster Chaffle | 183 |
| Simple Chaffles Without Maker | 183 |
| Heart Shape Chaffles | 184 |
| Bacon Chaffles With Herb Dip | 184 |
| Broccoli Chaffles On Pan | 185 |
| Chicken Chaffles With Tzatziki | 185 |
| Cereal And Walnut Chaffle | 186 |
| Cornbread Chaffle | 186 |
| Midday Chaffle Snacks | 187 |
| Spinach Chaffle | 187 |
| Bbq Chicken Chaffle | 188 |
| Shirataki Rice Chaffle | 188 |
| Ham Chaffle | 189 |
| Zucchini Bacon Chaffles | 189 |
| Spinach Artichoke Chaffle With Bacon | 190 |
| Chocolate Cannoli Chaffle | 190 |
| Broccoli And Cheese Chaffle | 191 |
| Eggnog Chaffle | 192 |
| Double Cheese Chaffles With Mayonnaise Dip | 192 |
| Carrot Cake Chaffle | 193 |
| Chaffles With Chocolate Balls | 194 |
| Bacon Jalapeno Popper Chaffle | 194 |
| Apple Pie Chaffle | 195 |
| French Toast Chaffle Sticks | 195 |
| Sweet Brownie Chaffle | 196 |
| Savory Chaffle Stick | 197 |
| Keto Avocado Chaffle Toast | 197 |
| Okonomiyaki Chaffle | 198 |
| Blt Chaffle Sandwich | 199 |
| CONVERSION TABLE | 201 |

# Introduction

Waffles are amazing. There are numerous sorts of waffles, it's easy to find one to love. Or even make a brand new flavor. Take a classic waffle, put something unique on top, or change a batter a little bit, and voila, you have invented a new waffle!

But what if you happen to be on a keto diet? How can you still enjoy waffles? The answer is the chaffle!

Chaffles are amazing on their own, with a unique, distinct taste. Like regular waffles, there are enough types for anyone to find a favorite.

The purpose of this book is to introduce the reader into the chaffle making process. To be a guide to everything related to this process. And I hope, it will do just that.

So, flip this page and get started! Chaffles are waiting to be baked and enjoyed!

# The Ketogenic Diet and its Benefits

The keto or ketogenic diet recommends eating high-fat, low-carbohydrate foods that give us healthy fats, proteins, and fewer carbohydrates. The calories we get comes mostly from fats (70%), proteins (20%), and carbs (10%). The diet typically doesn't count calories. Carbohydrates are counted instead and restricted.

The human body turns carbohydrates into glucose to produce energy. Fats, which can also be used for energy-making are largely ignored, which is why it gets deposited and makes us overweight. The ketogenic diet restricts the intake of carbs and pushes the body to burn fat for energy. For this reason, the ketogenic diet is considered to be very efficient for weight loss.

Also, when you eat fewer carbohydrates, the insulin level in the body goes down, so there is less glucose.

# Ketogenic Diet Health Benefits

Not just weight loss, the keto diet helps us in many ways -

Blood sugar - It can help us lower the blood sugar and insulin levels. A low-carb diet also prevents blood sugar spikes.

Cholesterol - It increases the level of healthy HDL cholesterol and lowers unhealthy LDL cholesterol. So it reduces the risk of heart disease.

The human brain - Studies have revealed that low-carb, high protein, and fatty foods make our brains more efficient. It can prevent or slow down Alzheimer's, dementia, autism, and other such cognitive diseases.

Inflammation - Inflammation improves immunity, but chronic inflammation can cause health problems. The keto diet lowers the production of free radicals and controls the negative effects of too much inflammation like arthritis, eczema, and psoriasis.

Stomach health - A low carbohydrate diet provides relief from heartburn and acid reflux. It can fight the key problems, such as bacterial issues and autoimmune responses. It also improves digestion.

Anti-Aging - The ketogenic diet may also promote longevity according to research findings.

Improves energy - The diet stabilizes the insulin level and provides more energy to the brain and tissues. It also improves the slow-wave sleep patterns and reduces REM (Rapid Eye Movement) or shallow sleep.

PCOS - Carbohydrate-rich foods are not recommended for those who are suffering from PCOS or Polycystic Ovary Syndrome. Studies have proved that Keto foods can improve PCOS markers.

Triglycerides - The triglycerides levels in the blood can shoot up when we consume too many carbohydrates, leading to an increased risk of heart disease. Lower the consumption and there is a drastic drop in its level.

Apart from the ones mentioned above, the ketogenic diet may also help us control the uric acid levels, improve the health of our eyes, and prevent acne breakouts.

# Foods Allowed and Disallowed in the Keto Diet

What you can eat :

1. Seafood, including sardines, salmon, shrimp, crabs, and tuna. Fatty fish like sardines and salmon are particularly good.

2. Fresh leafy vegetables, including broccoli, kale, spinach, cauliflower, turnips, cucumber, lettuce, asparagus, bell peppers.

3. Dairy products, including yogurt and cheese. Avoid flavored yogurts.

4. Meat, including pork, lamb, beef, chicken, and turkey is allowed.

5. Eggs are rich in protein and allowed in the keto diet.

6. You can eat nuts and seeds moderately. Avoid cashew nuts.

7. Tea and coffee are both allowed but without sugar.

8. Use coconut oil for frying and sautéing.

9. You can have dark chocolate with 80% cocoa.

Foods to avoid :

1. Restrict the intake of fruits because most of them have too much sugar.
2. Most cereals are sugar-rich and best avoided.
3. White starches only add empty calories.
4. Beans and legumes contain a lot of carbohydrates.
5. Restrict the intake of alcohol and honey.

# What is a "chaffle"?

A chaffle is a keto waffle. It's called a chaffle because one of its primary ingredients is shredded cheese, hence the CHaffle instead of Waffle because chaffles are cheese waffles. Pretty cool, right?

Waffles are usually made of a flour-based batter, but a chaffle is made of eggs and cheese. It sounds odd, but it actually works!

Chaffles are a great way for those on the keto diet to get their waffle fix. They're also a great way to eat fewer carbs while still eating what you want! Even if it is a modified version. There are also endless chaffle ingredient combinations.

HOW A BASIC CHAFFLE IS MADE

A basic chaffle is made of just two ingredients: ½ cup of shredded cheese, like mozzarella, and 1 large egg. Finely shredded cheese or thicker shreds work, it's completely up to you.

You whisk the egg, stir in the cheese, and place half the mixture in a waffle maker at a time for 2-3 minutes. Then, after removing from the waffle maker, let them sit for 1-2 minutes. They'll crisp up like a normal waffle would as they set.

You can add almond or coconut flour to give it a more bread-like texture. One teaspoon of either is a good place to start and adjust to your preferences.

# How To Eat/Serve A Basic Chaffle

Even though they are as simple as it can get, there are a lot of ways to eat chaffles.

Here are some ways to enjoy chaffles -Fruit-topped - Add berries, bananas, apples, or peaches on top.

Chaffle sandwich - You can use chaffles like buns or bread when you cut in half or make them in small sizes. Stuff them with the sandwich fillings you like. They can also be served with burgers and hotdogs.

Chaffle pizza - Add pepperoni, tomatoes, extra cheese, and your favorite toppings to make a version you will like.

Dessert chaffle - Yogurt, frosting, or ice cream will add a different dimension to your chaffles. They are perfect for satisfying those who love sweets.

Chaffles will keep surprising you. They are perfect for people who follow the keto diet but still want to have waffles. You can have them for breakfast, as a snack, or dessert.

Chaffles also provide a lot of protein. They are filling, so they will keep you feeling full for a long time, thus preventing overeating.

The Chaffle Maker

You will need a special appliance to make them - the chaffle maker. There are many brands available online like Dash, Cuisinart, Hamilton Beach, Burgess Brothers, Holstein Housewares, Brentwood, and others. They come with different browning settings, non-stick versions, different cooking times, a varied number of chaffles produced, and other features. Most of them are small enough to be tucked into your kitchen drawer.

You can also use a waffle maker to make chaffles. There are, however, some differences between these two appliances. For example, a classic waffle maker and chaffle maker will give you chaffles in different sizes. The grates are also smaller in chaffle makers, which helps to make them crisper. So it's best to use a chaffle maker.

Can Chaffles Be Frozen?

Yes, you can freeze them for up to 3-5 days. Simply keep them in a freezer bag with a parchment paper piece between each chaffle. You can also freeze in small freezer bags. Don't keep more than two in each bag.

You can reheat in a toaster oven, skillet, or conventional oven before eating them. You can also microwave for 30 to 60 seconds. Allow them to thaw before reheating.

Can the Eggy Flavor Be Replaced?

One difference between the chaffle and waffle is in the distinct eggy taste that you will find in this high-protein keto version. However, some people don't like this egg smell. That can be fixed easily by increasing the sugar quantity and adding milk powder.

Lime, lemon, or orange juice and/or rind can also be used. Use a teaspoon of juice or quarter teaspoon of rind per 3 eggs.

## Chaffle Making Tips, Frequently Asked Questions

**CAN YOU TASTE THE CHEESE IN A SWEET KETO CHAFFLE?**

Of course, this question is subjective as one person's taste buds are different from others, but it partly depends on how distinct the taste of the cheese that was used is.

**WHAT DO YOU MEAN BY SAVORY?**

Unlike chaffles served with sugar-free syrup or fresh berries, savory chaffles aren't sweet. Instead, they taste more like a traditional bread and can be used to make personal pan pizzas, crispy keto taco shells, and more.

**VARIETIES OF CHEESE FOR CHAFFLES:**

There are many different kinds of cheese that you can use in keto chaffle recipes. The most suitable are listed below. You can also mix different cheeses together.

So:

- Colby Jack
- Monterey Jack
- White Cheddar Cheese
- Mild Cheddar & Sharp Cheddar
- Parmesan Cheese
- Mozzarella

You can use cream cheese like Philadelphia in place of cheese, but the texture will be different. Cream cheese makes much softer, unstructured chaffles.

**ALMOND/COCONUT FLOUR IN CHAFFLES: WHY DO SOME RECIPES REQUIRE ADDING FLOUR, AND SOME DON'T?**

Coconut flour gives chaffles a bit of a bread-like texture, especially in sweet chaffle recipes. Usually, just 1 tsp of coconut flour along with ¼ tsp of baking powder is enough.

If using almond flour instead, you should make an amount conversion. The standard conversion in keto recipes is one part coconut flour to four parts almond flour, but that isn't the case with chaffles. Since you only use a small amount of coconut flour in recipes, the overall conversion rate is just one teaspoon coconut flour equals one tablespoon almond flour.

Why do some recipes require adding flour, and some don't?

While both adding and not adding flour to the same recipe may result okay, sometimes a bit of coconut or almond flour garners a better overall taste, especially in sweet recipes.

**WHAT IS THE PURPOSE OF BAKING POWDER?**

The baking powder adds bubbles to the chaffle batter, causing them to puff up a bit and be less dense.

**HOW DO I STORE CHAFFLES?**

Any plastic container that you find okay to use in the freezer will do. Even freezer bags. If they are basic chaffles, let them cool before setting them in the freezer. The heat and condensation will make them stick. Other chaffles covered in crazy ingredients, however, you may want to separate them with parchment paper or something similar.

**HOW DO I REHEAT CHAFFLES?**

You can reheat chaffles in several different ways, such as in the oven, toaster, air fryer, or skillet. You can also put them back into the waffle maker to heat up and make them crispy again.

Just don't use a microwave, they don't taste fresh after that.

**HOW DO I CLEAN MY WAFFLE MAKER?**

There is a lot of ways. One of them is putting a wet cloth in and letting the steam loosen everything up after unplugging it. Then, when it's cool, use it to wipe it off. The heat will kill everything on it. There are also all sorts of dishwashing gadgets out there that can get between the grooves if needed.

**WHY DOES THE CHAFFLE STICK?**

There are a few reasons why it may happen:

- Your waffle maker's surface may be wearing out from general use.
- You may not be letting the batter to cook long enough.
- The type of chaffle you're cooking is just a bit stickier.

# RECIPES

## Basic Keto Chaffles

Prep Time: 5 mins

Cook Time: 8 mins

Servings: 1

**Ingredients:**

1 egg

1/2 cup cheddar cheese, shredded

**Directions:**

Turn waffle maker on or plug it in so that it heats and grease both sides.

In a small bowl, crack an egg, then add the 1/2 cup cheddar cheese and stir to combine. Pour 1/2 of the batter in the waffle maker and close the top.

Cook for 3-4 minutes or until it reaches desired doneness.

Carefully remove from waffle maker and set aside for 2-3 minutes to give it time to crisp. Follow the Directions again to make the second chaffle.

Nutritional Value (per serving):

Calories: 291kcal Carbohydrates: 1g Protein: 20g Fat: 23g

Variations to the Basic Keto Chaffle Recipe:

Experiment with different kinds of cheese such as Monterrey Jack, Colby, mozzarella cheese, etc. You could even combine two different kinds of cheese for added flavor.

Add spices such as garlic powder, Italian seasoning, Everything But the Bagel seasoning, or red pepper flakes to turn it up a notch

Add a tsp of coconut flour or a tablespoon of almond flour along with 1/4 tsp baking powder and a pinch of salt.

Thinly chopped peppers, onions, or jalapenos can add flavor and texture.

Keep it sugar-free by adding keto-friendly sweeteners like Lakanto Monkfruit or Swerve to make a sweet Chaffle.

## Chocolate Chip Chaffle Keto Recipe

Prep Time: 5 mins

Cook Time: 8 mins

Serving: 1

**Ingredients**:

1 egg

1 tbsp heavy whipping cream 1/2 tsp coconut flour

1 3/4 tsp Lakanto monk fruit golden can use more or less to adjust sweetness 1/4 tsp baking powder

pinch of salt

1 tbsp Lily's Chocolate Chips

**Directions:**

Turn on the waffle maker so that it heats up.

In a small bowl, combine all ingredients except the chocolate chips and stir well until combined. Grease waffle maker, then pour half of the batter onto the bottom plate of the waffle maker. Sprinkle a few chocolate chips on top and then close.

Cook for 3-4 minutes or until the chocolate chip chaffle dessert is golden brown, then remove from waffle maker with a fork, being careful not to burn your fingers.

Repeat with the rest of the batter.

Let chaffle sit for a few minutes so that it begins to crisp. If desired, serve with sugar-free whipped topping.

Nutritional Value (per serving):

Calories: 146kcal Carbohydrates: 7g Protein: 6g Fat: 10g

## Keto Blueberry Chaffle

Prep Time: 3 minutes

Cook Time: 15 minutes

Servings: 5

**Ingredients**:

1 cup of mozzarella cheese

2 tablespoons almond flour

1 tsp baking powder

2 eggs

1 tsp cinnamon

2 tsp of Swerve

3 tablespoon blueberries

**Directions:**

Heat up your Dash mini waffle maker.

In a mixing bowl, add the mozzarella cheese, almond flour, baking powder, eggs, cinnamon, swerve, and blueberries. Mix well, so all the ingredients are mixed together.

Spray your mini waffle maker with nonstick cooking spray.

Add in a little bit less than 1/4 a cup of blueberry keto waffle batter.

Close the lid and cook the chaffle for 3-5 minutes. Check it at the 3-minute mark to see if it is crispy and brown. If it is not or it sticks to the top of the waffle machine, close the lid and cook for 1-2 minutes longer.

Serve with a sprinkle of swerve confectioners sugar or keto syrup.

Nutritional Value (per serving):

Calories: 116kcal Carbohydrates: 3g Protein: 8g Fat: 8g

## Crispy Chaffles With Egg & Asparagus

Servings:1

Cooking Time: 10 Minutes

**Ingredients**:

1 egg

1/4 cup cheddar cheese

2 tbsps. almond flour

½ tsp. baking powder

TOPPING

1 egg

4-5 stalks asparagus

1 tsp avocado oil

**Directions:**

1. Preheat waffle maker to medium-high heat.

2. Whisk together egg, mozzarella cheese, almond flour, and baking powder

3. Pour chaffles mixture into the center of the waffle iron. Close the waffle maker and let cook for 5 minutes or until waffle is golden brown and set.

4. Remove chaffles from the waffle maker and serve.

5. Meanwhile, heat oil in a nonstick pan.

6. Once the pan is hot, fry asparagus for about 4-5 minutes until golden brown.

7. Poach the egg in boil water for about 2-3 minutes.

8. Once chaffles are cooked, remove from the maker.

9. Serve chaffles with the poached egg and asparagus.

Nutrition Value per Servings:

Protein: 85 kcal Fat: 226 kcal Carbohydrates:

16 kcal

## Cinnamon Roll Chaffles

Servings: 3

Prep time: 15 min.

Cook time: 25 min.

**Ingredients**

FOR THE BATTER:

½ cup shredded mozzarella cheese

2 Tbsp golden monk fruit sweetener

2 Tbsp SunButter

1 egg

1 Tbsp coconut flour

2 tsp cinnamon

¼ tsp vanilla extract

⅛ tsp baking powder

FOR THE FROSTING:

¼ cup powdered monk fruit sweetener

1 Tbsp cream cheese

¾ Tbsp butter, melted

¼ tsp vanilla extract

1 Tbsp unsweetened coconut milk

FOR THE COATING

1 tsp cinnamon

1 tsp golden monk fruit sweetener

**Directions:**

Turn on waffle maker to heat and oil it with cooking spray.

Combine all batter components in a bowl, then set aside and leave for 3-5 minutes. In another bowl, whisk all frosting components until well-combined.

Divide batter into 3 portions and spoon 1 part into the waffle maker. Cook for 2-4 minutes, until golden brown.

Open and let chaffle cool for 30 seconds in waffle maker before you transfer it to a plate. Repeat with remaining batter.

While chaffles are warm, sprinkle with cinnamon and sweetener coating. When cooled a little, drizzle with icing.

Nutrition Value per servings:

 Carbs - 31 G  Fat - 15 G  Protein - 9 G  Calories – 195

## Yogurt Chaffles

Servings: 3

Prep time: 5 min. + overnight

Cook time: 10 min.

**Ingredients**

½ cup shredded mozzarella

1 egg

2 Tbsp ground almonds

½ tsp psyllium husk

¼ tsp baking powder

1 Tbsp yogurt

**Directions:**

Turn on waffle maker to heat and oil it with cooking spray. Whisk eggs in a bowl.

Add in remaining ingredients except mozzarella and mix well. Add mozzarella and mix once again. Let it sit for 5 minutes. Add ☐ cup batter into each waffle mold.

Close and cook for 4-5 minutes.

Repeat with remaining batter.

 Nutrition Value per servings:

Carbs - 2 G  Fat - 5 G  Protein - 4 G  Calories - 93

## Raspberry Chaffles

Servings: 2

Prep time: 5 min.

Cook time: 5 min.

**Ingredients**

4 Tbsp almond flour

4 large eggs

2 ☐ cup shredded mozzarella cheese

1 tsp vanilla extract

1 Tbsp erythritol sweetener

1½ tsp baking powder

½ cup raspberries

**Directions:**

Turn on waffle maker to heat and oil it with cooking spray.

Mix almond flour, sweetener, and baking powder in a bowl.

Add cheese, eggs, and vanilla extract, and mix until well-combined.

Add 1 portion of batter to waffle maker and spread it evenly. Close and cook for 3-4 minutes, or until golden.

Repeat until remaining batter is used. Serve with raspberries.

## Coconut Chaffles

Servings: 2

Cooking Time: 5 Minutes

**Ingredients**:

1 egg

1 oz. cream cheese,

1 oz. cheddar cheese

2 tbsps. coconut flour

1 tsp. stevia

1 tbsp. coconut oil, melted

1/2 tsp. coconut extract

2 eggs, soft boil for serving

**Directions:**

1. Heat you minutesi Dash waffle maker and grease with cooking spray.

2. Mix together all chaffles ingredients in a bowl.

3. Pour chaffle batter in a preheated waffle maker.

4. Close the lid.

5. Cook chaffles for about 2-3 minutes until golden brown.

6. Serve with boil egg and enjoy!

Nutrition Value per Servings:

Protein: 32 kcal Fat: 117 kcal Carbohydrates: 4 kcal

## Garlic And Parsley Chaffles

Servings: 1

Cooking Time: 5 Minutes

**Ingredients**:

1 large egg

1/4 cup cheese mozzarella

1 tsp. coconut flour

¼ tsp. baking powder

½ tsp. garlic powder

1 tbsp. minutesced parsley

For Serving

1 Poach egg

4 oz. smoked salmon

**Directions:**

1. Switch on yourDash minutesiwaffle maker and let it preheat.

2. Grease waffle maker with cooking spray.

3. Mix together egg, mozzarella, coconut flour, baking powder, and garlic powder, parsley to a mixing bowl until combined well.

4. Pour batter in circle chaffle maker.

5. Close the lid.

6. Cook for about 2-3 minutes or until the chaffles are cooked.

7. Serve with smoked salmon and poached egg.

8. Enjoy!

Nutrition Value per Servings: Protein:

140 kcal Fat: 160 kcal Carbohydrates: 14 kcal

## Scrambled Eggs On A Spring Onion Chaffle

Servings: 4

Cooking Time: 7-9 Minutes

**Ingredients:**

Batter

4 eggs

2 cups grated mozzarella cheese

2 spring onions, finely chopped Salt and pepper to taste

½ teaspoon dried garlic powder

2 tablespoons almond flour

2 tablespoons coconut flour

Other

2 tablespoons butter for brushing the waffle maker

6-8 eggs

Salt and pepper

1 teaspoon Italian spice mix

1 tablespoon olive oil

1 tablespoon freshly chopped parsley

**Directions:**

1. Preheat the waffle maker.

2. Crack the eggs into a bowl and add the grated cheese.

3. Mix until just combined, then add the chopped spring onions and season with salt and pepper and dried garlic powder.

4. Stir in the almond flour and mix until everything is combined.

5. Brush the heated waffle maker with butter and add a few tablespoons of the batter.

6. Close the lid and cook for about 7-8 minutes depending on your waffle maker.

7. While the chaffles are cooking, prepare the scrambled eggs by whisking the eggs in a bowl until frothy, about 2 minutes. Season with salt and black pepper to taste and add the Italian spice mix. Whisk to blend in the spices.

8. Warm the oil in a non-stick pan over medium heat.

9. Pour the eggs in the pan and cook until eggs are set to your liking.

10. Serve each chaffle and top with some scrambled eggs. Top with freshly chopped parsley.

Nutrition Value per Servings:

Calories 194, fat 14.7 g, carbs 5 g, Protein 1 g

## Strawberry Shortcake Chaffles

Servings: 1

Prep time: 20 min.

Cook time: 25 min.

**Ingredients**

FOR THE BATTER:

1 egg

¼ cup mozzarella cheese

1 Tbsp cream cheese

¼ tsp baking powder

2 strawberries, sliced

1 tsp strawberry extract

FOR THE GLAZE:

1 Tbsp cream cheese

¼ tsp strawberry extract

1 Tbsp monk fruit confectioners blend

FOR THE WHIPPED CREAM:

1 cup heavy whipping cream

1 tsp vanilla

1 Tbsp monk fruit

**Directions:**

Turn on waffle maker to heat and oil it with cooking spray. Beat egg in a small bowl.

Add remaining batter components. Divide the mixture in half.

Cook one half of the batter in a waffle maker for 4 minutes, or until golden brown. Repeat with remaining batter

Mix all glaze ingredients and spread over each warm chaffle. Mix all whipped cream ingredients and whip until it starts to form peaks. Top each waffle with whipped cream and strawberries.

Nutrition Value per Servings:

Carbs - 5 G  Fat - 14 G  Protein - 12 G  Calories - 218

## Glazed Chaffles

Servings: 2

Prep time: 10 min.

Cook time: 5 min.

**Ingredients:**

½ cup mozzarella shredded cheese ⅛ cup cream cheese

2 Tbsp unflavored whey protein isolate

2 Tbsp swerve confectioners sugar substitute ½ tsp baking powder

½ tsp vanilla extract

1 egg

FOR THE GLAZE TOPPING:

2 Tbsp heavy whipping cream

3-4 Tbsp swerve confectioners sugar substitute ½ tsp vanilla extract

**Directions:**

Turn on waffle maker to heat and oil it with cooking spray.

In a microwave-safe bowl, mix mozzarella and cream cheese. Heat at 30 second intervals until melted and fully combined.

Add protein, 2 Tbsp sweetener, baking powder to cheese. Knead with hands until well incorporated. Place dough into a mixing bowl and beat in egg and vanilla until a smooth batter forms.

Put ☐ of the batter into waffle maker, and cook for 3-5 minutes, until golden brown. Repeat until all 3 chaffles are made.

Beat glaze ingredients in a bowl and pour over chaffles before serving.

Nutrition Value per Servings:

Carbs - 4 G  Fat - 6 G  Protein - 4 G  Calories – 130

## Cream Mini-Chaffles

Servings: 2

Prep time: 5 min.

Cook time: 10 min.

**Ingredients:**

2 tsp coconut flour

4 tsp swerve/monk fruit

¼ tsp baking powder

1 egg

1 oz cream cheese

½ tsp vanilla extract

**Directions:**

Turn on waffle maker to heat and oil it with cooking spray.

Mix swerve/monk fruit, coconut flour, and baking powder in a small mixing bowl. Add cream cheese, egg, vanilla extract, and whisk until well-combined.

Add batter into waffle maker and cook for 3-4 minutes, until golden brown. Serve with your favorite toppings.

Nutrition Value per Servings:

Carbs - 4 G  Fat - 6 G  Protein - 2 G  Calories – 73

## Lemon Curd Chaffles

Servings: 1

prep time: 45 min.

Cook time: 5 min.

**Ingredients:**

3 large eggs

4 oz cream cheese, softened

1 Tbsp low carb sweetener

1 tsp vanilla extract

¾ cup mozzarella cheese, shredded

3 Tbsp coconut flour

1 tsp baking powder

☐ tsp salt

FOR THE LEMON CURD:

½-1 cup water

5 egg yolks

½ cup lemon juice

½ cup powdered sweetener

2 Tbsp fresh lemon zest

1 tsp vanilla extract Pinch of salt

8 Tbsp cold butter, cubed

**Directions:**

Pour water into a saucepan and heat over medium until it reaches a soft boil. Start with ½ cup and add more if needed.

Whisk yolks, lemon juice, lemon zest, powdered sweetener, vanilla, and salt in a medium heat-proof bowl. Leave to set for 5-6 minutes.

Place bowl onto saucepan and heat. The bowl shouldn't be touching water. Whisk mixture for 8-10 minutes, or until it begins to thicken.

Add butter cubes and whisk for 5-7 minutes, until it thickens. When it lightly coats the back of a spoon, remove from heat. Refrigerate until cool, allowing it to continue thickening.

Turn on waffle maker to heat and oil it with cooking spray.

Add baking powder, coconut flour, and salt in a small bowl. Mix well and set aside.

Add eggs, cream cheese, sweetener, and vanilla

in a separate bowl. Using a hand beater, beat until frothy.

Add mozzarella to egg mixture and beat again.

Add dry ingredients and mix until well-combined.

Add batter to waffle maker and cook for 3-4 minutes.

Transfer to a plate and top with lemon curd before serving

Nutrition Value per Servings:

Carbs - 6 G  Fat - 24 G  Protein - 15 G  Calories -302

## Egg On A Cheddar Cheese Chaffle

Servings: 4

Cooking Time: 7-9 Minutes

**Ingredients:**

Batter

4 eggs

2 cups shredded white cheddar cheese Salt and pepper to taste

Other

2 tablespoons butter for brushing the waffle maker

4 large eggs

2 tablespoons olive oil

**Directions:**

1. Preheat the waffle maker.
2. Crack the eggs into a bowl and whisk them with a fork.
3. Stir in the grated cheddar cheese and season with salt and pepper.
4. Brush the heated waffle maker with butter and add a few tablespoons of the batter.
5. Close the lid and cook for about 7-8 minutes depending on your waffle maker.
6. While chaffles are cooking, cook the eggs.
7. Warm the oil in a large non-stick pan that has a lid over medium-low heat for 2-3 minutes
8. Crack an egg in a small ramekin and gently add it to the pan. Repeat the same way for the other 3 eggs.
9. Cover and let cook for 2 to 2 ½ minutes for set eggs but with runny yolks.
10. Remove from heat.
11. To serve, place a chaffle on each plate and top with an egg. Season with salt and black pepper to taste.

Nutrition Value per Servings:

Calories 4 fat 34 g, carbs 2 g, sugar 0.6 g, Protein 26 g

## Avocado Chaffle Toast

Servings: 3

Cooking Time: 10 Minutes

**Ingredients:**

4 tbsps. avocado mash

1/2 tsp lemon juice

1/8 tsp salt

1/8 tsp black pepper

2 eggs

1/2 cup shredded cheese

For serving

3 eggs

½ avocado thinly sliced

1 tomato, sliced

**Directions:**

1. Mash avocado mash with lemon juice, salt, and black pepper in mixing bowl, until well

combined.

2. In a small bowl beat egg and pour eggs in avocado mixture and mix well.

3. Switch on Waffle Maker to pre-heat.

4. Pour 1/8 of shredded cheese in a waffle maker and then pour ½ of egg and avocado mixture and then 1/8 shredded cheese.

5. Close the lid and cook chaffles for about 3 - 4 minutes.

6. Repeat with the remaining mixture.

7. Meanwhile, fry eggs in a pan for about 1-2 minutes.

8. For serving, arrange fried egg on chaffle toast with avocado slice and tomatoes.

9. Sprinkle salt and pepper on top and enjoy!

Nutrition Value per Servings :

Protein: 66 kcal Fat: 169 kcal Carbohydrates: 15 kcal

## Cajun & Feeta Chaffles

Servings:1

Cooking Time: 10 Minutes

**Ingredients:**

1 egg white

1/4 cup shredded mozzarella cheese

2 tbsps. almond flour

1 tsp Cajun Seasoning

FOR SERVING

1 egg

4 oz. feta cheese

1 tomato, sliced

**Directions:**

1. Whisk together egg, cheese, and seasoning in a bowl.

2. Switch on and grease waffle maker with cooking spray.

3. Pour batter in a preheated waffle maker.

4. Cook chaffles for about 2-3 minutes until the chaffle is cooked through.

5. Meanwhile, fry the egg in a non-stick pan for about 1-2 minutes.

6. For serving set fried egg on chaffles with feta cheese and tomatoes slice.

Nutrition Value per Servings:

Protein: 119 kcal Fat 2 kcal Carbohydrates: 31 kcal

## Crispy Chaffles With Sausage

Servings:2

Cooking Time: 10 Minutes

**Ingredients:**

1/2 cup cheddar cheese

1/2 tsp. baking powder

1/4 cup egg whites

2 tsp. pumpkin spice

1 egg, whole

2 chicken sausage

2 slice bacon

salt and pepper to taste

1 tsp. avocado oil

**Directions:**

1. Mix together all ingredients in a bowl.

2. Allow batter to sit while waffle iron warms.

3. Spray waffle iron with nonstick spray.

4. Pour batter in the waffle maker and cook according to the directions of the manufacturer.

5. Meanwhile, heat oil in a pan and fry the

egg, according to your choice and transfer it to a plate.

6. In the same pan, fry bacon slice and sausage on medium heat for about 2-3 minutes until cooked.

7. Once chaffles are cooked thoroughly, remove them from the maker.

8. Serve with fried egg, bacon slice, sausages and enjoy!

Nutrition Value per Servings:

Calories 208  Fat 13.5g Carbohydrate 0.7g Protein 8.2g Sugars 0.6g

## Chili Chaffle

Servings: 4

Cooking Time: 7-9 Minutes

**Ingredients:**

Batter

4 eggs

½ cup grated parmesan cheese

1½ cups grated yellow cheddar cheese

1 hot red chili pepper

Salt and pepper to taste

½ teaspoon dried garlic powder

1 teaspoon dried basil

2 tablespoons almond flour

Other

2 tablespoons olive oil for brushing the waffle maker

**Directions:**

1. Preheat the waffle maker.

2. Crack the eggs into a bowl and add the grated parmesan and cheddar cheese.

3. Mix until just combined and add the chopped chili pepper. Season with salt and pepper, dried garlic powder and dried basil. Stir in the almond flour.

4. Mix until everything is combined.

5. Brush the heated waffle maker with olive oil and add a few tablespoons of the batter.

6. Close the lid and cook for about 7-8 minutes depending on your waffle maker.

Nutrition Value per Servings:

Calories 36 fat 30.4 g, carbs 3.1 g

## Simple Savory Chaffle

Servings: 4

Cooking Time: 7-9 Minutes

**Ingredients:**

Batter

4 eggs

1 cup grated mozzarella cheese

1 cup grated provolone cheese ½ cup almond flour

2 tablespoons coconut flour

2½ teaspoons baking powder

Salt and pepper to taste

Other

2 tablespoons butter to brush the waffle maker

**Directions:**

1. Preheat the waffle maker.

2. Add the grated mozzarella and provolone cheese to a bowl and mix.

3. Add the almond and coconut flour and baking powder and season with salt and pepper.

4. Mix with a wire whisk and crack in the eggs.

5. Stir everything together until batter forms.

6. Brush the heated waffle maker with butter and add a few tablespoons of the batter.

7. Close the lid and cook for about 8 minutes depending on your waffle maker.

8. Serve and enjoy.

Nutrition value per Servings:

Calories 352, fat 27.2 g, carbs 8.3 g, Protein 15 g

## Pizza Chaffle

Servings: 4

Cooking Time: 7-9 Minutes

**Ingredients:**

Batter

4 eggs

1½ cups grated mozzarella cheese

½ cup grated parmesan cheese

2 tablespoons tomato sauce ¼ cup almond flour

1½ teaspoons baking powder

Salt and pepper to taste

1 teaspoon dried oregano

¼ cup sliced salami

Other

2 tablespoons olive oil for brushing the waffle maker ¼ cup tomato sauce for serving

**Directions:**

1. Preheat the waffle maker.

2. Add the grated mozzarella and grated parmesan to a bowl and mix.

3. Add the almond flour and baking powder and season with salt and pepper and dried oregano.

4. Mix with a wooden spoon or wire whisk and crack in the eggs.

5. Stir everything together until batter forms.

6. Stir in the chopped salami.

7. Brush the heated waffle maker with olive oil and add a few tablespoons of the batter.

8. Close the lid and cook for about 7-minutes depending on your waffle maker.

9. Serve with extra tomato sauce on top and enjoy.

Nutrition value per Servings:

Calories 319, fat 25.2 g, carbs 5.9 g, Protein 19.3 g

## Bacon Chaffle

Servings: 4

Cooking Time: 7-9 Minutes

**Ingredients:**

Batter

4 eggs

2 cups shredded mozzarella

2 ounces finely chopped bacon Salt and pepper to taste

1 teaspoon dried oregano

Other

2 tablespoons olive oil for brushing the waffle maker

**Directions:**

1. Preheat the waffle maker.

2. Crack the eggs into a bowl and add the grated mozzarella cheese.

3. Mix until just combined and stir in the chopped bacon.

4. Season with salt and pepper and dried oregano.

5. Brush the heated waffle maker with olive oil and add a few tablespoons of the batter.

6. Close the lid and cook for about 7-8 minutes depending on your waffle maker.

Nutrition value per Servings:

Calories 241, fat 19.8 g, carbs 1.3 g, Protein 14.8 g

## Chaffles Breakfast Bowl

Servings: 2

Cooking Time: 5 Minutes

**Ingredients:**

1 egg

1/2 cup cheddar cheese shredded pinch of Italian seasoning

1 tbsp. pizza sauce

TOPPING

1/2 avocado sliced

2 eggs boiled

1 tomato, halves

4 oz. fresh spinach leaves

**Directions:**

1. Preheat yourwaffle maker and grease with cooking spray.

2. Crack an egg in a small bowl and beat with Italian seasoning and pizza sauce.

3. Add shredded cheese to the egg and spices mixture.

4. Pour 1 tbsp. shredded cheese in a waffle maker and cook for 30 sec.

5. Pour Chaffles batter inthe waffle maker and close the lid.

6. Cook chaffles for about 4 minutes until crispy and brown.

7. Carefully remove chaffles from the maker.

8. Serve on the bed of spinach with boil egg, avocado slice, and tomatoes.

9. Enjoy!

Nutrition value per Servings:

Protein: 77 kcal Fat: 222 kcal Carbohydrates: 39 kcal

## Morning Chaffles With Berries

Servings: 4

Cooking Time: 5 Minutes

**Ingredients:**

1 cup egg whites

1 cup cheddar cheese, shredded ¼ cup almond flour

¼ cup heavy cream

TOPPING

4 oz. raspberries

4 oz. strawberries.

1 oz. keto chocolate flakes

1 oz. feta cheese.

**Directions:**

1. Preheat your square waffle maker and grease with cooking spray.

2. Beat egg white in a small bowl with flour.

3. Add shredded cheese to the egg whites and flour mixture and mix well.

4. Add cream and cheese tothe egg mixture.

5. Pour Chaffles batter in a waffle maker and close the lid.

6. Cook chaffles for about 4 minutes until crispy and brown.

7. Carefully remove chaffles from the maker.

8. Serve with berries, cheese, and chocolate on top.

9. Enjoy!

Nutrition value per Servings:

Protein: 68 kcal Fat: 163 kcal Carbohydrates: 12 kcal

## Chocolate Vanilla Chaffles

Servings: 2

Prep time: 5 min.

Cook time: 5 min.

**Ingredients:**

½ cup shredded mozzarella cheese

1 egg

1 Tbsp granulated sweetener

1 tsp vanilla extract

1 Tbsp sugar-free chocolate chips

2 Tbsp almond meal/flour

**Directions:**

Turn on waffle maker to heat and oil it with cooking spray. Mix all components in a bowl until combined.

Pour half of the batter into waffle maker.

Cook for 2-4 minutes, then remove and repeat with remaining batter. Top with more chips and favorite toppings.

Nutrition Value per Servings:

Carbs - 23 G  Fat - 3 G  Protein - 4 G  Calories – 134

## Keto Chaffle Breakfast Sandwich

Prep Time: 3 minutes

Cook Time: 6 minutes

Servings: 1

**Ingredients:**

1 egg

1/2 cup Monterey Jack Cheese

1 tablespoon almond flour

2 tablespoons butter

**Directions:**

In a small bowl, mix the egg, almond flour, and Monterey Jack Cheese.

Pour half of the batter into your mini waffle maker and cook for 3-4 minutes. Then cook the rest of the batter to make a second chaffle.

In a small pan, melt 2 tablespoons of butter. Add the chaffles and cook on each side for 2 minutes. Pressing down while they are cooking lightly on the top of them, so they crisp up better.

Remove from the pan and let sit for 2 minutes.

Nutritional Value (per serving):

Calories: 514kcal Carbohydrates: 2g  Protein: 21g Fat: 47g

## Keto Chaffle Taco Shells

Prep Time: 5 minutes

Cook Time: 20 minutes

Servings: 5

**Ingredients:**

1 tablespoon almond flour

1 cup taco blend cheese

2 eggs

1/4 tsp taco seasoning

**Directions:**

In a bowl, mix almond flour, taco blend cheese, eggs, and taco seasoning. I find it easiest to mix everything using a fork.

Add 1.5 tablespoons of taco chaffle batter to the waffle maker at a time — Cook chaffle batter in the waffle maker for 4 minutes.

Remove the taco chaffle shell from the waffle maker and drape over the side of a bowl. I used my pie pan because it was what I had on hand, but just about any bowl will work.

Continue making chaffle taco shells until you are out of batter. Then fill your taco shells with taco meat, your favorite toppings, and enjoy!

Nutritional Value (per serving):

Calories: 113kcal Carbohydrates: 1g Protein: 8g Fat: 9g

## Peanut Butter Chaffle

Prep Time: 3 minutes

Cook Time: 8 minutes

Servings: 2

**Ingredients:**

1 egg

1/2 cup mozzarella cheese shredded

3 tablespoons swerve granulated

2 tbsp peanut butter

**Directions:**

Heat up your waffle maker.

In a bowl, mix the peanut butter, egg, granulated swerve, and mozzarella cheese.

Pour half of the chaffle batter into the waffle maker and cook for 4 minutes.

Carefully remove once cooked and place on a plate to cool. The chaffle will be a little flimsy when you remove it, but it will stiffen up as it cools.

Next, cook your second chaffle and let it sit for 2 minutes after you cook it.

Nutritional Value (per serving):

Calories: 210kcal Carbohydrates: 4g Protein: 13g Fat: 16g

## Pumpkin Chocolate Chip Chaffles

Prep Time: 4 minutes

Cook Time: 12 minutes

Servings: 3

**Ingredients:**

1/2 cup shredded mozzarella cheese

4 teaspoons pumpkin puree

1 egg

2 tablespoons granulated Swerve 1/4 tsp pumpkin pie spice

4 teaspoons sugar-free chocolate chips

1 tablespoon almond flour

**Directions:**

Plug in your waffle maker.

In a small bowl, mix the pumpkin puree and egg. Make sure you mix it well, so all the pumpkin is mixed with the egg.

Next, add in the mozzarella cheese, almond flour, swerve and add pumpkin spice and mix well. Then add in your sugar-free chocolate chips

Add half the keto pumpkin pie Chaffle mix to the Dish Mini waffle maker at a time. Cook chaffle batter in the waffle maker for 4 minutes.

Do not open before the 4 minutes is up. It is very important that you do not open the waffle maker before the 4-minute mark. After that you can open it to check it and make sure it is cooked all the way, but with these chaffles keeping the lid closed the whole time is very important.

When the first one is completely done cooking cook the second one.

Enjoy with some swerve confectioners sweetener or whipped cream on top.

Nutritional Value (per serving):

Calories: 93kcal Carbohydrates: 2g Protein: 7g Fat: 7g

## Broccoli & Cheese Chaffle

Prep Time: 2 minutes

Cook Time: 8 minutes

Servings: 2

**Ingredients:**

1/2 cup cheddar cheese

1/4 cup fresh chopped broccoli

1 egg

1/4 teaspoon garlic powder

1 tablespoon almond flour

**Directions:**

In a bowl, mix almond flour, cheddar cheese, egg, and garlic powder. I find it easiest to mix everything using a fork.

Add half the Broccoli and Cheese Chaffle batter to the Dish Mini waffle maker at a time. Cook chaffle batter in the waffle maker for 4 minutes.

Let each chaffle sit for 1-2 minutes on a plate to firm up. Enjoy alone or dipping in sour cream or ranch dressing.

Nutritional Value (per serving):

Calories: 170kcal Carbohydrates: 2g Protein: 11g Fat: 13g

## French Dip Keto Chaffle Sandwich

Prep Time: 5 mins

Cook Time: 12 mins

Servings: 2

**Ingredients:**

1 egg white

1/4 cup mozzarella cheese, shredded (packed)

1/4 cup sharp cheddar cheese, shredded (packed) 3/4 tsp water

1 tsp coconut flour

1/4 tsp baking powder

Pinch of salt

**Directions:**

Preheat oven to 425 degrees. Plug the Dash Mini Waffle Maker in the wall and grease lightly once it is hot.

Combine all of the ingredients in a bowl and stir to combine.

Spoon out 1/2 of the batter on the waffle maker and close lid. Set a timer for 4 minutes and do not lift the lid until the cooking time is complete. Lifting beforehand can cause the Chaffle keto sandwich recipe to separate and stick to the waffle iron. You have to let it cook the entire 4 minutes before lifting the lid.

Remove the chaffle from the waffle iron and set aside. Repeat the same steps above with the rest of the chaffle batter.

Cover a cookie sheet with parchment paper and place chaffles a few inches apart.

Add 1/4 to 1/3 cup of the slow cooker keto roast beef from the following recipe. Make sure to drain the excess broth/gravy before adding to the top of the chaffle.

Add a slice of deli cheese or shredded cheese on top. Swiss and provolone are both great options. Place on the top rack of the oven for 5 minutes so that the cheese can melt. If you'd like the cheese to bubble and begin to brown, turn oven to broil for 1 min. (The swiss cheese may not brown) Enjoy open-faced with a small bowl of beef broth for dipping.

Nutritional Value (per serving):

Calories: 118kcal Carbohydrates: 2g Protein: 9g Fat: 8g

# Fudgy Chocolate Chaffles

Prep Time: 5 mins

Cook Time: 8 mins

Servings: 2

**Ingredients:**

1 egg

2 tbsp mozzarella cheese, shredded

2 tbsp cocoa

2 tbsp Lakanto monk fruit powdered

1 tsp coconut flour

1 tsp heavy whipping cream

1/4 tsp baking powder

1/4 tsp vanilla extract

pinch of salt

**Directions:**

Turn on waffle or chaffle maker. I use the Dash Mini Waffle Maker. Grease lightly or use a cooking spray.

In a small bowl, combine all ingredients.

Cover the dash mini waffle maker with 1/2 of the batter. Close the mini waffle maker and cook for

4 minutes. Remove the chaffle from the waffle maker carefully as it is very hot. Repeat the steps above.

Serve with sugar-free strawberry ice cream or sugar-free whipped topping.

Nutritional Value (per serving):

Calories: 109kcal Carbohydrates: 5g Protein: 7g Fat: 7g

# Keto Cornbread Chaffle

Ingredients:

1 egg

1/2 cup cheddar cheese shredded (or mozzarella)

5 slices jalapeno optional - picked or fresh

1 tsp Frank's Red hot sauce

1/4 tsp corn extract

pinch salt

**Directions:**

Preheat the mini waffle maker

In a small bowl, whip the egg.

Add the remaining ingredients and mix it until it's well incorporated.

Add a teaspoon of shredded cheese to the waffle maker for 30 seconds before adding the mixture. This will create a nice and crisp crust that is absolutely fantastic!

Add half the mixture to the preheated waffle maker.

Cook it for a minimum of 3 to 4 minutes. The longer you cook it, the crispier it gets. Serve warm and enjoy!

# Keto Chaffle Stuffing Recipe

Servings: 4

**Ingredients:**

Basic Chaffle ingredients:

1/2 cup cheese mozzarella, cheddar or a combo of both

2 eggs

1/4 tsp garlic powder

1/2 tsp onion powder

1/2 tsp dried poultry seasoning

1/4 tsp salt

1/4 tsp pepper

Stuffing ingredients:

1 small onion diced

2 celery stalks

4 oz mushrooms diced

4 tbs butter for sauteing

3 eggs

**Directions:**

First, make your chaffles.

Preheat the mini waffle iron.

Preheat the oven to 350F

In a medium-size bowl, combine the chaffle ingredients.

Pour a 1/4 of the mixture into a mini waffle maker and cook each chaffle for about 4 minutes each.

Once they are all cooked, set them aside.

In a small frying pan, saute the onion, celery, and mushrooms until they are soft.

In a separate bowl, tear up the chaffles into small pieces, add the sauteed veggies, and 3 eggs. Mix until the ingredients are fully combined.

Add the stuffing mixture to a small casserole dish (about a 4 x 4) and bake it at 350 degrees for about 30 to 40 minutes.

## Banana Nut Chaffle Recipe

Servings: 2

**Ingredients:**

1 egg

1 tbs cream cheese, softened and room temp

1 tbs sugar-free cheesecake pudding optional ingredient because it is dirty keto 1/2 cup mozzarella cheese

1 tbs Monkfruit confectioners 1/4 tsp vanilla extract

1/4 tsp banana extract

Optional Toppings:

Sugar-free caramel sauce

Pecans

**Directions:**

Preheat the mini waffle maker

In a small bowl, whip the egg.

Add the remaining ingredients to the egg mixture and mix it until it's well incorporated.

Add half the batter to the waffle maker and cook it for a minimum of 4 minutes until it's golden brown.

Remove the finished chaffle and add the other half of the batter to cook the other chaffle. Top with your optional ingredients and serve warm!

Enjoy!

Nutritional Value (per serving):

Total Fat: 7.8g  Total Carbohydrate: 2.7g  Protein: 8.8g

## Crispy Bagel Chaffle Chips

Servings: 1

**Ingredients:**

3 Tbs Parmesan cheese shredded

1 tsp Everything Bagel Seasoning

**Directions:**

Preheat the mini waffle maker.

Place the Parmesan cheese on the griddle and allow it to bubble. About 3 minutes. Be sure to leave it long enough, or else it won't turn crispy when it cools. Important step!

Sprinkle the melted cheese with about 1 teaspoon of Everything Bagel Seasoning. Leave the waffle iron open when it cooks!

Unplug the mini waffle maker and allow it to cool for a few minutes. This will allow the cheese to cool enough to bind together and get crispy.

After about 2 minutes of it cooling off, it will still be warm.

Use a mini spatula to peel the warm (but not hot cheese from the mini waffle iron.

Allow it to cool completely for crispy chips! These chips pack a powerful crunch, which is something I tend to miss on Keto!

Nutritional Value (per serving):

Total Fat 5.6g Total Carbohydrate 1.2g Protein 6.2g

## Chaffle Churros

Servings: 2

Prep time: 10 min.

Cook time: 5 min.

**Ingredients:**

1 egg

1 Tbsp almond flour

½ tsp vanilla extract

1 tsp cinnamon, divided

¼ tsp baking powder

½ cup shredded mozzarella

1 Tbsp swerve confectioners sugar substitute

1 Tbsp swerve brown sugar substitute

1 Tbsp butter, melted

**Directions:**

Turn on waffle maker to heat and oil it with cooking spray.

Mix egg, flour, vanilla extract, ½ tsp cinnamon, baking powder, mozzarella, and sugar substitute in a bowl.

Place half of the mixture into waffle maker and cook for 3-5 minutes, or until desired doneness. Remove and place the second half of the batter into the maker.

Cut chaffles into strips.

Place strips in a bowl and cover with melted butter.

Mix brown sugar substitute and the remaining cinnamon in a bowl. Pour sugar mixture over the strips and toss to coat them well.

Nutrition Value per Servings:

Carbs - 5 G  Fat - 6 G  Protein - 5 G  Calories – 76

## Peanut Butter Chaffle

Servings: 2

Prep time: 5 min.

Cook time: 5 min

**Ingredients:**

1 egg

1 Tbsp heavy cream

1 Tbsp unsweetened cocoa

1 Tbsp lakanto powdered sweetener

1 tsp coconut flour

½ tsp vanilla extract

½ tsp cake batter flavor

¼ tsp baking powder

FOR THE FILLING:

3 Tbsp all-natural peanut butter

2 tsp lakanto powdered sweetener

2 Tbsp heavy cream

**Directions:**

Turn on waffle maker to heat and oil it with cooking spray. Mix all chaffle components in a small bowl.

Pour half of the mixture into waffle maker. Cook for 3-5 minutes. Remove and repeat for remaining batter.

Allow chaffles to sit for 4-5 minutes so that

they crisp up.

Mix filling ingredients together and spread it between chaffles.

Nutrition Value per Servings:

Carbs - 7 G  Fat - 21 G  Protein - 9 G  Calories - 264

## Cinnamon Pecan Chaffles

Servings: 1

Prep time: 20 min. + 12 h.

Cook time: 40 min.

**Ingredients:**

1 Tbsp butter

1 egg

½ tsp vanilla

2 Tbsp almond flour

1 Tbsp coconut flour

⅛ tsp baking powder

1 Tbsp monk fruit

FOR THE CRUMBLE:

½ tsp cinnamon

1 Tbsp melted butter

1 tsp monk fruit

1 Tbsp chopped pecans

**Directions:**

Turn on waffle maker to heat and oil it with cooking spray. Melt butter in a bowl, then mix in the egg and vanilla.

Mix in remaining chaffle ingredients.

Combine crumble ingredients in a separate bowl.

Pour half of the chaffle mix into waffle maker. Top with half of crumble mixture. Cook for 5 minutes, or until done.

Repeat with the other half of the batter.

Nutrition Value per Servings:

Carbs - 8 G  Fat - 35 G  Protein - 10 G  Calories - 391

## Almond Flour Chaffles

Servings: 2

Prep time: 10 min.

Cook time: 20 min.

**Ingredients:**

1 large egg

1 Tbsp blanched almond flour ¼ tsp baking powder

½ cup shredded mozzarella cheese

**Directions:**

Whisk egg, almond flour, and baking powder together. Stir in mozzarella and set batter aside.

Turn on waffle maker to heat and oil it with cooking spray.

Pour half of the batter onto waffle maker and spread it evenly with a spoon. Cook for 3 minutes, or until it reaches desired doneness.

Transfer to a plate and repeat with remaining batter. Let chaffles cool for 2-3 minutes to crisp up.

Nutrition Value per Servings:

Carbs - 2 G  Fat - 13 G  Protein - 10 G  Calories - 131

## Oreo Keto Chaffles

Servings: 2

Prep time: 5 min.

Cook time: 5 min.

**Ingredients:**

1 egg

1½ Tbsp unsweetened cocoa

2 Tbsp lakanto monk fruit, or choice of sweetener

1 Tbsp heavy cream

1 tsp coconut flour

½ tsp baking powder

½ tsp vanilla

FOR THE CHEESE CREAM:

1 Tbsp lakanto powdered sweetener

2 Tbsp softened cream cheese ¼ tsp vanilla

**Directions:**

Turn on waffle maker to heat and oil it with cooking spray. Combine all chaffle ingredients in a small bowl.

Pour one half of the chaffle mixture into waffle maker. Cook for 3-5 minutes.

Remove and repeat with the second half if the mixture. Let chaffles sit for 2-3 to crisp up.

Combine all cream ingredients and spread on chaffle when they have cooled to room temperature.

 Nutrition Value per Servings:

Carbs - 3 G  Fat - 4 G  Protein - 7 G  Calories – 66

## Chicken Bites With Chaffles

Servings: 2

Cooking Time: 10 minutes

**Ingredients:**

1 chicken breastscut into 2 x2 inch chunks

1 egg, whisked

1/4 cup almond flour

2 tbsps. onion powder

2 tbsps. garlic powder

1 tsp. dried oregano

1 tsp. paprika powder

1 tsp. salt

1/2 tsp. black pepper

2 tbsps. avocado oil

**Directions:**

1.   Add all the dry ingredients together into a large bowl. Mix well.

2.   Place the eggs into a separate bowl.

3.   Dip each chicken piece into the egg and then into the dry ingredients.

4.   Heat oil in 10-inch skillet, add oil.

5.   Once avocado oil is hot, place the coated chicken nuggets onto a skillet and cook for 6-8 minutes until cooked and golden brown.

6.   Serve with chaffles and raspberries.

7.   Enjoy!

Nutrition value per Servings: :

Calories 401 Kcal Fats 219 G Protein 32.35 G Net Carbs 1.46 G

## Crunchy Fish And Chaffle Bites

Servings: 4

Cooking Time: 15 Minutes

**Ingredients:**

1 lb. cod fillets, sliced into 4 slice

1 tsp. sea salt

1 tsp. garlic powder

1 egg, whisked

1 cup almond flour

2 tbsp. avocado oil

CHAFFLE Ingredients:

2 eggs

1/2 cup cheddar cheese

2 tbsps. almond flour

½ tsp. Italian seasoning

**Directions:**

1. Mix together chaffle ingredients in a bowl and make 4 square

2. Put the chaffles in a preheated chaffle maker.

3. Mix together the salt, pepper, and garlic powder in a mixing bowl. Toss the cod cubes in this mixture and let sit for 10 minutes.

4. Then dip each cod slice into the egg mixture and then into the almond flour.

5. Heat oil in skillet and fish cubes for about 2-3 minutes, until cooked and browned

6. Serve on chaffles and enjoy!

Nutrition value perServings:

Protein: 38% 121 Kcal Fat: 59% 189 Kcal Carbohydrates: 3% 11 Kcal


## Grill Pork Chaffle Sandwich

Servings:2

Cooking Time: 15 Minutes

**Ingredients:**

1/2 cup mozzarella, shredded

1 egg

I pinch garlic powder

PORK PATTY

1/2 cup pork, minutesced

1 tbsp. green onion, diced

1/2 tsp Italian seasoning

Lettuce leaves

**Directions:**

1. Preheat the square waffle maker and grease with

2. Mix together egg, cheese and garlic powder in a small mixing bowl.

3. Pour batter in a preheated waffle maker and close the lid.

4. Make 2 chaffles from thisbatter.

5. Cook chaffles for about 2-3 minutes until cooked through.

6. Meanwhile, mix together pork patty ingredients in a bowl and make 1 large patty.

7. Grill pork patty in a preheated grill for about 3-4 minutes per side until cooked through.

8. Arrange pork patty between two chaffles with lettuce leaves. Cut sandwich to make a triangular sandwich.

9. Enjoy!

Nutrition value per Servings:

Protein: 85 Kcal Fat: 86 Kcal Carbohydrates: 7 Kcal


## Chaffle & Chicken Lunch Plate

Servings:1

Cooking Time: 15 Minutes

**Ingredients:**

1 large egg

1/2 cup jack cheese, shredded

1 pinch salt

For Serving

1 chicken leg

salt

pepper

1 tsp. garlic, minutesced

1 egg

I tsp avocado oil

**Directions:**

1. Heat your square waffle maker and grease with cooking spray.

2. Pour Chaffle batter intothe skillet and cook for about 3 minutes.

3. Meanwhile,heat oil in a pan, over medium heat.

4. Once the oil is hot, add chicken thigh and garlicthen, cook for about 5 minutes. Flip and cook for another 3-4 minutes.

5. Season with salt and pepper and give them a good mix.

6. Transfer cooked thigh to plate.

7. Fry the egg in the same pan for about 1-2 minutes according to your choice.

8. Once chaffles are cooked, serve with fried egg and chicken thigh

9. Enjoy!

Nutrition value per Servings:

Protein: 31% 138 Kcal Fat: 66% 292 Kcal Carbohydrates: 2% Kcal

## Keto Blt Chaffle Sandwich

**Ingredients:**

Chaffle bread ingredients:

1/2 cup mozzarella shredded

1 egg

1 tbs green onion diced

1/2 tsp Italian seasoning

Sandwich ingredients:

Bacon pre-cooked

Lettuce

Tomato sliced

1 tbs mayo

**Directions:**

Preheat the mini waffle maker

In a small bowl, whip the egg.

Add the cheese, seasonings, and onion. Mix it until it's well incorporated.

Place half the batter in the mini waffle maker and cook it for 4 minutes.

If you want a crunchy bread, add a tsp of shredded cheese to the mini waffle iron for 30 seconds before adding the batter. The extra cheese on the outside creates the best crust!

After the first chaffle is complete, add the remaining batter to the mini waffle maker and cook it for 4 minutes.

Add the mayo, bacon, lettuce, and tomato to your sandwich.

Enjoy!

## Keto Lemon Chaffle Recipe

Servings: 4

**Ingredients:**

Chaffle Cake:

2 oz cream cheese room temp and softened

2 eggs

2 tsp butter melted

2 tbs coconut flour

1 tsp monk fruit powdered confectioners blend (add more if you like it sweeter)

1 tsp baking powder

1/2 tsp lemon extract

20 drops cake batter extract

Chaffle Frosting:

1/2 cup heavy whipping cream

1 tbs monk fruit powdered confectioners blend
1/4 tsp lemon extract

**Directions:**

Preheat the mini waffle maker

Add all of the ingredients for the chaffle cake in a blender and mix it until the batter is nice and smooth. This should only take a couple of minutes.

Use an ice cream scoop and fill the waffle iron with one full scoop of batter. This size of the ice cream scoop is about 3 tablespoons and fits perfectly in the mini waffle maker.

While the chaffles are cooking, start making the frosting.

In a medium-size bowl, add the chaffle frosting ingredients.

Mix the ingredients until the frosting is thick with peaks.

All the chaffles to completely cool before frosting the cake. Optional: Add lemon peel for extra flavor!

Nutritional Value (per serving):

Total Fat 20.3g Cholesterol 146.1mg Total Carbohydrate 5.2g Protein 5.6g


## Bacon Cheddar Bay Biscuits Chaffle Recipe

Servings: 6

**Ingredients:**

1/2 cup Almond Flour

1/4 cup Oat Fiber

3 strips of bacon cooked and crumbled

1 Egg, beaten

1/4 cup Sour Cream

1 T Bacon Grease melted

1 1/2 T Kerrygold Butter melted

1/2 cup Sharp Cheddar Cheese shredded 1/2 cup Smoked Gouda Cheese shredded 1/4 tsp Swerve Confectioners

1/2 tsp Garlic Salt

1/2 tsp Onion Powder

1/2 T Parsley dried

1/2 T Baking Powder

1/4 tsp Baking Soda

**Directions:**

Preheat mini waffle maker.

Mix almond flour, baking powder, baking soda, onion powder, and garlic salt to a bowl and mix using a whisk.

In another bowl, add the eggs, bacon, sour cream, parsley, bacon grease, melted butter, and cheese. Mix until combined.

Add the dry ingredients into the wet and mix.

Scoop 2-3 T of the mix into hot waffle iron and cook for 5-6 minutes.

Nutritional Value (per serving):

Total Fat 12.5g Total Carbohydrate 4.3g Protein 7.7g


## Lime Pie Chaffle Recipe

Servings: 2

**Ingredients:**

Key Lime Pie Chaffle Recipe ingredients:

1 egg

1/4 cup Almond flour

2 tsp cream cheese room temp

1 tsp powdered sweetener swerve or monk

fruit

1/2 tsp lime extract or 1 tsp fresh squeezed lime juice 1/2 tsp baking powder

1/2 tsp lime zest

Pinch of salt to bring out the flavors

Cream Cheese Lime Frosting Ingredients:

4 oz cream cheese softened

4 tbs butter

2 tsp powdered sweetener swerve or monk fruit

1 tsp lime extract

1/2 tsp lime zest

**Directions:**

Preheat the mini waffle iron.

In a blender, add all the chaffle ingredients and blend on high until the mixture is smooth and creamy.

Cook each chaffle about 3 to 4 minutes until it's golden brown. While the chaffles are cooking, make the frosting.

In a small bowl, combine all the ingredients for the frosting and mix it until it's smooth. Allow the chaffles to completely cool before frosting them.

Optional:

Top with whipped cream or the cream cheese frosting. Add a small amount of lime zest for an extra touch!

Nutritional Value (per serving):

Total Fat 5.7g Total Carbohydrate 4.9g Protein 5.5g

## Jicama Hash Brown Chaffle

Servings: 4

**Ingredients:**

1 large jicama root

1/2 medium onion minced

2 garlic cloves pressed

1 cup cheese of choice

2 eggs whisked

Salt and Pepper

**Directions:**

Peel jicama

Shred in food processor

Place shredded jicama in a large colander, sprinkle with 1-2 tsp of salt. Mix well and allow to drain.

Squeeze out as much liquid as possible (very important step) Microwave for 5-8 minutes.

Mix all ingredients together

Sprinkle a little cheese on waffle iron before adding 3 T of the mixture, sprinkle a little more cheese on top of mixture.

Nutritional Value (per serving):

Total Fat 11.8g Total Carbohydrate 5.1g Protein 10g

## Easy Corndog Chaffle Recipe

Servings: 5

**Ingredients:**

2 eggs

1 cup Mexican cheese blend

1 tbs almond flour

1/2 tsp cornbread extract

1/4 tsp salt

hot dogs with hot dog sticks

**Directions:**

Preheat corndog waffle maker.

In a small bowl, whip the eggs.

Add the remaining ingredients except the hotdogs

Spray the corndog waffle maker with non-stick cooking spray. Fill the corndog waffle maker with the batter halfway filled. Place a stick in the hot dog.

Place the hot dog in the batter and slightly press down.

Spread a small amount of better on top of the hot dog, just enough to fill it. Makes about 4 to 5 chaffle corndogs.

Cook the corndog chaffles for about 4 minutes or until golden brown.

When done, they will easily remove from the corndog waffle maker with a pair of tongs. Serve with mustard, mayo, or sugar-free ketchup!

Nutritional Value (per serving):

Total Fat 5.5g Total Carbohydrate 1.8g Protein 6.8g

## Sloppy Joe Chaffle Recipe

Ingredients:

Sloppy Joe Ingredients:

1 lb ground beef

1 tsp onion powder you can substitute for 1/4 cup real onion

1 tsp garlic minced

3 tbs tomato paste

1/2 tsp salt

1/4 tsp pepper

1 tbs chili powder

1 tsp cocoa powder, this is optional but highly recommended! It intensifies the flavor! 1/2 cup bone broth beef flavor

1 tsp coconut aminos or soy sauce if you prefer

1 tsp mustard powder

1 tsp Swerve brown or Sukrin golden 1/2 tsp paprika

Cornbread Chaffle Ingredients:

Makes 2 chaffles

1 egg

1/2 cup cheddar cheese

5 slices jalapeno diced very small (can be pickled or fresh)

1 tsp Franks Red Hot Sauce

1/4 tsp corn extract optional but tastes like real cornbread!

Pinch salt

**Directions:**

Cook the ground beef with salt and pepper first. Add all the remaining ingredients.

Allow the mixture to simmer while you make the chaffles. Preheat waffle maker.

In a small bowl, whip the egg.

Add the remaining ingredients.

Spray the waffle maker with nonstick cooking spray. Divide mixture in half.

Cook half the mixture for about 4 minutes or until golden brown.

For a crispy outer crust on the chaffle, add 1 tsp cheese to the waffle maker for 30 seconds before adding the mixture.

Pour the warm sloppy joe mix onto a hot chaffle.

Tip: you can add diced jalapenos (fresh or pickled) to this basic chaffle recipe and make it a jalapeno cornbread chaffle recipe too!)

## Keto Smores Chaffle

Servings: 2

**Ingredients:**

1 large Egg

½ c. Mozzarella cheese shredded ½ tsp Vanilla extract

2 tbs swerve brown

½ tbs Psyllium Husk Powder optional ¼ tsp Baking Powder

Pinch of pink salt

¼ Lily's Original Dark Chocolate Bar

2 tbs Keto Marshmallow Creme Fluff Recipe

**Directions:**

Make the batch of Keto Marshmallow Creme Fluff. Whisk the egg until creamy.

Add vanilla and Swerve Brown, mix well.

Mix in the shredded cheese and blend.

Then add Psyllium Husk Powder, baking powder, and salt. Mix until well incorporated, let the batter rest 3-4 minutes. Prep/plug in your waffle maker to preheat.

Spread ½ batter on the waffle maker and cook 3-4 minutes. Remove and set on a cooling rack.

Cook second half of batter same, then remove to cool.

Once cool, assemble the chaffles with the marshmallow fluff and chocolate: Using 2 tbs marshmallow and ¼ bar of Lily's Chocolate.

Eat as is, or toast for a melty and gooey Smore sandwich!

Nutritional Value (per serving):

Total Fat 8.1g Total Carbohydrate 3.1g Protein 8.3g

## Pumpkin Chaffle With Cream Cheese Frosting

Servings: 3

**Ingredients:**

1 egg

1/2 cup mozzarella cheese

1/2 tsp pumpkin pie spice

1 tbs pumpkin solid packed with no sugar added

Optional Cream Cheese Frosting Ingredients:

2 tbs cream cheese softened and room temperature

2 tbs monk fruit confectioners blend or any of your favorite keto-friendly sweetener 1/2 tsp clear vanilla extract

**Directions:**

Preheat the mini waffle maker.

In a small bowl, whip the egg.

Add the cheese, pumpkin pie spice, and the pumpkin.

Mix well.

Add 1/2 of the mixture to the mini waffle maker and cook it for at least 3 to 4 minutes until it's golden brown.

While the chaffle is cooking, add all of the cream cheese frosting ingredients in a bowl and mix it until it's smooth and creamy.

Add the cream cheese frosting to the hot chaffle and serve it immediately.

Nutritional Value (per serving):

Calories 84 Total Fat 4.5g Total Carbohydrate 5.3g Protein 6.1g

## Keto Vanilla Twinkie Copycat Chaffle Recipe

Servings: 4

**Ingredients:**

2 tablespoons butter melted (cooled)

2 ounces cream cheese softened

2 large eggs room temp

1 teaspoon vanilla extract

1/2 teaspoon Vanilla Cupcake Extract (optional)

1/4 cup Lakanto Confectioners

Pinch of pink salt

1/4 cup almond flour

2 tablespoons coconut flour

1 teaspoon baking powder

**Directions:**

Preheat the Corndog Maker.

Melt the butter and let it cool a minute.

Whisk the eggs into the butter until creamy.

Add vanilla, extract, sweetener, salt, and then blend well. Add Almond flour, coconut flour, and baking powder. Blend until well incorporated.

Add 2 tbsp batter to each well and spread across evenly. Close lid, lock, and let cook 4 minutes.

Remove and cool on a rack.

Nutritional Value (per serving):

Calories 152 Total Fat 9g Total Carbohydrate 6.5g Protein 6.1g

## Peppermint Mocha Chaffles With Buttercream Frosting

Servings: 6

**Ingredients:**

Chaffles:

1 egg

1 ounce cream cheese at room temperature

1 tablespoon melted butter or coconut oil

1 tablespoon unsweetened cocoa powder or raw cacao

2 tablespoons powdered sweeteners such as Swerve or Lakanto

1 tablespoon almond flour

2 teaspoons coconut flour

1/4 teaspoon baking powder powder

1 teaspoon instant coffee granules

1/4 teaspoon vanilla extract

Pinch salt

Filling:

2 tablespoons butter at room temperature

2-3 tablespoons powdered sweeteners such as Swerve or Lakanto 1/4 teaspoon vanilla extract

1/8 teaspoon peppermint extract

Optional toppings: sugar-free starlight mints

**Directions:**

For the Mocha Chaffles:

Heat mini Dash waffle iron until thoroughly hot.

Beat all chaffle ingredients together in a small bowl until smooth.

Add a heaping 2 tablespoons of batter to waffle iron and cook until done about 4 minutes. Repeat to make 3 chaffles. Let cool on wire rack.

For the Buttercream Frosting:

In a small bowl with a hand mixer, beat the butter and sweetener until smooth.

Add the heavy cream and vanilla extract and beat at high speed for about 4 minutes, until light and fluffy.

Spread frosting on each chaffle and garnish with sugar-free starlight mints, if desired.

Nutritional Value (per serving):

Calories: 96kcal Carbohydrates: 3.8g Protein: 1.9g Fat: 8.9g

## Cranberry Swirl Chaffles With Orange Cream Cheese Frosting

Servings: 6

**Ingredients:**

Cranberry sauce:

1/2 cup cranberries fresh or frozen

2 Tbsp granulated erythritol 1/2 cup water

1/2 tsp vanilla extract

Chaffles:

1 egg

1 ounce cream cheese at room temperature

1 Tbsp erythritol blends such as Swerve, Pyure or Lakanto 1/2 tsp vanilla extract

1 tsp coconut flour

1/4 tsp baking powder

Frosting:

1 ounce cream cheese at room temperature

1 Tbsp butter room temperature

1 Tbsp confectioner's sweetener such as Swerve

1/8 tsp orange extract OR 2 drops orange essential oil A few strands of grated orange zest (optional)

**Directions:**

For the cranberry swirl:

Combine the cranberries, water, and erythritol in a medium saucepan. Bring to a boil, then reduce heat to a gentle simmer.

Simmer for 10-15 minutes, until the cranberries pop and the sauce thickens. Remove from heat and stir in the vanilla extract.

Mash the berries with the back of a spoon until a chunky sauce forms.

The sauce will thicken off the heat significantly.

For the chaffles:

Preheat mini Dash waffle iron until thoroughly hot.

In a medium bowl, whisk all chaffle ingredients together until well combined. Spoon 2 tablespoons of batter into a waffle iron.

Add 1/2 of the cranberry sauce in little dollops over the batter of each chaffle. Close and cook 3-5 minutes, until done. Remove to a wire rack.

Repeat for the second chaffle.

For the Frosting:

Mix all ingredients, except orange zest, together until smooth and spread over each chaffle. Orange zest (optional).

Nutritional Value (per serving):

Calories: 70kcal Carbohydrates: 4.9g Protein: 1.8g Fat: 6g

## Zucchini Nut Bread Chaffle Recipe

**Ingredients:**

1 cup shredded zucchini approximately 1 small zucchini

1 egg

1/2 teaspoon cinnamon

1 Tbsp plus 1 tsp erythritol blend such as Swerve, Pyure or Lakanto Dash ground nutmeg

2 tsp melted butter

1 ounce softened cream cheese

2 tsp coconut flour

1/2 tsp baking powder

3 tablespoons chopped walnuts or pecans

Frosting Ingredients:

2 ounces cream cheese at room temperature

2 Tbsp butter at room temperature 1/4 tsp cinnamon

2 Tbsp caramel sugar-free syrup such as Skinny Girl, or 1 Tbsp confectioner's sweetener, such as Swerve plus 1/8 tsp caramel extract

1 Tbsp chopped walnuts or pecans

**Directions:**

Grate zucchini and place in a colander over a

plate to drain for 15 minutes. With your hands, squeeze out as much moisture as possible.

Preheat mini Dash waffle iron until thoroughly hot.

In a medium bowl, whisk all chaffle ingredients together until well combined.

Spoon a heaping 2 tablespoons of batter into waffle iron, close and cook 3-5 minutes, until done. Remove to a wire rack. Repeat 3 times.

Frosting Directions:

Mix all ingredients together until smooth and spread over each chaffle. Top with additional chopped nuts.

## Keto Apple Fritter Chaffles

Sodium 117.7mg

Total Carbohydrate 8.5g

Servings: 5

**Ingredients:**

Apple Fritter Filling Ingredients:

2 cups diced jicama

1/4 cup plus 1 tablespoon Swerve sweetener blend

4 tablespoons butter

1 teaspoon cinnamon

1/8 teaspoon nutmeg

Dash ground cloves

1/2 teaspoon vanilla

20 drops Lorann Oils apple flavoring

Chaffle Ingredients:

2 eggs

1/2 cup grated mozzarella cheese

1 tablespoon almond flour

1 teaspoon coconut flour

1/2 teaspoon baking powder

Glaze Ingredients:

1 tablespoon butter

2 teaspoons heavy cream

3 tablespoons powdered sweetener such as Swerve Confectioners 1/4 teaspoon vanilla extract

**Directions:**

Keto Apple Fritter Chaffle Filling Directions

Peel the jicama and cut into small dice.

In a medium skillet over medium-low heat, melt the butter and add the diced jicama and sweetener.

Let simmer slowly for 10-20 minutes until the jicama is soft, stirring often. Do not use high heat, or the sweetener will caramelize quickly and burn. It should develop a light amber color and will thicken.

When the jicama is soft, remove from heat and stir in the spices and flavorings.

Keto Apple Fritter Chaffle Directions:

Preheat waffle iron until hot.

In a medium bowl, beat all ingredients except cheese. Stir the jicama mixture into the eggs. Place 1 tablespoon grated cheese on that waffle iron.

Spoon 2 heaping tablespoons of the egg/jicama mixture into the waffle iron and top with another tablespoon cheese.

Close the waffle maker and cook 5-7 minutes until nicely browned and crunchy. Remove to a wire rack.

Repeat 3-4 times.

Keto Apple Fritter Chaffle Icing Directions:

Melt butter in a small saucepan and add the Swerve and heavy cream.

Simmer over medium heat for 5 minutes or until slightly thickened.

Stir in vanilla.

Drizzle the hot icing over the chaffles. It will

harden as it cools.

Nutritional Value (per serving):

Calories 186 Total Fat 14.3g Total Carbohydrate 8.5g Protein 7g

## Monte Cristo Chaffle Crepes Recipe

Servings: 3

**Ingredients:**

1 egg

1 T almond flour

1/4 tsp vanilla extract

1/2 T Swerve Confectioners

1 T cream cheese softened

1 tsp heavy cream

Pinch of cinnamon

**Directions:**

Mix all ingredients in a small blender. Let batter rest for 5 minutes.

Pour 1 1/2 Tablespoons of batter in preheated dash griddle. Cook 30 seconds.

Flip with tongs and cook a few more seconds.

Place 1 slice of cheese, 1 slice of ham and 1 slice of turkey on each crepe. If desired, microwave for a few seconds to slightly melt the cheese.

Roll the crepes with the filling on the inside.

Serve the filled crepes sprinkled with Swerve Confectioners and drizzled with low carb raspberry jam.

Nutritional Value (per serving)

Calories 60 Total Fat 4g Total Carbohydrate 2.1g Protein 2.8g

## Easy Turkey Burger With Halloumi Cheese Chaffle Recipe

Servings 4

**Ingredients:**

1 lb Ground Turkey raw (no need to precook the turkey)

8 oz Halloumi shredded

1 zucchini medium, shredded

2 tbsp Chives chopped

1/2 tsp Salt

1/4 tsp Pepper

**Directions:**

Add all ingredients to a bowl mix thoroughly together. Shape into 8 evenly sized patties.

Preheat mini griddle.

Cook the patties for 5-7 minutes.

Nutritional Value (per serving):

Calories 222 Total Fat 18g Total Carbohydrate 0.3g Protein 14.2g

## Rice Krispie Treat Chaffle Copycat Recipe

Servings: 2

**Ingredients:**

Chaffle batter:

1 Large Egg room temp

2 oz. Cream Cheese softened

1/4 tsp Pure Vanilla Extract

2 tbs Lakanto Confectioners Sweetener

1 oz. Pork Rinds crushed

1 tsp Baking Powder

**Marshmallow Frosting:**

1/4 c. Heavy Whipping Cream

1/4 tsp Pure Vanilla Extract

1 tbs Lakanto Confectioners Sweetener 1/2 tsp Xanthan Gum

**Directions:**

Plug in the mini waffle maker to preheat.

In a medium mixing bowl- Add egg, cream cheese, and vanilla. Whisk until blended well.

Add sweetener, crushed pork rinds, and baking powder. Mix until well incorporated.

Sprinkle extra crushed pork rinds onto waffle maker (optional).

Then add about 1/4 scoop of batter over, sprinkle a bit more pork rinds. Cook 3-4 minutes, then remove and cool on a wire rack.

Repeat for remaining batter.

Make the Marshmallow Frosting:

Whip the HWC, vanilla, and confectioners until thick and fluffy.

Slowly sprinkle over the xanthan gum and fold until well incorporated. Spread frosting over chaffles and cut as desired, then refrigerate until set. Enjoy cold or warm slightly in the microwave for 10 seconds.

Nutritional Value (per serving):

Calories: 334kcal Carbohydrates: 24g Protein: 13g Fat: 29g

## Biscuits & Gravy Chaffle Recipe

Servings: 4

**Ingredients:**

2 tbs Unsalted Butter melted

2 Large Eggs

1 c. Mozzarella Cheese shredded

1 tbs Garlic minced

10 drops Cornbread Extract optional

1/2 tbs Lakanto Confectioners optional

1 tbs Almond Flour

1/4 tsp Granulated Onion

1/4 tsp Granulated Garlic

1 tsp Dried Parsley

1 tsp Baking Powder

1 batch Keto Sausage Biscuits and Gravy Recipe

**Directions:**

Preheat Mini Waffle Maker.

Melt the butter, let cool.

Whisk in the eggs, then fold in the shredded cheese.

Add the rest of ingredients and mix thoroughly.

Scoop 1/4 of batter onto waffle maker and cook 4 minutes. Remove and let cool on wire rack.

Repeat for the remaining 3 chaffles.

Nutritional Value (per serving):

Calories: 195kcal Carbohydrates: 2g Protein: 12g Fat: 15g

## Bbq Chicken Chaffle

Prep Time: 3 minutes

Cook Time: 8 minutes

Servings: 2

**Ingredients:**

1/3 cup cooked chicken diced

1/2 cup shredded cheddar cheese

1 tbsp sugar-free bbq sauce

1 egg

1 tbsp almond flour

**Directions:**

Heat up your Dash mini waffle maker.

In a small bowl, mix the egg, almond flour, BBQ sauce, diced chicken, and Cheddar Cheese.

Add 1/2 of the batter into your mini waffle maker and cook for 4 minutes. If they are still a bit uncooked, leave it cooking for another 2 minutes. Then cook the rest of the batter to make a second chaffle.

Do not open the waffle maker before the 4 minute mark.

Enjoy alone or dip in BBQ Sauce or ranch dressing!

Nutritional Value (per serving):

Calories: 205kcal Carbohydrates: 2g Protein: 18g Fat: 14g

## Cheddar Chicken And Broccoli Chaffle

Prep Time: 2 minutes

Cook Time: 8 minutes

Servings: 2

**Ingredients:**

1/4 cup cooked diced chicken

1/4 cup fresh broccoli chopped

Shredded Cheddar cheese

1 egg

1/4 tsp garlic powder

**Directions:**

Heat up your Dash mini waffle maker.

In a small bowl, mix the egg, garlic powder, and cheddar cheese. Add the broccoli and chicken and mix well.

Add 1/2 of the batter into your mini waffle maker and cook for 4 minutes. If they are still a bit uncooked, leave it cooking for another 2 minutes. Then cook the rest of the batter to make a second chaffle and then cook the third chaffle.

After cooking, remove from the pan and let sit for 2 minutes. Dip in ranch dressing, sour cream, or enjoy alone.

Nutritional Value (per serving):

Calories: 58kcal Carbohydrates: 1g Protein: 7g Fat: 3g

## Gingerbread Chaffle

Servings: 2

Prep time: 5 min.

Cook time: 5 min.

**Ingredients:**

½ cup mozzarella cheese grated

1 medium egg

½ tsp baking powder

1 tsp erythritol powdered

½ tsp ground ginger

¼ tsp ground nutmeg

½ tsp ground cinnamon

⅛ tsp ground cloves

2 Tbsp almond flour

1 cup heavy whipped cream

¼ cup keto-friendly maple syrup

**Directions:**

Turn on waffle maker to heat and oil it with cooking spray. Beat egg in a bowl.

Add flour, mozzarella, spices, baking powder, and erythritol. Mix well.

Spoon one half of the batter into waffle maker and spread out evenly.

Close and cook for 5 minutes.

Remove cooked chaffle and repeat with remaining batter. Serve with whipped cream and maple syrup.

Nutrition Value per Servings:

Carbs - 5 G  Fat - 15 G  Protein - 12 G  Calories - 103

# Chocolate Peanut Butter Chaffle

Servings: 2

Prep time: 5 min.

Cook time: 10 min

**Ingredients:**

½ cup shredded mozzarella cheese

1 Tbsp cocoa powder

2 Tbsp powdered sweetener

2 Tbsp peanut butter

½ tsp vanilla

1 egg

2 Tbsp crushed peanuts

2 Tbsp whipped cream

¼ cup sugar-free chocolate syrup

**Directions:**

Combine mozzarella, egg, vanilla, peanut butter, cocoa powder, and sweetener in a bowl. Add in peanuts and mix well.

Turn on waffle maker and oil it with cooking spray.

Pour one half of the batter into waffle maker and cook for 4 minutes, then transfer to a plate. Top with whipped cream, peanuts, and sugar-free chocolate syrup.

Nutrition Value per Servings:

Carbs - 6 G  Fat - 17 G  Protein - 15 G  Calories - 236

# Pumpkin Pecan Chaffles

Servings: 2

Prep time: 10 min.

Cook time: 10 min.

**Ingredients:**

1 egg

½ cup mozzarella cheese grated

1 Tbsp pumpkin puree

½ tsp pumpkin spice

1 tsp erythritol low carb sweetener

2 Tbsp almond flour

2 Tbsp pecans, toasted chopped

1 cup heavy whipped cream

¼ cup low carb caramel sauce

**Directions:**

Turn on waffle maker to heat and oil it with cooking spray. In a bowl, beat egg.

Mix in mozzarella, pumpkin, flour, pumpkin spice, and erythritol. Stir in pecan pieces.

Spoon one half of the batter into waffle maker and spread evenly. Close and cook for 5 minutes.

Remove cooked waffles to a plate. Repeat with remaining batter.

Serve with pecans, whipped cream, and low carb caramel sauce.

Nutrition Value per Servings:

Carbs - 4 G  Fat - 17 G  Protein - 11 G  Calories - 210

# Italian Cream Chaffle Sandwich-Cake

**Ingredients:**

4 oz cream cheese, softened, at room temperature

4 eggs

1 Tbsp melted butter

1 tsp vanilla extract

½ tsp cinnamon

1 Tbsp monk fruit sweetener

4 Tbsp coconut flour

1 Tbsp almond flour

1½ teaspoons baking powder

1 Tbsp coconut, shredded and unsweetened

1 Tbsp walnuts, chopped

<u>FOR THE ITALIAN CREAM FROSTING:</u>

2 oz cream cheese, softened, at room temperature

2 Tbsp butter room temp

2 Tbsp monk fruit sweetener ½ tsp vanilla

**Directions:**

Combine cream cheese, eggs, melted butter, vanilla, sweetener, flours, and baking powder in a blender. Add walnuts and coconut to the mixture.

Blend to get a creamy mixture.

Turn on waffle maker to heat and oil it with cooking spray.

Add enough batter to fill waffle maker. Cook for 2-3 minutes, until chaffles are done. Remove and let them cool.

Mix all frosting ingredients in another bowl. Stir until smooth and creamy. Frost the chaffles once they have cooled.

Top with cream and more nuts.

Nutrition Value per Servings:

Carbs - 31 G   Fat - 2 G   Protein - 5 G   Calories – 168

# Chocolate Cherry Chaffles

Servings: 1

Prep time: 5 min.

Cook time: 5 min.

**Ingredients:**

1 Tbsp almond flour

1 Tbsp cocoa powder

1 Tbsp sugar free sweetener ½ tsp baking powder

1 whole egg

½ cup mozzarella cheese shredded

2 Tbsp heavy whipping cream whipped

2 Tbsp sugar free cherry pie filling

1 Tbsp chocolate chips

**Directions:**

Turn on waffle maker to heat and oil it with cooking spray. Mix all dry components in a bowl.

Add egg and mix well.

Add cheese and stir again.

Spoon batter into waffle maker and close. Cook for 5 minutes, until done.

Top with whipping cream, cherries, and chocolate chips.

Nutrition Value per Servings:

Carbs - 6 G   Fat - 1 G   Protein - 1 G   Calories – 130

## Banana Nut Chaffle

Servings: 1

Prep time: 15 min.

Cook time: 10 min.

**Ingredients:**

1 egg

1 Tbsp cream cheese, softened and room temp

1 Tbsp sugar-free cheesecake pudding ½ cup mozzarella cheese

1 Tbsp monk fruit confectioners sweetener ¼ tsp vanilla extract

¼ tsp banana extract

toppings of choice

**Directions:**

Turn on waffle maker to heat and oil it with cooking spray. Beat egg in a small bowl.

Add remaining ingredients and mix until well incorporated.

Add one half of the batter to waffle maker and cook for 4 minutes, until golden brown. Remove chaffle and add the other half of the batter.

Top with your optional toppings and serve warm!

Nutrition Value per Servings:

Carbs - 2 G  Fat - 7 G  Protein - 8 G  Calories – 119

## Belgium Chaffles

Servings: 1

Prep time: 5 min.

Cook time: 6 min.

**Ingredients:**

2 eggs

1 cup Reduced-fat Cheddar cheese, shredded

**Directions:**

Turn on waffle maker to heat and oil it with cooking spray.

Whisk eggs in a bowl, add cheese. Stir until well-combined.

Pour mixture into waffle maker and cook for 6 minutes until done. Let it cool a little to crisp before serving.

Nutrition Value per Servings:

Carbs - 2 G  Fat - 33 G  Protein - 44 G  Calories – 460

## Bacon Chaffles

Servings: 2

Prep time: 5 min.

Cook time: 5 min.

**Ingredients:**

2 eggs

½ cup cheddar cheese

½ cup mozzarella cheese

¼ tsp baking powder

½ Tbsp almond flour

1 Tbsp butter, for waffle maker

FOR THE FILLING:

¼ cup bacon, chopped

2 Tbsp green onions, chopped

**Directions:**

Turn on waffle maker to heat and oil it with

cooking spray.

Add eggs, mozzarella, cheddar, almond flour, and baking powder to a blender and pulse 10 times, so cheese is still chunky.

Add bacon and green onions. Pulse 2-3 times to combine.

Add one half of the batter to the waffle maker and cook for 3 minutes, until golden brown.

Repeat with remaining batter.

Add your toppings and serve hot.

Nutrition Value per Servings:

Carbs - 3 G   Fat - 38 G   Protein - 23 G   Calories – 446

## Chaffle Egg Sandwich

Servings: 2

Cooking Time: 10 Minutes

**Ingredients:**

2 minutesI keto chaffle

2 slice cheddar cheese

1 egg simple omelet

**Directions:**

1.   Prepare your oven on 4000 F.

2.   Arrange egg omelet and cheese slice between chaffles.

3.   Bake in the preheated oven for about 4-5 minutes until cheese is melted.

4.   Once the cheese is melted, remove from the oven.

5.   Serve and enjoy!

Nutrition value per Servings:

Protein: 144 kcal Fat: 337 kcal Carbohydrates: 14 kcal

## Chaffle Minutesi Sandwich

Servings: 2

Cooking Time: 10 Minutes

**Ingredients:**

1 large egg

1/8 cup almond flour

1/2 tsp. garlic powder

3/4 tsp. baking powder

1/2 cup shredded cheese

SANDWICH FILLING:

2 slices deli ham

2 slices tomatoes

1 slice cheddar cheese

**Directions:**

1.   Grease your square waffle maker and pre-heat it on medium heat.

2.   Mix together chaffle ingredients in a mixing bowl until well combined.

3.   Pour batter intoa square waffle and make two chaffles.

4.   Once chaffles are cooked, remove from the maker.

5.   For a sandwich,arrange deli ham, tomato slice and cheddar cheese between two chaffles.

6.   Cut sandwich from the center.

7.   Serve and enjoy!

Nutrition value per Servings:

Calories 208  Fat 13.5g Carbohydrate 0.7g Protein 8.2g Sugars 0.6g

## Chaffle Cheese Sandwich

Servings: 1

Cooking Time: 10 Minutes

**Ingredients:**

2 square keto chaffle

2 slice cheddar cheese

2 lettuce leaves

**Directions:**

1. Prepare your oven on 4000 F.

2. Arrange lettuce leave and cheese slice between chaffles.

3. Bake in the preheated oven for about 4-5 minutes until cheese is melted.

4. Once the cheese is melted, remove from the oven.

5. Serve and enjoy!

Nutrition value per Servings:

Calories 208  Fat 13.5g Carbohydrate 0.7g Protein 8.2g Sugars 0.6g

## Chicken Zinger Chaffle

Servings: 2

Cooking Time: 15 Minutes

**Ingredients:**

1 chicken breast, cut into 2 pieces 1/2 cup coconut flour

1/4 cup finely grated Parmesan

1 tsp. paprika

1/2 tsp. garlic powder

1/2 tsp. onion powder

1 tsp. salt& pepper

1 egg beaten

Avocado oil for frying Lettuce leaves

BBQ sauce

CHAFFLE Ingredients:

4 oz. cheese

2 whole eggs

2 oz. almond flour

1/4 cup almond flour

1 tsp baking powder

**Directions:**

1. Mix together chaffle ingredients in a bowl.

2. Pour the chaffle batter in preheated greased square chaffle maker.

3. Cook chaffles for about 2-minutes until cooked through.

4. Make square chaffles from this batter.

5. Meanwhile mix together coconut flour, parmesan, paprika, garlic powder, onion powder salt and pepper in a bowl.

6. Dip chicken first in coconut flour mixture then in beaten egg.

7. Heat avocado oil in a skillet and cook chicken from both sides. until lightly brown and cooked

8. Set chicken zinger between two chaffles with lettuce and BBQ sauce.

9. Enjoy!

Nutrition value per Servings:

Calories 208  Fat 13.5g Carbohydrate 0.7g Protein 8.2g Sugars 0.6g

## Double Chicken Chaffles

Servings: 2

Cooking Time: 5 Minutes

**Ingredients:**

1/2 cup boil shredded chicken

1/4 cup cheddar cheese

1/8 cup parmesan cheese

1 egg

1 tsp. Italian seasoning

1/8 tsp. garlic powder

1 tsp. cream cheese

**Directions:**

1. Preheat the Belgian waffle maker.

2. Mix together in chaffle ingredients in a bowl and mix together.

3. Sprinkle 1 tbsp. of cheese in a waffle maker and pour in chaffle batter.

4. Pour 1 tbsp. of cheese over batter and close the lid.

5. Cook chaffles for about 4 to minutes.

6. Serve with a chicken zinger and enjoy the double chicken flavor.

Nutrition value per Servings:

Calories 208  Fat 13.5g Carbohydrate 0.7g Protein 8.2g Sugars 0.6g

## Chaffles With Topping

Servings: 3

Cooking Time: 10 Minutes

**Ingredients:**

1 large egg

1 tbsp. almond flour

1 tbsp. full-fat Greek yogurt

1/8 tsp baking powder

1/4 cup shredded Swiss cheese

TOPPING

4oz. grillprawns

4 oz. steamed cauliflower mash 1/2 zucchini sliced

3 lettuce leaves

1 tomato, sliced

1 tbsp. flax seeds

**Directions:**

1. Make 3 chaffles with the given chaffles ingredients.

2. For serving, arrange lettuce leaves on each chaffle.

3. Top with zucchini slice, grill prawns, cauliflower mash and a tomato slice.

4. Drizzle flax seeds on top.

5. Serve and enjoy!

Nutrition value per Servings:

Calories 208  Fat 13.5g Carbohydrate 0.7g Protein 8.2g Sugars 0.6g

## Chaffle With Cheese & Bacon

Servings: 2

Cooking Time: 15 Minutes

**Ingredients:**

1 egg

1/2 cup cheddar cheese, shredded

1 tbsp. parmesan cheese

3/4 tsp coconut flour

1/4 tsp baking powder

1/8 tsp Italian Seasoning

pinch of salt

1/4 tsp garlic powder

FOR TOPPING

1 bacon sliced, cooked and chopped

1/2 cup mozzarella cheese, shredded

1/4 tsp parsley, chopped

**Directions:**

1. Preheat oven to 400 degrees.

2. Switch on your minutesi waffle maker and grease with cooking spray.

3. Mix together chaffle ingredients in a mixing bowl until combined.

4. Spoon half of the batter in the center of the waffle maker and close the lid. Cook chaffles for about 3-minutes until cooked.

5. Carefully remove chaffles from the maker.

6. Arrange chaffles in a greased baking tray.

7. Top with mozzarella cheese, chopped bacon and parsley.

8. And bake in the oven for 4 -5 minutes.

9. Once the cheese is melted, remove from the oven.

10. Serve and enjoy!

Nutrition value per Servings:

Calories 208  Fat 13.5g Carbohydrate 0.7g Protein 8.2g Sugars 0.6g

## Grill Beefsteak And Chaffle

Servings: 1

Cooking Time: 10 Minutes

**Ingredients:**

1 beefsteak rib eye

1 tsp salt

1 tsp pepper

1 tbsp. lime juice

1 tsp garlic

**Directions:**

1. Prepare your grill for direct heat.

2. Mix together all spices and rub over beefsteak evenly.

3. Place the beef on the grill rack over medium heat.

4. Cover and cook steak for about 6 to 8 minutes. Flip and cook for another 5 minutes until cooked through.

5. Serve with keto simple chaffle and enjoy!

Nutrition value per Servings:

Calories 208  Fat 13.5g Carbohydrate 0.7g Protein 8.2g Sugars 0.6g

## Cauliflower Chaffles And Tomatoes

Servings: 2

Cooking Time: 15 Minutes

**Ingredients:**

1/2 cup cauliflower

1/4 tsp. garlic powder

1/4 tsp. black pepper

1/4 tsp. Salt

1/2 cup shredded cheddar cheese

1 egg

FOR TOPPING

1 lettuce leave

1 tomato sliced

4 oz. cauliflower steamed, mashed

1 tsp sesame seeds

**Directions:**

1. Add all chaffle ingredients into a blender and mix well.

2. Sprinkle 1/8 shredded cheese on the waffle maker and pour cauliflower mixture in a preheated waffle maker and sprinkle the rest of the cheese over it.

3. Cook chaffles for about 4-5 minutes until cooked

4. For serving, lay lettuce leaves over chaffle top with steamed cauliflower and tomato.

5. Drizzle sesame seeds on top.

6. Enjoy!

Nutrition value per Servings:

Calories 208  Fat 13.5g Carbohydrate 0.7g Protein 8.2g Sugars 0.6g

## Layered Cheese Chaffles

Servings: 1

Cooking Time: 5 Minutes

**Ingredients:**

1 organic egg, beaten

1/3 cup Cheddar cheese, shredded

½ teaspoon ground flaxseed

¼ teaspoon organic baking powder

2 tablespoons Parmesan cheese, shredded

**Directions:**

1. Preheat a mini waffle iron and then grease it.

2. In a bowl, place all the ingredients except Parmesan and beat until well combined.

3. Place half the Parmesan cheese in the bottom of preheated waffle iron.

4. Place half of the egg mixture over cheese and top with the remaining Parmesan cheese.

5. Cook for about 3-minutes or until golden brown.

6. Serve warm.

Nutrition value per Servings:

Calories 208  Fat 13.5g Carbohydrate 0.7g Protein 8.2g Sugars 0.6g

## Chaffles With Keto Ice Cream

Servings: 2

Cooking Time: 14 Minutes

**Ingredients:**

1 egg, beaten

½ cup finely grated mozzarella cheese ¼ cup almond flour

2 tbsp swerve confectioner's sugar 1/8 tsp xanthan gum

Low-carb ice cream (flavor of your choice) for serving

**Directions:**

1. Preheat the waffle iron.

2. In a medium bowl, mix all the ingredients except the ice cream.

3. Open the iron and add half of the mixture. Close and cook until crispy, 7 minutes.

4. Transfer the chaffle to a plate and make second one with the remaining batter.

5. On each chaffle, add a scoop of low carb ice cream, fold into half-moons and enjoy.

Nutrition value:

Calories 89 Fats 48g Carbs 1.67g Net Carbs 1.37g Protein 5.91g

## Vanilla Mozzarella Chaffles

Servings: 2

Cooking Time: 12 Minutes

**Ingredients:**

1 organic egg, beaten

1 teaspoon organic vanilla extract

1 tablespoon almond flour

1 teaspoon organic baking powder Pinch of ground cinnamon

1 cup Mozzarella cheese, shredded

**Directions:**

1. Preheat a mini waffle iron and then grease it.

2. In a bowl, place the egg and vanilla extract and beat until well combined.

3. Add the flour, baking powder and cinnamon and mix well.

4. Add the Mozzarella cheese and stir to combine.

5. In a small bowl, place the egg and Mozzarella cheese and stir to combine.

6. Place half of the mixture into preheated waffle iron and cook for about 5-minutes or until golden brown.

7. Repeat with the remaining mixture.

8. Serve warm.

Nutrition value per Servings:

Calories 208  Fat 13.5g Carbohydrate 0.7g Protein 8.2g Sugars 0.6g

## Bruschetta Chaffle

Servings: 2

Cooking Time: 5 Minutes

**Ingredients:**

2 basic chaffles

2 tablespoons sugar-free marinara sauce

2 tablespoons mozzarella, shredded

1 tablespoon olives, sliced

1 tomato sliced

1 tablespoon keto friendly pesto sauce

Basil leaves

**Directions:**

1. Spread marinara sauce on each chaffle.

2. Spoon pesto and spread on top of the marinara sauce.

3. Top with the tomato, olives and mozzarella.

4. Bake in the oven for 3 minutes or until the cheese has melted.

5. Garnish with basil.

6. Serve and enjoy.

Nutrition value:

Calories 208  Fat 13.5g Carbohydrate 0.7g Protein 8.2g Sugars 0.6g

## Egg-Free Psyllium Husk Chaffles

Servings: 1

Cooking Time: 4 Minutes

**Ingredients:**

1 ounce Mozzarella cheese, shredded

1 tablespoon cream cheese, softened

1 tablespoon psyllium husk powder

**Directions:**

1. Preheat a waffle iron and then grease it.

2. In a blender, place all ingredients and pulse until a slightly crumbly mixture forms.

3. Place the mixture into preheated waffle iron and cook for about 4 minutes or until golden brown.

4. Serve warm.

Nutrition value per Servings:

Calories 208  Fat 13.5g Carbohydrate 0.7g Protein 8.2g Sugars 0.6g

## Mozzarella & Almond Flour Chaffles

Servings: 2

Cooking Time: 8 Minutes

**Ingredients:**

½ cup Mozzarella cheese, shredded

1 large organic egg

2 tablespoons blanched almond flour

¼ teaspoon organic baking powder

**Directions:**

1. Preheat a mini waffle iron and then grease it.

2. In a medium bowl, place all ingredients and with a fork, mix until well combined.

3. Place half of the mixture into preheated waffle iron and cook for about 4 minutes or until golden brown.

4. Repeat with the remaining mixture.

5. Serve warm.

Nutrition value per Servings:

Calories: 98 Fat: 7.1g Carbohydrates: 2.2g Sugar: 0.2g Protein: 7g

## Pulled Pork Chaffle Sandwiches

Servings: 4

Cooking Time: 28 Minutes

**Ingredients:**

2 eggs, beaten

1 cup finely grated cheddar cheese ¼ tsp baking powder

2 cups cooked and shredded pork

1 tbsp sugar-free BBQ sauce

2 cups shredded coleslaw mix

2 tbsp apple cider vinegar

½ tsp salt

¼ cup ranch dressing

**Directions:**

1. Preheat the waffle iron.

2. In a medium bowl, mix the eggs, cheddar cheese, and baking powder.

3. Open the iron and add a quarter of the mixture. Close and cook until crispy, 7 minutes.

4. Transfer the chaffle to a plate and make 3 more chaffles in the same manner.

5. Meanwhile, in another medium bowl, mix the pulled pork with the BBQ sauce until well combined. Set aside.

6. Also, mix the coleslaw mix, apple cider vinegar, salt, and ranch dressing in another medium bowl.

7. When the chaffles are ready, on two pieces, divide the pork and then top with the ranch coleslaw. Cover with the remaining chaffles and insert mini skewers to secure the sandwiches.

8. Enjoy afterward.

Nutrition value:

Calories 374 Fats 23.61g Carbs 8.2g Net Carbs 8.2g Protein 28.05g

## Cheddar & Egg White Chaffles

Servings: 4

Cooking Time: 12 Minutes

**Ingredients:**

2 egg whites

1 cup Cheddar cheese, shredded

**Directions:**

1. Preheat a mini waffle iron and then grease it.

2. In a small bowl, place the egg whites and cheese and stir to combine.

3. Place ¼ of the mixture into preheated waffle iron and cook for about 4 minutes or until golden brown.

4. Repeat with the remaining mixture.

5. Serve warm.

Nutrition value per Servings:

Calories: 122 Fat: 9.4g Carbohydrates: 0.5g Sugar: 0.3g Protein: 8.8g

## Spinach & Artichoke Chicken Chaffle

Prep Time: 3 minutes

Cook Time: 8 minutes

Servings: 2

**Ingredients:**

1/3 cup cooked diced chicken

1/3 cup cooked spinach chopped

1/3 cup marinated artichokes chopped

1/3 cup shredded mozzarella cheese

1 ounce softened cream cheese

1/4 teaspoon garlic powder

1 egg

**Directions:**

Heat up your Dash mini waffle maker.

In a small bowl, mix the egg, garlic powder, cream cheese, and Mozzarella Cheese. Add the spinach, artichoke, and chicken and mix well.

Add 1/3 of the batter into your mini waffle maker and cook for 4 minutes. If they are still a bit uncooked, leave it cooking for another 2 minutes. Then cook the rest of the batter to make a second chaffle and then cook the third chaffle.

After cooking, remove from the pan and let sit for 2 minutes. Dip in ranch dressing, sour cream, or enjoy alone.

Nutritional Value (per serving):

Calories: 172kcal Carbohydrates: 3g Protein: 11g Fat: 13g

## Chickfila Copycat Chaffle Sandwich

**Ingredients:**

Ingredients for the Chicken:

1 Chicken Breast

4 T of Dill Pickle Juice

2 T Parmesan Cheese powdered

2 T Pork Rinds ground

1 T Flax Seed ground

Salt and Pepper

2 T butter melted

Ingredients for Chaffle Sandwich Bun:

1 Egg room temperature

1 Cup Mozzarella Cheese shredded

3 -5 drops of Stevia Glycerite 1/4 tsp Butter Extract

**Directions:**

Directions for the Chicken:

Pound chicken to 1/2 inch thickness.

Cut in half and place in zip lock baggie with pickle juice.

Seal baggie and place in the fridge for 1 hour to overnight. Preheat Airfryer for 5 mins at 400 degrees F

In a small shallow bowl, mix together Parmesan cheese, pork rinds, flaxseed, and S&P. Remove chicken from the baggie and discard pickle juice.

Dip chicken in melted butter then in seasoning mix.

Place parchment paper round in Airfryer basket, brush the paper lightly with oil. (I used coconut) Place chicken in preheated Airfryer and cook for 7 mins.

Flip chicken and Airfry for an additional 7-8 mins.

Directions for Chaffle Bun:

Mix everything together in a small bowl. Put 1/4 of the mixture in the preheated mini dash waffle iron. Cook for 4 mins. Remove to a cooling rack. Repeat x3

Assemble Sandwich's: Place rested chicken on one Chaffle bun, add 3 dill pickle slices. Cover with other buns. Repeat. Enjoy!

## Strawberry Shortcake Chaffle

Prep Time: 4 minutes

Cook Time: 12 minutes

Servings: 3

**Ingredients:**

Strawberry topping Ingredients:

3 fresh strawberries

1/2 tablespoon granulated swerve

Sweet Chaffle Ingredients:

1 tablespoon almond flour

1/2 cup mozzarella cheese

1 egg

1 tablespoon granulated swerve

1/4 teaspoon vanilla extract

Keto Whipped Cream

**Directions:**

Heat up your waffle maker. If you are using a mini waffle maker, this recipe will make 2 chaffles; if using a large waffle maker, this recipe will make 1 large sweet chaffle.

Rinse and chop up your fresh strawberries. Place the strawberries in a small bowl and add 1/2 tablespoon granulated swerve. Mix the strawberries with the swerve and set aside.

In a bowl mix the almond flour, egg, mozzarella cheese, granulated swerve and vanilla extract. Pour 1/3 of the batter into your mini waffle maker and cook for 3-4 minutes. Then cook another 1/3 of the batter and the rest of the batter to make 3 keto chaffles.

While your second chaffle is cooking, make your keto whipped cream if you do not have any on hand.

Assemble your Strawberry Shortcake Chaffle by placing whipped cream and strawberries on top

of your sweet chaffle. Then drizzle the juice that will also be in the bowl with the strawberries on top.

Nutritional Value (per serving):

Calories: 112kcal Carbohydrates: 2g Protein: 7g Fat: 8g

## Chocolate Chaffle Cake

Prep Time: 2 minutes

Cook Time: 8 minutes

Servings: 2

**Ingredients:**

Chocolate Chaffle Cake Ingredients:

2 tablespoons cocoa powder

2 tablespoons Swerve granulated sweetener

1 egg

1 tablespoon heavy whipping cream

1 tablespoon almond flour

1/4 tsp baking powder

1/2 tsp vanilla extract

Cream Cheese Frosting:

2 tablespoons cream cheese

2 teaspoons swerve confectioners 1/8 tsp vanilla extract

1 tsp heavy cream

**Directions:**

How to Make Chocolate Chaffle Cake:

In a small bowl, whisk together cocoa powder, swerve, almond flour, and baking powder. Add in the vanilla extract and heavy whipping cream and mix well.

Add in the egg and mix well. Be sure to scrape the sides of the bowl to get all of the ingredients mixed well.

Let sit for 3-4 minutes while the mini waffle maker heats up.

Add half of the waffle mixture to the waffle maker and cook for 4 minutes. Then cook the second waffle. While the second chocolate keto waffle is cooking, make your frosting.

How to Make Cream Cheese Frosting:

In a small microwave-safe bowl add 2 tablespoons cream cheese. Microwave the cream cheese for 8 seconds to soften the cream cheese.

Add in heavy whipping cream and vanilla extract and use a small hand mixer to mix well.

Then add in the confectioners swerve and use the hand mixer to incorporate and fluffy the frosting.

Assembling Keto Chocolate Chaffle cake:

Place one chocolate chaffle on a plate, top with a layer of frosting. You can spread it with a knife or use a pastry bag and pipe the frosting.

Put the second chocolate chaffle on top of the frosting layer and then spread or pipe the rest of the frosting on top.

Nutritional Value (per serving):

Calories: 151kcal Carbohydrates: 5g Protein: 6g Fat: 13g

## Keto Birthday Cake Chaffle

Servings: 4

**Ingredients:**

Chaffle Cake Ingredients:

2 eggs

1/4 cup almond flour

1 tsp coconut flour

2 tbsp melted butter

2 tbsp cream cheese room temp

1 tsp cake batter extract

1/2 tsp vanilla extract

1/2 tsp baking powder

2 tbsp swerve confectioners sweetener or monk fruit 1/4 tsp Xanthan powder

Whipped Cream Vanilla Frosting Ingredients:

1/2 cup heavy whipping cream

2 tbs 2 tbsp swerve confectioners sweetener or monk fruit 1/2 tsp vanilla extract

**Directions:**

Preheat the mini waffle maker.

In a medium-size blender, add all of the chaffle cake ingredients and blend it on high until it's smooth and creamy. Allow the batter to sit for just a minute. It may seem a bit watery, but it will work just fine.

Add about 2 to 3 tablespoons of batter to your waffle maker and cook it for about 2 to 3 minutes until it's golden brown.

In a separate bowl, start making the whipped cream vanilla frosting.

Add all of the ingredients and mix it with a hand mixer until the whipping cream is thick and forms soft peaks.

Allow the keto birthday cake chaffles to cool completely before frosting your cake. If you frost it too soon, it will melt the frosting.

Enjoy!

## Chocolate Chip Cookie Chaffle Cake

**Ingredients:**

Ingredients for cake layers:

1 T butter melted

1 T Golden Monkfruit sweetener

1 Egg Yolk

1/8 tsp Vanilla Extract

1/8 tsp Cake Batter Extract

3 T Almond Flour

1/8 tsp Baking Powder

1 T Chocolate Chips sugar-free

Whipped Cream Frosting Ingredients:

1 tsp unflavored gelatin

4 tsp Cold Water

1 Cup HWC

2 T Confectioners Sweetener

**Directions:**

Cake Directions:

Mix everything together and cook in a mini waffle iron for 4 mins. Repeat for each layer. I chose

to make 3.

Whipped Cream Frosting Directions:

Place your beaters and your mixing bowl in the freezer for about 15 minutes to allow them to cool.

In a microwave-safe bowl, sprinkle the gelatin over the cold water. Stir, and allow to "bloom." This takes about 5 minutes.

Microwave the gelatin mixture for 10 seconds. It will become a liquid. Stir to make sure everything is dissolved.

In your chilled mixing bowl, begin whipping the cream on a low speed. Add in the confectioner's sugar.

Move to a higher speed and watch for good peaks to begin to form.

Once the whipping cream is starting to peak, switch back to a lower speed and slowly drizzle the melted liquid gelatin mixture in. Once it's in, switch back to a higher speed and continue to beat until it's reached stiff peaks.

Place in piping bags and pipe on your cake.

## Cap'n Crunch Cereal Chaffle Cake

Servings: 2

**Ingredients:**

1 egg

2 tablespoons almond flour

1/2 teaspoon coconut flour

1 tablespoon butter melted

1 tablespoon cream cheese room temp

20 drops Captain Cereal flavoring

1/4 teaspoon vanilla extract

1/4 teaspoon baking powder

1 tablespoon confectioners sweetener 1/8 teaspoon xanthan gum

**Directions:**

Preheat the mini waffle maker.

Mix or blend all of the ingredients until smooth and creamy. Allow the batter to rest for a few minutes for the flour to absorb the liquid.

Add about 2 to 3 tablespoons of batter to your waffle maker and cook it for about 2 1/2 minutes. Top with fresh whipped cream

Nutritional Value (per serving):

Calories 154 Total Fat 11.2g Total arbohydrate 5.9g Protein 4.6g

## Jicama Loaded Baked Potato Chaffle

Servings: 4

**Ingredients:**

1 large jicama root

1/2 medium onion minced

2 garlic cloves pressed

1 cup cheese of choice

2 eggs whisked

Salt and Pepper

**Directions:**

Peel jicama and shred in food processor

Place shredded jicama in a large colander, sprinkle with 1-2 tsp of salt. Mix well and allow to drain.

Squeeze out as much liquid as possible (very important step) Microwave for 5-8 minutes Mix all ingredients together

Sprinkle a little cheese on waffle iron before adding 3 T of the mixture, sprinkle a little more cheese on top of the mixture Cook for 5 minutes. Flip and cook 2 more.

Top with a dollop of sour cream, bacon pieces, cheese, and chives!

Nutritional Value (per serving):

Calories 168 Total Fat 11.8g Total Carbohydrate 5.1g Sugars 1.2g Protein 10g

## German Chocolate Chaffle Cake Recipe

Servings: 4

**Ingredients:**

German Chocolate Chaffle Cake Ingredients:

2 eggs

1 tablespoon melted butter

1 tablespoon cream cheese softened to room temperature

2 tablespoons unsweetened cocoa powder or unsweetened raw cacao powder

2 tablespoons almond flour

2 teaspoons coconut flour

2 tablespoons Pyure granulated sweetener blend 1/2 teaspoon baking powder

1/2 teaspoon instant coffee granules dissolved in 1 tablespoon hot water 1/2 teaspoon vanilla extract

2 pinches salt

German Chocolate Chaffle Cake Filling Ingredients:

1 egg yolk

1/4 cup heavy cream

2 tablespoons Pyure granulated sweetener blend

1 tablespoon butter

1/2 teaspoon caramel or maple extract 1/4 cup chopped pecans

1/4 cup unsweetened flaked coconut

1 teaspoon coconut flour

**Directions:**

Chaffle Directions:

Preheat mini Dash waffle iron until thoroughly hot.

In a medium bowl, whisk all ingredients together until well combined.

Spoon a heaping 2 tablespoons of batter into waffle iron, close and cook 3-5 minutes, until done. Remove to a wire rack.

Repeat 3 times.

Filling Directions:

In a small saucepan over medium heat, combine the egg yolk, heavy cream, butter, and sweetener. Simmer slowly, constantly stirring for 5 minutes.

Remove from heat and stir in extract, pecans, flaked coconut, and coconut flour.

Assembly:

Spread one-third of the filling in between each of 2 layers of chaffles and the remaining third on top chaffle and serve.

Nutritional Value (per serving):

Calories 271 Total Fat 23.7g Carbohydrate 8.4g Sugars 1.8g Protein 7.6g

## Keto Peanut Butter Chaffle Cake

Servings: 2

**Ingredients:**

Peanut Butter Chaffle Ingredients:

2 Tbs sugar-free Peanut Butter Powder

2 Tbs Monkfruit Confectioner's

1 egg

1/4 Tsp Baking Powder

1 Tbs heavy whipping cream

1/4 tsp Peanut Butter extract

Peanut Butter Frosting Ingredients:

2 Tbs Monkfruit Confectioners

1 Tbs butter softened and room temp

1 tbs sugar-free natural peanut butter or peanut butter powder

2 Tbs Cream Cheese softened and room temp

1/4 tsp vanilla

**Directions:**

In a small bowl, whip up the egg.

Add the remaining ingredients and mix well until the batter is smooth and creamy.

If you don't have the peanut butter extract, you can skip it. It does add a more intense peanut butter flavor that is absolutely wonderful and makes this extract worth investing in.

Pour half the batter in a mini waffle maker and cook it for 2 to 3 minutes until it's fully cooked. In a separate small bowl, add the sweetener, cream cheese, sugar-free natural peanut butter, and vanilla. Mix the frosting until everything is well incorporated.

Spread the frosting on the waffle cake after it has completely cooled down to room temperature. Or you can pipe the frosting too!

Or you can heat the frosting and add a 1/2 teaspoon of water to make it a peanut butter glaze you can drizzle on your peanut butter chaffle too!

Nutritional Value (per serving):

Total Fat 7g Total Carbohydrate 3.6g Sugars 1.8g Protein 5.5g

## Keto Boston Cream Pie Chaffle Cake Recipe

Servings: 4

**Ingredients:**

Chaffle Cake Ingredients:

2 eggs

1/4 cup almond flour

1 tsp coconut flour

2 tbsp melted butter

2 tbsp cream cheese room temp

20 drops Boston Cream extract 1/2 tsp vanilla extract

1/2 tsp baking powder

2 tbsp swerve confectioners sweetener or monk fruit 1/4 tsp Xanthan powder

Custard Ingredients:

1/2 cup heavy whipping cream 1/2 tsp Vanilla extract

1 /2 tbs Swerve confectioners Sweetener

2 Egg Yolks

1/8 tsp Xanthan Gum

Ganache Ingredients:

2 tbs heavy whipping cream

2 tbs Unsweetened Baking chocolate bar chopped

1 tbs Swerve Confectioners Sweetener

**Directions:**

Preheat the mini waffle iron to make cake chaffles first.

In a blender, combine all the cake ingredients and blend it on high until it's smooth and creamy. This should only take a couple of minutes.

On the stovetop, heat the heavy whipping cream to a boil. While it's heating, whisk the egg yolks and Swerve together in a separate small bowl.

Once the cream is boiling, pour half of it into the egg yolks. Make sure you are whisking it together while you pour in the mixture slowly.

Pour the egg and cream mixture back into the stovetop pan into the rest of the cream and stir continuously for another 2-3 minutes.

Take the custard off the heat and whisk in your vanilla & xanthan gum. Then set it aside to cool and thicken.

Put ingredients for the ganache in a small bowl. Microwave for 20 seconds, stir. Repeat if needed.

Careful not to overheat the ganache and burn it. Only do 20 seconds at a time until it's fully melted.

Serve your Boston Cream Pie Chaffle Cake and Enjoy!

Nutritional Value (per serving):

Total Fat 53.3g  Carbohydrate 10.1g Sugars 3.6g Protein 12.4g

## Coconut Cream Cake Chaffle Recipe

Servings: 6

**Ingredients:**

Chaffles:

2 eggs

1 ounce cream cheese softened to room temperature

2 tablespoons finely shredded unsweetened coconut

2 tablespoons powdered sweetener blends such as Swerve or Lakanto

1 tablespoon melted butter or coconut oil

1/2 teaspoon coconut extract

1/2 teaspoon vanilla extract

Filling:

1/3 cup coconut milk

1/3 cup unsweetened almond or cashew milk

2 eggs yolks

2 tablespoons powdered sweetener blends such

as Swerve or Lakanto 1/4 teaspoon xanthan gum

2 teaspoons butter

Pinch of salt

1/4 cup finely shredded unsweetened coconut

Optional toppings:

Sugar-free whipped cream

1 tablespoon finely shredded unsweetened coconut toasted until lightly brown

**Directions:**

For the chaffles:

Heat mini Dash waffle iron until thoroughly hot.

Beat all chaffle ingredients together in a small bowl.

Add a heaping 2 tablespoons batter to waffle iron and cook until golden brown and the waffle iron stops steaming, about 5 minutes.

Repeat 3 times to make 4 chaffles. You only need 3 for the recipe.

For the filling:

Heat the coconut and almond milk in a small saucepan over medium-low heat. It should be steaming hot, but not simmering or boiling.

In a separate bowl, beat the egg yolks together lightly. While whisking the milk constantly, slowly drizzle the egg yolks into the milk.

Heat, constantly stirring until the mixture thickens slightly. Do not boil. Whisk in the sweetener. While constantly whisking, slowly sprinkle in the xanthan gum. Continue to cook for 1 minute. Remove from the heat and add the remaining ingredients.

Pour coconut cream filling into a container, cover the surface with plastic wrap and refrigerate until cool. The plastic wrap prevents a skin from forming on the filling. The mixture will thicken as is cools.

Cake assembly:

Spread 1/3 of the filling over each of 3 chaffles, stack them together to make a cake Top with whipped cream and garnish with toasted coconut.

Nutritional Value (per serving):

Calories: 157kcal Carbohydrates: 5.7g Protein: 5.1g Fat: 14.1g

## Almond Joy Cake Chaffle Recipe

Servings: 6

**Ingredients:**

Chocolate Chaffles:

1 egg

1 ounce cream cheese

1 tablespoon almond flour

1 tablespoon unsweetened cocoa powder

1 tablespoon erythritol sweeteners blends such as Swerve, Pyure or Lakanto 1/2 teaspoon vanilla extract

1/4 teaspoon instant coffee powder

Coconut Filling:

1 1/2 teaspoons coconut oil melted

1 tablespoon heavy cream

1/4 cup unsweetened finely shredded coconut

2 ounces cream cheese

1 tablespoon confectioner's sweetener such as Swerve 1/4 teaspoon vanilla extract

14 whole almonds

**Directions:**

For the Chaffles:

Preheat mini Dash waffle iron until thoroughly hot.

In a medium bowl, whisk all chaffle ingredients together until well combined. Pour half of the batter into the waffle iron.

Close and cook 3-5 minutes, until done. Remove to a wire rack. Repeat for the second chaffle.

For the Filling:

Soften cream to room temperature or warm in the microwave for 10 seconds.

Add all ingredients to a bowl and mix until smooth and well-combined.

Assembly:

Spread half the filling on one chaffle and place 7 almonds evenly on top of the filling. Repeat with the second chaffle and stack together.

Nutritional Value (per serving):

Calories: 130kcal Carbohydrates: 6.3g Protein: 3g  Fat: 10.6g

## Pumpkin Chaffle Keto Sugar Cookies Recipe

**Ingredients:**

Keto Sugar Cookie Ingredients:

1 T butter melted

1 T Sweetener

1 Egg Yolk

1/8 tsp Vanilla Extract

1/8 tsp Cake Batter Extract

3 T Almond Flour

1/8 tsp Baking Powder

Icing Ingredients:

1 T Confectioners Sweetener 1/4 tsp Vanilla Extract

1-2 tsp Water

Sprinkles Ingredients:

1 T Granular Sweetener mixed with 1 drop of food coloring. Mix well.

**Directions:**

Stir all ingredients together. Let rest for 5 min.

Stir again.

Refrigerate for 15 mins.

Put 1/2 of dough in the pumpkin waffle maker. Cook 4 minutes.

Repeat. Let cool.

Add icing and sprinkles, if desired

## Maple Iced Soft Gingerbread Cookies Chaffle

Servings: 2

**Ingredients:**

Chaffles Ingredients:

1 egg

1 ounce cream cheese softened to room temperature

2 teaspoons melted butter

1 tablespoon Swerve Brown sweetener

1 tablespoon almond flour

2 teaspoons coconut flour

1/4 teaspoon baking powder

3/4 teaspoon ground ginger

1/2 teaspoon ground cinnamon

Generous dash ground nutmeg

Generous dash ground clove

Icing Ingredients:

2 tablespoons powdered sweeteners such as Swerve or Lakanto

1 1/2 teaspoons heavy cream

1/8 teaspoon maple extract

Water as needed to thin the frosting

**Directions:**

Heat mini Dash waffle iron until thoroughly hot.

Beat all chaffle ingredients together in a small

bowl until smooth.

Add a heaping 2 tablespoons of batter to waffle iron and cook until done about 4 minutes. Repeat to make 2 chaffles. Let cool on wire rack.

Maple Icing Directions:

In a small bowl, whisk together sweetener, heavy cream, and maple extract until smooth. Add enough water to thin to a spreadable consistency.

Spread icing on each chaffle and sprinkle with additional ground cinnamon, if desired.

Nutritional Value (per serving):

Calories 161 Total Fat 12.5g Carbohydrate 7.6g Protein 5.2g

## Spicy Shrimp And Chaffles

Servings: 4

Cooking Time: 31 Minutes

**Ingredients:**

For the shrimp:

1 tbsp olive oil

1 lb jumbo shrimp, peeled and deveined

1 tbsp Creole seasoning

Salt to taste

2 tbsp hot sauce

3 tbsp butter

2 tbsp chopped fresh scallions to garnish For the chaffles:

2 eggs, beaten

1 cup finely grated Monterey Jack cheese

**Directions:**

1. For the shrimp:
2. Heat the olive oil in a medium skillet over medium heat.
3. Season the shrimp with the Creole seasoning and salt. Cook in the oil until pink and opaque on both sides, 2 minutes.
4. Pour in the hot sauce and butter. Mix well until the shrimp is adequately coated in the sauce, 1 minute.
5. Turn the heat off and set aside.
6. For the chaffles:
7. Preheat the waffle iron.
8. In a medium bowl, mix the eggs and Monterey Jack cheese.
9. Open the iron and add a quarter of the mixture. Close and cook until crispy, 7 minutes.
10. Transfer the chaffle to a plate and make 3 more chaffles in the same manner.
11. Cut the chaffles into quarters and place on a plate.
12. Top with the shrimp and garnish with the scallions.
13. Serve warm.

Nutrition value:

Calories 342 Fats 19.75g Carbs 2.8g Net Carbs 2.3g Protein 36.01g

## Creamy Chicken Chaffle Sandwich

Servings: 2

Cooking Time: 10 Minutes

**Ingredients:**

Cooking spray

1 cup chicken breast fillet, cubed

Salt and pepper to taste

¼ cup all-purpose cream

4 garlic chaffles

Parsley, chopped

**Directions:**

1. Spray your pan with oil.
2. Put it over medium heat.
3. Add the chicken fillet cubes.
4. Season with salt and pepper.
5. Reduce heat and add the cream.
6. Spread chicken mixture on top of the chaffle.
7. Garnish with parsley and top with another chaffle.

Nutrition value:

Calories 273 Fat 34g Saturated Fat 4.1g Carbohydrate 22. Sugars 3.2g Protein 17.5g

## Chaffle Cannoli

Servings: 4

Cooking Time: 28 Minutes

**Ingredients:**

For the chaffles:

1 large egg

1 egg yolk

3 tbsp butter, melted

1 tbso swerve confectioner's

1 cup finely grated Parmesan cheese

2 tbsp finely grated mozzarella cheese For the cannoli filling:

½ cup ricotta cheese

2 tbsp swerve confectioner's sugar

1 tsp vanilla extract

2 tbsp unsweetened chocolate chips for garnishing

**Directions:**

1. Preheat the waffle iron.
2. Meanwhile, in a medium bowl, mix all the ingredients for the chaffles.
3. Open the iron, pour in a quarter of the mixture, cover, and cook until crispy, 7 minutes.
4. Remove the chaffle onto a plate and make 3 more with the remaining batter.
5. Meanwhile, for the cannoli filling:
6. Beat the ricotta cheese and swerve confectioner's sugar until smooth. Mix in the vanilla.
7. On each chaffle, spread some of the filling and wrap over.
8. Garnish the creamy ends with some chocolate chips.
9. Serve immediately.

Nutrition value:

Calories 308 Fats 25.05g Carbs 5.17g Net Carbs 5.17g Protein 15.18g

## Strawberry Shortcake Chaffle Bowls

Servings: 4

Cooking Time: 28 Minutes

**Ingredients:**

1 egg, beaten

½ cup finely grated mozzarella cheese

1 tbsp almond flour

¼ tsp baking powder

2 drops cake batter extract

1 cup cream cheese, softened

1 cup fresh strawberries, sliced

1 tbsp sugar-free maple syrup

**Directions:**

1. Preheat a waffle bowl maker and grease lightly with cooking spray.

2. Meanwhile, in a medium bowl, whisk all the ingredients except the cream cheese and strawberries.

3. Open the iron, pour in half of the mixture, cover, and cook until crispy, 6 to 7 minutes.

4. Remove the chaffle bowl onto a plate and set aside.

5. Make a second chaffle bowl with the remaining batter.

6. To serve, divide the cream cheese into the chaffle bowls and top with the strawberries.

7. Drizzle the filling with the maple syrup and serve.

Nutrition value:

Calories 235 Fats 20.62g Carbs 5.9g Net Carbs 5g Protein 7.51g

## Chocolate Melt Chaffles

Servings: 4

Cooking Time: 36 Minutes

**Ingredients:**

For the chaffles:

2 eggs, beaten

¼ cup finely grated Gruyere cheese

2 tbsp heavy cream

1 tbsp coconut flour

2 tbsp cream cheese, softened

3 tbsp unsweetened cocoa powder

2 tsp vanilla extract

A pinch of salt

For the chocolate sauce:

1/3 cup + 1 tbsp heavy cream

1 ½ oz unsweetened baking chocolate, chopped

1 ½ tsp sugar-free maple syrup

1 ½ tsp vanilla extract

**Directions:**

1. For the chaffles:

2. Preheat the waffle iron.

3. In a medium bowl, mix all the ingredients for the chaffles.

4. Open the iron and add a quarter of the mixture. Close and cook until crispy, 7 minutes.

5. Transfer the chaffle to a plate and make 3 more with the remaining batter.

6. For the chocolate sauce:

7. Pour the heavy cream into saucepan and simmer over low heat, 3 minutes.

8. Turn the heat off and add the chocolate. Allow melting for a few minutes and stir until fully melted, 5 minutes.

9. Mix in the maple syrup and vanilla extract.

10. Assemble the chaffles in layers with the chocolate sauce sandwiched between each layer.

11. Slice and serve immediately.

Nutrition value:

Calories 172 Fats 13.57g Carbs 6.65g Net Carbs 3.65g Protein 5.76g

## Pumpkin & Pecan Chaffle

Servings: 2

Cooking Time: 10 Minutes

**Ingredients:**

1 egg, beaten

½ cup mozzarella cheese, grated

½ teaspoon pumpkin spice

1 tablespoon pureed pumpkin

2 tablespoons almond flour

1 teaspoon sweetener

2 tablespoons pecans, chopped

**Directions:**

1. Turn on the waffle maker.
2. Beat the egg in a bowl.
3. Stir in the rest of the ingredients.
4. Pour half of the mixture into the device.
5. Seal the lid.
6. Cook for 5 minutes.
7. Remove the chaffle carefully.
8. Repeat the steps to make the second chaffle.

Nutrition value:

Calories 210 Total Fat 17 g Carbohydrate 4.6 g Protein 11 g Total Sugars 2 g

## Spicy Jalapeno & Bacon Chaffles

Servings: 2

Cooking Time: 5 Minutes

**Ingredients:**

1 oz. cream cheese

1 large egg

1/2 cup cheddar cheese

2 tbsps. bacon bits

1/2 tbsp. jalapenos

1/4 tsp baking powder

**Directions:**

1. Switch on your waffle maker.
2. Grease your waffle maker with cooking spray and let it heat up.
3. Mix together egg and vanilla extract in a bowl first.
4. Add baking powder, jalapenos and bacon bites.
5. Add in cheese last and mix together.
6. Pour the chaffles batter intothe maker and cook the chaffles for about 2-3 minutes.
7. Once chaffles are cooked, remove from the maker.
8. Serve hot and enjoy!

Nutrition value per Servings:

Calories 172 Fats 13.57g Carbs 6.65g Net Carbs 3.65g Protein 5.76g

## Zucchini Parmesan Chaffles

Servings: 2

Cooking Time: 14 Minutes

**Ingredients:**

1 cup shredded zucchini

1 egg, beaten

½ cup finely grated Parmesan cheese

Salt and freshly ground black pepper to taste

**Directions:**

1. Preheat the waffle iron.
2. Put all the ingredients in a medium bowl and mix well.
3. Open the iron and add half of the mixture. Close and cook until crispy, 7 minutes.
4. Remove the chaffle onto a plate and make another with the remaining mixture.
5. Cut each chaffle into wedges and serve afterward.

Nutrition value per Servings:

Calories 138 Fats 9.07g Carbs 3.81g Net Carbs 3.71g Protein 10.02g

## Cheddar & Almond Flour Chaffles

Servings: 2

Cooking Time: 10 Minutes

**Ingredients:**

1 large organic egg, beaten

½ cup Cheddar cheese, shredded

2 tablespoons almond flour

**Directions:**

1. Preheat a mini waffle iron and then grease it.

2. In a bowl, place the egg, Cheddar cheese and almond flour and beat until well combined.

3. Place half of the mixture into preheated waffle iron and cook for about 5 minutes or until golden brown.

4. Repeat with the remaining mixture.

5. Serve warm.

Nutrition value per Servings:

Calories: 195  Fat: 15g Carbohydrates: 1.8g Sugar: 0.6g Protein: 10.2g

## Simple & Beginner Chaffle

Servings: 2

Cooking Time: 5 Minutes

**Ingredients:**

1 large egg

1/2 cup mozzarella cheese, shredded Cooking spray

**Directions:**

1. Switch on your waffle maker.

2. Beat the egg with a fork in a small mixing bowl.

3. Once the egg is beaten, add the mozzarella and mix well.

4. Spray the waffle maker with cooking spray.

5. Pour the chaffles mixture in a preheated waffle maker and let it cook for about 2-3 minutes.

6. Once the chaffles are cooked, carefully remove them from the maker and cook the remaining batter.

7. Serve hot with coffee and enjoy!

Nutrition value per Servings:

Protein: 36% 42 kcal Fat: 60% 71 kcal Carbohydrates: 4% 5 kcal

## Asian Cauliflower Chaffles

Servings: 4

Cooking Time: 28 Minutes

**Ingredients:**

For the chaffles:

1 cup cauliflower rice, steamed

1 large egg, beaten

Salt and freshly ground black pepper to taste

1 cup finely grated Parmesan cheese

1 tsp sesame seeds

¼ cup chopped fresh scallions For the dipping sauce:

3 tbsp coconut aminos

1 ½ tbsp plain vinegar

1 tsp fresh ginger puree

1 tsp fresh garlic paste

3 tbsp sesame oil

1 tsp fish sauce

1 tsp red chili flakes

**Directions:**

1. Preheat the waffle iron.

2. In a medium bowl, mix the cauliflower rice, egg, salt, black pepper, and Parmesan cheese.

3. Open the iron and add a quarter of the mixture. Close and cook until crispy, 7 minutes.

4. Transfer the chaffle to a plate and make 3 more chaffles in the same manner.

5. Meanwhile, make the dipping sauce.

6. In a medium bowl, mix all the ingredients for the dipping sauce.

7. Plate the chaffles, garnish with the sesame seeds and scallions and serve with the dipping sauce.

Nutrition value:

Calories 231 Fats 188g Carbs 6.32g Net Carbs 5.42g Protein 9.66g

## Sharp Cheddar Chaffles

Servings: 2

Cooking Time: 10 Minutes

**Ingredients:**

1 organic egg, beaten

½ cup sharp Cheddar cheese, shredded

**Directions:**

1. Preheat a mini waffle iron and then grease it.

2. In a small bowl, place the egg and cheese and stir to combine.

3. Place half of the mixture into preheated waffle iron and cook for about 5 minutes or until golden brown.

4. Repeat with the remaining mixture.

5. Serve warm.

Nutrition value per Servings:

Calories: 145 Fat: 11. Carbohydrates: 8.5g Protein: 9.8g

## Egg-Free Almond Flour Chaffles

Servings: 2

Cooking Time: 10 Minutes

**Ingredients:**

2 tablespoons cream cheese, softened

1 cup mozzarella cheese, shredded

2 tablespoons almond flour

1 teaspoon organic baking powder

**Directions:**

1. Preheat a mini waffle iron and then grease it.

2. In a medium bowl, place all ingredients and with a fork, mix until well combined.

3. Place half of the mixture into preheated waffle iron and cook for about 4-5 minutes or until golden brown.

4. Repeat with the remaining mixture.

5. Serve warm.

Nutrition value per Servings:

Calories: 77 Fat: 9.8g Carbohydrates: 3.2g Sugar: 0.3g Protein: 4.8g

## Mozzarellas & Psyllium Husk Chaffles

Servings: 2

Cooking Time: 8 Minutes

**Ingredients:**

½ cup Mozzarella cheese, shredded

1 large organic egg, beaten

2 tablespoons blanched almond flour

½ teaspoon Psyllium husk powder

¼ teaspoon organic baking powder

**Directions:**

1. Preheat a mini waffle iron and then grease it.

2. In a bowl, place all the ingredients and beat until well combined.

3. Place half of the mixture into preheated waffle iron and cook for about 4 minutes or until golden brown.

4. Repeat with the remaining mixture.

5. Serve warm.

Nutrition value per Servings:

Calories: 101 Net Carb: 1. Fat: 7g Carbohydrates: 2.9g Sugar: 0.2g Protein: 6.7g

## Pumpkin-Cinnamon Churro Sticks

Servings: 2

Cooking Time: 14 Minutes

**Ingredients:**

3 tbsp coconut flour

¼ cup pumpkin puree

1 egg, beaten

½ cup finely grated mozzarella cheese

2 tbsp sugar-free maple syrup + more for serving

1 tsp baking powder

1 tsp vanilla extract

½ tsp pumpkin spice seasoning

1/8 tsp salt

1 tbsp cinnamon powder

**Directions:**

1. Preheat the waffle iron.

2. Mix all the ingredients in a medium bowl until well combined.

3. Open the iron and add half of the mixture. Close and cook until golden brown and crispy, 7 minutes.

4. Remove the chaffle onto a plate and make 1 more with the remaining batter.

5. Cut each chaffle into sticks, drizzle the top with more maple syrup and serve after.

Nutrition value per Servings:

Calories 219 Fats 9.72g Carbs 8.g Net Carbs 4.34g Protein 25.27g

## Chicken Jalapeño Chaffles

Servings: 2

Cooking Time: 14 Minutes

**Ingredients:**

1/8 cup finely grated Parmesan cheese

¼ cup finely grated cheddar cheese

1 egg, beaten

½ cup cooked chicken breasts, diced

1 small jalapeño pepper, deseeded and minced

1/8 tsp garlic powder

1/8 tsp onion powder

1 tsp cream cheese, softened

**Directions:**

1. Preheat the waffle iron.

2. In a medium bowl, mix all the ingredients until adequately combined.

3. Open the iron and add half of the mixture. Close and cook until crispy, 7 minutes.

4. Transfer the chaffle to a plate and make a second chaffle in the same manner.

5. Allow cooling and serve afterward.

Nutrition value:

Calories 201 Fats 11.49g Carbs 3.7 Net Carbs 3.36g Protein 20.11g

## Chocolate & Almond Chaffle

Servings: 3

Cooking Time: 12 Minutes

**Ingredients:**

1 egg

¼ cup mozzarella cheese, shredded

1 oz. cream cheese

2 teaspoons sweetener

1 teaspoon vanilla

2 tablespoons cocoa powder

1 teaspoon baking powder

2 tablespoons almonds, chopped

4 tablespoons almond flour

**Directions:**

1. Blend all the ingredients in a bowl while the waffle maker is preheating.

2. Pour some of the mixture into the waffle maker.

3. Close and cook for 4 minutes.

4. Transfer the chaffle to a plate. Let cool for 2 minutes.

5. Repeat steps using the remaining mixture.

Nutrition value:

Calories 219 Total Fat 13.1g Carbohydrate 9.1g Fiber 3.8g Protein 7.8g Sugars 0.8g

## Keto Chocolate Fudge Chaffle

Servings: 2

Cooking Time: 14 Minutes

**Ingredients:**

1 egg, beaten

¼ cup finely grated Gruyere cheese

2 tbsp unsweetened cocoa powder ¼ tsp baking powder

¼ tsp vanilla extract

2 tbsp erythritol

1 tsp almond flour

1 tsp heavy whipping cream A pinch of salt

**Directions:**

1. Preheat the waffle iron.

2. Add all the ingredients to a medium bowl and mix well.

3. Open the iron and add half of the mixture. Close and cook until golden brown and crispy, 7 minutes.

4. Remove the chaffle onto a plate and make another with the remaining batter.

5. Cut each chaffle into wedges and serve after.

Nutrition value per Servings:

Calories 173 Fats 13.08g Carbs 3.98g Net Carbs 2.28g Protein 12.27g

## Broccoli & Cheese Chaffle

Servings: 2

Cooking Time: 8 Minutes

**Ingredients:**

¼ cup broccoli florets

1 egg, beaten

1 tablespoon almond flour

¼ teaspoon garlic powder

½ cup cheddar cheese

**Directions:**

1. Preheat your waffle maker.
2. Add the broccoli to the food processor.
3. Pulse until chopped.
4. Add to a bowl.
5. Stir in the egg and the rest of the ingredients.
6. Mix well.
7. Pour half of the batter to the waffle maker.
8. Cover and cook for 4 minutes.
9. Repeat procedure to make the next chaffle.

Nutrition value:

Calories 170 Total Fat 13 g Carbohydrate 2 g Protein 11 g Total Sugars 1 g

## Chaffled Brownie Sundae

Servings: 4

Cooking Time: 30 Minutes

**Ingredients:**

For the chaffles:

2 eggs, beaten

1 tbsp unsweetened cocoa powder

1 tbsp erythritol

1 cup finely grated mozzarella cheese For the topping:

3 tbsp unsweetened chocolate, chopped

3 tbsp unsalted butter

½ cup swerve sugar

Low-carb ice cream for topping

1 cup whipped cream for topping

3 tbsp sugar-free caramel sauce

**Directions:**

1. For the chaffles:
2. Preheat the waffle iron.
3. Meanwhile, in a medium bowl, mix all the ingredients for the chaffles.
4. Open the iron, pour in a quarter of the mixture, cover, and cook until crispy, 7 minutes.
5. Remove the chaffle onto a plate and make 3 more with the remaining batter.
6. Plate and set aside.
7. For the topping:
8. Meanwhile, melt the chocolate and butter in a medium saucepan with occasional stirring, 2 minutes.
9. To Servings:
10. Divide the chaffles into wedges and top with the ice cream, whipped cream, and swirl the chocolate sauce and caramel sauce on top.
11. Serve immediately.

Nutrition value:

Calories 165 Fats 11.39g Carbs 3.81g Net Carbs 2.91g Protein 79g

## Cream Cheese Chaffle

Servings: 2

Cooking Time: 8 Minutes

**Ingredients:**

1 egg, beaten

1 oz. cream cheese

½ teaspoon vanilla

4 teaspoons sweetener

¼ teaspoon baking powder Cream cheese

**Directions:**

1. Preheat your waffle maker.
2. Add all the ingredients in a bowl.
3. Mix well.
4. Pour half of the batter into the waffle maker.
5. Seal the device.
6. Cook for 4 minutes.
7. Remove the chaffle from the waffle maker.
8. Make the second one using the same steps.
9. Spread remaining cream cheese on top before serving.

Nutrition value:

Calories 169 Total Fat 14.3g Carbohydrate 4g Fiber 4g Protein 7.7g Sugars 0.7g

## Garlic Chaffles

Servings: 4

Cooking Time: 5 Minutes

**Ingredients:**

1/2 cup mozzarella cheese, shredded 1/3 cup cheddar cheese

1 large egg

½ tbsp. garlic powder

1/2 tsp Italian seasoning

1/4 tsp baking powder

**Directions:**

1. Switch on your waffle maker and lightly grease your waffle maker with a brush.
2. Beat the egg with garlic powder, Italian seasoning and baking powder in a small mixing bowl.
3. Add mozzarella cheese and cheddar cheese to the egg mixture and mix well.
4. Pour half of the chaffles batter into the middle of your waffle iron and close the lid.
5. Cook chaffles for about 2-3 minutes until crispy.
6. Once cooked, remove chaffles from the maker.
7. Sprinkle garlic powder on top and enjoy!

Nutrition value per Servings:

Calories 169 Total Fat 14.3g Carbohydrate 4g Fiber 4g Protein 7.7g Sugars 0.7g

## Cinnamon Powder Chaffles

Servings: 2

Cooking Time: 5 Minutes

**Ingredients:**

1 large egg

3/4 cup cheddar cheese, shredded

2 tbsps. coconut flour

1/2 tbsps. coconut oil melted

1 tsp. stevia

1/2 tsp cinnamon powder

1/2 tsp vanilla extract

1/2 tsp psyllium husk powder 1/4 tsp baking powder

**Directions:**

1. Switch on your waffle maker.

2. Grease your waffle maker with cooking spray and heat up on medium heat.

3. In a mixing bowl, beat egg with coconut flour, oil, stevia, cinnamon powder, vanilla, husk powder, and baking powder.

4. Once the egg is beaten well, add in cheese- and mix again.

5. Pour half of the waffle batter into the middle of your waffle iron and close the lid.

6. Cook chaffles for about 2-3 minutes until crispy.

7. Once chaffles are cooked, carefully remove them from the maker.

8. Serve with keto hot chocolate and enjoy!

Nutrition value per Servings:

Protein: 25% 62 kcal Fat: 72% 175 kcal Carbohydrates: 3% 7 kcal

## Chaffles With Raspberry Syrup

Servings: 4

Cooking Time: 38 Minutes

**Ingredients:**

For the chaffles:

1 egg, beaten

½ cup finely shredded cheddar cheese

1 tsp almond flour

1 tsp sour cream

For the raspberry syrup:

1 cup fresh raspberries

¼ cup swerve sugar

¼ cup water

1 tsp vanilla extract

**Directions:**

1. For the chaffles:

2. Preheat the waffle iron.

3. Meanwhile, in a medium bowl, mix the egg, cheddar cheese, almond flour, and sour cream.

4. Open the iron, pour in half of the mixture, cover, and cook until crispy, 7 minutes.

5. Remove the chaffle onto a plate and make another with the remaining batter.

6. For the raspberry syrup:

7. Meanwhile, add the raspberries, swerve sugar, water, and vanilla extract to a medium pot. Set over low heat and cook until the raspberries soften and sugar becomes syrupy. Occasionally stir while mashing the raspberries as you go. Turn the heat off when your desired consistency is achieved and set aside to cool.

8. Drizzle some syrup on the chaffles and enjoy when ready.

Nutrition value:

Calories 105 Fats 7.11g Carbs 4.31g Net Carbs 2.21g Protein 5.83g

## Crispy Bagel Chaffles

Servings: 1

Prep time: 10 min. + day

Cook time: 30 min.

**Ingredients:**

2 eggs

½ cup parmesan cheese

1 tsp bagel seasoning

½ cup mozzarella cheese

2 teaspoons almond flour

**Directions:**

Turn on waffle maker to heat and oil it with cooking spray.

Evenly sprinkle half of cheeses to a griddle and let them melt. Then toast for 30 seconds and leave them wait for batter.

Whisk eggs, other half of cheeses, almond flour, and bagel seasoning in a small bowl. Pour batter into the waffle maker. Cook for 4 minutes.

Let cool for 2-3 minutes before serving.

Nutrition Value per Servings:

Carbs - 6 G   Fat - 20 G   Protein - 21 G   Calories – 287

## Bacon And Ham Chaffle Sandwich

Servings: 2

Prep time: 10 min.

Cook time: 5 min.

**Ingredients:**

3 egg

½ cup grated Cheddar cheese

1 Tbsp almond flour

½ tsp baking powder

FOR THE TOPPINGS:

4 strips cooked bacon

2 pieces Bibb lettuce

2 slices preferable ham

2 slices tomato

**Directions:**

Turn on waffle maker to heat and oil it with cooking spray. Combine all chaffle components in a small bowl.

Add around ¼ of total batter to waffle maker and spread to fill the edges. Close and cook for 4 minutes. Remove and let it cool on a rack.

Repeat for the second chaffle.

Top one chaffle with a tomato slice, a piece of lettuce, and bacon strips, then cover it with second chaffle. Plate and enjoy.

Nutrition Value per Servings:

Carbs - 5 G   Fat - 60 G   Protein - 31 G   Calories – 631

## Parmesan Garlic Chaffle

Servings: 2

Prep time: 5 min.

Cook time: 5 min.

**Ingredients:**

1 Tbsp fresh garlic minced

2 Tbsp butter

1-oz cream cheese, cubed

2 Tbsp almond flour

1 tsp baking soda

2 large eggs

1 tsp dried chives

½ cup parmesan cheese, shredded

¾ cup mozzarella cheese, shredded

**Directions:**

Heat cream cheese and butter in a saucepan over medium-low until melted. Add garlic and cook, stirring, for 2 minutes.

Turn on waffle maker to heat and oil it with cooking spray.

In a small mixing bowl, whisk together flour and baking soda, then set aside.

In a separate bowl, beat eggs for 1 minute 30 seconds on high, then add in cream cheese mixture and beat for 60 seconds more.

Add flour mixture, chives, and cheeses to the bowl and stir well. Add ¼ cup batter to waffle maker.

Close and cook for 4 minutes, until golden brown. Repeat for remaining batter.

Add favorite toppings and serve.

Nutrition Value per Servings:

Carbs - 5 G  Fat - 33 G  Protein - 19 G  Calories - 385

## Buffalo Chicken Chaffles

Servings: 4

Prep time: 5 min.

Cook time: 5 min.

**Ingredients:**

¼ cup almond flour

1 tsp baking powder

2 large eggs

½ cup chicken, shredded

¾ cup sharp cheddar cheese, shredded

¼ cup mozzarella cheese, shredded

¼ cup Red-Hot Sauce + 1 Tbsp for topping ¼ cup feta cheese, crumbled

¼ cup celery, diced

**Directions:**

Whisk baking powder and almond flour in a small bowl and set aside. Turn on waffle maker to heat and oil it with cooking spray.

Beat eggs in a large bowl until frothy.

Add hot sauce and beat until combined. Mix in flour mixture.

Add cheeses and mix until well combined.

Fold in chicken.

Pour batter into waffle maker and cook for 4 minutes. Remove and repeat until all batter is used up.

Top with celery, feta, and hot sauce.

Nutrition Value per Servings:

Carbs - 4 G  Fat - 26 G  Protein - 22 G  Calories - 337

## Garlic Cheese Chaffle Bread Sticks

Servings: 8

Prep time: 5 min.

Cook time: 5 min.

**Ingredients:**

1 medium egg

½ cup mozzarella cheese, grated

2 Tbsp almond flour

½ tsp garlic powder

½ tsp oregano

½ tsp salt

<u>FOR THE TOPPINGS:</u>

2 Tbsp butter, unsalted softened ½ tsp garlic powder

¼ cup grated mozzarella cheese

2 tsp dried oregano for sprinkling

**Directions:**

Turn on waffle maker to heat and oil it with cooking spray. Beat egg in a bowl.

Add mozzarella, garlic powder, flour, oregano, and salt, and mix.

Spoon half of the batter into the waffle maker.

Close and cook for 5 minutes. Remove cooked chaffle. Repeat with remaining batter.

Place chaffles on a tray and preheat the grill.

Mix butter with garlic powder and spread over the chaffles.

Sprinkle mozzarella over top and cook under the broiler for 2-3 minutes, until cheese has melted.

Nutrition Value per Servings:

Carbs - 1 G  Fat - 7 G  Protein - 4 G  Calories – 74

## Egg-Free Coconut Flour Chaffles

Servings: 2

Cooking Time: 10 Minutes

**Ingredients:**

1 tablespoon flaxseed meal

2½ tablespoons water

¼ cup Mozzarella cheese, shredded

1 tablespoon cream cheese, softened

2 tablespoons coconut flour

**Directions:**

1. Preheat a waffle iron and then grease it.

2. In a bowl, place the flaxseed meal and water and mix well.

3. Set aside for about 5 minutes or until thickened.

4. In the bowl of flaxseed mixture, add the remaining ingredients and mix until well combined.

5. Place half of the mixture into preheated waffle iron and cook for about 3-minutes or until golden brown.

6. Repeat with the remaining mixture.

7. Serve warm.

Nutrition value per Servings:

Calories: 76 Net Carb: 2.3g Fat: 4.2g Carbohydrates:6.3g Sugar: 0.1g Protein: 3g

## Cheeseburger Chaffle

Servings: 2

Cooking Time: 15 Minutes

**Ingredients:**

1 lb. ground beef

1 onion, minced

1 tsp. parsley, chopped

1 egg, beaten

Salt and pepper to taste

1 tablespoon olive oil

4 basic chaffles

2 lettuce leaves

2 cheese slices

1 tablespoon dill pickles

Ketchup

Mayonnaise

**Directions:**

1. In a large bowl, combine the ground beef, onion, parsley, egg, salt and pepper.

2. Mix well.

3. Form 2 thick patties.

4. Add olive oil to the pan.

5. Place the pan over medium heat.

6. Cook the patty for 3 to 5 minutes per side or until fully cooked.

7. Place the patty on top of each chaffle.

8. Top with lettuce, cheese and pickles.

9. Squirt ketchup and mayo over the patty and veggies.

10. Top with another chaffle.

Nutrition value:

Calories 325 Total Fat 16.3g Carbohydrate 3g Sugars 1.4g Protein 39.6g

## Buffalo Hummus Beef Chaffles

Servings: 4

Cooking Time: 32 Minutes

**Ingredients:**

2 eggs

1 cup + ¼ cup finely grated cheddar cheese, divided

2 chopped fresh scallions

Salt and freshly ground black pepper to taste

2 chicken breasts, cooked and diced ¼ cup buffalo sauce

3 tbsp low-carb hummus

2 celery stalks, chopped

¼ cup crumbled blue cheese for topping

**Directions:**

1. Preheat the waffle iron.

2. In a medium bowl, mix the eggs, 1 cup of the cheddar cheese, scallions, salt, and black pepper,

3. Open the iron and add a quarter of the mixture. Close and cook until crispy, 7 minutes.

4. Transfer the chaffle to a plate and make 3 more chaffles in the same manner.

5. Preheat the oven to 400 F and line a baking sheet with parchment paper. Set aside.

6. Cut the chaffles into quarters and arrange on the baking sheet.

7. In a medium bowl, mix the chicken with the buffalo sauce, hummus, and celery.

8. Spoon the chicken mixture onto each quarter of chaffles and top with the remaining cheddar cheese.

9. Place the baking sheet in the oven and bake until the cheese melts, 4 minutes.

10. Remove from the oven and top with the blue cheese.

11. Serve afterward.

Nutrition value:

Calories 552 Fats 28.37g Carbs 6.97g Net Carbs 6.07g Protein 59.8g

## Basic Mozzarella Chaffles

Servings: 2

Cooking Time: 6 Minutes

**Ingredients:**

1 large organic egg, beaten

½ cup Mozzarella cheese, shredded finely

**Directions:**

1. Preheat a mini waffle iron and then grease it.

2. In a small bowl, place the egg and Mozzarella cheese and stir to combine.

3. Place half of the mixture into preheated waffle iron and cook for about 2-minutes or until golden brown.

4. Repeat with the remaining mixture.

5. Serve warm.

Nutrition value per Servings:

Calories: 5 Net Carb: 0.4g Fat: 3.7g Carbohydrates: 0.4g Sugar: 0.2g Protein: 5.2g

## Brie And Blackberry Chaffles

Servings: 4

Cooking Time: 36 Minutes

**Ingredients:**

For the chaffles:

2 eggs, beaten

1 cup finely grated mozzarella cheese For the topping:

1 ½ cups blackberries

1 lemon, 1 tsp zest and 2 tbsp juice

1 tbsp erythritol

4 slices Brie cheese

**Directions:**

1. For the chaffles:
2. Preheat the waffle iron.
3. Meanwhile, in a medium bowl, mix the eggs and mozzarella cheese.
4. Open the iron, pour in a quarter of the mixture, cover, and cook until crispy, 7 minutes.
5. Remove the chaffle onto a plate and make 3 more with the remaining batter.
6. Plate and set aside.
7. For the topping:
8. In a medium pot, add the blackberries, lemon zest, lemon juice, and erythritol. Cook until the blackberries break and the sauce thickens, 5 minutes. Turn the heat off.
9. Arrange the chaffles on the baking sheet and place two Brie cheese slices on each. Top with blackberry mixture and transfer the baking sheet to the oven.
10. Bake until the cheese melts, 2 to 3 minutes.
11. Remove from the oven, allow cooling and serve afterward.

Nutrition value:

Calories 576 Fats 42.22g Carbs 7.07g Net Carbs 3.67g Protein 42.35g

## Turkey Chaffle Burger

Servings: 2

Cooking Time: 10 Minutes

**Ingredients:**

2 cups ground turkey

Salt and pepper to taste

1 tablespoon olive oil

4 garlic chaffles

1 cup Romaine lettuce, chopped

1 tomato, sliced

Mayonnaise

Ketchup

**Directions:**

1. Combine ground turkey, salt and pepper.
2. Form thick burger patties.
3. Add the olive oil to a pan over medium heat.
4. Cook the turkey burger until fully cooked on both sides.
5. Spread mayo on the chaffle.
6. Top with the turkey burger, lettuce and tomato.
7. Squirt ketchup on top before topping with another chaffle.

Nutrition value:

Calories 555 Total Fat 21.5g Carbohydrate 4.1g Protein 31.7g Total Sugars 1g

## Double Choco Chaffle

Servings: 2

Cooking Time: 10 Minutes

**Ingredients:**

1 egg

2 teaspoons coconut flour

2 tablespoons sweetener

1 tablespoon cocoa powder

¼ teaspoon baking powder

1 oz. cream cheese

½ teaspoon vanilla

1 tablespoon sugar-free chocolate chips

**Directions:**

1. Put all the ingredients in a large bowl.

2. Mix well.

3. Pour half of the mixture into the waffle maker.

4. Seal the device.

5. Cook for 4 minutes.

6. Uncover and transfer to a plate to cool.

7. Repeat the procedure to make the second chaffle.

Nutrition value:

Calories 171 Total Fat 10.7g Carbohydrate 3g Protein 5.8g Total Sugars 0.4g

## Guacamole Chaffle Bites

Servings: 2

Cooking Time: 14 Minutes

**Ingredients:**

1 large turnip, cooked and mashed

2 bacon slices, cooked and finely chopped

½ cup finely grated Monterey Jack cheese

1 egg, beaten

1 cup guacamole for topping

**Directions:**

1. Preheat the waffle iron.

2. Mix all the ingredients except for the guacamole in a medium bowl.

3. Open the iron and add half of the mixture. Close and cook for 4 minutes. Open the lid, flip the chaffle and cook further until golden brown and crispy, minutes.

4. Remove the chaffle onto a plate and make another in the same manner.

5. Cut each chaffle into wedges, top with the guacamole and serve afterward.

Nutrition value per Servings:

Calories 311 Fats 22.52g Carbs 8.29g Net Carbs 5.79g Protein 13.g

## Mayonnaise & Cream Cheese Chaffles

Servings: 4

Cooking Time: 20 Minutes

**Ingredients:**

4 organic eggs large

4 tablespoons mayonnaise

1 tablespoon almond flour

2 tablespoons cream cheese, cut into small cubes

**Directions:**

1. Preheat a waffle iron and then grease it.

2. In a bowl, place the eggs, mayonnaise and almond flour and with a hand mixer, mix until smooth.

3. Place about ¼ of the mixture into preheated waffle iron.

4. Place about ¼ of the cream cheese cubes on top of the mixture evenly and cook for about 5 minutes or until golden brown.

5. Repeat with the remaining mixture and cream cheese cubes.

6. Serve warm.

Nutrition value per Servings:

Calories: 190 Fat: 17g Carbohydrates: 0.8g Sugar: 0.5g Protein: 6.7g

## Blue Cheese Chaffle Bites

Servings: 2

Cooking Time: 14 Minutes

**Ingredients:**

1 egg, beaten

½ cup finely grated Parmesan cheese ¼ cup crumbled blue cheese

1 tsp erythritol

**Directions:**

1. Preheat the waffle iron.

2. Mix all the ingredients in a bowl.

3. Open the iron and add half of the mixture. Close and cook until crispy, 7 minutes.

4. Remove the chaffle onto a plate and make another with the remaining mixture.

5. Cut each chaffle into wedges and serve afterward.

Nutrition value per Servings:

Calories 19  Fats 13.91g  Carbs 4.03g Net Carbs 4.03g Protein 13.48g

## Raspberries Chaffles

Servings: 2

Cooking Time: 5 Minutes

**Ingredients:**

1 egg

1/2 cup mozzarella cheese, shredded

1 tbsp. almond flour

1/4 cup raspberry puree

1 tbsp. coconut flour for topping

**Directions:**

1. Preheat your waffle makerin line with the manufacturer's Directions.

2. Grease your waffle maker with cooking spray.

3. Mix together egg, almond flour, and raspberry purée.

4. Add cheese and mix until well combined.

5. Pour batter intothe waffle maker.

6. Close the lid.

7. Cook for about 3-4 minutes or until waffles are cooked and not soggy.

8. Once cooked, remove from the maker.

9. Sprinkle coconut flour on top and enjoy!

Nutrition value per Servings:

Calories: 190 Fat: 17g Carbohydrates: 0.8g Sugar: 0.5g Protein: 6.7g

## Simple Chaffle Toast

Servings: 2

Cooking Time: 5 Minutes

**Ingredients:**

1 large egg

1/2 cup shredded cheddar cheese FOR TOPPING

1 egg

3-4 spinach leaves

¼ cup boil and shredded chicken

**Directions:**

1. Preheat your square waffle maker on medium-high heat.

2. Mix together egg and cheese in a bowl and make two chaffles in a chaffle maker

3. Once chaffle are cooked, carefully remove them from the maker.

4. Serve with spinach, boiled chicken, and fried egg.

5. Serve hot and enjoy!

Nutrition value per Servings:

Protein: 39% 99 kcal  Fat: % 153 kcal Carbohydrates: 1% 3 kcal


## Savory Beef Chaffle

Servings: 2

Cooking Time: 15 Minutes

**Ingredients:**

1 teaspoon olive oil

2 cups ground beef

Garlic salt to taste

1 red bell pepper, sliced into strips

1 green bell pepper, sliced into strips

1 onion, minced

1 bay leaf

2 garlic chaffles

Butter

**Directions:**

1. Put your pan over medium heat.

2. Add the olive oil and cook ground beef until brown.

3. Season with garlic salt and add bay leaf.

4. Drain the fat, transfer to a plate and set aside.

5. Discard the bay leaf.

6. In the same pan, cook the onion and bell peppers for 2 minutes.

7. Put the beef back to the pan.

8. Heat for 1 minute.

9. Spread butter on top of the chaffle.

10. Add the ground beef and veggies.

11. Roll or fold the chaffle.

Nutrition value:

Calories 220 Fat 17.8g Carbohydrate 3g Sugars 5.4g  Protein 27.1g


## Chaffles With Almond Flour

Servings: 4

Cooking Time: 5 Minutes

**Ingredients:**

2 large eggs

1/4 cup almond flour

3/4 tsp baking powder

1 cup cheddar cheese, shredded Cooking spray

**Directions:**

1. Switch on your waffle maker and grease with cooking spray.

2. Beat eggs with almond flour and baking powder in a mixing bowl.

3. Once the eggs and cheese are mixed together, add in cheese and mix again.

4. Pour 1/cup of the batter in the dash mini waffle maker and close the lid.

5. Cook chaffles for about 2-3 minutes until crispy and cooked

6. Repeat with the remaining batter

7. Carefully transfer the chafflesto plate.

8. Serve with almonds and enjoy!

Nutrition value per Servings:

Protein: 23% 52 kcal Fat: 72% 15kcal Carbohydrates: 5% 11 kcal

## Nutter Butter Chaffles

Servings: 2

Cooking Time: 14 Minutes

**Ingredients:**

For the chaffles:

2 tbsp sugar-free peanut butter powder

2 tbsp maple (sugar-free) syrup

1 egg, beaten

¼ cup finely grated mozzarella cheese ¼ tsp baking powder

¼ tsp almond butter

¼ tsp peanut butter extract

1 tbsp softened cream cheese For the frosting:

½ cup almond flour

1 cup peanut butter

3 tbsp almond milk

½ tsp vanilla extract

½ cup maple (sugar-free) syrup

**Directions:**

1. Preheat the waffle iron.

2. Meanwhile, in a medium bowl, mix all the ingredients until smooth.

3. Open the iron and pour in half of the mixture.

4. Close the iron and cook until crispy, 6 to 7 minutes.

5. Remove the chaffle onto a plate and set aside.

6. Make a second chaffle with the remaining batter.

7. While the chaffles cool, make the frosting.

8. Pour the almond flour in a medium saucepan and stir-fry over medium heat until golden.

9. Transfer the almond flour to a blender and top with the remaining frosting ingredients. Process until smooth.

10. Spread the frosting on the chaffles and serve afterward.

Nutrition value:

Calories 239 Fats 15.48g Carbs 17.42g Net Carbs 15.92g Protein 7.52g

## Hot Dog Chaffles

Servings: 2

Cooking Time: 14 Minutes

**Ingredients:**

1 egg, beaten

1 cup finely grated cheddar cheese

2 hot dog sausages, cooked

Mustard dressing for topping

8 pickle slices

**Directions:**

1. Preheat the waffle iron.

2. In a medium bowl, mix the egg and cheddar cheese.

3. Open the iron and add half of the mixture. Close and cook until crispy, 7 minutes.

4. Transfer the chaffle to a plate and make a second chaffle in the same manner.

5. To serve, top each chaffle with a sausage, swirl the mustard dressing on top, and then divide the pickle slices on top.

6. Enjoy!

Nutrition value:

Calories 231 Fats 18.29g Carbs 2.8g Net Carbs 2.6g Protein 13.39g

## Keto Reuben Chaffles

Servings: 4

Cooking Time: 28 Minutes

**Ingredients:**

For the chaffles:

2 eggs, beaten

1 cup finely grated Swiss cheese

2 tsp caraway seeds

1/8 tsp salt

½ tsp baking powder For the sauce:

2 tbsp sugar-free ketchup

3 tbsp mayonnaise

1 tbsp dill relish

1 tsp hot sauce

For the filling:

6 oz pastrami

2 Swiss cheese slices

¼ cup pickled radishes

**Directions:**

1. For the chaffles:

2. Preheat the waffle iron.

3. In a medium bowl, mix the eggs, Swiss cheese, caraway seeds, salt, and baking powder.

4. Open the iron and add a quarter of the mixture. Close and cook until crispy, 7 minutes.

5. Transfer the chaffle to a plate and make 3 more chaffles in the same manner.

6. For the sauce:

7. In another bowl, mix the ketchup, mayonnaise, dill relish, and hot sauce.

8. To assemble:

9. Divide on two chaffles; the sauce, the pastrami, Swiss cheese slices, and pickled radishes.

10. Cover with the other chaffles, divide the sandwich in halves and serve.

Nutrition value:

Calories 316Fats 21.78gCarbs 6.52gNet Carbs 5.42gProtein 23.56g

## Carrot Chaffle Cake

Servings: 6

Cooking Time: 24 Minutes

**Ingredients:**

1 egg, beaten

2 tablespoons melted butter

½ cup carrot, shredded

¾ cup almond flour

1 teaspoon baking powder

2 tablespoons heavy whipping cream

2 tablespoons sweetener

1 tablespoon walnuts, chopped

1 teaspoon pumpkin spice

2 teaspoons cinnamon

**Directions:**

1. Preheat your waffle maker.

2. In a large bowl, combine all the ingredients.

3. Pour some of the mixture into the waffle maker.

4. Close and cook for minutes.

5. Repeat steps until all the remaining batter has been used.

Nutrition value:

Calories 294 Total Fat 27g Carbohydrate 11.6g Protein 6.8g Total Sugars 1.7g

## Colby Jack Slices Chaffles

Servings: 1

Cooking Time: 6 Minutes

**Ingredients:**

2 ounces Colby Jack cheese, cut into thin triangle slices

1 large organic egg, beaten

**Directions:**

1. Preheat a waffle iron and then grease it.

2. Arrange 1 thin layer of cheese slices in the bottom of preheated waffle iron.

3. Place the beaten egg on top of the cheese.

4. Now, arrange another layer of cheese slices on top to cover evenly.

5. Cook for about 6 minutes or until golden brown.

6. Serve warm.

Nutrition value per Servings:

Calories: 292 Fat: 23g Carbohydrates: 2.4g Sugar: 0.4g Protein: 18.3g

## Egg & Chives Chaffle Sandwich Roll

Servings: 2

Cooking Time: 0 Minute

**Ingredients:**

2 tablespoons mayonnaise

1 hard-boiled egg, chopped

1 tablespoon chives, chopped

2 basic chaffles

**Directions:**

1. In a bowl, mix the mayo, egg and chives.

2. Spread the mixture on top of the chaffles.

3. Roll the chaffle.

Nutrition value:

Calories 258 Fat 12g Carbohydrate 7.5g Protein 5.9g

## Basic Chaffles Recipe For Sandwiches

Servings: 2

Cooking Time: 5 Minutes

**Ingredients:**

1/2 cup mozzarella cheese, shredded

1 large egg

2 tbsps. almond flour

1/2 tsp psyllium husk powder 1/4 tsp baking powder

**Directions:**

1. Grease your Belgian waffle maker with cooking spray.

2. Beat the egg with a fork; once the egg is beaten, add almond flour, husk powder, and baking powder.

3. Add cheesetothe egg mixture and mix until combined.

4. Pour batter in the center of Belgian waffle and close the lid.

5. Cook chaffles for about 2-3 minutes until well cooked.

6. Carefully transfer the chaffles to plate.

7. The chaffles are perfect for a sandwich base.

Nutrition value per Servings:

Calories 258 Fat 12g Carbohydrate 7.5g Protein 5.9g

## Cereal Chaffle Cake

Servings: 2

Cooking Time: 8 Minutes

**Ingredients:**

1 egg

2 tablespoons almond flour

½ teaspoon coconut flour

1 tablespoon melted butter

1 tablespoon cream cheese

1 tablespoon plain cereal, crushed

¼ teaspoon vanilla extract

¼ teaspoon baking powder

1 tablespoon sweetener

1/8 teaspoon xanthan gum

**Directions:**

1. Plug in your waffle maker to preheat.

2. Add all the ingredients in a large bowl.

3. Mix until well blended.

4. Let the batter rest for 2 minutes before cooking.

5. Pour half of the mixture into the waffle maker.

6. Seal and cook for 4 minutes.

7. Make the next chaffle using the same steps.

Nutrition value:

Calories 154 Fat 21.2g Carbohydrate 5.9g Protein 4.6g Total Sugars 2.7g

## Okonomiyaki Chaffles

Servings: 4

Cooking Time: 28 Minutes

**Ingredients:**

For the chaffles:

2 eggs, beaten

1 cup finely grated mozzarella cheese ½ tsp baking powder

¼ cup shredded radishes For the sauce:

2 tsp coconut aminos

2 tbsp sugar-free ketchup

1 tbsp sugar-free maple syrup

2 tsp Worcestershire sauce For the topping:

1 tbsp mayonnaise

2 tbsp chopped fresh scallions

2 tbsp bonito flakes

1 tsp dried seaweed powder

1 tbsp pickled ginger

**Directions:**

1. For the chaffles:

2. Preheat the waffle iron.

3. In a medium bowl, mix the eggs, mozzarella cheese, baking powder, and radishes.

4. Open the iron and add a quarter of the mixture. Close and cook until crispy, 7 minutes.

5. Transfer the chaffle to a plate and make a 3 more chaffles in the same manner.

6. For the sauce:

7. Combine the coconut aminos, ketchup, maple syrup, and Worcestershire sauce in a medium bowl and mix well.

8. For the topping:

9. In another mixing bowl, mix the mayonnaise, scallions, bonito flakes, seaweed powder, and ginger

10. To Servings:

11. Arrange the chaffles on four different plates and swirl the sauce on top. Spread the topping on the chaffles and serve afterward.

Nutrition value:

Calories 90 Fats 3.32g Carbs 2.97g Net Carbs 2.17g Protein 09g

## Bacon & Chicken Ranch Chaffle

Servings: 2

Cooking Time: 8 Minutes

**Ingredients:**

1 egg

¼ cup chicken cubes, cooked

1 slice bacon, cooked and chopped

¼ cup cheddar cheese, shredded

1 teaspoon ranch dressing powder

**Directions:**

1. Preheat your waffle maker.

2. In a bowl, mix all the ingredients.

3. Add half of the mixture to your waffle maker.

4. Cover and cook for minutes.

5. Make the second chaffle using the same steps.

Nutrition value:

Calories 200 Fat 14 g Carbohydrate 2 g Protein 16 g Total Sugars 1 g

## Keto Cocoa Chaffles

Servings: 2

Cooking Time: 5 Minutes

**Ingredients:**

1 large egg

1/2 cup shredded cheddar cheese

1 tbsp. cocoa powder

2 tbsps. almond flour

**Directions:**

1. Preheat your round waffle maker on medium-high heat.

2. Mix together egg, cheese, almond flour, cocoa powder and vanilla in a small mixing bowl.

3. Pour chaffles mixture into the center of the waffle iron.

4. Close the waffle maker and let cook for 3-5 minutes or until waffle is golden brown and set.

5. Carefully remove chaffles from the waffle

maker.

6. Serve hot and enjoy!

Nutrition value per Servings:

Calories 258 Fat 12g Carbohydrate 7.5g Protein 5.9g

## Barbecue Chaffle

Servings: 2

Cooking Time: 8 Minutes

**Ingredients:**

1 egg, beaten

½ cup cheddar cheese, shredded

½ teaspoon barbecue sauce

¼ teaspoon baking powder

**Directions:**

1. Plug in your waffle maker to preheat.

2. Mix all the ingredients in a bowl.

3. Pour half of the mixture to your waffle maker.

4. Cover and cook for minutes.

5. Repeat the same steps for the next barbecue chaffle.

Nutrition value:

Calories 295 Fat 23 g Carbohydrate 2 g Protein 20 g  Total Sugars 1 g

## Chicken And Chaffle Nachos

Servings: 4

Cooking Time: 33 Minutes

**Ingredients:**

For the chaffles:

2 eggs, beaten

1 cup finely grated Mexican cheese blend For the chicken-cheese topping:

2 tbsp butter

1 tbsp almond flour

¼ cup unsweetened almond milk

1 cup finely grated cheddar cheese + more to garnish

3 bacon slices, cooked and chopped

2 cups cooked and diced chicken breasts

2 tbsp hot sauce

2 tbsp chopped fresh scallions

**Directions:**

1. For the chaffles:

2. Preheat the waffle iron.

3. In a medium bowl, mix the eggs and Mexican cheese blend.

4. Open the iron and add a quarter of the mixture. Close and cook until crispy, 7 minutes.

5. Transfer the chaffle to a plate and make 3 more chaffles in the same manner.

6. Place the chaffles on serving plates and set aside for serving.

7. For the chicken-cheese topping:

8. Melt the butter in a large skillet and mix in the almond flour until brown, 1 minute.

9. Pour the almond milk and whisk until well combined. Simmer until thickened, 2 minutes.

10. Stir in the cheese to melt, 2 minutes and then mix in the bacon, chicken, and hot sauce.

11. Spoon the mixture onto the chaffles and top with some more cheddar cheese.

12. Garnish with the scallions and serve immediately.

Nutrition value:

Calories 524 Fats 37.51g Carbs 3.55g Net Carbs 3.25g Protein 41.86g

## Ham, Cheese & Tomato Chaffle Sandwich

Servings: 2

Cooking Time: 10 Minutes

**Ingredients:**

1 teaspoon olive oil

2 slices ham

4 basic chaffles

1 tablespoon mayonnaise

2 slices Provolone cheese

1 tomato, sliced

**Directions:**

1. Add the olive oil to a pan over medium heat.

2. Cook the ham for 1 minute per side.

3. Spread the chaffles with mayonnaise.

4. Top with the ham, cheese and tomatoes.

5. Top with another chaffle to make a sandwich.

Nutrition value:

Calories 198 Fat 14.7g Carbohydrate 4.6g Sugars 1.5g Protein 12.2g

## Pizza Chaffle

Servings: 2

Prep time: 5 min.

Cook time: 5 min.

**Ingredients:**

1 egg

½ cup mozzarella cheese shredded Pinch of Italian seasoning

1 Tbsp no sugar added pizza sauce

more shredded cheese, pepperoni for topping

**Directions:**

Turn on waffle maker to heat and oil it with cooking spray. Mix egg and seasonings in a small bowl.

Mix in cheese.

Add 1 tsp cheese to hot waffle maker and melt for 30 seconds, then add half batter mixture to waffle maker and cook for 4 minutes, until golden brown.

Remove and repeat with remaining mixture.

Top with pizza sauce, cheese, and pepperoni. Microwave for 20 seconds on high and serve.

Nutrition Value per Servings:

Carbs - 4 G  Fat - 8g  Protein - 4 G  Calories – 178

## Eggs Benedict Chaffle

Servings: 2

Prep time: 20 min.

Cook time: 10 min.

**Ingredients:**

FOR THE CHAFFLE:

2 egg whites

2 Tbsp almond flour

1 Tbsp sour cream

½ cup mozzarella cheese

**FOR THE HOLLANDAISE:**

½ cup salted butter

4 egg yolks

2 Tbsp lemon juice

**FOR THE POACHED EGGS:**

2 eggs

1 Tbsp white vinegar

3 oz deli ham

**Directions:**

Whip egg white until frothy, then mix in remaining ingredients. Turn on waffle maker to heat and oil it with cooking spray.

Cook for 7 minutes until golden brown.

Remove chaffle and repeat with remaining batter. Fill half the pot with water and bring to a boil.

Place heat-safe bowl on top of pot, ensuring bottom doesn't touch the boiling water. Heat butter to boiling in a microwave.

Add yolks to double boiler bowl and bring to boil.

Add hot butter to the bowl and whisk briskly. Cook until the egg yolk mixture has thickened.

Remove bowl from pot and add in lemon juice. Set aside.

Add more water to pot if needed to make the poached eggs (water should completely cover the eggs).

Bring to a simmer. Add white vinegar to water.

Crack eggs into simmering water and cook for 1 minute 30 seconds. Remove using slotted spoon.

Warm chaffles in toaster for 2-3 minutes. Top with ham, poached eggs, and hollandaise sauce.

Nutrition Value per Servings:

Carbs - 4 G  Fat - 26 G  Protein - 26 G  Calories – 365

## Breakfast Chaffle

Servings: 2

Prep time: 5 min.

Cook time: 5 min.

**Ingredients:**

2 eggs

½ cup shredded mozzarella cheese

FOR THE TOPPINGS:

2 ham slices

1 fried egg

**Directions:**

Mix eggs and cheese in a small bowl.

Turn on waffle maker to heat and oil it with cooking spray. Pour half of the batter into the waffle maker.

Cook for 2-4 minutes, remove, and repeat with remaining batter. Place egg and ham between two chaffles to make a sandwich.

Nutrition Value per Servings:

Carbs - 1 G  Fat - 8 G  Protein - 9 G  Calories – 115

## Cheddar Jalapeño Chaffle

Servings: 2

Prep time: 5 min.

Cook time: 5 min.

**Ingredients:**

2 large eggs

½ cup shredded mozzarella ¼ cup almond flour

½ tsp baking powder

¼ cup shredded cheddar cheese

2 Tbsp diced jalapeños jarred or canned

FOR THE TOPPINGS:

½ cooked bacon, chopped

2 Tbsp cream cheese

¼ jalapeño slices

**Directions:**

Turn on waffle maker to heat and oil it with cooking spray.

Mix mozzarella, eggs, baking powder, almond flour, and garlic powder in a bowl. Sprinkle 2 Tbsp cheddar cheese in a thin layer on waffle maker, and ½ jalapeño. Ladle half of the egg mixture on top of the cheese and jalapeños.

Cook for 5 minutes, or until done. Repeat for the second chaffle.

Top with cream cheese, bacon, and jalapeño slices.

Nutrition Value per Servings:

Carbs - 5 G  Fat - 18 G  Protein - 18 G  Calories – 307

## Broccoli And Cheese Chaffles

Servings: 1

Prep time: 5 min.

Cook time: 5 min.

**Ingredients:**

☐ cup raw broccoli, finely chopped

¼ cup shredded cheddar cheese

1 egg

½ tsp garlic powder

½ tsp dried minced onion

Salt and pepper, to taste

**Directions:**

Turn on waffle maker to heat and oil it with cooking spray. Beat egg in a small bowl.

Fold in cheese, broccoli, onion, garlic powder, salt, and pepper. Pour egg mixture into waffle maker. Cook for 4 minutes, or until done. Remove from waffle maker with a fork.

Serve with sour cream or butter.

Nutrition Value per Servings:

Carbs - 4 G  Fat - 9 G  Protein - 7 G  Calories – 125

## Hash Brown Chaffle

Servings: 2

Prep time: 20 min.

Cook time: 10 min.

**Ingredients:**

1 large jicama root, peeled and shredded ½ medium onion, minced

2 garlic cloves, pressed

1 cup cheddar shredded cheese

2 eggs

Salt and pepper, to taste

**Directions:**

Place jicama in a colander, sprinkle with 1-2 tsp salt, and let drain. Squeeze out all excess liquid.

Microwave jicama for 5-8 minutes.

Mix ¾ of cheese and all other ingredients in a bowl.

Sprinkle 1-2 tsp cheese on waffle maker, add 3 Tbsp mixture, and top with 1-2 tsp cheese. Cook for 5-6 minutes, or until done.

Remove and repeat for remaining batter.

Serve while hot with preferred toppings.

Nutrition Value per Servings:

Carbs - 9 G  Fat - 6 G  Protein - 4 G  Calories – 194

## Chicken Parmesan Chaffle

Servings: 2

Prep time: 5 min.

Cook time: 10 min.

**Ingredients:**

☐ cup cooked chicken

1 egg

☐ cup shredded mozzarella cheese ¼ tsp basil, chopped

¼ garlic, minced

2 Tbsp tomato sauce

2 Tbsp mozzarella cheese

**Directions:**

Turn on waffle maker to heat and oil it with cooking spray.

Mix egg, basil, chicken, garlic, and ☐ cup mozzarella in a small bowl. Add half of the batter to the waffle maker and cook for 4 minutes, or until done. Remove and repeat for remaining batter.

Let each chaffle sit for 2 minutes.

Top each chaffle with sauce and sprinkle with 2 Tbsp mozzarella cheese. Preheat oven to 400°F and bake chaffles until cheese is melted.

Nutrition Value per Servings:

Carbs - 2g  Fat - 13 G  Protein - 14 G  Calories – 135

## Red Velvet Chaffles

Servings: 2

Cooking Time: 8 Minutes

**Ingredients:**

2 tablespoons cacao powder

2 tablespoons erythritol

1 organic egg, beaten

2 drops super red food coloring

¼ teaspoon organic baking powder

1 tablespoon heavy whipping cream

**Directions:**

1. Preheat a mini waffle iron and then grease it.

2. In a medium bowl, put all ingredients and with a fork, mix until well combined.

3. Place half of the mixture into preheated waffle iron and cook for about 4 minutes.

4. Repeat with the remaining mixture.

5. Serve warm.

Nutrition value:

Calories 70 Fat 9 g  Carbs 3.2 g  Sugar 0.2 g  Protein 3.9 g

## Mayonnaise Chaffles

Servings: 2

Cooking Time: 10 Minutes

**Ingredients:**

1 large organic egg, beaten 1 tablespoon mayonnaise

2 tablespoons almond flour

1/8 teaspoon organic baking powder

1 teaspoon water 2-4 drops liquid stevia

**Directions:**

1. Preheat a mini waffle iron and then grease it.

2. In a medium bowl, put all ingredients and with a fork, mix until well combined. Place half of the mixture into preheated waffle iron and cook for about 4-5 minutes.

3. Repeat with the remaining mixture.

4. Serve warm.

Nutrition value:

Calories 110 Fat 8.7 g  Carbs 3.4 g  Protein 3.2 g

## Layered Chaffles

Servings: 2

Cooking Time: 10 Minutes

**Ingredients:**

1 organic egg, beaten and divided

½ cup cheddar cheese, shredded and divided

Pinch of salt

**Directions:**

1. Preheat a mini waffle iron and then grease it.

2. Place about 1/8 cup of cheese in the bottom of the waffle iron and top with half of the beaten egg.

3. Now, place 1/8 cup of cheese on top and cook for about 4-5 minutes.

4. Repeat with the remaining cheese and egg.

5. Serve warm.

Nutrition value:

Calories 145 Fat 11.g Carbs 0.5 g  Protein 9.8 g

## Cream Mini-Chaffles

Servings: 2

Cooking Time: 10 Minutes

**Ingredients:**

2 tsp coconut flour

4 tsp swerve/monk fruit

¼ tsp baking powder

1 egg

1 oz cream cheese

½ tsp vanilla extract

**Directions:**

1. Turn on waffle maker to heat and oil it with cooking spray.

2. Mix swerve/monk fruit, coconut flour, and baking powder in a small mixing bowl.

3. Add cream cheese, egg, vanilla extract, and whisk until well-combined.

4. Add batter into waffle maker and cook for 3-minutes, until golden brown.

5. Serve with your favorite toppings.

Nutrition value:

Carbs: 4 g ;Fat: 8 g ; Protein: 2 g ; Calories: 73

## Pumpkin & Psyllium Husk Chaffles

Servings: 4

Cooking Time: 16 Minutes

**Ingredients:**

2 organic eggs

½ cup mozzarella cheese, shredded

1 tablespoon homemade pumpkin puree

2 teaspoons Erythritol

½ teaspoon psyllium husk powder

1/3 teaspoon ground cinnamon

Pinch of salt

½ teaspoon organic vanilla extract

**Directions:**

1. Preheat a mini waffle iron and then grease it.

2. In a bowl, place all ingredients and beat until well combined.

3. Place ¼ of the mixture into preheated waffle iron and cook for about 4 minutes or until golden brown.

4. Repeat with the remaining mixture.

5. Serve warm.

Nutrition value per Servings:

Calories: 214 Fat: 2.8g Carbohydrates: 1.8g Protein: 3.9g

## Blackberry Chaffles

Servings: 2

Cooking Time: 8 Minutes

**Ingredients:**

1 organic egg, beaten

1/3 cup Mozzarella cheese, shredded

1 teaspoon cream cheese, softened

1 teaspoon coconut flour

¼ teaspoon organic baking powder

¾ teaspoon powdered Erythritol

¼ teaspoon ground cinnamon

¼ teaspoon organic vanilla extract

Pinch of salt

1 tablespoon fresh blackberries

**Directions:**

1. Preheat a mini waffle iron and then grease it.

2. In a bowl, place all ingredients except for blackberries and beat until well combined.

3. Fold in the blackberries.

4. Place half of the mixture into preheated waffle iron and cook for about minutes or until golden brown.

5. Repeat with the remaining mixture.

6. Serve warm.

Nutrition value per Servings:

Calories: 121 Fat: 7.5g Carbohydrates: 4.5g Protein: 8.9g

## Pumpkin Cream Cheese Chaffles

Servings: 2

Cooking Time: 10 Minutes

**Ingredients:**

1 organic egg, beaten

½ cup Mozzarella cheese, shredded

1½ tablespoon sugar-free pumpkin puree

2 teaspoons heavy cream

1 teaspoon cream cheese, softened

1 tablespoon almond flour

1 tablespoon Erythritol

½ teaspoon pumpkin pie spice

½ teaspoon organic baking powder

1 teaspoon organic vanilla extract

**Directions:**

1. Preheat a mini waffle iron and then grease it.

2. In a medium bowl, place all ingredients and with a fork, mix until well combined.

3. Place half of the mixture into preheated waffle iron and cook for about 5 minutes or until golden brown.

4. Repeat with the remaining mixture.

5. Serve warm.

Nutrition value per Servings:

Calories: 110 Fat: 4.3g Carbohydrates: 3.3g Sugar: 1g Protein: 5.2g

## Cinnamon Sugar Chaffles

Servings: 2

Cooking Time: 12 Minutes

**Ingredients:**

2 eggs

1 cup Mozzarella cheese, shredded

2 tbsp blanched almond flour ½ tbsp butter, melted

2 tbsp Erythritol

½ tsp cinnamon

½ tsp vanilla extract

½ tsp psyllium husk powder, optional ¼ tsp baking powder, optional

1 tbsp melted butter, for topping

¼ cup Erythritol, for topping

¾ tsp cinnamon, for topping

**Directions:**

1. Pour enough batter into the waffle maker and cook for 4 minutes.

2. Once the cooked, carefully remove the chaffle and set aside.

3. Repeat with the remaining batter the same steps.

4. Stir together the cinnamon and erythritol.

5. Finish by brushing your chaffles with the melted butter and then sprinkle with cinnamon sugar.

Nutrition value: Calories per Servings:

208 Kcal ; Fats: 16 g ; Carbs: 4 g ; Protein: 11 g

## Cream Cheese Chaffles

Servings: 2

Cooking Time: 8 Minutes

**Ingredients:**

2 teaspoons coconut flour

3 teaspoons Erythritol

¼ teaspoon organic baking powder

1 organic egg, beaten

1 ounce cream cheese, softened

½ teaspoon organic vanilla extract

**Directions:**

1. Preheat a mini waffle iron and then grease it.

2. In a bowl, place flour, Erythritol and baking powder and mix well.

3. Add the egg, cream cheese and vanilla extract and beat until well combined.

4. Place half of the mixture into preheated waffle iron and cook for about 3-minutes or until golden brown.

5. Repeat with the remaining mixture.

6. Serve warm.

Nutrition value per Servings:

Calories: 95  Fat: 4g Carbohydrates: 2.6g Sugar: 0.3g Protein: 4.2g

## Mozzarella & Butter Chaffles

Servings: 2

Cooking Time: 8 Minutes

**Ingredients:**

1 large organic egg, beaten

¾ cup Mozzarella cheese, shredded

½ tablespoon unsalted butter, melted

2 tablespoons blanched almond flour

2 tablespoons Erythritol

½ teaspoon ground cinnamon

½ teaspoon Psyllium husk powder

¼ teaspoon organic baking powder

½ teaspoon organic vanilla extract

**Directions:**

1. Preheat a waffle iron and then grease it.

2. In a medium bowl, place all ingredients and with a fork, mix until well combined.

3. Place half of the mixture into preheated waffle iron and cook for about 5 minutes or until golden brown.

4. Repeat with the remaining mixture.

5. Serve warm.

Nutrition value per Servings:

Calories 208  Fat 13.5g Carbohydrate 0.7g Protein 8.2g Sugars 0.6g

## Pumpkin Pecan Chaffles

Servings: 2

Cooking Time: 10 Minutes

**Ingredients:**

1 egg

½ cup mozzarella cheese grated

1 Tbsp pumpkin puree

½ tsp pumpkin spice

1 tsp erythritol low carb sweetener

2 Tbsp almond flour

2 Tbsp pecans, toasted chopped

1 cup heavy whipped cream

¼ cup low carb caramel sauce

**Directions:**

1. Turn on waffle maker to heat and oil it with cooking spray.

2. In a bowl, beat egg.

3. Mix in mozzarella, pumpkin, flour, pumpkin spice, and erythritol.

4. Stir in pecan pieces.

5. Spoon one half of the batter into waffle maker and spread evenly.

6. Close and cook for 5 minutes.

7. Remove cooked waffles to a plate.

8. Repeat with remaining batter.

9. Serve with pecans, whipped cream, and low carb caramel sauce.

Nutrition value:

Carbs: 4 g ; Fat: 17 g ; Protein: 11 g ; Calories: 210

## Taco Chaffle Shell

Servings: 1

Prep time: 5 min.

Cook time: 8 min.

**Ingredients:**

1 egg white

¼ cup shredded Monterey jack cheese

¼ cup shredded sharp cheddar cheese

¾ tsp water

1 tsp coconut flour

¼ tsp baking powder

⅛ tsp chili powder

Pinch of salt

**Directions:**

Turn on waffle maker to heat and oil it with cooking spray. Mix all components in a bowl.

Spoon half of the batter on the waffle maker and cook for 4 minutes.

Remove chaffle and set aside. Repeat for remaining chaffle batter.

Turn over a muffin pan and set chaffle between the cups to form a shell. Allow to set for 2-4 minutes. Remove and serve with your favorite taco recipe.

Nutrition Value per Servings:

Carbs - 4 G   Fat - 19 G   Protein - 18 G   Calories – 258

## Pulled Pork Chaffle

Servings: 8

Prep time: 10 min.

Cook time: 8 h.

**Ingredients:**

1 cup shredded cheddar cheese

2 eggs

½ tsp BBQ Rub

5 lbs pork butt

¼ cup BBQ Rub

2 Tbsp yellow mustard

½ cup sweet BBQ Sauce

**Directions:**

Brush mustard on each side of pork butt and season with rub.

Set smoker to 250°F. Smoke, uncovered, for about 4 hours, then wrap tightly, using butcher paper, and cook until internal temperature is 205°F.

Let pork rest for at least 1 hour before shredding it. Mix cheese and eggs in a small bowl.

Scoop out ¼ cup of the mixture and pour into waffle maker. Cook for 5 minutes. Top chaffles with shredded pork and BBQ sauce.

Nutrition Value per Servings:

Carbs - 5 G   Fat - 14 G   Protein - 36 G   Calories – 279

## Chicken Bacon Chaffle

Servings: 2

Prep time: 5 min.

Cook time: 5 min.

**Ingredients:**

1 egg

☐ cup cooked chicken, diced

1 piece of bacon, cooked and crumbled

☐ cup shredded cheddar jack cheese

1 tsp powdered ranch dressing

**Directions:**

Turn on waffle maker to heat and oil it with cooking spray. Mix egg, dressing, and Monterey cheese in a small bowl. Add bacon and chicken.

Add half of the batter to the waffle maker and cook for 3-4 minutes. Remove and cook remaining batter to make a second chaffle.

Let chaffles sit for 2 minutes before serving.

Nutrition Value per Servings:

Carbs - 2 G  Fat - 14 G  Protein - 16 G  Calories - 200

## Spiced Pumpkin Chaffles

Servings: 2

Cooking Time: 8 Minutes

**Ingredients:**

1 organic egg, beaten

½ cup Mozzarella cheese, shredded

1 tablespoon sugar-free canned solid pumpkin

¼ teaspoon ground cinnamon

Pinch of ground cloves

Pinch of ground nutmeg

Pinch of ground ginger

**Directions:**

1. Preheat a mini waffle iron and then grease it.

2. In a medium bowl, place all ingredients and with a fork, mix until well combined.

3. Place half of the mixture into preheated waffle iron and cook for about 4 minutes or until golden brown.

4. Repeat with the remaining mixture.

5. Serve warm.

Nutrition value per Servings:

Calories: 98  Fat: 3.5g Carbohydrates: 1.4g Sugar: 0.5g Protein: 4.9g

## Vanilla Chaffle

Servings: 2

Cooking Time: 8 Minutes

**Ingredients:**

2 tbsp butter, softened

2 oz cream cheese, softened

2 eggs

¼ cup almond flour

2 tbsp coconut flour

1 tsp baking powder

1 tsp vanilla extract

¼ cup confectioners

Pinch of pink salt

**Directions:**

1. Preheat the waffle maker and spray with non-stick cooking spray.

2. Melt the butter and set aside for a minute to cool.

3. Add the eggs into the melted butter and whisk until creamy.

4. Pour in the sweetener, vanilla, extract, and salt. Blend properly.

5. Next add the coconut flour, almond flour, and baking powder. Mix well.

6. Pour into the waffle maker and cook for 4 minutes.

7. Repeat the process with the remaining batter.

8. Remove and set aside to cool.
9. Enjoy.

Nutrition value:

Calories: 202 Kcal ; Fats: 27 g ; Carbs: 9 g ; Protein: 23 g

## Whipping Cream Pumpkin Chaffles

Servings: 4

Cooking Time: 12 Minutes

**Ingredients:**

2 organic eggs

2 tablespoons homemade pumpkin puree

2 tablespoons heavy whipping cream

1 tablespoon coconut flour

1 tablespoon Erythritol

1 teaspoon pumpkin pie spice

½ teaspoon organic baking powder

½ teaspoon organic vanilla extract

Pinch of salt

½ cup Mozzarella cheese, shredded

**Directions:**

1. Preheat a mini waffle iron and then grease it.

2. In a bowl, place all the ingredients except Mozzarella cheese and beat until well combined.

3. Add the Mozzarella cheese and stir to combine.

4. Place half of the mixture into preheated waffle iron and cook for about 6 minutes or until golden brown.

5. Repeat with the remaining mixture.

6. Serve warm.

Nutrition value per Servings:

Calories: 81 Fat: 5.9g Carbohydrates: 3.1g Sugar: 0.5g Protein: 4.3g

## Chocolate Vanilla Chaffles

Servings: 2

Cooking Time: 5 Minutes

**Ingredients:**

½ cup shredded mozzarella cheese

1 egg

1 Tbsp granulated sweetener

1 tsp vanilla extract

1 Tbsp sugar-free chocolate chips

2 Tbsp almond meal/flour

**Directions:**

1. Turn on waffle maker to heat and oil it with cooking spray.

2. Mix all components in a bowl until combined.

3. Pour half of the batter into waffle maker.

4. Cook for 2-minutes, then remove and repeat with remaining batter.

5. Top with more chips and favorite toppings.

Nutrition value:

Carbs: 23 g ;Fat: 3 g ;Protein: 4 g ;Calories: 134

## Churro Waffles

Servings: 1

Cooking Time: 10 Minutes

**Ingredients:**

1 tbsp coconut cream

1 egg

6 tbsp almond flour

¼ tsp xanthan gum

½ tsp cinnamon

2 tbsp keto brown sugar

Coating:

2 tbsp butter, melt

1 tbsp keto brown sugar

Warm up your waffle maker.

**Directions:**

Pour half of the batter to the waffle pan and cook for 5 minutes.

Carefully remove the cooked waffle and repeat the steps with the remaining batter.

Allow the chaffles to cool and spread with the melted butter and top with the brown sugar.

Enjoy.

Nutrition value:

Calories: 178 Kcal ; Fats: 15.7 g ; Carbs: 3.9 g ; Protein: 2 g

## Chocolate Chips Lemon Chaffles

Servings: 4

Cooking Time: 8 Minutes

**Ingredients:**

2 organic eggs

½ cup Mozzarella cheese, shredded

¾ teaspoon organic lemon extract

½ teaspoon organic vanilla extract

2 teaspoons Erythritol

½ teaspoon psyllium husk powder

Pinch of salt

1 tablespoon 70% dark chocolate chips

¼ teaspoon lemon zest, grated finely

**Directions:**

1.  Preheat a mini waffle iron and then grease it.

2.  In a bowl, place all ingredients except chocolate chips and lemon zest and beat until well combined.

3.  Gently, fold in the chocolate chips and lemon zest.

4.  Place ¼ of the mixture into preheated waffle iron and cook for about minutes or until golden brown.

5.  Repeat with the remaining mixture.

6.  Serve warm.

Nutrition value per Servings:

Calories: 111 Fat: 4.8g Carbohydrates: 1.5g Sugar: 0.3g Protein: 4.3g

## Mocha Chaffles

Servings: 3

Cooking Time: 9 Minutes

**Ingredients:**

1 organic egg, beaten

1 tablespoon cacao powder

1 tablespoon Erythritol

¼ teaspoon organic baking powder

2 tablespoons cream cheese, softened

1 tablespoon mayonnaise

¼ teaspoon instant coffee powder

Pinch of salt

1 teaspoon organic vanilla extract

**Directions:**

1. Preheat a mini waffle iron and then grease it.

2. In a medium bowl, place all ingredients and with a fork, mix until well combined.

3. Place 1/of the mixture into preheated waffle iron and cook for about 2½-3 minutes or until golden brown.

4. Repeat with the remaining mixture.

5. Serve warm.

Nutrition value per Servings:

Calories: 83 Fat: 7.5g Carbohydrates: 1.5g Sugar: 0.3g Protein: 2.7g

## Carrot Chaffles

Servings: 6

Cooking Time: 18 Minutes

**Ingredients:**

¾ cup almond flour

1 tablespoon walnuts, chopped

2 tablespoons powdered Erythritol

1 teaspoon organic baking powder

½ teaspoon ground cinnamon

½ teaspoon pumpkin pie spice

1 organic egg, beaten

2 tablespoons heavy whipping cream

2 tablespoons butter, melted

½ cup carrot, peeled and shredded

**Directions:**

1. Preheat a mini waffle iron and then grease it.

2. In a bowl, place the flour, walnut, Erythritol, cinnamon, baking powder and spices and mix well.

3. Add the egg, heavy whipping cream and butter and mix until well combined.

4. Gently, fold in the carrot.

5. Add about 3 tablespoons of the mixture into preheated waffle iron and cook for about 2½-3 minutes or until golden brown.

6. Repeat with the remaining mixture.

7. Serve warm.

Nutrition value per Servings:

Calories: 165 Fat: 14.7g Carbohydrates: 4.4g Sugar: 1g Protein: 1.5g

## Ube Chaffles With Ice Cream

Servings: 2

Cooking Time: 10 Minutes

**Ingredients:**

1/3 cup mozzarella cheese, shredded

1 tbsp whipped cream cheese

2 tbsp sweetener

1 egg

2-3 drops ube or pandan extract 1/2 tsp baking powder

Keto ice cream

**Directions:**

1. Add in 2 or 3 drops of ube extract, mix until creamy and smooth.

2. Pour half of the batter mixture in the mini waffle maker and cook for about 5 minutes.

3. Repeat the same steps with the remaining batter mixture.

4. Top with keto ice cream and enjoy.

Nutrition value:

Calories 265 ; Fats: 16 g ; Carbs: 7 g ; Protein: 22 g

## Berries Chaffles

Servings: 2

Cooking Time: 10 Minutes

**Ingredients:**

1 organic egg

1 teaspoon organic vanilla extract

1 tablespoon of almond flour

1 teaspoon organic baking powder Pinch of ground cinnamon

1 cup Mozzarella cheese, shredded

2 tablespoons fresh blueberries

2 tablespoons fresh blackberries

**Directions:**

1. Preheat a waffle iron and then grease it.

2. In a bowl, place thee egg and vanilla extract and beat well.

3. Add the flour, baking powder and cinnamon and mix well.

4. Add the Mozzarella cheese and mix until just combined.

5. Gently, fold in the berries.

6. Place half of the mixture into preheated waffle iron and cook for about 4-5 minutes or until golden brown.

7. Repeat with the remaining mixture.

8. Serve warm.

Nutrition value per Servings:

Calories: 112 Fat: 6.7g Carbohydrates: 5g

Sugar: 1.Protein: 7g

## Cinnamon Swirl Chaffles

Servings: 3

Cooking Time: 12 Minutes

**Ingredients:**

For Chaffles:

1 organic egg

½ cup Mozzarella cheese, shredded

1 tablespoon almond flour

¼ teaspoon organic baking powder

1 teaspoon granulated Erythritol

1 teaspoon ground cinnamon For Topping:

1 tablespoon butter

1 teaspoon ground cinnamon

2 teaspoons powdered Erythritol

**Directions:**

1. Preheat a waffle iron and then grease it.

2. For chaffles: in a bowl, place all ingredients and mix until well combined.

3. For topping: in a small microwave-safe bowl, place all ingredients and microwave for about 15 seconds.

4. Remove from microwave and mix well.

5. Place 1/3 of the chaffles mixture into preheated waffle iron.

6. Top with 1/3 of the butter mixture and with a skewer, gently swirl into the chaffles mixture.

7. Cook for about 3-4 minutes or until golden brown.

8. Repeat with the remaining chaffles and topping mixture.

9. Serve warm.

Nutrition value per Servings:

Calories: 87  Fat: 7.4g  Carbohydrates: 2.1g  Sugar: 0.2g  Protein: 3.3g

## Colby Jack Chaffles

Servings: 1

Cooking Time: 6 Minutes

**Ingredients:**

2 ounces colby jack cheese, sliced thinly in triangles

1 large organic egg, beaten

**Directions:**

1. Preheat a waffle iron and then grease it.
2. Arrange 1 thin layer of cheese slices in the bottom of preheated waffle iron.
3. Place the beaten egg on top of the cheese.
4. Now, arrange another layer of cheese slices on top to cover evenly.
5. Cook for about 6 minutes.
6. Serve warm.

Nutrition value:

Calories 292  Fat 23 g  Carbs 2.4 g  Sugar 0.4 g  Protein 18.3 g

## Acocado Chaffle Toast

Servings: 2

Cooking Time: 8 Minutes

**Ingredients:**

½ avocado

1 egg

½ cup cheddar cheese, finely shredded

1 tbsp almond flour

1 tsp lemon juice, fresh

Salt, ground pepper to taste

Parmesan cheese, finely shredded for garnishing

**Directions:**

1. Warm up your mini waffle maker.
2. Mix the egg, almond flour with cheese in a small bowl.
3. For a crispy crust, add a teaspoon of shredded cheese to the waffle maker and cook for seconds.
4. Then, pour the mixture into the waffle maker and cook for 5 minutes or until crispy.
5. Repeat with remaining batter.
6. Mash avocado with a fork until well combined and add lemon juice, salt, pepper
7. Top each chaffle with avocado mixture. Sprinkle with parmesan and enjoy!

Nutrition value:

Calories  250  Fat:  23 g  ;  Carbs: 9 g  ;  Protein: 14 g

## Bacon And Ham Chaffle Sandwich

Servings: 2

Cooking Time: 5 Minutes

**Ingredients:**

3 egg

½ cup grated Cheddar cheese

1 Tbsp almond flour

½ tsp baking powder

For the toppings:

4 strips cooked bacon

2 pieces Bibb lettuce

2 slices preferable ham

2 slices tomato

**Directions:**

1. Turn on waffle maker to heat and oil it with cooking spray.

2. Combine all chaffle components in a small bowl.

3. Add around ¼ of total batter to waffle maker and spread to fill the edges. Close and cook for 4 minutes.

4. Remove and let it cool on a rack.

5. Repeat for the second chaffle.

6. Top one chaffle with a tomato slice, a piece of lettuce, and bacon strips, then cover it with second chaffle.

7. Plate and enjoy.

Nutrition value:

Carbs: 5 g ;Fat: 60 g ;Protein: 31 g ;Calories: 631

## Ham And Jalapenos Chaffle

Servings: 3

Cooking Time: 9 Minutes

**Ingredients:**

2 lbs cheddar cheese, finely grated

2 large eggs

½ jalapeno pepper, finely grated

2 ounces ham steak

1 medium scallion

2 tsp coconut flour

**Directions:**

1. Spray your waffle iron with cooking spray and heat for 3 minutes.

2. Pour 1/4 of the batter mixture into the waffle iron.

3. Cook for 3 minutes, until crispy around the edges.

4. Remove the waffles from the heat and repeat until all the batter is finished.

5. Once done, allow them to cool to room temperature and enjoy.

6. Shred the cheddar cheese using a fine grater.

7. Deseed the jalapeno and grate using the same grater.

8. Finely chop the scallion and ham.

Nutrition value:

Calories 120 ; Fat: 10 g ; Carbs: 2 g ; Protein: 12

## Burger Chaffle

Servings: 1

Cooking Time: 10 Minutes

**Ingredients:**

For the Cheeseburgers:

1/3 lb beef, ground

½ tsp garlic salt

3 slices American cheese For the Chaffles:

1 large egg

½ cup mozzarella, finely shredded Salt and ground pepper to taste For the Big Mac Sauce:

2 tsp mayonnaise

1 tsp ketchup

To Assemble:

2 tbsp lettuce, shredded

4 dill pickles

2 tsp onion, minced

To assemble burgers:

**Directions:**

1. Take your burger patties and place them on one chaffle. Top with shredded lettuce, onions and pickles.

2. Spread the sauce over the other chaffle and place it on top of the veggies, sauce side down.

3. Enjoy.

Nutrition value:

Calories : 850 ; Fat: 56 g ; Carbs: 8 g ; Protein: 67 g

## Bbq Chicken Chaffles

Servings: 2

Cooking Time: 8 Minutes

**Ingredients:**

1 1/3 cups grass-fed cooked chicken, chopped
½ cup Cheddar cheese, shredded

1 tablespoon sugar-free BBQ sauce

1 organic egg, beaten

1 tablespoon almond flour

**Directions:**

1. Preheat a mini waffle iron and then grease it.

2. In a bowl, place all ingredients and mix until well combined.

3. Place half of the mixture into preheated waffle iron and cook for about 4 minutes or until golden brown.

4. Repeat with the remaining mixture.

5. Serve warm.

Nutrition value per Servings:

Calories: 320 Fat: 16.3g Carbohydrates: 4g Sugar: 2g Protein: 36.9g

## Avocado Chaffle

Servings: 2

Cooking Time: 10 Minutes

**Ingredients:**

½ avocado, sliced

½ tsp lemon juice

⅛ tsp salt

⅛ tsp black pepper

1 egg

½ cup shredded cheese

¼ crumbled feta cheese

1 cherry tomato, halved

**Directions:**

1. Mash together avocado, lemon juice, salt, and pepper until well-combined.

2. Turn on waffle maker to heat and oil it with cooking spray.

3. Beat egg in a small mixing bowl.

4. Place ⅛ cup of cheese on waffle maker, then spread half of the egg mixture over it and top with ⅛ cup of cheese.

5. Close and cook for 3-4 minutes. Repeat for remaining batter.

6. Let chaffles cool for 3-4 minutes, then spread avocado mix on top of each.

7. Top with crumbled feta and cherry tomato halves.

Nutrition value:

Carbs: 5 g ;Fat: 19 g ;Protein: 7 g ;Calories: 232

## Zucchini & Onion Chaffles

Servings: 4

Cooking Time: 16 Minutes

**Ingredients:**

2 cups zucchini, grated and squeezed

½ cup onion, grated and squeezed

2 organic eggs

½ cup Mozzarella cheese, shredded

½ cup Parmesan cheese, grated

**Directions:**

1. Preheat a waffle iron and then grease it.

2. In a medium bowl, place all ingredients and, mix until well combined.

3. Place ¼ of the mixture into preheated waffle iron and cook for about 4 minutes or until golden brown.

4. Repeat with the remaining mixture.

5. Serve warm.

Nutrition value per Servings:

Calories: 92 Fat: 5.3g Carbohydrates: 3.5g Sugar: 1.8gProtein: 8.6g

## Chaffle Cuban Sandwich

Servings: 1

Prep time: 10 min.

Cook time: 10 min.

**Ingredients:**

1 large egg

1 Tbsp almond flour

1 Tbsp full-fat Greek yogurt ⅛ tsp baking powder

¼ cup shredded Swiss cheese

FOR THE FILLING:

3 oz roast pork

2 oz deli ham

1 slice Swiss cheese

3-5 sliced pickle chips

½ Tbsp Dijon mustard

**Directions:**

Turn on waffle maker to heat and oil it with cooking spray.

Beat egg, yogurt, almond flour, and baking powder in a bowl.

Sprinkle ¼ Swiss cheese on hot waffle maker. Top with half of the egg mixture, then add ¼ of the cheese on top. Close and cook for 3-5 minutes, until golden brown and crispy.

Repeat with remaining batter.

Layer pork, ham, and cheese slice in a small microwaveable bowl. Microwave for 50 seconds, until cheese melts.

Spread the inside of chaffle with mustard and top with pickles. Invert bowl onto chaffle top so that cheese is touching pickles. Place bottom chaffle onto pork and serve.

Nutrition Value per Servings:

Carbs - 4 G  Fat - 46 G  Protein - 33 G  Calories – 522

## Salmon Chaffles

Servings: 2

Prep time: 10 min.

Cook time: 10 min.

**Ingredients:**

1 large egg

½ cup shredded mozzarella

1 Tbsp cream cheese

2 slices salmon

1 Tbsp everything bagel seasoning

**Directions:**

Turn on waffle maker to heat and oil it with cooking spray. Beat egg in a bowl, then add ½ cup mozzarella.

Pour half of the mixture into the waffle maker and cook for 3-4 minutes. Remove and repeat with remaining mixture.

Let chaffles cool, then spread cream cheese, sprinkle with seasoning, and top with salmon.

Nutrition Value per Servings:

Carbs - 3 G  Fat - 10 G  Protein - 5 G  Calories – 201

## 3 Cheeses Herbed Chaffles

Servings: 4

Cooking Time: 12 Minutes

**Ingredients:**

4 tablespoons almond flour

1 tablespoon coconut flour

1 teaspoon mixed dried herbs

½ teaspoon organic baking powder ¼ teaspoon garlic powder

¼ teaspoon onion powder

Salt and freshly ground black pepper, to taste ¼ cup cream cheese, softened

3 large organic eggs

½ cup Cheddar cheese, grated

1/3 cup Parmesan cheese, grated

**Directions:**

1. Preheat a waffle iron and then grease it.

2. In a bowl, mix together the flours, dried herbs, baking powder and seasoning and mix well.

3. In a separate bowl, put cream cheese and eggs and beat until well combined.

4. Add the flour mixture, cheddar and Parmesan cheese and mix until well combined.

5. Place the desired amount of the mixture into preheated waffle iron and cook for about 2-3 minutes or until golden brown.

6. Repeat with the remaining mixture.

7. Serve warm

Nutrition value per Servings:

Calories: 240 Fat: 19g Carbohydrates: 4g Sugar: 0.7g Protein: 12.3g

## Bagel Seasoning Chaffles

Servings: 4

Cooking Time: 20 Minutes

**Ingredients:**

1 large organic egg

1 cup Mozzarella cheese, shredded

1 tablespoon almond flour

1 teaspoon organic baking powder

2 teaspoons bagel seasoning

¼ teaspoon garlic powder

¼ teaspoon onion powder

**Directions:**

1. Preheat a mini waffle iron and then grease it.

2. In a medium bowl, place all ingredients and with a fork, mix until well combined.

3. Place ¼ of the mixture into preheated waffle iron and cook for about 4 minutes or until golden brown.

4. Repeat with the remaining mixture.

5. Serve warm.

Nutrition value per Servings:

Calories: 73 Fat: 5.5g Carbohydrates: 2.3g Sugar: 0.9gProtein: 3.7g

# Grilled Cheese Chaffle

Servings: 1

Cooking Time: 10 Minutes

**Ingredients:**

1 large egg

½ cup mozzarella cheese

2 slices yellow American cheese

2-3 slices cooked bacon, cut in half

1 tsp butter

½ tsp baking powder

**Directions:**

1. Turn on waffle maker to heat and oil it with cooking spray.

2. Beat egg in a bowl.

3. Add mozzarella, and baking powder.

4. Pour half of the mix into the waffle maker and cook for minutes.

5. Remove and repeat to make the second chaffle.

6. Layer bacon and cheese slices in between two chaffles.

7. Melt butter in a skillet and add chaffle sandwich to the pan. Fry on each side for 2-3 minutes covered, until cheese has melted.

8. Slice in half on a plate and serve.

Nutrition value:

Carbs: 4 g ;Fat: 18 g ;Protein: 7 g ;Calories: 233

# Pandan Asian Chaffles

Servings: 2

Cooking Time: 8 Minutes

**Ingredients:**

½ cup cheddar cheese, finely shredded

1 egg

3 drops of pandan extract

1 tbsp almond flour

1/3 tsp garlic powder

**Directions:**

1. Warm up your mini waffle maker.

2. Mix the egg, almond flour, garlic powder with cheese in a small bowl.

3. Add pandan extract to the cheese mixture and mix well.

4. For a crispy crust, add a teaspoon of shredded cheese to the waffle maker and cook for 30 seconds.

5. Then, pour the mixture into the waffle maker and cook for minutes or until crispy.

6. Repeat with remaining batter.

7. Serve with fried chicken wings with bbq sauce and enjoy!

8. Note: more keto stuffing you can find in my air fryer cookbook here:

Nutrition value:

Calories 170 Fat: 13 g ; Carbs: 2 g ; Protein: 11 g

## Ham Chaffles

Servings: 4

Cooking Time: 16 Minutes

**Ingredients:**

2 large organic eggs (yolks and whites separated)

6 tablespoons butter, melted

2 scoops unflavored whey protein powder

1 teaspoon organic baking powder

Salt, to taste

1 ounce sugar-free ham, chopped finely

1 ounce Cheddar cheese, shredded 1/8 teaspoon paprika

**Directions:**

1. Preheat a waffle iron and then grease it.
2. In a bowl place egg yolks, butter, protein powder, baking powder and salt and beat until well combined.
3. Add the ham steak pieces, cheese and paprika and stir to combine.
4. In another bowl, place 2 egg whites and a pinch of salt and with an electric hand mixer and beat until stiff peaks form.
5. Gently fold the whipped egg whites into the egg yolk mixture in 2 batches.
6. Place ¼ of the mixture into preheated waffle iron and cook for about 3-4 minutes or until golden brown.
7. Repeat with the remaining mixture.
8. Serve warm.

Nutrition value per Servings:

Calories: 288 Fat: 22.8g Carbohydrates:1.7g Sugar: 0.3g Protein: 20.3g

## Chaffle Katsu Sandwich

Servings: 4

Prep time: 30 min.

Cook time: 20 min.

**Ingredients:**

FOR THE CHICKEN:

¼ lb boneless and skinless chicken thigh

⅛ tsp salt

⅛ tsp black pepper

½ cup almond flour

1 egg

3 oz unflavored pork rinds

2 cup vegetable oil for deep frying

FOR THE BRINE:

2 cup of water

1 Tbsp salt

FOR THE SAUCE:

2 Tbsp sugar-free ketchup

1½ Tbsp Worcestershire Sauce

1 Tbsp oyster sauce

1 tsp swerve/monkfruit

FOR THE CHAFFLE:

2 egg

1 cup shredded mozzarella cheese

**Directions:**

Add brine ingredients in a large mixing bowl. Add chicken and brine for 1 hour.

Pat chicken dry with a paper towel. Sprinkle with salt and pepper. Set aside. Mix ketchup, oyster sauce, Worcestershire sauce, and swerve in a small mixing bowl. Pulse pork rinds in a food processor, making fine crumbs.

Fill one bowl with flour, a second bowl with beaten eggs, and a third with crushed pork rinds. Dip and coat each thigh in: flour, eggs, crushed pork rinds. Transfer on holding a plate.

Add oil to cover ½ inch of frying pan. Heat to 375°F.

Once oil is hot, reduce heat to medium and add chicken. Cooking time depends on the chicken thickness.

Transfer to a drying rack.

Turn on waffle maker to heat and oil it with cooking spray.

Beat egg in a small bowl.

Place ⅛ cup of cheese on waffle maker, then add ¼ of the egg mixture and top with ⅛ cup of cheese.

Cook for 3-4 minutes.

Repeat for remaining batter.

Top chaffles with chicken katsu, 1 Tbsp sauce, and another piece of chaffle.

## Spinach & Cauliflower Chaffles

Servings: 2

Cooking Time: 10 Minutes

**Ingredients:**

½ cup frozen chopped spinach, thawed and squeezed ½ cup cauliflower, chopped finely

½ cup Cheddar cheese, shredded

½ cup Mozzarella cheese, shredded

1/3 cup Parmesan cheese, , shredded

2 organic eggs

1 tablespoon butter, melted

1 teaspoon garlic powder

1 teaspoon onion powder

Salt and freshly ground black pepper, to taste

**Directions:**

1. Preheat a waffle iron and then grease it.

2. In a medium bowl, place all ingredients and, mix until well combined.

3. Place half of the mixture into preheated waffle iron and cook for about 4-5 minutes or until golden brown.

4. Repeat with the remaining mixture.

5. Serve warm.

Nutrition value per Servings:

Calories 170 Fat: 13 g ; Carbs: 2 g ; Protein: 11 g

## Rosemary Chaffles

Servings: 2

Cooking Time: 8 Minutes

**Ingredients:**

1 organic egg, beaten

½ cup Cheddar cheese, shredded

1 tablespoon almond flour

1 tablespoon fresh rosemary, chopped

Pinch of salt and freshly ground black pepper

**Directions:**

1. Preheat a mini waffle iron and then grease it.

2. For chaffles: In a medium bowl, place all ingredients and with a fork, mix until well combined.

3. Place half of the mixture into preheated waffle iron and cook for about 4 minutes or until golden brown.

4. Repeat with the remaining mixture.

5. Serve warm.

Nutrition value per Servings:

Calories: 173 Fat: 13.7g Carbohydrates: 2.2g

Sugar: 0.4g Protein: 9.9g

## Zucchini Chaffles With Peanut Butter

Servings: 2

Cooking Time: 5 Minutes

**Ingredients:**

1 cup zucchini grated

1 egg beaten

1/2 cup shredded parmesan cheese

1/4 cup shredded mozzarella cheese

1 tsp dried basil

1/2 tsp. salt

1/2 tsp. black pepper

2 tbsps. peanut butter for topping

**Directions:**

1. Sprinkle salt over zucchini and let it sit for minutes.

2. Squeeze out water from zucchini.

3. Beat egg with zucchini, basil. saltmozzarella cheese, and pepper.

4. Sprinkle ½ of the parmesan cheese over preheated waffle maker and pour zucchini batter over it.

5. Sprinkle the remaining cheese over it.

6. Close the lid.

7. Cook zucchini chaffles for about 4-8 minutes.

8. Remove chaffles from the maker and repeat with the remaining batter.

9. Serve with peanut butter on top and enjoy!

Nutrition value per Servings:

Calories 170 Fat: 13 g ; Carbs: 2 g ; Protein: 11 g

## Pepperoni & Cauliflower Chaffles

Servings: 4

Cooking Time: 16 Minutes

**Ingredients:**

6 turkey pepperoni slices, chopped ¼ cup cauliflower rice

1 organic egg, beaten

¼ cup Cheddar cheese, shredded

¼ cup Mozzarella cheese, shredded

2 tablespoons Parmesan cheese, grated ½ teaspoon Italian seasoning

¼ teaspoon onion powder

¼ teaspoon garlic powder

**Directions:**

1. Preheat a mini waffle iron and then grease it.

2. In a medium bowl, place all ingredients and mix until well combined.

3. Place ¼ of the mixture into preheated waffle iron and cook for about 4 minutes or until golden brown.

4. Repeat with the remaining mixture.

5. Serve warm.

Nutrition value per Servings:

Calories: 103 Fat: 8g Carbohydrates: 0.8g Sugar: 0.4g Protein: 10.2g

## Pulled Pork Chaffle

Servings: 8

Cooking Time: 8 Hours.

**Ingredients:**

1 cup shredded cheddar cheese

2 eggs

½ tsp BBQ Rub

5 lbs pork butt

¼ cup BBQ Rub

2 Tbsp yellow mustard

½ cup sweet BBQ Sauce

**Directions:**

1. Brush mustard on each side of pork butt and season with rub.

2. Set smoker to 0°F. Smoke, uncovered, for about 4 hours, then wrap tightly, using butcher paper, and cook until internal temperature is 205°F.

3. Let pork rest for at least 1 hour before shredding it.

4. Mix cheese and eggs in a small bowl.

5. Scoop out ¼ cup of the mixture and pour into waffle maker. Cook for minutes.

6. Top chaffles with shredded pork and BBQ sauce.

Nutrition value:

Carbs: 5 g ;Fat: 14 g ;Protein: 36 g ;Calories: 2

## Buffalo Chicken Chaffles

Servings: 4

Cooking Time: 5 Minutes

**Ingredients:**

¼ cup almond flour

1 tsp baking powder

2 large eggs

½ cup chicken, shredded

¾ cup sharp cheddar cheese, shredded

¼ cup mozzarella cheese, shredded

¼ cup Red-Hot Sauce + 1 Tbsp for topping ¼ cup feta cheese, crumbled

¼ cup celery, diced

**Directions:**

1. Whisk baking powder and almond flour in a small bowl and set aside.

2. Turn on waffle maker to heat and oil it with cooking spray.

3. Beat eggs in a large bowl until frothy.

4. Add hot sauce and beat until combined.

5. Mix in flour mixture.

6. Add cheeses and mix until well combined.

7. Fold in chicken.

8. Pour batter into waffle maker and cook for 4 minutes.

9. Remove and repeat until all batter is used up.

10. Top with celery, feta, and hot sauce.

Nutrition value:

Carbs: 4 g ;Fat: 26 g ;Protein: 22 g ;Calories: 337

## Japanese Breakfast Chaffle

Servings: 2

Cooking Time: 10 Minutes

**Ingredients:**

1 egg

½ cup shredded mozzarella cheese

1 Tbsp kewpie mayo

1 stalk of green onion, chopped

1 slice bacon, chopped

**Directions:**

1. Turn on waffle maker to heat and oil it with cooking spray.

2. Beat egg in a small bowl.

3. Add 1 Tbsp mayo, bacon, and ½ green onion. Mix well.

4. Place ⅛ cup of cheese on waffle maker, then spread half of the egg mixture over it and top with ⅛ cup cheese.

5. Close and cook for 3-4 minutes.

6. Repeat for remaining batter.

7. Transfer to a plate and sprinkle with remaining green onion.

Nutrition value:

Carbs: 1 g ;Fat: 16 g ;Protein: g ;Calories: 183

## Garlic And Spinach Chaffles

Servings:2

Cooking Time:5minutes

**Ingredients:**

1 cup egg whites

1 tsp. Italian spice

2 tsps. coconut flour ½ tsp.vanilla

1 tsp. baking powder

1 tsp. baking soda

1 cup mozzarella cheese, grated 1/2 tsp. garlic powder

1 cup chopped spinach

**Directions:**

1. Switch on your square waffle maker. Spray with non-stick spray.

2. Beat egg whites with beater, until fluffy and white.

3. Add pumpkin puree, pumpkin pie spice, coconut flour in egg whites and beat again.

4. Stir in the cheese, powder, garlic powder, baking soda, and powder.

5. Sprinkle chopped spinach on a waffle maker

6. Pour the batter in waffle maker over chopped spinach

7. Close the maker and cook for about 4-5 minutes.

8. Remove chaffles from the maker.

9. Serve hot and enjoy!

Nutrition value per Servings:

Calories 170 Fat: 13 g ; Carbs: 2 g ; Protein: 11 g

## Cauliflower Chaffle

Servings: 3

Prep time: 5 min.

Cook time: 1 min.

**Ingredients:**

2 cup cauliflower, minced

2 cup shredded mozzarella cheese

2 eggs

2 Tbsp almond flour ½ tsp paprika

½ tsp onion powder

½ tsp oregano

Salt and pepper, to taste

3 egg for topping

**Directions:**

Turn on waffle maker to heat and oil it with cooking spray.

Combine cauliflower, eggs, cheese, flour, onion powder, paprika, oregano, salt, and pepper. Add 1 cup mixture to waffle maker. Cook for 6 minutes.

Remove the first chaffle, repeat with the remaining batter. Fry eggs well.

Place a fried egg on top of each chaffle and serve.

Nutrition Value per Servings:

Carbs - 9 G  Fat - 19 G  Protein - 22 G  Calories - 304

## Cauliflower & Italian Seasoning Chaffles

Servings: 4

Cooking Time: 20 Minutes

**Ingredients:**

1 cup cauliflower rice

¼ teaspoon garlic powder

½ teaspoon Italian seasoning

Salt and freshly ground black pepper, to taste

½ cup Mexican blend cheese, shredded

1 organic egg, beaten

½ cup Parmesan cheese, shredded

**Directions:**

1. Preheat a mini waffle iron and then grease it.

2. In a blender, add all the ingredients except Parmesan cheese and pulse until well combined.

3. Place 1½ tablespoon of the Parmesan cheese in the bottom of preheated waffle iron.

4. Place ¼ of the egg mixture over cheese and sprinkle with the ½ tablespoon of the Parmesan cheese.

5. Cook for about 4-minutes or until golden brown.

6. Repeat with the remaining mixture and Parmesan cheese.

7. Serve warm.

Nutrition value per Servings:

Calories: 127 Fat: 9g Carbohydrates: 2.7g Sugar: 1.5g Protein: 9.2g

## Chaffle Cuban Sandwich

Servings: 1

Cooking Time: 10 Minutes

**Ingredients:**

1 large egg

1 Tbsp almond flour

1 Tbsp full-fat Greek yogurt ⅛ tsp baking powder

¼ cup shredded Swiss cheese For the Filling:

3 oz roast pork

2 oz deli ham

1 slice Swiss cheese

3-5 sliced pickle chips

½ Tbsp Dijon mustard

**Directions:**

1. Turn on waffle maker to heat and oil it with cooking spray.

2. Beat egg, yogurt, almond flour, and baking powder in a bowl.

3. Sprinkle ¼ Swiss cheese on hot waffle maker. Top with half of the egg mixture, then add ¼ of the cheese on top. Close and cook for 5 minutes, until golden brown and crispy.

4. Repeat with remaining batter.

5. Layer pork, ham, and cheese slice in a small microwaveable bowl. Microwave for seconds, until cheese melts.

6. Spread the inside of chaffle with mustard and top with pickles. Invert bowl onto chaffle top so that cheese is touching pickles. Place bottom chaffle onto pork and serve.

Nutrition value:

Carbs: 4 g ;Fat: 46 g ;Protein: 33 g ;Calories: 522

## Protein Chaffles

Servings: 1

Cooking Time: 4 Minutes

**Ingredients:**

¼ cup almond milk

¼ cup plant-based protein powder

2 tbsp almond butter

1 tbsp psyllium husk

**Directions:**

1. Preheat the waffle maker.

2. Combine almond milk, protein powder, psyllium husk and mix thoroughly until the mixture gets the form of a paste.

3. Add in butter, combine well and form round balls

4. Place the ball in the center of preheated waffle maker.

5. Cook for 4 minutes.

6. Remove, top as prefer and enjoy.

Nutrition value:

Calories: 310 Kcal ; Fats: 19 g ; Carbs: 5 g ; Protein: 25 g

## Garlic Powder & Oregano Chaffles

Servings: 2

Cooking Time: 10 Minutes

**Ingredients:**

½ cup Mozzarella cheese, grated

1 medium organic egg, beaten

2 tablespoons almond flour

½ teaspoon dried oregano, crushed ½ teaspoon garlic powder

Salt, to taste

**Directions:**

1. Preheat a mini waffle iron and then grease it.

2. In a medium bowl, place all ingredients and mix until well combined.

3. Place half of the mixture into preheated waffle iron and cook for about 4-5 minutes or until golden brown.

4. Repeat with the remaining mixture.

5. Serve warm.

Nutrition value per Servings:

Calories: 100 Fat: 7.2g Carbohydrates:2.4g Sugar: 0,5g Protein: 4.9g

## Tuna Chaffles

Servings: 2

Cooking Time: 9 Minutes

**Ingredients:**

1 organic egg, beaten

½ cup plus 2 teaspoons Mozzarella cheese, shredded and divided 1 (2.6-ounce) can water-packed tuna, drained

Pinch of salt

**Directions:**

1. Preheat a mini waffle iron and then grease it.

2. In a bowl, place the egg, ½ cup of Mozzarella cheese, tuna and salt and mix well.

3. Place 1 teaspoon of Mozzarella cheese in the bottom of preheated waffle iron and cook for about seconds.

4. Place the egg mixture over cheese and cook for about minutes or until golden brown.

5. Repeat with the remaining mixture.

6. Serve warm.

Nutrition value per Servings:

Calories: 94 Fat: 3g Carbohydrates: 0.4g Sugar: 0.2g Protein: 14.2g

## Sausage & Veggie Chaffles

Servings: 4

Cooking Time: 20 Minutes

**Ingredients:**

1/3 cup unsweetened almond milk

4 medium organic eggs

2 tablespoons gluten-free breakfast sausage, cut into slices

2 tablespoons broccoli florets, chopped

2 tablespoons bell peppers, seeded and chopped

2 tablespoons mozzarella cheese, shredded

**Directions:**

1. Preheat a waffle iron and then grease it.

2. In a medium bowl, add the almond milk and eggs and beat well.

3. Place the remaining ingredients and stir to combine well.

4. Place desired amount of the mixture into preheated waffle iron.

5. Cook for about minutes.

6. Repeat with the remaining mixture.

7. Serve warm.

Nutrition value:

Calories 132 Fat 9.2 g Carbs 1.4 g Sugar 0.5 g Protein 11.1 g

## Crispy Bagel Chaffles

Servings: 1

Cooking Time: 30 Minutes

**Ingredients:**

2 eggs

½ cup parmesan cheese

1 tsp bagel seasoning

½ cup mozzarella cheese

2 teaspoons almond flour

**Directions:**

1. Turn on waffle maker to heat and oil it with cooking spray.

2. Evenly sprinkle half of cheeses to a griddle and let them melt. Then toast for 30 seconds and leave them wait for batter.

3. Whisk eggs, other half of cheeses, almond flour, and bagel seasoning in a small bowl.

4. Pour batter into the waffle maker. Cook for minutes.

5. Let cool for 2-3 minutes before serving.

Nutrition value:

Carbs: 8g ;Fat: 20 g ;Protein: 21 g ; Calories: 287

## Vegan Chaffle

Servings: 1

Prep time: 15 min.

Cook time: 25 min.

**Ingredients:**

1 Tbsp flaxseed meal

2 ½ Tbsp water

¼ cup low carb vegan cheese

2 Tbsp coconut flour

1 Tbsp low carb vegan cream cheese, softened
Pinch of salt

**Directions:**

Turn on waffle maker to heat and oil it with cooking spray.

Mix flaxseed and water in a bowl. Leave for 5 minutes, until thickened and gooey. Whisk remaining ingredients for chaffle.

Pour one half of the batter into the center of the waffle maker. Close and cook for 3-5 minutes. Remove chaffle and serve

Nutrition Value per Servings:

Carbs - 33 G  Fat - 25 G  Protein - 25 G  Calories – 450

## Turkey Chaffle Sandwich

Servings: 6

Prep time: 1 h.

Cook time: 10 min.

**Ingredients:**

2 egg whites

2 Tbsp almond flour

1 Tbsp mayonnaise

1 tsp water

¼ tsp baking powder Pinch of salt

FOR THE SANDWICH:

2 Tbsp mayonnaise

1 slice deli turkey

1 slice cheddar cheese

1 slice tomato

1 leaf green leaf lettuce

**Directions:**

Turn on waffle maker to heat and oil it with cooking spray. Mix all chaffle ingredients in a small bowl.

Pour half of the batter into waffle maker and cook for 3-5 minutes. Remove and repeat with remaining batter.

Spread mayonnaise on one side of each chaffle. Layer on turkey, tomato and green leaf lettuce.

Nutrition Value per Servings:

Carbs - 12 G  Fat - 9 G  Protein - 11 G  Calories – 246

## Sausage & Veggies Chaffles

Servings: 4

Cooking Time: 20 Minutes

**Ingredients:**

1/3 cup unsweetened almond milk

4 medium organic eggs

2 tablespoons gluten-free breakfast sausage, cut into slices

2 tablespoons broccoli florets, chopped

2 tablespoons bell peppers, seeded and chopped

2 tablespoons Mozzarella cheese, shredded

**Directions:**

1. Preheat a waffle iron and then grease it.

2. In a medium bowl, place the almond milk and eggs and beat well.

3. Place the remaining ingredients and stir to combine well.

4. Place ¼ of the mixture into preheated waffle iron and cook for about 5 minutes or until golden brown.

5. Repeat with the remaining mixture.

6. Serve warm.

Nutrition value per Servings:

Calories: 132 Fat: 9.2g Carbohydrates: 1.4g Sugar: 0.5g Protein: 11.1g

## Broccoli & Almond Flour Chaffles

Servings: 2

Cooking Time: 8 Minutes

**Ingredients:**

1 organic egg, beaten

½ cup Cheddar cheese, shredded

¼ cup fresh broccoli, chopped

1 tablespoon almond flour

¼ teaspoon garlic powder

**Directions:**

1. Preheat a mini waffle iron and then grease it.

2. In a bowl, place all ingredients and mix until well combined.

3. Place half of the mixture into preheated waffle iron and cook for about 4 minutes or until golden brown.

4. Repeat with the remaining mixture.

5. Serve warm.

Nutrition value per Servings:

Calories: 173 Fat: 13.5g Carbohydrates: 2.2g Sugar: 0.7g Protein: 10.2g

## Bacon & Serrano Pepper Chaffles

Servings: 2

Cooking Time: 10 Minutes

**Ingredients:**

1 organic egg, beaten

½ cup Swiss/Gruyere cheese blend, shredded

2 tablespoons cooked bacon slices, chopped

1 tablespoon Serrano pepper, chopped

**Directions:**

1. Preheat a mini waffle iron and then grease it.

2. In a medium bowl, place all ingredients and mix well.

3. Place half of the mixture into preheated waffle iron and cook for about 5 minutes or until golden brown.

4. Repeat with the remaining mixture.

5. Meanwhile, for dip: in a bowl, mix together the cream and stevia.

6. Serve warm.

Nutrition value per Servings:

Calories: 141 Fat: 10.2g Carbohydrates:1.8g Sugar: 0.7g Protein: 10.5g

## Bacon Chaffle Omelettes

Servings: 2

Cooking Time: 10 Minutes

**Ingredients:**

2 slices bacon, raw

1 egg

1 tsp maple extract, optional

1 tsp all spices

**Directions:**

1. Put the bacon slices in a blender and turn it on.

2. Once ground up, add in the egg and all spices. Go on blending until liquefied.

3. Heat your waffle maker on the highest setting and spray with non-stick cooking spray.

4. Pour half the omelette into the waffle maker and cook for 5 minutes max.

5. Remove the crispy omelette and repeat the same steps with rest batter.

6. Enjoy warm.

Nutrition value:

Calories 59 ; Fats: 4.4 g ; Carbs: 1 g ; Protein: 5 g

## Aioli Chicken Chaffle Sandwich

Servings: 1

Cooking Time: 6 Minutes

**Ingredients:**

¼ cup shredded rotisserie chicken

2 Tbsp Kewpie mayo

½ tsp lemon juice

1 grated garlic clove

¼ green onion, chopped

1 egg

½ cup shredded mozzarella cheese

**Directions:**

1. Mix lemon juice and mayo in a small bowl.

2. Turn on waffle maker to heat and oil it with cooking spray.

3. Beat egg in a small bowl.

4. Place ⅛ cup of cheese on waffle maker, then spread half of the egg mixture over it and top with ⅛ cup of cheese. Close and cook for 3-minutes.

5. Repeat for remaining batter.

6. Place chicken on chaffles and top with sauce. Sprinkle with chopped green onion.

Nutrition value:

Carbs: 3 g ;Fat: 42 g ;Protein: 34 g ;Calories: 545

## Sage & Coconut Milk Chaffles

Servings: 6

Cooking Time: 24 Minutes

**Ingredients:**

¾ cup coconut flour, sifted

1½ teaspoons organic baking powder

½ teaspoon dried ground sage

1/8 teaspoon garlic powder

1/8 teaspoon salt

1 organic egg

1 cup unsweetened coconut milk

¼ cup water

1½ tablespoons coconut oil, melted

½ cup cheddar cheese, shredded

**Directions:**

1. Preheat a waffle iron and then grease it.

2. In a bowl, add the flour, baking powder, sage, garlic powder and salt and mix well.

3. Add the egg, coconut milk, water and coconut oil and mix until a stiff mixture forms.

4. Add the cheese and gently stir to combine.

5. Divide the mixture into 6 portions.

6. Place 1 portion of the mixture into preheated waffle iron and cook for about 4 minutes or until golden brown.

7. Repeat with the remaining mixture.

8. Serve warm.

Nutrition value per Servings: Calories: 147Net Carb: 2.2gFat: 13gSaturated Fat: 10.7gCarbohydrates: 2.Dietary Fiber: 0.7g Sugar: 1.3gProtein: 4g


## Hot Ham Chaffles

Servings: 2

Cooking Time: 4 Minutes

**Ingredients:**

½ cup mozzarella cheese, shredded

1 egg

¼ cup ham, chopped

¼ tsp salt

2 tbsp mayonnaise

1 tsp Dijon mustard

**Directions:**

1. Preheat your waffle iron.

2. In the meantime, add the egg in a small mixing bowl and whisk.

3. Add in the ham, cheese, and salt. Mix to combine.

4. Scoop half the mixture using a spoon and pour into the hot waffle iron.

5. Close and cook for 4 minutes.

6. Remove the waffle and place on a large plate. Repeat the process with the remaining batter.

7. In a separate small bowl, add the mayo and mustard. Mix together until smooth.

8. Slice the waffles in quarters and use the mayo mixture as the dip.

Nutrition value:

Calories: 110 ; Fats: 12 g ; Carbs: 6 g ; Protein: 12 g


## Japanese Breakfast Chaffle

Servings: 2

Prep time: 5 min.

Cook time: 10 min.

**Ingredients:**

1 egg

½ cup shredded mozzarella cheese

1 Tbsp kewpie mayo

1 stalk of green onion, chopped

1 slice bacon, chopped

**Directions:**

Turn on waffle maker to heat and oil it with cooking spray. Beat egg in a small bowl.

Add 1 Tbsp mayo, bacon, and ½ green onion. Mix well.

Place ⅛ cup of cheese on waffle maker, then

spread half of the egg mixture over it and top with ⅛ cup cheese.

Close and cook for 3-4 minutes. Repeat for remaining batter.

Transfer to a plate and sprinkle with remaining green onion.

Nutrition Value per Servings:

Carbs - 1 G  Fat - 16 G  Protein - 8 G  Calories – 183

## Scallion Cream Cheese Chaffle

Servings: 2

Prep time: 15 min. + 1 h.

Cook time: 20 min.

**Ingredients:**

1 large egg

½ cup of shredded mozzarella

2 Tbsp cream cheese

1 Tbsp everything bagel seasoning

1-2 sliced scallions

**Directions:**

Turn on waffle maker to heat and oil it with cooking spray. Beat egg in a small bowl.

Add in ½ cup mozzarella.

Pour half of the mixture into the waffle maker and cook for 3-4 minutes. Remove chaffle and repeat with remaining mixture.

Let them cool, then cover each chaffle with cream cheese, sprinkle with seasoning and scallions.

Nutrition Value per Servings:

Carbs - 8 G  Fat - 11 G  Protein - 5 G  Calories – 168

## Grilled Cheese Chaffle

Servings: 1

Prep time: 10 min.

Cook time: 10 min.

**Ingredients:**

1 large egg

½ cup mozzarella cheese

2 slices yellow American cheese

2-3 slices cooked bacon, cut in half

1 tsp butter

½ tsp baking powder

**Directions:**

Turn on waffle maker to heat and oil it with cooking spray. Beat egg in a bowl.

Add mozzarella, and baking powder.

Pour half of the mix into the waffle maker and cook for 4 minutes. Remove and repeat to make the second chaffle.

Layer bacon and cheese slices in between two chaffles.

Melt butter in a skillet and add chaffle sandwich to the pan. Fry on each side for 2-3 minutes covered, until cheese has melted.

Slice in half on a plate and serve.

Nutrition Value per Servings:

Carbs - 4 G  Fat - 18 G  Protein - 7 G  Calories - 233

## Lemony Fresh Herbs Chaffles

Servings: 6

Cooking Time: 24 Minutes

**Ingredients:**

½ cup ground flaxseed

2 organic eggs

½ cup goat cheddar cheese, grated

2-4 tablespoons plain Greek yogurt

1 tablespoon avocado oil

½ teaspoon baking soda

1 teaspoon fresh lemon juice

2 tablespoons fresh chives, minced

1 tablespoon fresh basil, minced

½ tablespoon fresh mint, minced

¼ tablespoon fresh thyme, minced

¼ tablespoon fresh oregano, minced

Salt and freshly ground black pepper, to taste

**Directions:**

1. Preheat a waffle iron and then grease it.

2. In a medium bowl, place all ingredients and with a fork, mix until well combined.

3. Divide the mixture into 6 portions.

4. Place 1 portion of the mixture into preheated waffle iron and cook for about minutes or until golden brown.

5. Repeat with the remaining mixture.

6. Serve warm.

Nutrition value per Servings:

Calories: 11 Fat: 7.9g Carbohydrates: 3.7g Sugar: 0.7gProtein: 6.4g

## Basil Chaffles

Servings: 3

Cooking Time: 16 Minutes

**Ingredients:**

2 organic eggs, beaten

½ cup Mozzarella cheese, shredded

1 tablespoon Parmesan cheese, grated

1 teaspoon dried basil, crushed

Pinch of salt

**Directions:**

1. Preheat a mini waffle iron and then grease it.

2. In a medium bowl, place all ingredients and mix until well combined.

3. Place 1/of the mixture into preheated waffle iron and cook for about 3-4 minutes or until golden brown.

4. Repeat with the remaining mixture.

5. Serve warm.

Nutrition value per Servings:

Calories: 99 Fat: 4.2g Carbohydrates: 0.4g Sugar: 0.2g Protein: 5.7g

## Scallion Cream Cheese Chaffle

Servings: 2

Cooking Time: 20 Minutes

**Ingredients:**

1 large egg

½ cup of shredded mozzarella

2 Tbsp cream cheese

1 Tbsp everything bagel seasoning

1-2 sliced scallions

**Directions:**

1. Turn on waffle maker to heat and oil it with cooking spray.

2. Beat egg in a small bowl.

3. Add in ½ cup mozzarella.

4. Pour half of the mixture into the waffle maker and cook for 3-minutes.

5. Remove chaffle and repeat with remaining mixture.

6. Let them cool, then cover each chaffle with cream cheese, sprinkle with seasoning and scallions.

Nutrition value:

Carbs: 8 g ;Fat: 11 g ;Protein: 5 g ;Calories: 168

## Chicken Taco Chaffles

Servings: 2

Cooking Time: 8 Minutes

**Ingredients:**

1/3 cup cooked grass-fed chicken, chopped

1 organic egg

1/3 cup Monterrey Jack cheese, shredded ¼ teaspoon taco seasoning

**Directions:**

1. Preheat a mini waffle iron and then grease it.

2. In a bowl, place all the ingredients and mix until well combined.

3. Place half of the mixture into preheated waffle iron and cook for about 4 minutes or until golden brown.

4. Repeat with the remaining mixture.

5. Serve warm.

Nutrition value per Servings:

Calories: 141 Fat: 8.9g Carbohydrates:1.1g Sugar: 0.2g Protein: 13.5g

## Crab Chaffles

Servings: 6

Cooking Time: 25 Minutes

**Ingredients:**

1 lb crab meat

1/3 cup Panko breadcrumbs

1 egg

2 tbsp fat greek yogurt

1 tsp Dijon mustard

2 tbsp parsley and chives, fresh

1 tsp Italian seasoning

1 lemon, juiced

**Directions:**

Salt, pepper to taste

Add the meat. Mix well.

Form the mixture into round patties. Cook 1 patty for 3 minutes.

Remove it and repeat the process with the remaining crab chaffle mixture. Once ready, remove and enjoy warm.

Nutrition value:

Calories 99 ; Fats: 8 g ; Carbs: 4 g ; Protein: 16 g

## Bacon & Egg Chaffles

Servings: 2

Cooking Time: 10 Minutes

**Ingredients:**

2 eggs

4 tsp collagen peptides, grass-fed

2 tbsp pork panko

3 slices crispy bacon

**Directions:**

1. Warm up your mini waffle maker.

2. Combine the eggs, pork panko, and collagen peptides. Mix well. Divide the batter in two small bowls.

3. Once done, evenly distribute ½ of the crispy chopped bacon on the waffle maker.

4. Pour one bowl of the batter over the bacon. Cook for 5 minutes and immediately repeat this step for the second chaffle.

5. Plate your cooked chaffles and sprinkle with extra Panko for an added crunch.

6. Enjoy!

Nutrition value:

Calories : 266 ; Fats: 1g ; Carbs: 11.2 g ; Protein: 27 g

## Chicken & Bacon Chaffles

Servings: 2

Cooking Time: 8 Minutes

**Ingredients:**

1 organic egg, beaten

1/3 cup grass-fed cooked chicken, chopped

1 cooked bacon slice, crumbled

1/3 cup Pepper Jack cheese, shredded

1 teaspoon powdered ranch dressing

**Directions:**

1. Preheat a mini waffle iron and then grease it.

2. In a medium bowl, place all ingredients and with a fork, mix until well combined.

3. Place half of the mixture into preheated waffle iron and cook for about 4 minutes or until golden brown.

4. Repeat with the remaining mixture.

5. Serve warm.

Nutrition value per Servings:

Calories: 145 Fat: 9.4g Carbohydrates: 1g Sugar: 0.2g Protein: 14.3g

## Belgium Chaffles

Servings: 1

Cooking Time: 6 Minutes

**Ingredients:**

2 eggs

1 cup Reduced-fat Cheddar cheese, shredded

**Directions:**

1. Turn on waffle maker to heat and oil it with cooking spray.

2. Whisk eggs in a bowl, add cheese. Stir until well-combined.

3. Pour mixture into waffle maker and cook for 6 minutes until done.

4. Let it cool a little to crisp before serving.

Nutrition value:

Carbs: 2 g ;Fat: 33 g ;Protein: 44 g ;Calories: 460

## Chaffle Katsu Sandwich

Servings: 4

Cooking Time: 00 Minutes

**Ingredients:**

For the chicken:

¼ lb boneless and skinless chicken thigh

⅛ tsp salt

⅛ tsp black pepper

½ cup almond flour

1 egg

3 oz unflavored pork rinds

2 cup vegetable oil for deep frying For the brine:

2 cup of water

1 Tbsp salt

For the sauce:

2 Tbsp sugar-free ketchup

1½ Tbsp Worcestershire Sauce

1 Tbsp oyster sauce

1 tsp swerve/monkfruit For the chaffle:

2 egg

1 cup shredded mozzarella cheese

**Directions:**

1. Add brine ingredients in a large mixing bowl.

2. Add chicken and brine for 1 hour.

3. Pat chicken dry with a paper towel. Sprinkle with salt and pepper. Set aside.

4. Mix ketchup, oyster sauce, Worcestershire sauce, and swerve in a small mixing bowl.

5. Pulse pork rinds in a food processor, making fine crumbs.

6. Fill one bowl with flour, a second bowl with beaten eggs, and a third with crushed pork rinds.

7. Dip and coat each thigh in: flour, eggs, crushed pork rinds. Transfer on holding a plate.

8. Add oil to cover ½ inch of frying pan. Heat to 375°F.

9. Once oil is hot, reduce heat to medium and add chicken. Cooking time depends on the chicken thickness.

10. Transfer to a drying rack.

11. Turn on waffle maker to heat and oil it with cooking spray.

12. Beat egg in a small bowl.

13. Place ⅛ cup of cheese on waffle maker, then add ¼ of the egg mixture and top with ⅛ cup of cheese.

14. Cook for 3-4 minutes.

15. Repeat for remaining batter.

16. Top chaffles with chicken katsu, 1 Tbsp sauce, and another piece of chaffle.

Nutrition value:

Carbs: 12 g ; Fat: 1 g ; Protein: 2 g ; Calories: 57

## Pork Rind Chaffles

Servings: 2

Cooking Time: 10 Minutes

**Ingredients:**

1 organic egg, beaten

½ cup ground pork rinds

1/3 cup Mozzarella cheese, shredded

Pinch of salt

**Directions:**

1. Preheat a mini waffle iron and then grease it.

2. In a bowl, place all the ingredients and beat until well combined.

3. Place half of the mixture into preheated waffle iron and cook for about 5 minutes or until golden brown.

4. Repeat with the remaining mixture.

5. Serve warm.

Nutrition value per Servings:

Calories: 91 Fat: 5.9g Carbohydrates: 0.3g Sugar: 0.2g Protein: 9.2g

## Chicken & Ham Chaffles

Servings: 4

Cooking Time: 16 Minutes

**Ingredients:**

¼ cup grass-fed cooked chicken, chopped

1 ounce sugar-free ham, chopped

1 organic egg, beaten

¼ cup Swiss cheese, shredded

¼ cup Mozzarella cheese, shredded

**Directions:**

1. Preheat a mini waffle iron and then grease it.

2. In a medium bowl, place all ingredients and mix until well combined.

3. Place ¼ of the mixture into preheated waffle iron and cook for about 4 minutes or until golden brown.

4. Repeat with the remaining mixture.

5. Serve warm.

Nutrition value per Servings:

Calories: 71 Fat: 4.2g Carbohydrates: 0.8g Sugar: 0.2g Protein: 7.4g

## Eggs Benedict Chaffle

Servings: 2

Cooking Time: 10 Minutes

**Ingredients:**

For the chaffle:

2 egg whites

2 Tbsp almond flour

1 Tbsp sour cream

½ cup mozzarella cheese

For the hollandaise:

½ cup salted butter

4 egg yolks

2 Tbsp lemon juice

For the poached eggs:

2 eggs

1 Tbsp white vinegar

3 oz deli ham

**Directions:**

1. Whip egg white until frothy, then mix in remaining ingredients.

2. Turn on waffle maker to heat and oil it with cooking spray.

3. Cook for 7 minutes until golden brown.

4. Remove chaffle and repeat with remaining batter.

5. Fill half the pot with water and bring to a boil.

6. Place heat-safe bowl on top of pot, ensuring bottom doesn't touch the boiling water.

7. Heat butter to boiling in a microwave.

8. Add yolks to double boiler bowl and bring to boil.

9. Add hot butter to the bowl and whisk briskly. Cook until the egg yolk mixture has thickened.

10. Remove bowl from pot and add in lemon juice. Set aside.

11. Add more water to pot if needed to make the poached eggs (water should completely cover the eggs). Bring to a simmer. Add white vinegar to water.

12. Crack eggs into simmering water and cook for 1 minute 30 seconds. Remove using slotted spoon.

13. Warm chaffles in toaster for 2-3 minutes. Top with ham, poached eggs, and hollandaise sauce.

Nutrition value:

Carbs: 4 g ;Fat: 26 g ;Protein: 26 g ;Calories: 365

## Chicken & Veggies Chaffles

Servings: 3

Cooking Time: 15 Minutes

**Ingredients:**

1/3 cup cooked grass-fed chicken, chopped

1/3 cup cooked spinach, chopped

1/3 cup marinated artichokes, chopped

1 organic egg, beaten

1/3 cup Mozzarella cheese, shredded

1 ounce cream cheese, softened

¼ teaspoon garlic powder

**Directions:**

1. Preheat a mini waffle iron and then grease it.

2. In a medium bowl, place all ingredients and mix until well combined.

3. Place 1/of the mixture into preheated waffle iron and cook for about 4-5 minutes or until golden brown.

4. Repeat with the remaining mixture.

5. Serve warm.

Nutrition value per Servings:

Calories: 95 Fat: 5.8g Carbohydrates: 2.2g Sugar: 0.3g Protein: 8g

## Turkey Chaffles

Servings: 4

Cooking Time: 16 Minutes

**Ingredients:**

½ cup cooked turkey meat, chopped

2 organic eggs, beaten

½ cup Parmesan cheese, grated

½ cup Mozzarella, shredded

¼ teaspoon poultry seasoning

¼ teaspoon onion powder

**Directions:**

1. Preheat a mini waffle iron and then grease it.

2. In a medium bowl, place all ingredients and mix until well combined.

3. Place ¼ of the mixture into preheated waffle iron and cook for about 4 minutes or until golden brown.

4. Repeat with the remaining mixture.

5. Serve warm.

Nutrition value per Servings:

Calories: 108 Fat: 1g Carbohydrates: 0.5g Sugar: 0.2g Protein: 12.9g

## Pepperoni Chaffles

Servings: 1

Cooking Time: 5 Minutes

**Ingredients:**

1 organic egg, beaten

½ cup Mozzarella cheese, shredded

2 tablespoons turkey pepperoni slice, chopped

1 tablespoon sugar-free pizza sauce ¼ teaspoon Italian seasoning

**Directions:**

1. Preheat a waffle iron and then grease it.

2. In a bowl, place all the ingredients and mix well.

3. Place the mixture into preheated waffle iron and cook for about 5 minutes or until golden brown.

4. Serve warm.

Nutrition value per Servings:

Calories: 119 Fat: 7.g Carbohydrates: 2.7g Sugar: 0.9g Protein: 10.3g

## Hot Sauce Jalapeño Chaffles

Servings: 2

Cooking Time: 8 Minutes

**Ingredients:**

½ cup plus 2 teaspoons Cheddar cheese, shredded and divided

1 organic egg, beaten

6 jalapeño pepper slices

¼ teaspoon hot sauce

Pinch of salt

**Directions:**

1. Preheat a mini waffle iron and then grease it.

2. In a bowl, place ½ cup of cheese and remaining ingredients and mix until well combined.

3. Place about 1 teaspoon of cheese in the bottom of the waffle maker for about  seconds before adding the mixture.

4. Place half of the mixture into preheated waffle iron and cook for about 3-minutes or until golden brown.

5. Repeat with the remaining cheese and mixture.

6. Serve warm.

Nutrition value per Servings:

Calories: 153 Fat: 12.2g Carbohydrates: 0.7g Sugar: 0.4g Protein: 10.3g

## Garlic Herb Blend Seasoning Chaffles

Servings: 2

Cooking Time: 8 Minutes

**Ingredients:**

1 large organic egg, beaten

¼ cup Parmesan cheese, shredded

¼ cup Mozzarella cheese, shredded

½ tablespoon butter, melted

1 teaspoon garlic herb blend seasoning

Salt, to taste

**Directions:**

1. Preheat a mini waffle iron and then grease it.

2. In a bowl, place all the ingredients and beat until well combined.

3. Place half of the mixture into preheated waffle iron and cook for about 4 minutes or until golden brown.

4. Repeat with the remaining mixture.

5. Serve warm.

Nutrition value per Servings:

Calories: 115 Fat: 8.8g Carbohydrates: 1.2g Sugar: 0.2g Protein: 8g

## Protein Cheddar Chaffles

Servings: 8

Cooking Time: 48 Minutes

**Ingredients:**

½ cup golden flax seeds meal ½ cup almond flour

2 tablespoons unflavored whey protein powder

1 teaspoon organic baking powder

Salt and ground black pepper, to taste

¾ cup cheddar cheese, shredded

1/3 cup unsweetened almond milk

2 tablespoons unsalted butter, melted

2 large organic eggs, beaten

**Directions:**

1. Preheat a mini waffle iron and then grease it.

2. In a large bowl, add flax seeds meal, flour, protein powder, and baking powder, and mix well.

3. Stir in the cheddar cheese.

4. In another bowl, add the remaining ingredients and beat until well combined.

5. Add the egg mixture into the bowl with flax seeds meal mixture and mix until well combined.

6. Place desired amount of the mixture into preheated waffle iron.

7. Cook for about 4-6 minutes.

8. Repeat with the remaining mixture.

9. Serve warm.

Nutrition value:

Calories 187 Fat 14.5 g Carbs 4.9 g Sugar 0.4 g Protein 8 g

## Cheese-Free Breakfast Chaffle

Servings: 1

Cooking Time: 12 Minutes

**Ingredients:**

1 egg

½ cup almond milk ricotta, finely shredded.

1 tbsp almond flour

2 tbsp butter

**Directions:**

1. Mix the egg, almond flour and ricotta in a small bowl.

2. Separate the chaffle batter into two and cook each for 4 minutes.

3. Melt the butter and pour on top of the chaffles.

4. Put them back in the pan and cook on each side for 2 minutes.

5. Remove from the pan and allow them sit for 2 minutes.

6. Enjoy while still crispy

Nutrition value:

Calories 530 ; Fats: 50 g ; Carbs: 3 g ; Protein: 23 g

## Savory Bagel Seasoning Chaffles

Servings: 4

Cooking Time: 5 Minutes

**Ingredients:**

2 tbsps. everything bagel seasoning

2 eggs

1 cup mozzarella cheese

1/2 cup grated parmesan

**Directions:**

1. Preheat the square waffle maker and grease with cooking spray.

2. Mix together eggs, mozzarella cheese and grated cheese in a bowl.

3. Pour half of the batter in the waffle maker.

4. Sprinkle 1 tbsp. of the everything bagel seasoning over batter.

5. Close the lid.

6. Cook chaffles for about 3-4 minutes.

7. Repeat with the remaining batter.

8. Serve hot and enjoy!

Nutrition value per Servings:

Calories 170 Fat: 13 g ; Carbs: 2 g ; Protein: 11 g

## Dried Herbs Chaffles

Servings: 2

Cooking Time: 8 Minutes

**Ingredients:**

1 organic egg, beaten

½ cup Cheddar cheese, shredded

1 tablespoon almond flour

Pinch of dried thyme, crushed

Pinch of dried rosemary, crushed

**Directions:**

1. Preheat a mini waffle iron and then grease it.

2. In a bowl, place all the ingredients and beat until well combined.

3. Place half of the mixture into preheated waffle iron and cook for about 4 minutes or until golden brown.

4. Repeat with the remaining mixture.

5. Serve warm.

Nutrition value per Servings:

Calories: 112 Fat: 13.4g Carbohydrates: 1.3g Sugar: 0.4g Protein: 9.8g

## Cookie Dough Chaffle

Servings: 4

Cooking Time: 7-9 Minutes

**Ingredients:**

Batter

4 eggs

¼ cup heavy cream

1 teaspoon vanilla extract ¼ cup stevia

6 tablespoons coconut flour

1 teaspoon baking powder

Pinch of salt

¼ cup unsweetened chocolate chips

Other

2 tablespoons cooking spray to brush the waffle maker ¼ cup heavy cream, whipped

**Directions:**

1. Preheat the waffle maker.

2. Add the eggs and heavy cream to a bowl and stir in the vanilla extract, stevia, coconut flour, baking powder, and salt. Mix until just combined.

3. Stir in the chocolate chips and combine.

4. Brush the heated waffle maker with cook-

ing spray and add a few tablespoons of the batter.

5. Close the lid and cook for about 7-8 minutes depending on your waffle maker.

6. Serve with whipped cream on top.

Nutrition value per Servings:

Calories 30 fat 32.3 g carbs 12.6 g, sugar 0.5 g, Protein 9 g

## Thanksgiving Pumpkin Spice Chaffle

Servings: 4

Cooking Time: 5 minutes

**Ingredients:**

1 cup egg whites

¼ cup pumpkin puree

2 tsps. pumpkin pie spice

2 tsps. coconut flour ½ tsp. vanilla

1 tsp. baking powder

1 tsp. baking soda

1/8 tsp cinnamon powder

1 cup mozzarella cheese, grated 1/2 tsp. garlic powder

**Directions:**

1. Switch on your square waffle maker. Spray with non-stick spray.

2. Beat egg whites with beater, until fluffy and white.

3. Add pumpkin puree, pumpkin pie spice, coconut flour in egg whites and beat again.

4. Stir in the cheese, cinnamon powder, garlic powder, baking soda, and powder.

5. Pour ½ of the batter in the waffle maker.

6. Close the maker and cook for about 3 minutes.

7. Repeat with the remaining batter.

8. Remove chaffles from the maker.

9. Serve hot and enjoy!

Nutrition value per Servings: Protein: 51% 66 kcal Fat: 41% 53 kcal Carbohydrates: 8% kcal

## Pumpkin Spice Chaffles

Servings: 2

Cooking Time: 14 Minutes

**Ingredients:**

1 egg, beaten

½ tsp pumpkin pie spice

½ cup finely grated mozzarella cheese

1 tbsp sugar-free pumpkin puree

**Directions:**

1. Preheat the waffle iron.

2. In a medium bowl, mix all the ingredients.

3. Open the iron, pour in half of the batter, close, and cook until crispy, 6 to 7 minutes.

4. Remove the chaffle onto a plate and set aside.

5. Make another chaffle with the remaining batter.

6. Allow cooling and serve afterward.

Nutrition value:

Calories 90 Fats 6.46g Carbs 1.98g Protein 5.94g

# Chaffle Fruit Snacks

Servings: 2

Cooking Time: 14 Minutes

**Ingredients:**

1 egg, beaten

½ cup finely grated cheddar cheese

½ cup Greek yogurt for topping

8 raspberries and blackberries for topping

**Directions:**

1. Preheat the waffle iron.
2. Mix the egg and cheddar cheese in a medium bowl.
3. Open the iron and add half of the mixture. Close and cook until crispy, 7 minutes.
4. Remove the chaffle onto a plate and make another with the remaining mixture.
5. Cut each chaffle into wedges and arrange on a plate.
6. Top each waffle with a tablespoon of yogurt and then two berries.
7. Serve afterward.

Nutrition value:

Calories 207 Fats 15.29g Carbs 4.36g Protein 12.91g

# Open-Faced Ham & Green Bell Pepper Chaffle Sandwich

Servings: 2

Cooking Time: 10 Minutes

**Ingredients:**

2 slices ham

Cooking spray

1 green bell pepper, sliced into strips

2 slices cheese

1 tablespoon black olives, pitted and sliced

2 basic chaffles

**Directions:**

1. Cook the ham in a pan coated with oil over medium heat.
2. Next, cook the bell pepper.
3. Assemble the open-faced sandwich by topping each chaffle with ham and cheese, bell pepper and olives.
4. Toast in the oven until the cheese has melted a little.

Nutrition value:

Calories 36 Fat 24.6g Carbohydrate 8g Protein 24.5g Sugars 6.3g

# Christmas Morning Choco Chaffle Cake

Servings: 8

Cooking Time: 5 minutes

**Ingredients:**

8 keto chocolate square chaffles

2 cups peanut butter

16 oz. raspberries

**Directions:**

1. Assemble chaffles in layers.
2. Spread peanut butter in each layer.
3. Top with raspberries.
4. Enjoy cake on Christmas morning with keto coffee!

Nutrition value per Servings:

Calories 170 Fat: 13 g ; Carbs: 2 g ; Protein: 11 g

## Lt Chaffle Sandwich

Servings: 2

Cooking Time: 15 Minutes

**Ingredients:**

Cooking spray

4 slices bacon

1 tablespoon mayonnaise

4 basic chaffles

2 lettuce leaves

2 tomato slices

**Directions:**

1. Coat your pan with foil and place it over medium heat.
2. Cook the bacon until golden and crispy.
3. Spread mayo on top of the chaffle.
4. Top with the lettuce, bacon and tomato.
5. Top with another chaffle.

Nutrition value:

Calories 238 Fat 18.4g Carbohydrate 3g Protein 14.3g Sugars 0.9g

## Mozzarella Peanut Butter Chaffle

Servings: 2

Cooking Time: 15 Minutes

**Ingredients:**

1 egg, lightly beaten

2 tbsp peanut butter

2 tbsp Swerve

1/2 cup mozzarella cheese, shredded

**Directions:**

1. Preheat your waffle maker.
2. In a bowl, mix egg, cheese, Swerve, and peanut butter until well combined.
3. Spray waffle maker with cooking spray.
4. Pour half batter in the hot waffle maker and cook for minutes or until golden brown. Repeat with the remaining batter.
5. Serve and enjoy.

Nutrition value:

Calories 150 Fat 11.5 g Carbohydrates 5.g Sugar 1.7 g Protein 8.8 g

## Double Decker Chaffle

Servings: 2

Cooking Time: 10 Minutes

**Ingredients:**

1 large egg

1 cup shredded cheese

TOPPING

1 keto chocolate ball

2 oz. cranberries

2 oz. blueberries

4 oz. cranberries puree

**Directions:**

1. Make 2 minutesi dash waffles.
2. Put cranberries and blueberries in the freezer for about hours.

3. For serving, arrange keto chocolate ball between 2 chaffles.

4. Top with frozen berries,

5. Serve and enjoy!

Nutrition value per Servings:

Calories 170 Fat: 13 g ; Carbs: 2 g ; Protein: 11 g

## Cinnamon And Vanilla Chaffle

Servings: 4

Cooking Time: 7-9 Minutes

**Ingredients:**

Batter

4 eggs

4 ounces sour cream

1 teaspoon vanilla extract

1 teaspoon cinnamon ¼ cup stevia

5 tablespoons coconut flour

Other

2 tablespoons coconut oil to brush the waffle maker

½ teaspoon cinnamon for garnishing the chaffles

**Directions:**

1. Preheat the waffle maker.

2. Add the eggs and sour cream to a bowl and stir with a wire whisk until just combined.

3. Add the vanilla extract, cinnamon, and stevia and mix until combined.

4. Stir in the coconut flour and stir until combined.

5. Brush the heated waffle maker with coconut oil and add a few tablespoons of the batter.

6. Close the lid and cook for about 7-8 minutes depending on your waffle maker.

7. Serve and enjoy.

Nutrition value per Servings:

Calories 224, fat 11 g, carbs 8.4 g, sugar 0.5 g, Protein 7.7 g

## New Year Cinnamon Chaffle With Coconut Cream

Servings: 2

Cooking Time: 5 minutes

**Ingredients:**

2 large eggs

1/8 cup almond flour

1 tsp. cinnamon powder

1 tsp. sea salt

1/2 tsp. baking soda

1 cup shredded mozzarella FOR TOPPING

2 tbsps. coconut cream

1 tbsp. unsweetened chocolate sauce

**Directions:**

1. Preheat waffle maker according to the manufacturer's directions.

2. Mix together recipe ingredients in a mixing bowl.

3. Add cheese and mix well.

4. Pour about ½ cup mixture into the center of the waffle maker and cook for about 2-3 minutes until golden and crispy.

5. Repeat with the remaining batter.

6. For serving, coat coconut cream over chaffles. Drizzle chocolate sauce over chaffle.

7. Freeze chaffle in the freezer for about 10

minutes.

8. Serve on Christmas morning and enjoy!

Nutrition value per Servings:

Calories 170 Fat: 13 g ; Carbs: 2 g ; Protein: 11 g

## Chaffles And Ice-Cream Platter

Servings: 2

Cooking Time: 5 minutes

**Ingredients:**

2 keto brownie chaffles

2 scoop vanilla keto ice cream

8 oz. strawberries, sliced

keto chocolate sauce

**Directions:**

1. Arrange chaffles, ice-cream, strawberries slice in serving plate.

2. Drizzle chocolate sauce on top.

3. Serve and enjoy!

Nutrition value per Servings:

Calories 170 Fat: 13 g ; Carbs: 2 g ; Protein: 11 g

## Choco Chip Pumpkin Chaffle

Servings: 2

Cooking Time: 15 Minutes

**Ingredients:**

1 egg, lightly beaten

1 tbsp almond flour

1 tbsp unsweetened chocolate chips 1/4 tsp pumpkin pie spice

2 tbsp Swerve

1 tbsp pumpkin puree

1/2 cup mozzarella cheese, shredded

**Directions:**

1. Preheat your waffle maker.

2. In a small bowl, mix egg and pumpkin puree.

3. Add pumpkin pie spice, Swerve, almond flour, and cheese and mix well.

4. Stir in chocolate chips.

5. Spray waffle maker with cooking spray.

6. Pour half batter in the hot waffle maker and cook for 4 minutes. Repeat with the remaining batter.

7. Serve and enjoy.

Nutrition value:

Calories 130 Fat 9.2 g Carbohydrates 5.9 g Sugar 0.6 g Protein 6.6 g

## Sausage & Pepperoni Chaffle Sandwich

Servings: 4

Cooking Time: 10 Minutes

**Ingredients:**

Cooking spray

2 cervelat sausage, sliced into rounds

12 pieces pepperoni

6 mushroom slices

4 teaspoons mayonnaise

4 big white onion rings

4 basic chaffles

**Directions:**

1. Spray your skillet with oil.
2. Place over medium heat.
3. Cook the sausage until brown on both sides.
4. Transfer on a plate.
5. Cook the pepperoni and mushrooms for 2 minutes.
6. Spread mayo on top of the chaffle.
7. Top with the sausage, pepperoni, mushrooms and onion rings.
8. Top with another chaffle.

Nutrition value:

Calories 373  Fat 24.4g Carbohydrate 28g Protein 8.1g Sugars 4.5g

## Maple Chaffle

Servings: 2

Cooking Time: 15 Minutes

**Ingredients:**

1 egg, lightly beaten

2 egg whites

1/2 tsp maple extract

2 tsp Swerve

1/2 tsp baking powder, gluten-free

2 tbsp almond milk

2 tbsp coconut flour

**Directions:**

1. Preheat your waffle maker.
2. In a bowl, whip egg whites until stiff peaks form.
3. Stir in maple extract, Swerve, baking powder, almond milk, coconut flour, and egg.
4. Spray waffle maker with cooking spray.
5. Pour half batter in the hot waffle maker and cook for 3-minutes or until golden brown. Repeat with the remaining batter.
6. Serve and enjoy.

Nutrition value:

Calories 122 Fat 6.6 g Carbohydrates 9 g Sugar 1 g Protein 7 g

## Red Velvet Chaffle

Servings: 3

Cooking Time: 12 Minutes

**Ingredients:**

1 egg

¼ cup mozzarella cheese, shredded

1 oz. cream cheese

4 tablespoons almond flour

1 teaspoon baking powder

2 teaspoons sweetener

1 teaspoon red velvet extract

2 tablespoons cocoa powder

**Directions:**

1. Combine all the ingredients in a bowl.
2. Plug in your waffle maker.
3. Pour some of the batter into the waffle maker.
4. Seal and cook for minutes.
5. Open and transfer to a plate.
6. Repeat the steps with the remaining batter.

Nutrition value:

Calories 126 Fat 10.1g  Carbohydrate 6.5g Protein 5.9g  Sugars 0.2g

## Walnuts Lowcarb Chaffles

Servings: 2

Cooking Time: 5 minutes

**Ingredients:**

2 tbsps. cream cheese

½ tsp almonds flour

¼ tsp. baking powder

1 large egg

¼ cup chopped walnuts

Pinch of stevia extract powder

**Directions:**

1. Preheat your waffle maker.

2. Spray waffle maker with cooking spray.

3. In a bowl, add cream cheese, almond flour, baking powder, egg, walnuts, and stevia.

4. Mix all ingredients,

5. Spoon walnut batter in the waffle maker and cook for about 2-3 minutes.

6. Let chaffles cool at room temperature before serving.

Nutrition value per Servings:

Calories 170 Fat: 13 g ; Carbs: 2 g ; Protein: 11 g

## Beginner Brownies Chaffle

Servings: 2

Cooking Time: 5 minutes

**Ingredients:**

1 cup cheddar cheese

1 tbsp. cocoa powder

½ tsp baking powder

1 large egg.

¼ cup melted keto chocolate chips for topping

**Directions:**

1. Preheat dash minutesi waffle iron and grease it.

2. Blend all ingredients in a blender until mixed.

3. Pour 1 tsp. cheese in a waffle maker and then pour the mixture in the center of greased waffle.

4. Again sprinkle cheese on the batter.

5. Close the waffle maker.

6. Cook chaffles for about 4-5 minutes until cooked and crispy.

7. Once chaffles are cooked remove.

8. Top with melted chocolate and enjoy!

Nutrition value per Servings:

Calories 170 Fat: 13 g ; Carbs: 2 g ; Protein: 11 g

## Holidays Chaffles

Servings: 4

Cooking Time: 5minutes

**Ingredients:**

1 cup egg whites

2 tsps. coconut flour ½ tsp. vanilla

1 tsp. baking powder

1 tsp. baking soda

1/8 tsp cinnamon powder

1 cup mozzarella cheese, grated

TOPPING:

Cranberries

keto Chocolate sauce

**Directions:**

1. Make 4 minutesi chaffles from the chaffle ingredients.

2. Top with chocolate sauce and cranberries

3. Serve hot and enjoy!

Nutrition value per Servings:

Calories: 145 Fat: 9.4g Carbohydrates: 1g Sugar: 0.2g Protein: 14.3g

## Cherry Chocolate Chaffle

Servings: 1

Cooking Time: 10 Minutes

**Ingredients:**

1 egg, lightly beaten

1 tbsp unsweetened chocolate chips

2 tbsp sugar-free cherry pie filling

2 tbsp heavy whipping cream

1/2 cup mozzarella cheese, shredded

1/2 tsp baking powder, gluten-free

1 tbsp Swerve

1 tbsp unsweetened cocoa powder

1 tbsp almond flour

**Directions:**

1. Preheat the waffle maker.

2. In a bowl, whisk together egg, cheese, baking powder, Swerve, cocoa powder, and almond flour.

3. Spray waffle maker with cooking spray.

4. Pour batter in the hot waffle maker and cook until golden brown.

5. Top with cherry pie filling, heavy whipping cream, and chocolate chips and serve.

Nutrition value:

Calories 2 Fat 22 g Carbohydrates 8.5 g Sugar 0.5 g Protein 12.7 g

## Bacon, Egg & Avocado Chaffle Sandwich

Servings: 2

Cooking Time: 10 Minutes

**Ingredients:**

Cooking spray

4 slices bacon

2 eggs

½ avocado, mashed

4 basic chaffles

2 leaves lettuce

**Directions:**

1. Coat your skillet with cooking spray.

2. Cook the bacon until golden and crisp.

3. Transfer into a paper towel lined plate.

4. Crack the eggs into the same pan and cook until firm.

5. Flip and cook until the yolk is set.

6. Spread the avocado on the chaffle.

7. Top with lettuce, egg and bacon.

8. Top with another chaffle.

Nutrition value:

Calories 372 Fat 30.1g Carbohydrate 5.4g Sugars 0.6g Protein 20.6g

## Crunchy Coconut Chaffles Cake

Servings: 4

Cooking Time: 15 Minutes

**Ingredients:**

4 large eggs

1 cup shredded cheese

2 tbsps. coconut cream

2 tbsps. coconut flour.

1 tsp. stevia

TOPPING

1 cup heavy cream

8 oz. raspberries

4 oz. blueberries

2 oz. cherries

**Directions:**

1. Make 4 thin round chaffles with the chaffle ingredients. Once chaffles are cooked, set in layers on a plate.

2. Spread heavy cream in each layer.

3. Top with raspberries then blueberries and cherries.

4. Serve and enjoy!

Nutrition value per Servings:

Calories: 145 Fat: 9.4g Carbohydrates: 1g Sugar: 0.2g Protein: 14.3g

## Coffee Flavored Chaffle

Servings: 4

Cooking Time: 7-9 Minutes

**Ingredients:**

Batter

4 eggs

4 ounces cream cheese

½ teaspoon vanilla extract

6 tablespoons strong boiled espresso ¼ cup stevia

½ cup almond flour

1 teaspoon baking powder

Pinch of salt

Other

2 tablespoons butter to brush the waffle maker

**Directions:**

1. Preheat the waffle maker.

2. Add the eggs and cream cheese to a bowl and stir in the vanilla extract, espresso, stevia, almond flour, baking powder and a pinch of salt.

3. Stir just until everything is combined and fully incorporated.

4. Brush the heated waffle maker with butter and add a few tablespoons of the batter.

5. Close the lid and cook for about 7-8 minutes depending on your waffle maker.

6. Serve and enjoy.

Nutrition value per Servings:

Calories 300, fat 26.g, carbs 4.8 g, sugar 0.5 g, Protein 10.8 g

## Italian Sausage Chaffles

Servings: 2

Cooking Time: 8 Minutes

**Ingredients:**

1 egg, beaten

1 cup cheddar cheese, shredded

¼ cup Parmesan cheese, grated

1 lb. Italian sausage, crumbled

2 teaspoons baking powder

1 cup almond flour

**Directions:**

1. Preheat your waffle maker.
2. Mix all the ingredients in a bowl.
3. Pour half of the mixture into the waffle maker.
4. Cover and cook for minutes.
5. Transfer to a plate.
6. Let cool to make it crispy.
7. Do the same steps to make the next chaffle.

Nutrition value:

Calories 332 Fat 27.1g Carbohydrate 1.9g Sugars 0.1g Protein 19.6g

## Chaffles With Strawberry Frosty

Servings: 2

Cooking Time: 5 Minutes

**Ingredients:**

1 cup frozen strawberries

1/2 cup Heavy cream

1 tsp stevia

1 scoop protein powder

3 keto chaffles

**Directions:**

1. Mix together all ingredients in a mixing bowl.

2. Pour mixture in silicone molds and freeze in a freezer for about 4 hours to set.

3. Once frosty is set, top on keto chaffles and enjoy!

Nutrition value per Servings:

Calories: 145 Fat: 9.4g Carbohydrates: 1g Sugar: 0.2g Protein: 14.3g

## Hot Chocolate Breakfast Chaffle

Servings: 2

Cooking Time: 14 Minutes

**Ingredients:**

1 egg, beaten

2 tbsp almond flour

1 tbsp unsweetened cocoa powder

2 tbsp cream cheese, softened

¼ cup finely grated Monterey Jack cheese

2 tbsp sugar-free maple syrup

1 tsp vanilla extract

**Directions:**

1. Preheat the waffle iron.
2. In a medium bowl, mix all the ingredients.
3. Open the iron, lightly grease with cooking spray and pour in half of the mixture.
4. Close the iron and cook until crispy, 7 minutes.
5. Remove the chaffle onto a plate and set aside.
6. Pour the remaining batter in the iron and make the second chaffle.
7. Allow cooling and serve afterward.

Nutrition value per Servings:

Calories 47 Fats 3.67g Carbs 1.39g Protein

2.29g

## Pecan Pumpkin Chaffle

Servings: 2

Cooking Time: 15 Minutes

**Ingredients:**

1 egg

2 tbsp pecans, toasted and chopped

2 tbsp almond flour

1 tsp erythritol

1/4 tsp pumpkin pie spice

1 tbsp pumpkin puree

1/2 cup mozzarella cheese, grated

**Directions:**

1. Preheat your waffle maker.
2. Beat egg in a small bowl.
3. Add remaining ingredients and mix well.
4. Spray waffle maker with cooking spray.
5. Pour half batter in the hot waffle maker and cook for minutes or until golden brown. Repeat with the remaining batter.
6. Serve and enjoy.

Nutrition value:

Calories 121 Fat 9.g Carbohydrates 5.7 g Sugar 3.3 g Protein 6.7 g

## Swiss Bacon Chaffle

Servings: 2

Cooking Time: 8 Minutes

**Ingredients:**

1 egg

½ cup Swiss cheese

2 tablespoons cooked crumbled bacon

**Directions:**

1. Preheat your waffle maker.
2. Beat the egg in a bowl.
3. Stir in the cheese and bacon.
4. Pour half of the mixture into the device.
5. Close and cook for 4 minutes.
6. Cook the second chaffle using the same steps.

Nutrition value:

Calories 23 Fat 17.6g Carbohydrate 1.9g Sugars 0.5g Protein 17.1g

## Bacon, Olives & Cheddar Chaffle

Servings: 2

Cooking Time: 8 Minutes

**Ingredients:**

1 egg

½ cup cheddar cheese, shredded

1 tablespoon black olives, chopped

1 tablespoon bacon bits

**Directions:**

1. Plug in your waffle maker.
2. In a bowl, beat the egg and stir in the cheese.
3. Add the black olives and bacon bits.
4. Mix well.
5. Add half of the mixture into the waffle

maker.

6. Cover and cook for 4 minutes.

7. Open and transfer to a plate.

8. Let cool for 2 minutes.

9. Cook the other chaffle using the remaining batter.

Nutrition value:

Calories 202 Fat 16g Carbohydrate 0.9g Protein 13.4g Sugars 0.3g

## Breakfast Spinach Ricotta Chaffles

Servings: 4

Cooking Time: 28 Minutes

**Ingredients:**

4 oz frozen spinach, thawed, squeezed dry

1 cup ricotta cheese

2 eggs, beaten

½ tsp garlic powder

¼ cup finely grated Pecorino Romano cheese

½ cup finely grated mozzarella cheese

Salt and freshly ground black pepper to taste

**Directions:**

1. Preheat the waffle iron.

2. In a medium bowl, mix all the ingredients.

3. Open the iron, lightly grease with cooking spray and spoon in a quarter of the mixture.

4. Close the iron and cook until brown and crispy, 7 minutes.

5. Remove the chaffle onto a plate and set aside.

6. Make three more chaffles with the remaining mixture.

7. Allow cooling and serve afterward.

Nutrition value:

Calories 50 Fat 13.15g Carbs 5.06g Protein 12.79g

## Pumpkin Chaffle With Frosting

Servings: 2

Cooking Time: 15 Minutes

**Ingredients:**

1 egg, lightly beaten

1 tbsp sugar-free pumpkin puree 1/4 tsp pumpkin pie spice

1/2 cup mozzarella cheese, shredded For frosting:

1/2 tsp vanilla

2 tbsp Swerve

2 tbsp cream cheese, softened

**Directions:**

1. Preheat your waffle maker.

2. Add egg in a bowl and whisk well.

3. Add pumpkin puree, pumpkin pie spice, and cheese and stir well.

4. Spray waffle maker with cooking spray.

5. Pour 1/2 of the batter in the hot waffle maker and cook for 3-4 minutes or until golden brown. Repeat with the remaining batter.

6. In a small bowl, mix all frosting ingredients until smooth.

7. Add frosting on top of hot chaffles and serve.

Nutrition value:

Calories 97 Carbohydrates 3.6 g Sugar 0.6 g Protein 5.6 g

# Thanksgiving Pumpkin Latte With Chaffles

Servings: 1

Cooking Time: 5 minutes

**Ingredients:**

3/4 cup unsweetened coconut milk

2 tbsps. Heavy cream

2 tbsps. Pumpkin puree

1 tsp. stevia

1/4 tsp pumpkin spice

1/4 tsp Vanilla extract

1/4 cup espresso

FOR TOPPING:

2 scoop whipped cream Pumpkin spice

2 heart shape minutesi chaffles

**Directions:**

1. Mix together all recipe ingredients in mug and microwave for minutesute.

2. Pour thelatte intoa serving glass.

3. Top with a heavy cream scoop, pumpkin spice, and chaffle.

4. Serve and enjoy!

Nutrition value per Servings:

Calories: 145 Fat: 9.4g Carbohydrates: 1g Sugar: 0.2g Protein: 14.3g

# Choco And Strawberries Chaffles

Servings: 2

Cooking Time: 5 minutes

**Ingredients:**

1 tbsp. almond flour

1/2 cup strawberry puree

1/2 cup cheddar cheese

1 tbsp. cocoa powder

½ tsp baking powder

1 large egg.

2 tbsps. coconut oil. melted

1/2 tsp vanilla extract optional

**Directions:**

1. Preheat waffle iron while you are mixing the ingredients.

2. Melt oil in a microwave.

3. In a small mixing bowl, mix together flour, baking powder, flour, and vanilla until well combined.

4. Add egg, melted oil, ½ cup cheese and strawberry puree tothe flour mixture.

5. Pour 1/8 cup cheese in a waffle maker and then pour the mixture in the center of greased waffle.

6. Again sprinkle cheese on the batter.

7. Close the waffle maker.

8. Cook chaffles for about 4-5 minutes until cooked and crispy.

9. Once chaffles are cooked, remove and enjoy!

Nutrition value per Servings:

Calories: 145 Fat: 9.4g Carbohydrates: 1g Sugar: 0.2g Protein: 14.3g

# Lemon And Paprika Chaffles

Servings: 4

Cooking Time: 28 Minutes

**Ingredients:**

1 egg, beaten

1 oz cream cheese, softened

1/3 cup finely grated mozzarella cheese

1 tbsp almond flour

1 tsp butter, melted

1 tsp maple (sugar-free) syrup ½ tsp sweet paprika

½ tsp lemon extract

**Directions:**

1. Preheat the waffle iron.

2. Mix all the ingredients in a medium bowl

3. Open the iron and pour in a quarter of the mixture. Close and cook until crispy, 7 minutes.

4. Remove the chaffle onto a plate and make 3 more with the remaining mixture.

5. Cut each chaffle into wedges, plate, allow cooling and serve.

Nutrition value:

Calories 48 Fats 4.22g Carbs 8 Protein 2g

## Triple Chocolate Chaffle

Servings: 4

Cooking Time: 7-9 Minutes

**Ingredients:**

Batter

4 eggs

4 ounces cream cheese, softened

1 ounce dark unsweetened chocolate, melted

1 teaspoon vanilla extract

5 tablespoons almond flour

3 tablespoons cocoa powder

1 ½ teaspoons baking powder

¼ cup dark unsweetened chocolate chips

Other

2 tablespoons butter to brush the waffle maker

**Directions:**

1. Preheat the waffle maker.

2. Add the eggs and cream cheese to a bowl and stir with a wire whisk until just combined.

3. Add the vanilla extract and mix until combined.

4. Stir in the almond flour, cocoa powder, and baking powder and mix until combined.

5. Add the chocolate chips and stir.

6. Brush the heated waffle maker with butter and add a few tablespoons of the batter.

7. Close the lid and cook for about 8 minutes depending on your waffle maker.

8. Serve and enjoy.

Nutrition value per Servings:

Calories 385, fat 33 g, carbs 10.6 g, sugar 0.7 g, Protein 12.g,

## Mixed Berry-Vanilla Chaffles

Servings: 4

Cooking Time: 28 Minutes

**Ingredients:**

1 egg, beaten

½ cup finely grated mozzarella cheese

1 tbsp cream cheese, softened

1 tbsp sugar-free maple syrup

2 strawberries, sliced

2 raspberries, slices

¼ tsp blackberry extract

¼ tsp vanilla extract

½ cup plain yogurt for serving

**Directions:**

1. Preheat the waffle iron.

2. In a medium bowl, mix all the ingredients except the yogurt.

3. Open the iron, lightly grease with cooking spray and pour in a quarter of the mixture.

4. Close the iron and cook until golden brown and crispy, 7 minutes.

5. Remove the chaffle onto a plate and set aside.

6. Make three more chaffles with the remaining mixture.

7. To Servings: top with the yogurt and enjoy.

Nutrition value per Servings:

Calories 75 Carbs 12g Protein 4.5g Sugar 0.5g

## Nut Butter Chaffle

Servings: 2

Cooking Time: 8 Minutes

**Ingredients:**

1 egg

½ cup mozzarella cheese, shredded

2 tablespoons almond flour

½ teaspoon baking powder

1 tablespoon sweetener

1 teaspoon vanilla

2 tablespoons nut butter

**Directions:**

1. Turn on the waffle maker.

2. Beat the egg in a bowl and combine with the cheese.

3. In another bowl, mix the almond flour, baking powder and sweetener.

4. In the third bowl, blend the vanilla extract and nut butter.

5. Gradually add the almond flour mixture into the egg mixture.

6. Then, stir in the vanilla extract.

7. Pour the batter into the waffle maker.

8. Cook for 4 minutes.

9. Transfer to a plate and let cool for 2 minutes.

10. Repeat the steps with the remaining batter.

Nutrition value:

Calories 168  Fat 15.5g Carbohydrate 1.6g Protein 5.4g Sugars 0.6g

## Keto Coffee Chaffles

Servings: 2

Cooking Time: 5 minutes

**Ingredients:**

1 tbsp. almond flour

1 tbsp. instant coffee

1/2 cup cheddar cheese

½ tsp baking powder

1 large egg

**Directions:**

1. Preheat waffle iron and grease with cooking spray

2. Meanwhile, in a small mixing bowl, mix together all ingredients and ½ cup cheese.

3. Pour 1/8 cup cheese in a waffle maker and then pour the mixture in the center of greased waffle.

4. Again, sprinkle cheese on the batter.

5. Close the waffle maker.

6. Cook chaffles for about 4-5 minutes until cooked and crispy.

7. Once chaffles are cooked, remove and enjoy!

Nutrition value per Servings:

Calories: 145 Fat: 9.4g Carbohydrates: 1g Sugar: 0.2g Protein: 14.3g

## Scrambled Egg Stuffed Chaffles

Servings: 4

Cooking Time: 28 Minutes

**Ingredients:**

For the chaffles:

1 cup finely grated cheddar cheese

2 eggs, beaten

For the egg stuffing:

1 tbsp olive oil

1 small red bell pepper

4 large eggs

1 small green bell pepper

Salt and freshly ground black pepper to taste

2 tbsp grated Parmesan cheese

**Directions:**

1. For the chaffles:

2. Preheat the waffle iron.

3. In a medium bowl, mix the cheddar cheese and egg.

4. Open the iron, pour in a quarter of the mixture, close, and cook until crispy, 6 to 7 minutes.

5. Plate and make three more chaffles using the remaining mixture.

6. For the egg stuffing:

7. Meanwhile, heat the olive oil in a medium skillet over medium heat on a stovetop.

8. In a medium bowl, beat the eggs with the bell peppers, salt, black pepper, and Parmesan cheese.

9. Pour the mixture into the skillet and scramble until set to your likeness, 2 minutes.

10. Between two chaffles, spoon half of the scrambled eggs and repeat with the second set of chaffles.

11. Serve afterward.

Nutrition value per Servings:

Calories 387 Fat 22.52g Carbs 18g Protein 27.76g Sugar 2g

## Peanut Butter Sandwich Chaffle

Servings: 1

Cooking Time: 15 Minutes

**Ingredients:**

For chaffle:

1 egg, lightly beaten

1/2 cup mozzarella cheese, shredded 1/4 tsp espresso powder

1 tbsp unsweetened chocolate chips

1 tbsp Swerve

2 tbsp unsweetened cocoa powder

For filling:

1 tbsp butter, softened

2 tbsp Swerve

3 tbsp creamy peanut butter

**Directions:**

1. Preheat your waffle maker.

2. In a bowl, whisk together egg, espresso powder, chocolate chips, Swerve, and cocoa powder.

3. Add mozzarella cheese and stir well.

4. Spray waffle maker with cooking spray.

5. Pour 1/2 of the batter in the hot waffle maker and cook for 3-4 minutes or until golden brown. Repeat with the remaining batter.

6. For filling: In a small bowl, stir together butter, Swerve, and peanut butter until smooth.

7. Once chaffles is cool, then spread filling mixture between two chaffle and place in the fridge for 10 minutes.

8. Cut chaffle sandwich in half and serve.

Nutrition value:

Calories 70 Fat 16.1 g Carbohydrates 9.6 g Sugar 1.1 g Protein 8.2 g

## Easter Morning Simple Chaffles

Servings: 2

Cooking Time: 5 minutes

**Ingredients:**

1/2 cup egg whites

1 cup mozzarella cheese, melted

**Directions:**

1. Switch on your square waffle maker. Spray with non-stick spray.

2. Beat egg whites with beater, until fluffy and white.

3. Add cheese and mix well.

4. Pour batter in a waffle maker.

5. Close the maker and cook for about 3 minutes.

6. Repeat with the remaining batter.

7. Remove chaffles from the maker.

8. Serve hot and enjoy!

Nutrition value per Servings:

Calories: 145 Fat: 9.4g Carbohydrates: 1g Sugar: 0.2g Protein: 14.3g

## Apple Cinnamon Chaffles

Servings: 3

Cooking Time: 20 Minutes

**Ingredients:**

3 eggs, lightly beaten

1 cup mozzarella cheese, shredded ¼ cup apple, chopped

½ tsp monk fruit sweetener

1 ½ tsp cinnamon

¼ tsp baking powder, gluten-free

2 tbsp coconut flour

**Directions:**

1. Preheat your waffle maker.

2. Add remaining ingredients and stir until well combined.

3. Spray waffle maker with cooking spray.

4. Pour 1/3 of batter in the hot waffle maker and cook for minutes or until golden brown. Repeat with the remaining batter.

5. Serve and enjoy.

Nutrition value:

Calories 142 Fat 7.4 g Carbohydrates 9.7 g Sugar 3 g Protein 9.g

## Churro Chaffle

Servings: 2

Cooking Time: 8 Minutes

**Ingredients:**

1 egg

½ cup mozzarella cheese, shredded ½ teaspoon cinnamon

2 tablespoons sweetener

**Directions:**

1. Turn on your waffle iron.
2. Beat the egg in a bowl.
3. Stir in the cheese.
4. Pour half of the mixture into the waffle maker.
5. Cover the waffle iron.
6. Cook for 4 minutes.
7. While waiting, mix the cinnamon and sweetener in a bowl.
8. Open the device and soak the waffle in the cinnamon mixture.
9. Repeat the steps with the remaining batter.

Nutrition value:

Calories 98 Fat 6.9g Carbohydrate 5.8g Protein 9.6g Sugars 0.4g

## Super Easy Chocolate Chaffles

Servings: 2

Cooking Time: 5 minutes

**Ingredients:**

1/4 cup unsweetened chocolate chips

1 egg

2 tbsps. almond flour

1/2 cup mozzarella cheese

1 tbsp. Greek yogurts

1/2 tsp. baking powder

1 tsp. stevia

**Directions:**

1. Switch on your square chaffle maker.
2. Spray the waffle maker with cooking spray.
3. Mix together all recipe ingredients in a mixing bowl.
4. Spoon batter in a greased waffle maker and make two chaffles.
5. Once chaffles are cooked, remove from the maker.
6. Serve with coconut cream, shredded chocolate, and nuts on top.
7. Enjoy!

Nutrition value per Servings:

Calories: 145 Fat: 9.4g Carbohydrates: 1g Sugar: 0.2g Protein: 14.3g

## Mini Keto Pizza

Servings: 2

Cooking Time: 15 Minutes

**Ingredients:**

1 egg

½ cup mozzarella cheese, shredded ¼ teaspoon basil

¼ teaspoon garlic powder

1 tablespoon almond flour

½ teaspoon baking powder

2 tablespoons reduced-carb pasta sauce

2 tablespoons mozzarella cheese

**Directions:**

1. Preheat your waffle maker.

2. In a bowl, beat the egg.

3. Stir in the ½ cup mozzarella cheese, basil, garlic powder, almond flour and baking powder.

4. Add half of the mixture to your waffle maker.

5. Cook for 4 minutes.

6. Transfer to a baking sheet.

7. Cook the second mini pizza.

8. While both pizzas are on the baking sheet, spread the pasta sauce on top.

9. Sprinkle the cheese on top.

10. Bake in the oven until the cheese has melted.

Nutrition value:

Calories 195  Fat 14 g Carbohydrate 4 g Protein 13 g Sugars 1 g

## Keto Chaffle With Almond Flour

Servings: 2

Cooking Time: 8 Minutes

**Ingredients:**

1 egg, beaten

½ cup cheddar cheese, shredded

1 tablespoon almond flour

**Directions:**

1. Turn on your waffle maker.

2. Mix all the ingredients in a bowl.

3. Pour half of the batter into the waffle maker.

4. Close the device and cook for minutes.

5. Remove from the waffle maker.

6. Let sit for 2 to 3 minutes.

7. Repeat the steps with the remaining batter.

Nutrition value:

Calories 145  Fat 11 g  Carbohydrate 1 g  Protein 10 g  Total Sugars 1 g

## Chaffles With Caramelized Apples And Yogurt

Servings: 2

Cooking Time: 10 Minutes

**Ingredients:**

1 tablespoon unsalted butter

1 tablespoon golden brown sugar

1 Granny Smith apple, cored and thinly sliced

1 pinch salt

2 whole-grain frozen waffles, toasted

1/2 cup mozzarella cheese, shredded

1/4 cup Yoplait® Original French Vanilla yogurt

**Directions:**

Melt the butter in a large skillet over medium-high heat until starting to brown. Add mozzarella cheese and stir well.

Add the sugar, apple slices and salt and cook, stirring frequently, until apples are softened and tender, about 6 to 9 minutes.

Put one warm waffle each on a plate, top each with yogurt and apples. Serve warm.

Nutrition value:

Calories: 240  Fat: 10.4 g Carbohydrate: 33.8 g  Protein: 4.7 g

## Keto Chaffle With Ice-Cream

Servings: 2

Cooking Time: 5 Minutes

**Ingredients:**

1 egg

1/2 cup cheddar cheese, shredded

1 tbsp. almond flour

½ tsp. baking powder.

FOR SERVING

1/2 cup heavy cream

1 tbsp. keto chocolate chips.

2 oz. raspberries

2 oz. blueberries

**Directions:**

1. Preheat your minutesi waffle maker according to the manufacturer's Directions.

2. Mix together chaffle ingredients in a small bowl and make minutesi chaffles.

3. For an ice-cream ball, mix cream and chocolate chips in a bowl and pour this mixture in 2 silicone molds.

4. Freeze the ice-cream balls in a freezer for about 2-hours.

5. For serving, set ice-cream ball on chaffle.

6. Top with berries and enjoy!

Nutrition value per Servings:

Calories: 145 Fat: 9.4g Carbohydrates: 1g Sugar: 0.2g Protein: 14.3g

## Chaffle Tortilla

Servings: 2

Cooking Time: 8 Minutes

**Ingredients:**

1 egg

½ cup cheddar cheese, shredded

1 teaspoon baking powder

4 tablespoons almond flour

¼ teaspoon garlic powder

1 tablespoon almond milk Homemade salsa

Sour cream

Jalapeno pepper, chopped

**Directions:**

1. Preheat your waffle maker.

2. Beat the egg in a bowl.

3. Stir in the cheese, baking powder, flour, garlic powder and almond milk.

4. Pour half of the batter into the waffle maker.

5. Cover and cook for 4 minutes.

6. Open and transfer to a plate. Let cool for 2 minutes.

7. Do the same for the remaining batter.

8. Top the waffle with salsa, sour cream and jalapeno pepper.

9. Roll the waffle.

Nutrition value:

Calories 225 Fat 17.6g Carbohydrate 6g Protein 11.3g Sugars 1.9g

## Chicken Quesadilla Chaffle

Servings: 2

Cooking Time: 14 Minutes

**Ingredients:**

1 egg, beaten

¼ tsp taco seasoning

1/3 cup finely grated cheddar cheese

1/3 cup cooked chopped chicken

**Directions:**

1. Preheat the waffle iron.

2. In a medium bowl, mix the eggs, taco seasoning, and cheddar cheese. Add the chicken and combine well.

3. Open the iron, lightly grease with cooking spray and pour in half of the mixture.

4. Close the iron and cook until brown and crispy, 7 minutes.

5. Remove the chaffle onto a plate and set aside.

6. Make another chaffle using the remaining mixture.

7. Serve afterward.

Nutrition value per Servings:

Calories 314 Fat 20.64g Carbs 5.71g Protein 16.74g

# Chocolate Chip Chaffle

Servings: 2

Cooking Time: 8 Minutes

**Ingredients:**

1 egg

½ teaspoon coconut flour

¼ teaspoon baking powder

1 teaspoon sweetener

1 tablespoon heavy whipping cream

1 tablespoon chocolate chips

**Directions:**

1. Preheat your waffle maker.

2. Beat the egg in a bowl.

3. Stir in the flour, baking powder, sweetener and cream.

4. Pour half of the mixture into the waffle maker.

5. Sprinkle the chocolate chips on top and close.

6. Cook for 4 minutes.

7. Remove the chaffle and put on a plate.

8. Do the same procedure with the remaining batter.

Nutrition value:

Calories 146 Fat 10 g Carbohydrate 5 g Protein 6 g Sugars 1 g

# Cheese Garlic Chaffle

Servings: 2

Cooking Time: 8 Minutes

**Ingredients:**

Chaffle

1 egg

1 teaspoon cream cheese

½ cup mozzarella cheese, shredded ½ teaspoon garlic powder

1 teaspoon Italian seasoning

Topping

1 tablespoon butter

½ teaspoon garlic powder

½ teaspoon Italian seasoning

2 tablespoon mozzarella cheese, shredded

**Directions:**

1. Plug in your waffle maker to preheat.

2. Preheat your oven to 350 degrees F.

3. In a bowl, combine all the chaffle ingredients.

4. Cook in the waffle maker for minutes per

chaffle.
5. Transfer to a baking pan.
6. Spread butter on top of each chaffle.
7. Sprinkle garlic powder and Italian seasoning on top.
8. Top with mozzarella cheese.
9. Bake until the cheese has melted.

Nutrition value:

Calories141  Fat 13 g Carbohydrate 2.6g

## Lemon And Vanilla Chaffle

Servings:4

Cooking Time:7-9 Minutes

**Ingredients:**

Batter

4 eggs

4 ounces ricotta cheese

2 teaspoons vanilla extract

2 tablespoons fresh lemon juice Zest of ½ lemon

6 tablespoons stevia

5 tablespoons coconut flour

½ teaspoon baking powder

Other

2 tablespoons butter to brush the waffle maker

**Directions:**

1. Preheat the waffle maker.
2. Add the eggs and ricotta cheese to a bowl and stir with a wire whisk until just combined.
3. Add the vanilla extract, lemon juice, lemon zest, and stevia and mix until combined.
4. Stir in the coconut flour and baking powder until combined.
5. Brush the heated waffle maker with butter and add a few tablespoons of the batter.
6. Close the lid and cook for about 7-8 minutes depending on your waffle maker.
7. Serve and enjoy.

Nutrition value per Servings:

Calories 200, fat 13.4 g, carbs 9 g, sugar 0.9 g, Protein 10.2 g

## Christmas Smoothie With Chaffles

Servings: 2

Cooking Time: 10 Minutes

**Ingredients:**

1 cupcoconutmilk

2 tbsps. almonds chopped ¼ cup cherries

1 pinch sea salt

1/4 cup ice cubes

FOR TOPPING:

2 oz. keto chocolate chips

2 oz. cherries

2 minutesi chaffles

2 scoop heavy cream, frozen

**Directions:**

1. Add almond milk, almonds, cherries, salt and ice in a blender, blend for 2 minutes until smooth and fluffy.
2. Pour the smoothie into glasses.
3. Top with one scoop heavy cream, chocolate chips, cherries and chaffle in each glass.
4. Serve and enjoy!

Nutrition value per Servings:

Calories: 145 Fat: 9.4g Carbohydrates: 1g Sugar: 0.2g Protein: 14.3g

## Raspberry And Chocolate Chaffle

Servings: 4

Cooking Time: 7-9 Minutes

**Ingredients:**

Batter

4 eggs

2 ounces cream cheese, softened

2 ounces sour cream

1 teaspoon vanilla extract

5 tablespoons almond flour ¼ cup cocoa powder

1½ teaspoons baking powder

2 ounces fresh or frozen raspberries

2 tablespoons butter to brush the waffle maker Fresh sprigs of mint to garnish

**Directions:**

1. Preheat the waffle maker.

2. Add the eggs, cream cheese and sour cream to a bowl and stir with a wire whisk until just combined.

3. Add the vanilla extract and mix until combined.

4. Stir in the almond flour, cocoa powder, and baking powder and mix until combined.

5. Add the raspberries and stir until combined.

6. Brush the heated waffle maker with butter and add a few tablespoons of the batter.

7. Close the lid and cook for about 8 minutes depending on your waffle maker.

8. Serve with fresh sprigs of mint.

Nutrition value per Servings:

Calories 270, fat 23 g, carbs 8.g, sugar 1.3 g, Protein 10.2 g

## Pumkpin Chaffle With Maple Syrup

Servings: 2

Cooking Time: 16 Minutes

**Ingredients:**

2 eggs, beaten

½ cup mozzarella cheese, shredded

1 teaspoon coconut flour

¾ teaspoon baking powder

¾ teaspoon pumpkin pie spice

2 teaspoons pureed pumpkin

4 teaspoons heavy whipping cream ½ teaspoon vanilla

Pinch salt

2 teaspoons maple syrup (sugar-free)

**Directions:**

1. Turn your waffle maker on.

2. Mix all the ingredients except maple syrup in a large bowl.

3. Pour half of the batter into the waffle maker.

4. Close and cook for minutes.

5. Transfer to a plate to cool for 2 minutes.

6. Repeat the steps with the remaining mixture.

7. Drizzle the maple syrup on top of the chaffles before serving.

Nutrition value:

Calories 201  Fat 15 g  Carbohydrate 4 g   Protein 12 g  Sugars 1 g

## Maple Syrup & Vanilla Chaffle

Servings: 3

Cooking Time: 12 Minutes

**Ingredients:**

1 egg, beaten

¼ cup mozzarella cheese, shredded

1 oz. cream cheese

1 teaspoon vanilla

1 tablespoon keto maple syrup

1 teaspoon sweetener

1 teaspoon baking powder

4 tablespoons almond flour

**Directions:**

1. Preheat your waffle maker.
2. Add all the ingredients to a bowl.
3. Mix well.
4. Pour some of the batter into the waffle maker.
5. Cover and cook for 4 minutes.
6. Transfer chaffle to a plate and let cool for 2 minutes.
7. Repeat the same process with the remaining mixture.

Nutrition value:

Calories 146  Fat 9.5g Carbohydrate 10.6g Protein 5.6g Total Sugars 6.4g

## Garlic Mayo Vegan Chaffles

Servings: 2

Cooking Time: 5 minutes

**Ingredients:**

1 tbsp. chia seeds

2 ½ tbsps. water

¼ cup low carb vegan cheese

2 tbsps. coconut flour

1 cup low carb vegan cream cheese, softened

1 tsp. garlic powder

pinch of salt

2 tbsps. vegan garlic mayo for topping

**Directions:**

1. Preheat your square waffle maker.
2. In a small bowl, mix chia seeds and water, let it stand for 5 minutes.
3. Add all ingredients to the chia seeds mixture and mix well.
4. Pour vegan chaffle batter in a greased waffle maker
5. Close the waffle maker and cook for about 3-minutes.
6. Once chaffles are cooked, remove from the maker.
7. Top with garlic mayo and pepper.
8. Enjoy!

Nutrition value per Servings:

Calories: 145 Fat: 9.4g Carbohydrates: 1g Sugar: 0.2g Protein: 14.3g

## Broccoli Chaffle

Servings: 4

Cooking Time: 15 Minutes

**Ingredients:**

Batter

4 eggs

2 cups grated mozzarella cheese

1 cup steamed broccoli, chopped Salt and pepper to taste

1 clove garlic, minced

1 teaspoon chili flakes

2 tablespoons almond flour

2 teaspoons baking powder

2 tablespoons cooking spray to brush the waffle maker ¼ cup mascarpone cheese for serving

**Directions:**

1. Preheat the waffle maker.

2. Add the eggs, grated mozzarella, chopped broccoli, salt and pepper, minced garlic, chili flakes, almond flour and baking powder to a bowl.

3. Mix with a fork.

4. Brush the heated waffle maker with cooking spray and add a few tablespoons of the batter.

5. Close the lid and cook for about 7 minutes depending on your waffle maker.

6. Serve each chaffle with mascarpone cheese.

Nutrition value per Servings:

Calories 229, fat 15 g, carbs 6 g, sugar 1.1 g, Protein 13.1 g

## Celery And Cottage Cheese Chaffle

Servings: 4

Cooking Time: 15 Minutes

**Ingredients:**

Batter

4 eggs

2 cups grated cheddar cheese

1 cup fresh celery, chopped

Salt and pepper to taste

2 tablespoons chopped almonds

2 teaspoons baking powder

2 tablespoons cooking spray to brush the waffle maker ¼ cup cottage cheese for serving

**Directions:**

1. Preheat the waffle maker.

2. Add the eggs, grated mozzarella cheese, chopped celery, salt and pepper, chopped almonds and baking powder to a bowl.

3. Mix with a fork.

4. Brush the heated waffle maker with cooking spray and add a few tablespoons of the batter.

5. Close the lid and cook for about 7 minutes depending on your waffle maker.

6. Serve each chaffle with cottage cheese on top.

Nutrition value per Servings:

Calories 385, fat 31.6 g, carbs 4 g, sugar 1.5 g, Protein 22.2 g

## Mushroom And Almond Chaffle

Servings: 4

Cooking Time: 15 Minutes

**Ingredients:**

Batter

4 eggs

2 cups grated mozzarella cheese

1 cup finely chopped zucchini

3 tablespoons chopped almonds

2 teaspoons baking powder

Salt and pepper to taste

1 teaspoon dried basil

1 teaspoon chili flakes

2 tablespoons cooking spray to brush the waffle maker

**Directions:**

1. Preheat the waffle maker.

2. Add the eggs, grated mozzarella, mushrooms, almonds, baking powder, salt and pepper, dried basil and chili flakes to a bowl.

3. Mix with a fork.

4. Brush the heated waffle maker with cooking spray and add a few tablespoons of the batter.

5. Close the lid and cook for about 7 minutes depending on your waffle maker.

6. Serve and enjoy.

Nutrition value per Servings:

Calories 196, fat 16 g, carbs 4 g, sugar 1 g, Protein 10.8 g

# Spinach And Artichoke Chaffle

Servings: 4

Cooking Time: 15 Minutes

**Ingredients:**

Batter

4 eggs

2 cups grated provolone cheese

1 cup cooked and diced spinach

½ cup diced artichoke hearts

Salt and pepper to taste

2 tablespoons coconut flour

2 teaspoons baking powder

2 tablespoons cooking spray to brush the waffle maker ¼ cup of cream cheese for serving

**Directions:**

1. Preheat the waffle maker.

2. Add the eggs, grated provolone cheese, diced spinach, artichoke hearts, salt and pepper, coconut flour and baking powder to a bowl.

3. Mix with a fork.

4. Brush the heated waffle maker with cooking spray and add a few tablespoons of the batter.

5. Close the lid and cook for about 7 minutes depending on your waffle maker.

6. Serve each chaffle with cream cheese.

Nutrition value per Servings:

Calories 42 fat 32.8 g, carbs 9.5 g, sugar 1.1 g, Protein 25.7 g

# Avocado Croque Madam Chaffle

Servings: 4

Cooking Time: 15 Minutes

**Ingredients:**

Batter

4 eggs

2 cups grated mozzarella cheese

1 avocado, mashed

Salt and pepper to taste

6 tablespoons almond flour

2 teaspoons baking powder

1 teaspoon dried dill

2 tablespoons cooking spray to brush the waffle maker

4 fried eggs

2 tablespoons freshly chopped basil

**Directions:**

1. Preheat the waffle maker.

2. Add the eggs, grated mozzarella, avocado, salt and pepper, almond flour, baking powder and dried dill to a bowl.

3. Mix with a fork.

4. Brush the heated waffle maker with cooking spray and add a few tablespoons of the batter.

5. Close the lid and cook for about 7 minutes depending on your waffle maker.

6. Serve each chaffle with a fried egg and freshly chopped basil on top.

Nutrition value per Servings:

Calories 393, fat 32.1 g, carbs 9.2 g, sugar 1.3 g, Protein 18.8 g

## Fruity Vegan Chaffles

Servings:2

Cooking Time:5minutes

**Ingredients:**

1 tbsp. chia seeds

2 tbsps. warm water

¼ cup low carb vegan cheese

2 tbsps. strawberry puree

2 tbsps. Greek yogurt

pinch of salt

**Directions:**

1. Preheat minutesi waffle maker to medium-high heat.

2. In a small bowl, mix together chia seeds and water and let it stand for few minutes to be thickened.

3. Mix the rest of the ingredients in chia seed egg and mix well.

4. Spray waffle machine with cooking spray.

5. Pour vegan waffle batter into the center of the waffle iron.

6. Close the waffle maker and cook chaffles for about 3-5 minutes.

7. Once cooked, remove from the maker and serve with berries on top.

Nutrition value per Servings:

Calories: 145 Fat: 9.4g Carbohydrates: 1g Sugar: 0.2g Protein: 14.3g

## Almonds And Flaxseeds Chaffles

Servings:2

Cooking Time:5minutes

**Ingredients:**

1/4 cup coconut flour

1 tsp. stevia

1 tbsp. ground flaxseed

1/4 tsp baking powder

1/2 cup almond milk

1/4 tsp vanilla extract

1/ cup low carb vegan cheese

**Directions:**

1. Mix together flaxseed in warm water and set aside.

2. Add in the remaining ingredients.

3. Switch on waffle iron and grease with cooking spray.

4. Pour the batter in the waffle machine and close the lid.

5. Cook the chaffles for about 3-4 minutes.

6. Once cooked, remove from the waffle machine.

7. Serve with berries and enjoy!

Nutrition value per Servings:

Calories 42 fat 32.8 g, carbs 9.5 g, sugar 1.1 g, Protein 25.7 g

## Vegan Chocolate Chaffles

Servings: 2

Cooking Time: 5minutes

**Ingredients:**

1/2 cupcoconut flour

3 tbsps. cocoa powder

2 tbsps. whole psyllium husk

1/2 teaspoon baking powder

pinch of salt

1/2 cup vegan cheese, softened 1/4 cup coconut milk

**Directions:**

1. Prepare your waffle iron according to the manufacturer's Directions.

2. Mix together coconut flour, cocoa powder, baking powder, salt and husk in a bowl and set aside.

3. Add melted cheese and milk and mix well. Let it stand for a few minutes before cooking.

4. Pour batter in waffle machine and cook for about 3-minutes.

5. Once chaffles are cooked, carefully remove them from the waffle machine.

6. Serve with vegan icecream and enjoy!

Nutrition value per Servings:

Calories 196, fat 16 g, carbs 4 g, sugar 1 g, Protein 10.8 g

## Vegan Chaffles With Flaxseed

Servings: 2

Cooking Time: 5minutes

**Ingredients:**

1 tbsp. flaxseed meal

2 tbsps. warm water

¼ cup low carb vegan cheese

¼ cup chopped minutest

pinch of salt

2 oz. blueberries chunks

**Directions:**

1. Preheat waffle maker to medium-high heat and grease with cooking spray.

2. Mix together flaxseed meal and warm water and set aside to be thickened.

3. After 5 minutes' mix together all ingredients in flax egg.

4. Pour vegan waffle batter into the center of the waffle iron.

5. Close the waffle maker and let cook for 3-minutes

6. Once cooked, remove the vegan chaffle from the waffle maker and serve.

Nutrition value per Servings:

Calories 42 fat 32.8 g, carbs 9.5 g, sugar 1.1 g, Protein 25.7 g

## Asparagus Chaffle

Servings: 4

Cooking Time: 15 Minutes

**Ingredients:**

Batter

4 eggs

1½ cups grated mozzarella cheese

½ cup grated parmesan cheese

1 cup boiled asparagus, chopped Salt and pepper to taste

¼ cup almond flour

2 teaspoons baking powder

2 tablespoons cooking spray to brush the waffle maker ¼ cup Greek yogurt for serving

¼ cup chopped almonds for serving

**Directions:**

1. Preheat the waffle maker.

2. Add the eggs, grated mozzarella, grated parmesan, asparagus, salt and pepper, almond flour and baking powder to a bowl.

3. Mix with a fork.

4. Brush the heated waffle maker with cooking spray and add a few tablespoons of the batter.

5. Close the lid and cook for about 7 minutes depending on your waffle maker.

6. Serve each chaffle with Greek yogurt and chopped almonds.

Nutrition value per Servings:

Calories 316, fat 24.9 g, carbs 3 g, sugar 1.2 g, Protein 18.2 g

## Rosemary Pork Chops On Chaffle

Servings: 4

Cooking Time: 15 Minutes

**Ingredients:**

4 eggs

2 cups grated mozzarella cheese Salt and pepper to taste

Pinch of nutmeg

2 tablespoons sour cream

6 tablespoons almond flour

2 teaspoons baking powder

Pork chops

2 tablespoons olive oil

1 pound pork chops

Salt and pepper to taste

1 teaspoon freshly chopped rosemary

2 tablespoons cooking spray to brush the waffle maker

2 tablespoons freshly chopped basil for decoration

**Directions:**

1. Preheat the waffle maker.

2. Add the eggs, mozzarella cheese, salt and pepper, nutmeg, sour cream, almond flour and baking powder to a bowl.

3. Mix until combined.

4. Brush the heated waffle maker with cooking spray and add a few tablespoons of the batter.

5. Close the lid and cook for about 7 minutes depending on your waffle maker.

6. Meanwhile, heat the butter in a nonstick grill pan and season the pork chops with salt and pepper and freshly chopped rosemary.

7. Cook the pork chops for about 4-5 minutes on each side.

8. Serve each chaffle with a pork chop and sprinkle some freshly chopped basil on top.

Nutrition value per Servings:

Calories 666, fat 55.2 g, carbs 4.8 g, sugar 0.4 g, Protein 37.5 g

## Classic Beef Chaffle

Servings: 4

Cooking Time: 10 Minutes

**Ingredients:**

Batter

½ pound ground beef

4 eggs

4 ounces cream cheese

1 cup grated mozzarella cheese Salt and pepper to taste

1 clove garlic, minced

½ teaspoon freshly chopped rosemary

2 tablespoons butter to brush the waffle maker ¼ cup sour cream

2 tablespoons freshly chopped parsley for garnish

**Directions:**

1. Preheat the waffle maker.

2. Add the ground beef, eggs, cream cheese, grated mozzarella cheese, salt and pepper, minced garlic and freshly chopped rosemary to a bowl.

3. Brush the heated waffle maker with butter and add a few tablespoons of the batter.

4. Close the lid and cook for about 8-10 minutes depending on your waffle maker.

5. Serve each chaffle with a tablespoon of sour cream and freshly chopped parsley on top.

6. Serve and enjoy.

Nutrition value per Servings:

Calories 368, fat 24 g, carbs 2.1 g, sugar 0.4 g, Protein 27.4 g

## Beef And Tomato Chaffle

Servings: 4

Cooking Time: 15 Minutes

**Ingredients:**

Batter

4 eggs

¼ cup cream cheese

1 cup grated mozzarella cheese Salt and pepper to taste

¼ cup almond flour

1 teaspoon freshly chopped dill

Beef

1 pound beef loin

Salt and pepper to taste

1 tablespoon balsamic vinegar

2 tablespoons olive oil

1 teaspoon freshly chopped rosemary

2 tablespoons cooking spray to brush the waffle maker

4 tomato slices for serving

**Directions:**

1. Preheat the waffle maker.

2. Add the eggs, cream cheese, grated mozzarella cheese, salt and pepper, almond flour and freshly chopped dill to a bowl.

3. Mix until combined and batter forms.

4. Brush the heated waffle maker with cooking spray and add a few tablespoons of the batter.

5. Close the lid and cook for about 8-10 minutes depending on your waffle maker.

6. Meanwhile, heat the olive oil in a non-stick frying pan and season the beef loin with

salt and pepper and freshly chopped rosemary.

7. Cook the beef on each side for about 5 minutes and drizzle with some balsamic vinegar. 8. Serve each chaffle with a slice of tomato and cooked beef loin slices.

Nutrition value per Servings:

Calories 4, fat 35.8 g, carbs 3.3 g, sugar 0.8 g, Protein 40.3 g

## Classic Ground Pork Chaffle

Servings: 4

Cooking Time: 15 Minutes

**Ingredients:**

½ pound ground pork

3 eggs

½ cup grated mozzarella cheese Salt and pepper to taste

1 clove garlic, minced

1 teaspoon dried oregano

2 tablespoons butter to brush the waffle maker

2 tablespoons freshly chopped parsley for garnish

**Directions:**

1. Preheat the waffle maker.

2. Add the ground pork, eggs, mozzarella cheese, salt and pepper, minced garlic and dried oregano to a bowl.

3. Mix until combined.

4. Brush the heated waffle maker with butter and add a few tablespoons of the batter.

5. Close the lid and cook for about 7-8 minutes depending on your waffle maker.

6. Serve with freshly chopped parsley.

Nutrition value per Servings:

Calories 192, fat 11.g, carbs 1 g, sugar 0.3 g, Protein 20.2 g

## Spinach & Artichoke Chicken Chaffle

Servings: 2

Cooking Time: 8 Minutes

**Ingredients:**

1/3 cup cooked diced chicken

1/3 cup cooked spinach chopped

1/3 cup marinated artichokes chopped

1/3 cup shredded mozzarella cheese

1 ounce softened cream cheese

1/4 teaspoon garlic powder

1 egg

**Directions:**

1. Heat up your Dash mini waffle maker.

2. In a small bowl, mix the egg, garlic powder, cream cheese, and Mozzarella Cheese.

3. Add the spinach, artichoke, and chicken and mix well.

4. Add 1/3 of the batter into your mini waffle maker and cook for minutes. If they are still a bit uncooked, leave it cooking for another 2 minutes. Then cook the rest of the batter to make a second chaffle and then cook the third chaffle.

5. After cooking, remove from the pan and let sit for 2 minutes.

6. Dip in ranch dressing, sour cream, or enjoy alone.

Nutrition value:

Calories: 110 ;Carbohydrates:3g ;Protein: 11g;Fat: 13g Sugar: 1g

# Beef Chaffle Taco

Servings: 4

Cooking Time: 15 Minutes

**Ingredients:**

Batter

4 eggs

2 cups grated cheddar cheese ¼ cup heavy cream

Salt and pepper to taste

¼ cup almond flour

2 teaspoons baking powder

Beef

2 tablespoons butter

½ onion, diced

1 pound ground beef

Salt and pepper to taste

1 teaspoon dried oregano

1 tablespoon sugar-free ketchup

2 tablespoons cooking spray to brush the waffle maker

2 tablespoons freshly chopped parsley

**Directions:**

1. Preheat the waffle maker.

2. Add the eggs, grated cheddar cheese, heavy cream, salt and pepper, almond flour and baking powder to a bowl.

3. Brush the heated waffle maker with cooking spray and add a few tablespoons of the batter.

4. Close the lid and cook for about 5-7 minutes depending on your waffle maker.

5. Once the chaffle is ready, place it in a napkin holder to harden into the shape of a taco as it cools.

6. Meanwhile, melt and heat the butter in a nonstick frying pan and start cooking the diced onion.

7. Once the onion is tender, add the ground beef. Season with salt and pepper and dried oregano and stir in the sugar-free ketchup.

8. Cook for about 7 minutes.

9. Serve the cooked ground meat in each taco chaffle sprinkled with some freshly chopped parsley.

Nutrition value per Servings:

Calories 719, fat 51.7 g, carbs 7.3 g, sugar 1.3 g, Protein 56.1 g

# Cheddar Chicken And Broccoli Chaffle

Servings: 2

Cooking Time: 8 Minutes

**Ingredients:**

1/4 cup cooked diced chicken

1/4 cup fresh broccoli chopped

Shredded Cheddar cheese

1 egg

1/4 tsp garlic powder

**Directions:**

1. Heat up your Dash mini waffle maker.

2. In a small bowl, mix the egg, garlic powder, and cheddar cheese.

3. Add the broccoli and chicken and mix well.

4. Add 1/2 of the batter into your mini waffle maker and cook for minutes. If they are still a bit uncooked, leave it cooking for another 2 minutes. Then cook the rest of the batter to make a second chaffle and then cook the third chaffle.

5. After cooking, remove from the pan and let sit for 2 minutes.

6. Dip in ranch dressing, sour cream, or enjoy alone.

Nutrition value:

Calories: 58 ;Carbohydrates:1g ;Protein: ;Fat: 3g ;Sugar: 1g

## Turkey Chaffle Sandwich

Servings:4

Cooking Time:15 Minutes

**Ingredients:**

Batter

4 eggs

¼ cup cream cheese

1 cup grated mozzarella cheese Salt and pepper to taste

1 teaspoon dried dill

½ teaspoon onion powder

½ teaspoon garlic powder

Juicy chicken

2 tablespoons butter

1 pound chicken breast

Salt and pepper to taste

1 teaspoon dried dill

2 tablespoons heavy cream

2 tablespoons butter to brush the waffle maker

4 lettuce leaves to garnish the sandwich

4 tomato slices to garnish the sandwich

**Directions:**

1. Preheat the waffle maker.

2. Add the eggs, cream cheese, mozzarella cheese, salt and pepper, dried dill, onion powder and garlic powder to a bowl.

3. Mix everything with a fork just until batter forms.

4. Brush the heated waffle maker with butter and add a few tablespoons of the batter.

5. Close the lid and cook for about 7 minutes depending on your waffle maker.

6. Meanwhile, heat some butter in a nonstick pan.

7. Season the chicken with salt and pepper and sprinkle with dried dill. Pour the heavy cream on top.

8. Cook the chicken slices for about 10 minutes or until golden brown.

9. Cut each chaffle in half.

10. On one half add a lettuce leaf, tomato slice, and chicken slice. Cover with the other chaffle half to make a sandwich.

11. Serve and enjoy.

Nutrition value per Servings:

Calories 381, fat 26.3 g, carbs 2.5 g, sugar 1 g, Protein 32.9 g

## Bbq Sauce Pork Chaffle

Servings:4

Cooking Time:15 Minutes

**Ingredients:**

½ pound ground pork

3 eggs

1 cup grated mozzarella cheese Salt and pepper to taste

1 clove garlic, minced

1 teaspoon dried rosemary

3 tablespoons sugar-free BBQ sauce

2 tablespoons butter to brush the waffle maker

½ pound pork rinds for serving

¼ cup sugar-free BBQ sauce for serving

**Directions:**

1. Preheat the waffle maker.

2. Add the ground pork, eggs, mozzarella, salt and pepper, minced garlic, dried rosemary, and BBQ sauce to a bowl.

3. Mix until combined.

4. Brush the heated waffle maker with butter and add a few tablespoons of the batter.

5. Close the lid and cook for about 7-8 minutes depending on your waffle maker.

6. Serve each chaffle with some pork rinds and a tablespoon of BBQ sauce.

Nutrition value per Servings:

Calories 350, fat 21.1 g, carbs 2.g, sugar 0.3 g, Protein 36.9 g

## Chicken Bacon Ranch Chaffle

Servings: 2

Cooking Time: 8 Minutes

**Ingredients:**

1 egg

1/3 cup cooked chicken diced

1 piece bacon cooked and crumbled

1/3 cup shredded cheddar jack cheese

1 teaspoon powdered ranch dressing

**Directions:**

1. Heat up your Dash mini waffle maker.

2. In a small bowl, mix the egg, ranch dressing, and Monterey Jack Cheese.

3. Add the bacon and chicken and mix well.

4. Add half of the batter into your mini waffle maker and cook for 3-minutes. Then cook the rest of the batter to make a second chaffle.

5. Remove from the pan and let sit for 2 minutes.

6. Dip in ranch dressing, sour cream, or enjoy alone.

Nutrition value:

Calories: 200kcal ;Carbohydrates:2g ;Protein: 16g;Fat: 14g ;Sugar: 1g

## Chicken Taco Chaffle

Servings:4

Cooking Time:15 Minutes

**Ingredients:**

Batter

4 eggs

2 cups grated provolone cheese

6 tablespoons almond flour

2½ teaspoons baking powder

Salt and pepper to taste

Chicken topping

2 tablespoons olive oil

½ pound ground chicken

Salt and pepper to taste

1 garlic clove, minced

2 teaspoons dried oregano

2 tablespoons butter to brush the waffle maker

2 tablespoons freshly chopped spring onion for garnishing

**Directions:**

1. Preheat the waffle maker.

2. Add the eggs, grated provolone cheese, almond flour, baking powder and salt and pepper to a bowl.

3. Mix until just combined.

4. Brush the heated waffle maker with cooking spray and add a few tablespoons of the batter.

5. Close the lid and cook for about 7-9 minutes depending on your waffle maker.

6. Meanwhile, heat the olive oil in a nonstick pan over medium heat and start cooking the ground chicken.

7. Season with salt and pepper and stir in the minced garlic and dried oregano. Cook for 10 minutes.

8. Add some of the cooked ground chicken to each chaffle and serve with freshly chopped spring onion.

Nutrition value per Servings:

Calories 584, fat 44 g, carbs 6.4 g, sugar 0.8 g, Protein 41.3g

## Italian Chicken And Basil Chaffle

Servings: 4

Cooking Time: 7-9 Minutes

**Ingredients:**

Batter

½ pound ground chicken

4 eggs

3 tablespoons tomato sauce

Salt and pepper to taste

1 cup grated mozzarella cheese

1 teaspoon dried oregano

3 tablespoons freshly chopped basil leaves ½

teaspoon dried garlic

2 tablespoons butter to brush the waffle maker

¼ cup tomato sauce for serving

1 tablespoon freshly chopped basil for serving

**Directions:**

1. Preheat the waffle maker.

2. Add the ground chicken, eggs and tomato sauce to a bowl and season with salt and pepper.

3. Add the mozzarella cheese and season with dried oregano, freshly chopped basil and dried garlic.

4. Mix until fully combined and batter forms.

5. Brush the heated waffle maker with butter and add a few tablespoons of the chaffle batter.

6. Close the lid and cook for about 7-9 minutes depending on your waffle maker.

7. Repeat with the rest of the batter.

8. Serve with tomato sauce and freshly chopped basil on top.

Nutrition value per Servings:

Calories 250, fat 15.7 g, carbs 2.5 g, sugar 1.5 g, Protein 24.5 g

## Beef Meatballs On A Chaffle

Servings: 4

Cooking Time: 20 Minutes

**Ingredients:**

Batter

4 eggs

2½ cups grated gouda cheese ¼ cup heavy cream

Salt and pepper to taste

1 spring onion, finely chopped Beef meatballs

1 pound ground beef

Salt and pepper to taste

2 teaspoons Dijon mustard

1 spring onion, finely chopped

5 tablespoons almond flour

2 tablespoons butter

2 tablespoons cooking spray to brush the waffle maker

2 tablespoons freshly chopped parsley

**Directions:**

1. Preheat the waffle maker.

2. Add the eggs, grated gouda cheese, heavy cream, salt and pepper and finely chopped spring onion to a bowl.

3. Mix until combined and batter forms.

4. Brush the heated waffle maker with cooking spray and add a few tablespoons of the batter.

5. Close the lid and cook for about 7 minutes depending on your waffle maker.

6. Meanwhile, mix the ground beef meat, salt and pepper, Dijon mustard, chopped spring onion and

almond flour in a large bowl.

7. Form small meatballs with your hands.

8. Heat the butter in a nonstick frying pan and cook the beef meatballs for about 3-4 minutes on each side.

9. Serve each chaffle with a couple of meatballs and some freshly chopped parsley on top.

Nutrition value per Servings:

Calories 670, fat 47.4g, carbs 4.6 g, sugar 1.7 g, Protein 54.9 g

# Leftover Turkey Chaffle

Servings: 4

Cooking Time: 7-9 Minutes

**Ingredients:**

Batter

½ pound shredded leftover turkey meat

4 eggs

1 cup grated provolone cheese Salt and pepper to taste

1 teaspoon dried basil

½ teaspoon dried garlic

3 tablespoons sour cream

2 tablespoons coconut flour

2 tablespoons cooking spray for greasing the chaffle maker ¼ cup cream cheese for serving the chaffles

**Directions:**

1. Preheat the waffle maker.

2. Add the leftover turkey, eggs and provolone cheese to a bowl and season with salt and pepper, dried basil and dried garlic.

3. Add the sour cream and coconut flour and mix until batter forms.

4. Brush the heated waffle maker with cooking spray and add a few tablespoons of the chaffle batter.

5. Close the lid and cook for about 7-9 minutes depending on your waffle maker.

6. Repeat with the rest of the batter.

7. Serve with cream cheese on top of each chaffle.

Nutrition value per Servings:

Calories 372, fat 27.g, carbs 5.4 g, sugar 0.6 g, Protein 25 g

## Beef Meatza Chaffle

Servings: 4

Cooking Time: 15 Minutes

**Ingredients:**

Meatza chaffle batter

½ pound ground beef

4 eggs

2 cups grated cheddar cheese

Salt and pepper to taste

1 teaspoon Italian seasoning

2 tablespoons tomato sauce

2 tablespoons cooking spray to brush the waffle maker ¼ cup tomato sauce for serving

2 tablespoons freshly chopped basil for serving

**Directions:**

1. Preheat the waffle maker.
2. Add the ground beef, eggs, grated cheddar cheese, salt and pepper, Italian seasoning and tomato sauce to a bowl.
3. Mix until everything is fully combined.
4. Brush the heated waffle maker with cooking spray and add a few tablespoons of the batter.
5. Close the lid and cook for about 7-10 minutes depending on your waffle maker.
6. Serve with tomato sauce and freshly chopped basil on top.

Nutrition value per Servings:

Calories 4, fat 34.6 g, carbs 2.5 g, sugar 1.7 g, Protein 36.5 g

## Chicken Jalapeno Chaffle

Servings: 4

Cooking Time: 8-10 Minutes

**Ingredients:**

Batter

½ pound ground chicken

4 eggs

1 cup grated mozzarella cheese

2 tablespoons sour cream

1 green jalapeno, chopped

Salt and pepper to taste

1 teaspoon dried oregano

½ teaspoon dried garlic

2 tablespoons butter to brush the waffle maker ¼ cup sour cream to garnish

1 green jalapeno, diced, to garnish

**Directions:**

1. Preheat the waffle maker.
2. Add the ground chicken, eggs, mozzarella cheese, sour cream, chopped jalapeno, salt and pepper, dried oregano and dried garlic to a bowl.
3. Mix everything until batter forms.
4. Brush the heated waffle maker with butter and add a few tablespoons of the batter.
5. Close the lid and cook for about 8-10 minutes depending on your waffle maker.
6. Serve with a tablespoon of sour cream and sliced jalapeno on top.

Nutrition value per Servings:

Calories 284, fat 19.4 g, carbs 2.2 g, sugar 0.6 g, Protein 24.g

## Pork Tzatziki Chaffle

Servings: 4

Cooking Time: 25 Minutes

**Ingredients:**

4 eggs

2 cups grated provolone cheese Salt and pepper to taste

1 teaspoon dried rosemary

1 teaspoon dried oregano

Pork loin

2 tablespoons olive oil

1 pound pork tenderloin

Salt and pepper to taste

Tzatziki sauce

1 cup sour cream

Salt and pepper to taste

1 cucumber, peeled and diced

1 teaspoon garlic powder

1 teaspoon dried dill

2 tablespoons butter to brush the waffle maker

**Directions:**

1. Preheat the waffle maker.
2. Add the eggs, grated provolone cheese, dried rosemary, and dried oregano to a bowl. Season with salt and pepper to taste.
3. Mix until combined.
4. Brush the heated waffle maker with butter and add a few tablespoons of the batter.
5. Close the lid and cook for about 7 minutes depending on your waffle maker.
6. Meanwhile, heat the olive oil in a non-stick frying pan. Generously season the pork tenderloin with salt and pepper and cook it for about 7 minutes on each side.
7. Mix the sour cream, salt and pepper, diced cucumber, garlic powder and dried dill in a bowl.
8. Serve each chaffle with a few tablespoons of tzatziki sauce and slices of pork tenderloin.

Nutrition value per Servings:

Calories 700, fat 50.g, carbs 6 g, sugar 1.5 g, Protein 54.4 g

## Mediterranean Lamb Kebabs On Chaffle

Servings: 4

Cooking Time: 15 Minutes

**Ingredients:**

4 eggs

2 cups grated mozzarella cheese Salt and pepper to taste

1 teaspoon garlic powder

¼ cup Greek yogurt

½ cup coconut flour

2 teaspoons baking powder Lamb kebabs

1 pound ground lamb meat

Salt and pepper to taste

1 egg

2 tablespoons almond flour

1 spring onion, finely chopped ½ teaspoon dried garlic

2 tablespoons olive oil

2 tablespoons butter to brush the waffle maker ¼ cup sour cream for serving

4 sprigs of fresh dill for garnish

**Directions:**

1. Preheat the waffle maker.

2. Add the eggs, mozzarella cheese, salt and pepper, garlic powder, Greek yogurt, coconut flour and baking powder to a bowl.

3. Mix until combined.

4. Brush the heated waffle maker with butter and add a few tablespoons of the batter.

5. Close the lid and cook for about 7 minutes depending on your waffle maker.

6. Meanwhile, add the ground lamb, salt and pepper, egg, almond flour, chopped spring onion, and dried garlic to a bowl. Mix and form medium-sized kebabs.

7. Impale each kebab on a skewer. Heat the olive oil in a frying pan.

8. Cook the lamb kebabs for about 3 minutes on each side.

9. Serve each chaffle with a tablespoon of sour cream and one or two lamb kebabs. Decorate with fresh dill.

Nutrition value per Servings:

Calories 679, fat 49.9 g, carbs 15.8 g, sugar 0.8 g, Protein 42.6 g

## Beef And Sour Cream Chaffle

Servings: 4

Cooking Time: 15 Minutes

**Ingredients:**

Batter

4 eggs

2 cups grated mozzarella cheese

3 tablespoons coconut flour

3 tablespoons almond flour

2 teaspoons baking powder

Salt and pepper to taste

1 tablespoon freshly chopped parsley Seasoned beef

1 pound beef tenderloin

Salt and pepper to taste

2 tablespoons olive oil

1 tablespoon Dijon mustard

2 tablespoons olive oil to brush the waffle maker ¼ cup sour cream for garnish

2 tablespoons freshly chopped spring onion for garnish

**Directions:**

1. Preheat the waffle maker.

2. Add the eggs, grated mozzarella cheese, coconut flour, almond flour, baking powder, salt and pepper and freshly chopped parsley to a bowl.

3. Mix until just combined and batter forms.

4. Brush the heated waffle maker with olive oil and add a few tablespoons of the batter. 5. Close the lid and cook for about 7 minutes depending on your waffle maker.

6. Meanwhile, heat the olive oil in a nonstick pan over medium heat.

7. Season the beef tenderloin with salt and pepper and spread the whole piece of beef tenderloin with Dijon mustard.

8. Cook on each side for about 4-5 minutes.

9. Serve each chaffle with sour cream and slices of the cooked beef tenderloin.

10. Garnish with freshly chopped spring onion.

11. Serve and enjoy.

Nutrition value per Servings:

Calories 543, fat 37 g, carbs 7.9 g, sugar 0.5 g, Protein 44.9 g

## Pork Loin Chaffle Sandwich

Servings: 4

Cooking Time: 15 Minutes

**Ingredients:**

4 eggs

1 cup grated mozzarella cheese

1 cup grated parmesan cheese Salt and pepper to taste

2 tablespoons cream cheese

6 tablespoons coconut flour

2 teaspoons baking powder

Pork loin

2 tablespoons olive oil

1 pound pork loin

Salt and pepper to taste

2 cloves garlic, minced

1 tablespoon freshly chopped thyme

2 tablespoons cooking spray to brush the waffle maker

4 lettuce leaves for serving

4 slices of tomato for serving

¼ cup sugar-free mayonnaise for serving

**Directions:**

1. Preheat the waffle maker.

2. Add the eggs, mozzarella cheese, parmesan cheese, salt and pepper, cream cheese, coconut flour and baking powder to a bowl.

3. Mix until combined.

4. Brush the heated waffle maker with cooking spray and add a few tablespoons of the batter.

5. Close the lid and cook for about 7 minutes depending on your waffle maker.

6. Meanwhile, heat the olive oil in a non-stick frying pan and season the pork loin with salt and pepper, minced garlic and freshly chopped thyme.

7. Cook the pork loin for about 5-minutes on each side.

8. Cut each chaffle in half and add some mayonnaise, lettuce leaf, tomato slice and sliced pork loin on one half.

9. Cover the sandwich with the other chaffle half and serve.

Nutrition value per Servings:

Calories 7 fat 52.7 g, carbs 11.3 g, sugar 0.8 g, Protein 47.4 g

## Beef Chaffle Tower

Servings: 4

Cooking Time: 15 Minutes

**Ingredients:**

Batter

4 eggs

2 cups grated mozzarella cheese Salt and pepper to taste

2 tablespoons almond flour

1 teaspoon Italian seasoning

Beef

2 tablespoons butter

1 pound beef tenderloin

Salt and pepper to taste

1 teaspoon chili flakes

Other

2 tablespoons cooking spray to brush the waffle maker

**Directions:**

1. Preheat the waffle maker.

2. Add the eggs, grated mozzarella cheese, salt and pepper, almond flour and Italian seasoning to a bowl.

3. Mix until everything is fully combined.

4. Brush the heated waffle maker with cooking spray and add a few tablespoons of the batter.

5. Close the lid and cook for about 7 minutes depending on your waffle maker.

6. Meanwhile, heat the butter in a nonstick frying pan and season the beef tenderloin with salt and pepper and chili flakes.

7. Cook the beef tenderloin for about 5-minutes on each side.

8. When serving, assemble the chaffle tower by placing one chaffle on a plate, a layer of diced beef tenderloin, another chaffle, another layer of beef, and so on until you finish with the chaffles and beef.

9. Serve and enjoy.

Nutrition value per Servings:

Calories 412, fat 25 g, carbs 1.8 g, sugar 0.5 g, Protein 43.2 g

## Turkey Bbq Sauce Chaffle

Servings: 4

Cooking Time: 8-10 Minutes

**Ingredients:**

Batter

½ pound ground turkey meat

3 eggs

1 cup grated Swiss cheese

¼ cup cream cheese

¼ cup BBQ sauce

1 teaspoon dried oregano

Salt and pepper to taste

2 cloves garlic, minced

2 tablespoons butter to brush the waffle maker

¼ cup BBQ sauce for serving

2 tablespoons freshly chopped parsley for garnish

**Directions:**

1. Preheat the waffle maker.

2. Add the ground turkey, eggs, grated Swiss cheese, cream cheese, BBQ sauce, dried oregano, salt and pepper, and minced garlic to a bowl.

3. Mix everything until combined and batter forms.

4. Brush the heated waffle maker with butter and add a few tablespoons of the batter.

5. Close the lid and cook for about 8-10 minutes depending on your waffle maker.

6. Serve each chaffle with a tablespoon of BBQ sauce and a sprinkle of freshly chopped parsley.

Nutrition value per Servings:

Calories 365, fat 23.g, carbs 13.7 g, sugar 8.8 g, Protein 23.5 g

## Strawberry Cream Sandwich Chaffles

Servings: 2

Cooking Time: 6 Minutes

**Ingredients:**

Chaffles

1 large organic egg, beaten

½ cup mozzarella cheese, shredded finely

Filling

4 teaspoons heavy cream

2 tablespoons powdered erythritol

1 teaspoon fresh lemon juice

Pinch of fresh lemon zest, grated

2 fresh strawberries, hulled and sliced

**Directions:**

1. Preheat a mini waffle iron and then grease it.

2. For chaffles: in a small bowl, add the egg and mozzarella cheese and stir to combine.

3. Place half of the mixture into preheated waffle iron and cook for about 2-minutes.

4. Repeat with the remaining mixture.

5. Meanwhile, for filling: in a bowl, Place all the ingredients except the strawberry slices and with a hand mixer, beat until well combined.

6. Serve each chaffle with cream mixture and strawberry slices.

Nutrition value:

Calories 95  Fat 5 g  Carbs 1.7 g  Fiber 0.3 g  Sugar 0.9 g  Protein 5.5 g

## Ham Sandwich Chaffles

Servings: 2

Cooking Time: 8 Minutes

**Ingredients:**

1 organic egg, beaten

½ cup Monterrey Jack cheese, shredded

1 teaspoon coconut flour

Pinch of garlic powder

Filling

2 sugar-free ham slices

1 small tomato, sliced

2 lettuce leaves

**Directions:**

1. Preheat a mini waffle iron and then grease it.

2. For chaffles: In a medium bowl, put all ingredients and with a fork, mix until well combined. Place

half of the mixture into preheated waffle iron and cook for about 3-4 minutes.

3. Repeat with the remaining mixture.

4. Serve each chaffle with filling ingredients.

Nutrition value:

Calories 100  Fat 8.7 g  Carbs 5.5 g  Fiber 1.8 g  Sugar 1.5 g  Protein 13.9 g

## Chicken Sandwich Chaffles

Servings: 2

Cooking Time: 8 Minutes

**Ingredients:**

Chaffles

1 large organic egg, beaten

½ cup cheddar cheese, shredded

Pinch of salt and ground black pepper

Filling

1 (6-ounce) cooked chicken breast, halved

2 lettuce leaves

¼ of small onion, sliced

1 small tomato, sliced

**Directions:**

1. Preheat a mini waffle iron and then grease it.

2. For chaffles: In a medium bowl, put all ingredients and with a fork, mix until well combined.Place half of the mixture into preheated waffle iron and cook for about 3-4 minutes.

3. Repeat with the remaining mixture.

4. Serve each chaffle with filling ingredients.

Nutrition value:

Calories 159 Fat 14.1 g Carbs 3.3 g Sugar 2 g Protein 28.7 g

## Salmon & Cheese Sandwich Chaffles

Servings: 4

Cooking Time: 24 Minutes

**Ingredients:**

Chaffles

2 organic eggs

½ ounce butter, melted

1 cup mozzarella cheese, shredded

2 tablespoons almond flour

Pinch of salt

Filling

½ cup smoked salmon

1/3 cup avocado, peeled, pitted, and sliced

2 tablespoons feta cheese, crumbled

**Directions:**

1. Preheat a mini waffle iron and then grease it.

2. For chaffles: In a medium bowl, put all ingredients and with a fork, mix until well combined. Place ¼ of the mixture into preheated waffle iron and cook for about 5-6 minutes.

3. Repeat with the remaining mixture.

4. Serve each chaffle with filling ingredients.

Nutrition value:

Calories 169 Fat 13.g Carbs 2.8 g  Fiber 1.6 g Sugar 0.6 g  Protein 8.9 g

## Blueberry Peanut Butter Sandwich Chaffles

Servings: 2

Cooking Time: 10 Minutes

**Ingredients:**

1 organic egg, beaten

½ cup cheddar cheese, shredded

Filling

2 tablespoons erythritol

1 tablespoon butter, softened

1 tablespoon natural peanut butter

2 tablespoons cream cheese, softened

¼ teaspoon organic vanilla extract

2 teaspoons fresh blueberries

**Directions:**

1. Preheat a mini waffle iron and then grease it.

2. For chaffles: in a small bowl, add the egg and Cheddar cheese and stir to combine.

3. Place half of the mixture into preheated waffle iron and cook for about 5 minutes.

4. Repeat with the remaining mixture.

5. Meanwhile, for filling: In a medium bowl, put all ingredients and mix until well combined.

6. Serve each chaffle with peanut butter mixture.

Nutrition value:

Calories 143 Fat 10.1 g Carbs 4.1 g  Fiber 0.8 g Sugar 1.2 g  Protein 6 g

## Berry Sauce Sandwich Chaffles

Servings: 2

Cooking Time: 8 Minutes

**Ingredients:**

Filling

3 ounces frozen mixed berries, thawed with the juice

1 tablespoon erythritol

1 tablespoon water

¼ tablespoon fresh lemon juice

2 teaspoons cream

Chaffles

1 large organic egg, beaten

½ cup cheddar cheese, shredded

2 tablespoons almond flour

**Directions:**

1. For berry sauce: in a pan, add the berries, erythritol, water and lemon juice over medium heat and cook for about 8- minutes, pressing with the spoon occasionally.

2. Remove the pan of sauce from heat and set aside to cool before serving.

3. Preheat a mini waffle iron and then grease it.

4. In a bowl, add the egg, cheddar cheese and almond flour and beat until well combined. Place half of the mixture into preheated waffle iron and cook for about 3-5 minutes.

5. Repeat with the remaining mixture.

6. Serve each chaffle with cream and berry sauce.

Nutrition value:

Calories 222 Fat 16 g Carbs 7 g Fiber 2.3 g Sugar 3.8 g Protein 10.5 g

## Pork Sandwich Chaffles

Servings: 4

Cooking Time: 16 Minutes

**Ingredients:**

Chaffles

2 large organic eggs

¼ cup superfine blanched almond flour ¾ teaspoon organic baking powder ½ teaspoon garlic powder

1 cup cheddar cheese, shredded

Filling

12 ounces cooked pork, cut into slices

1 tomato, sliced

4 lettuce leaves

**Directions:**

1. Preheat a mini waffle iron and then grease it.

2. For chaffles: in a bowl, add the eggs, almond flour, baking powder, and garlic powder, and beat until well combined.

3. Add the cheese and stir to combine.

4. Place ¼ of the mixture into preheated waffle iron and cook for about 3-minutes.

5. Repeat with the remaining mixture.

6. Serve each chaffle with filling ingredients.

Nutrition value:

Calories 319 Fat 18.2g Carbs 3.5 g Fiber 1 g Sugar 0.9 g Protein 34.2 g

## Tomato Sandwich Chaffles

Servings: 2

Cooking Time: 6 Minutes

**Ingredients:**

Chaffles

1 large organic egg, beaten

½ cup colby jack cheese, shredded finely

1/8 teaspoon organic vanilla extract

Filling

1 small tomato, sliced

2 teaspoons fresh basil leaves

**Directions:**

1. Preheat a mini waffle iron and then grease it.

2. For chaffles: in a small bowl, place all the ingredients and stir to combine.

3. Place half of the mixture into preheated waffle iron and cook for about minutes.

4. Repeat with the remaining mixture.

5. Serve each chaffle with tomato slices and basil leaves.

Nutrition value:

Calories 155 Fat 11.g Carbs 3 g  Fiber 0.6 g Sugar 1.4 g  Protein 9.6 g

## Cheesy Garlic Chaffle Bread Recipe

Servings: 2

Cooking Time: 14 Minutes

**Ingredients:**

1 egg

1/2 cup mozzarella cheese, shredded

1 tbsp parmesan cheese

3/4 tsp coconut flour

1/4 tsp baking powder

1/8 tsp Italian Seasoning

Pinch of salt

1 tbsp butter, melted

1/4 tsp garlic powder

1/2 cup mozzarella cheese, shredded 1/4 tsp basil seasoning

**Directions:**

1. Preheat oven to 400 degrees. Plug the Dash Mini Waffle Maker in the wall and allow it to get hot. Lightly grease waffle maker.

2. Combine the first 7 ingredients in a small bowl and stir well to combine.

3. Spoon half of the batter on the waffle maker and close — Cook for 4 minutes or until golden brown.

4. Remove the chaffle bread carefully from the Dash Mini Waffle Maker, then repeat for the rest of the batter.

5. In a small bowl, melt the butter and add garlic powder.

6. Cut each chaffle in half (or thirds), and place on a baking sheet, then brush the tops with the garlic butter mixture.

7. Top with mozzarella cheese and pop in the oven for 4 -5 minutes.

8. Turn oven to broil and move the baking pan to the top shelf for 1-2 minutes so that the cheese begins to bubble and turn golden brown. Watch very carefully, as it can burn quickly on broil. (check every 30 seconds)

9. Remove from oven and sprinkle basil seasoning on top. Enjoy!

Nutrition value:

Calories: 270 Carbohydrates:3g  Protein: 16g Fat: 21g Sugar: 1g

## Best Keto Pizza Chaffle

Servings: 2

Cooking Time: 15 Minutes

**Ingredients:**

1 tsp coconut flour

1 egg white

1/2 cup mozzarella cheese, shredded

`1 tsp cream cheese, softened

1/4 tsp baking powder

1/8 tsp Italian seasoning

1/8 tsp garlic powder

pinch of salt

3 tsp low carb marinara sauce

1/2 cup mozzarella cheese

6 pepperonis cut in half

1 tbsp parmesan cheese, shredded 1/4 tsp basil seasoning

**Directions:**

1. Preheat oven to 400 degrees. Turn waffle maker on or plug it in so that it gets hot.

2. In a small bowl, add coconut flour, egg white, mozzarella cheese, softened cream cheese, baking powder, garlic powder, Italian seasonings, and a pinch of salt.

3. Pour 1/2 of the batter in the waffle maker, close the top, and cook for 4 minutes or until chaffle reaches desired doneness.

4. Carefully remove chaffle from the waffle maker, then follow the same Directions to make the second chaffle.

5. Top each chaffle with tomato sauce (I used 1 1/2 tsp per), pepperoni, mozzarella cheese, and parmesan cheese.

6. Place in the oven on a baking sheet (or straight on the baking rack) on the top shelf of the oven for 5-minutes. Then turn the oven to broil so that the cheese begins to bubble and brown. Keep a close eye as it can burn quickly. I broiled my pizza chaffle for approx 1 min and 30 seconds.

7. Remove from oven and sprinkle basil on top.

8. Enjoy!

Nutrition value:

Calories: 241 Carbohydrates:4g ;Protein: 17g; Fat: 18g ;Sugar: 1g

## Easy Keto Chaffle Sausage Gravy Recipe

Servings: 2

Cooking Time: 10 Minutes

**Ingredients:**

For the Chaffle:

1 egg

1/2 cup mozzarella cheese, grated

1 tsp coconut flour

1 tsp water

1/4 tsp baking powder

Pinch of salt

For the Keto Sausage Gravy:

1/4 cup breakfast sausage, browned

3 tbsp chicken broth

2 tbsp heavy whipping cream

2 tsp cream cheese, softened Dash garlic powder

Pepper to taste

Dash of onion powder (optional)

**Directions:**

1. Plug Dash Mini Waffle Maker into the wall and allow it to heat up. Grease lightly or use cooking spray.

2. Combine all the ingredients for the chaffle into a small bowl and stir to combine well.

3. Pour half of the chaffle batter onto the waffle maker, then shut the lid and cook for approximately 4 minutes.

4. Remove chaffle from waffle maker and repeat the same process to make the second chaffle. Set aside to crisp.

5. For the Keto Sausage Gravy:

6. Cook one pound of breakfast sausage and drain. Reserve 1/4 cup for this recipe.

7. Tip: Make sausage patties out of the rest of the sausage and reserve 1/4 a cup to brown for this recipe. If you aren't familiar with breakfast sausage, it is crumbled like ground beef.

8. Wipe excess grease from the skillet and add 1/4 cup browned breakfast sausage and the rest of the ingredients and bring to a boil stirring continuously.

9. Reduce heat to medium and continue to cook down with the lid off so that it begins to thicken for approx 5-7 minutes. If you'd like it very thick, you can add a bit of Xanthan Gum, but if you are patient with it simmering, the keto sausage gravy will thicken. Then, it will thicken even more as it cools.

10. Add salt and pepper to taste and spoon keto sausage gravy over chaffles.

11. Enjoy

Nutrition value:

Calories: 194 ;Carbohydrates:3g ;Protein: 11g; Fat: 17g; Sugar: 1g

## Fudgy Chocolate Chaffles

Servings: 2

Cooking Time: 8 Minutes

**Ingredients:**

1 egg

2 tbsp mozzarella cheese, shredded

2 tbsp cocoa

2 tbsp Lakanto monk fruit powdered

1 tsp coconut flour

1 tsp heavy whipping cream

1/4 tsp baking powder

1/4 tsp vanilla extract

pinch of salt

**Directions:**

1. Turn on waffle or chaffle maker. I use the Dash Mini Waffle Maker. Grease lightly or use a cooking spray.

2. In a small bowl, combine all ingredients.

3. Cover the dash mini waffle maker with 1/2 of the batter. Close the mini waffle maker and cook for 4 minutes. Remove the chaffle from the waffle maker carefully as it is very hot.

4. Repeat the steps above.

5. Serve with sugar-free strawberry ice cream or sugar-free whipped topping.

6. Note:

7. The nutritional information does not include the Lakanto Monkfruit powdered sugar as most subtract to calculate net carbs. The nutritional info is based on one chaffle per serving.

8. The nutritional information is provided for the fudgy chocolate chaffle recipe only.

Nutrition value:

Calories: 10cal ;Carbohydrates:5g ;Protein: 7g;Fat: 7g ; Sugar: 1g

## Mouthwatering Blueberry Chaffles

Servings: 2

Cooking Time: 8 Minutes

**Ingredients:**

1 egg

1/3 cup mozzarella cheese, shredded

1 tbsp blueberries

1 tsp cream cheese

1 tsp coconut flour

1/4 tsp baking powder

1/4 tsp vanilla extract

2 squirts liquid Pyure Sweetener (can substitute 3/4 tsp other sweeteners such as Monkfruit powdered) 1/4 tsp cinnamon

Pinch of salt

**Directions:**

1. Turn on waffle or chaffle maker. Grease lightly or use a cooking spray.

2. In a small bowl, combine all ingredients except the blueberries

3. Cover the dash mini waffle maker with 1/2 of the batter then sprinkle a couple of blueberries on top. Close the mini waffle maker and cook for 4 minutes. Remove the chaffle from the waffle maker carefully,

4. Repeat the steps above.

5. Serve with sugar-free maple syrup, whipped cream, or keto ice cream.

Nutrition value:

Calories: 113 ;Carbohydrates:3g ;Protein: 7g;Fat: 7g ; Sugar: 1g

## Open-Faced French Dip Keto Chaffle Sandwich

Servings: 2

Cooking Time: 12 Minutes

**Ingredients:**

1 egg white

1/4 cup mozzarella cheese, shredded (packed)

1/4 cup sharp cheddar cheese, shredded (packed) 3/4 tsp water

1 tsp coconut flour

1/4 tsp baking powder

Pinch of salt

**Directions:**

1. Preheat oven to 425 degrees. Plug the Dash Mini Waffle Maker in the wall and grease lightly once it is hot.

2. Combine all of the ingredients in a bowl and stir to combine.

3. Spoon out 1/2 of the batter on the waffle maker and close lid. Set a timer for 4 minutes and do not lift the lid until the cooking time is complete. Lifting beforehand can cause the Chaffle keto sandwich recipe to separate and stick to the waffle iron. You have to let it cook the entire 4 minutes before lifting the lid.

4. Remove the chaffle from the waffle iron and set aside. Repeat the same steps above with the rest of the chaffle batter.

5. Cover a cookie sheet with parchment paper and place chaffles a few inches apart.

6. Add 1/4 to 1/3 cup of the slow cooker keto roast beef from the following recipe. Make sure to drain the excess broth/gravy before adding to the top of the chaffle.

7. Add a slice of deli cheese or shredded cheese on top. Swiss and provolone are both great options.

8. Place on the top rack of the oven for 5 minutes so that the cheese can melt. If you'd like the cheese to bubble and begin to brown, turn oven to broil for 1 min. (The swiss cheese may not brown)

9. Enjoy open-faced with a small bowl of beef broth for dipping.

Nutrition value:

Calories: 118kcal ;Carbohydrates:2g ;Protein: 9g;Fat: 8g ;sugar: 1g

## Maple Pumpkin Keto Chaffle Recipe

Servings: 2

Cooking Time: 16 Minutes

**Ingredients:**

2 eggs

3/4 tsp baking powder

2 tsp pumpkin puree (100% pumpkin) 3/4 tsp pumpkin pie spice

4 tsp heavy whipping cream

2 tsp Lakanto Sugar-Free Maple Syrup

1 tsp coconut flour

1/2 cup mozzarella cheese, shredded 1/2 tsp vanilla

Pinch of salt

**Directions:**

1. Turn on chaffle maker.

2. In a small bowl, combine all ingredients.

3. Cover the dash mini waffle maker with 1/4 of the batter and cook for 4 minutes.

4. Repeat 3 more times until you have made Maple Syrup Pumpkin Keto Waffles (Chaffles).

5. Serve with sugar-free maple syrup or keto ice cream.

Nutrition value:

Calories: 201 ;Carbohydrates:4g; Protein: 12g; Fat: 15g; Sugar: 1g

## Basic Keto Low Carb Chaffle Recipe

Servings: 1

Cooking Time: 8 Minutes

**Ingredients:**

1 egg

1/2 cup cheddar cheese, shredded

**Directions:**

1. Turn waffle maker on or plug it in so that it heats and grease both sides.

2. In a small bowl, crack an egg, then add the 1/cup cheddar cheese and stir to combine.

3. Pour 1/2 of the batter in the waffle maker and close the top.

4. Cook for 3-minutes or until it reaches desired doneness.

5. Carefully remove from waffle maker and set aside for 2-3 minutes to give it time to crisp.

6. Follow the Directions again to make the second chaffle.

Nutrition value:

Calories: 291l;Carbohydrates:1g ;Protein: 20g;Fat: 23g; Sugar: 1g;

## Keto Protein Chaffle

Servings: 1

Cooking Time: 8 Minutes

**Ingredients:**

1 egg (beaten)

½ cup whey protein powder A pinch of salt

1 tsp baking powder

3 tbsp sour cream

½ tsp vanilla extract

Topping:

2 tbsp heavy cream

1 tbsp granulated swerve

**Directions:**

1. Plug the waffle maker to preheat it and spray it with a non-stick cooking spray.

2. In a mixing bowl, whisk together the egg, vanilla and sour cream.

3. In another mixing bowl, combine the protein powder, baking powder and salt.

4. Pour the flour mixture into the egg mixture and mix until the ingredients are well combined and you form a smooth batter.

5. Pour an appropriate amount of the batter into the waffle maker and spread the batter to

the edges to cover all the holes on the waffle maker.

6. Close the waffle maker and cook for about 4 minutes or according to your waffle maker's settings.

7. After the cooking cycle, use a plastic or silicone utensil to remove the chaffle from the waffle iron.

8. Repeat step 4 to 6 until you have cooked all the batter into chaffles.

9. For the topping, whisk together the cream and swerve in a mixing bowl until smooth and fluffy.

10. Top the chaffles with the cream and enjoy.

Nutrition value per Servings:

Calories 42 fat 32.8 g, carbs 9.5 g, sugar 1.1 g, Protein 25.7 g

## Chaffle Tacos

Servings: 4

Cooking Time: 15 Minutes

**Ingredients:**

Chaffle:

2 tbsp coconut flour

3 eggs (beaten)

½ cup shredded mozzarella cheese

½ cup shredded cheddar cheese

A pinch of salt

½ tsp oregano

Taco Filling:

1 garlic clove (minced)

1 small onion (finely chopped) ½ pound ground beef

1 tsp olive oil

1 tsp cumin

½ tsp Italian seasoning

1 tsp paprika

1 tsp chili powder

1 roma tomato (diced)

1 green bell pepper (diced)

4 tbsp sour cream

1 tbsp chopped green onions

**Directions:**

1. Plug the waffle maker to preheat it and spray it with a non-stick cooking spray.

2. In a mixing bowl, combine the mozzarella cheese, cheddar, coconut flour, salt and oregano. Add the eggs and mix until the ingredients are well combined.

3. Fill the waffle maker with an appropriate amount of the batter. Spread the batter to the edges to cover all the hole on the waffle maker.

4. Close the waffle maker and cook for about 5 minutes or according to waffle maker's settings.

5. After the cooking cycle, use a plastic or silicone utensil to remove the chaffle from the waffle maker. Set aside.

6. Repeat step 3 to 5 until you have cooked all the batter into chaffles.

7. Heat up a large skillet over medium to high heat.

8. Add the ground beef and saute until it is browned, breaking it apart while sautéing. Transfer the beef to a paper towel lined plate to drain and wipe the skillet clean.

9. Add the olive oil and leave it to get hot.

10. Add the onions and garlic and saute for 3-4 minutes or until the onion is translucent, stirring often.

11. Add the diced tomatoes and green pepper. Cook for 1 minute.

12. Add the browned ground beef. Stir in the cumin, paprika, chili powder and Italian seasoning.

13. Reduce the heat and cook on low for about 8 minutes, stirring often to prevent burning.

14. Remove the skillet from heat.

15. Scoop the taco mixture into the chaffles and top with chopped green onion and sour cream.

16. Enjoy.

Nutrition value per Servings:

Calories 42 fat 32.8 g, carbs 9.5 g, sugar 1.1 g, Protein 25.7 g

## Lettuce Chaffle Sandwich

Servings: 2

Cooking Time: 5 Minutes

**Ingredients:**

1 large egg

1 tbsp. almond flour

1 tbsp. full-fat Greek yogurt

1/8 tsp baking powder

1/4 cup shredded Swiss cheese

4 lettuce leaves

**Directions:**

1. Switch on your minutesi waffle maker.

2. Grease it with cooking spray.

3. Mix together egg, almond flour, yogurts, baking powder and cheese in mixing bowl.

4. Pour 1/2 cup of the batter into the center of your waffle iron and close the lid.

5. Cook chaffles for about 2-3 minutes until-cooked through.

6. Repeat with remaining batter

7. Once cooked, carefully transfer to plate. Serve lettuce leaves between 2 chaffles.

8. Enjoy!

Nutrition value per Servings:

Calories: 145 Fat: 9.4g Carbohydrates: 1g Sugar: 0.2g Protein: 14.3g

## Cocoa Chaffles With Coconut Cream

Servings: 2

Cooking Time: 5 Minutes

**Ingredients:**

1 egg

1/2 cup mozzarella cheese

1 tsp stevia

1 tsp vanilla

2 tbsps. almond flour

1 tbsp. sugar-free chocolate chips

2 tbsps. cocoa powder

TOPPING

1 scoop coconut cream

1 tbsp. coconut flour

**Directions:**

1. Mix together chaffle ingredients in a bowl and mix well.

2. Preheat your dash minutesi waffle maker. Spray waffle maker with cooking spray.

3. Pour 1/2 batter into the minutesi-waffle maker and close the lid.

4. Cook chaffles for about 2-minutes and remove from the maker.

5. Make chaffles from the rest of the batter.

6. Serve with a scoop of coconut cream between two chaffles.

7. Drizzle coconut flour on top.

8. Enjoy with afternoon coffee!

Nutrition value per Servings:

Calories: 145 Fat: 9.4g Carbohydrates: 1g Sugar: 0.2g Protein: 14.3g

## Shrimp Avocado Chaffle Sandwich

Servings: 4

Cooking Time: 32 Minutes

**Ingredients:**

2 cups shredded mozzarella cheese

4 large eggs

½ tsp curry powder

½ tsp oregano

Shrimp Sandwich Filling:

1-pound raw shrimp (peeled and deveined)

1 large avocado (diced)

4 slices cooked bacon

2 tbsp sour cream

½ tsp paprika

1 tsp Cajun seasoning

1 tbsp olive oil

¼ cup onion (finely chopped)

1 red bell pepper (diced)

**Directions:**

1. Plug the waffle maker to preheat it and spray it with a non-stick cooking spray.

2. Break the eggs into a mixing bowl and beat. Add the cheese, oregano and curry. Mix until the ingredients are well combined.

3. Pour an appropriate amount of the batter into the waffle maker and spread out the batter to the edges to cover all the holes on the waffle maker. This should make 8 mini waffles.

4. Close the waffle maker and cook for about minutes or according to your waffle maker's settings.

5. After the cooking cycle, use a silicone or plastic utensil to remove the chaffle from the waffle maker.

6. Repeat step 3 to 5 until you have cooked all the batter into chaffles.

7. Heat up the olive oil in a large skillet over medium to high heat.

8. Add the shrimp and cook until the shrimp is pink and tender.

9. Remove the skillet from heat and use a slotted spoon to transfer the shrimp to a paper towel lined plate to drain for a few minutes.

10. Put the shrimp in a mixing bowl. Add paprika and Cajun seasoning. Toss until the shrimps are all coated with seasoning.

11. To assemble the sandwich, place one chaffle on a flat surface and spread some sour cream over it. Layer some shrimp, onion, avocado, diced pepper and one slice of bacon over it. Cover with another chaffle.

12. Repeat step 10 until you have assembled all the ingredients into sandwiches.

13. Serve and enjoy.

Nutrition value per Servings:

Calories: 145 Fat: 9.4g Carbohydrates: 1g Sugar: 0.2g Protein: 14.3g

## Cuban Pork Sandwich

Servings: 1

Cooking Time: 10 Minutes

**Ingredients:**

Sandwich Filling:

25 g swiss cheese (sliced)

2 ounces cooked deli ham (thinly sliced)

3 slices pickle chips

½ tbsp Dijon mustard

½ tbsp mayonnaise

3 ounces pork roast

1 tsp paprika

1 stalk celery (diced)

Chaffle:

1 tsp baking powder

1 large egg (beaten)

1 tbsp full-fat Greek yogurt

4 tbsp mozzarella cheese

1 tbsp almond flour

**Directions:**

1. Preheat the oven to 350°F and grease a baking sheet.

2. Plug the waffle maker to preheat it and spray it with a non-stick cooking spray.

3. In a mixing bowl, combine the almond flour, cheese and baking powder.

4. Add the egg and yogurt. Mix until the ingredients are well combined.

5. Fill the waffle maker with an appropriate amount of the batter and spread the batter to the edges to cover all the holes on the waffle maker.

6. Close the waffle maker and cook the waffle until it is crispy. That will take about 5 minutes. The time may vary in some waffle makers.

7. After the cooking cycle, remove the chaffle from the waffle maker with a plastic or silicone utensil.

8. Repeat step 4 to 6 until you have cooked all the batter into chaffles.

9. In a small mixing bowl, combine the mustard, oregano and mayonnaise.

10. Brush the mustard-mayonnaise mixture over the surface of both chaffles.

11. Layer the pork, ham, pickles and celery over one of the chaffles. Layer the cheese slices on top and cover it with the second chaffle.

12. Place it on the baking sheet. Place it in oven and bake until the cheese melts. You can place a heavy stainless place over the chaffle to make the sandwich come out flat after baking

13. After the baking cycle, remove the chaffle sandwich from the oven and let it cool for a few minutes.

14. Serve warm and enjoy.

Nutrition value per Servings:

Calories: 145 Fat: 9.4g Carbohydrates: 1g Sugar: 0.2g Protein: 14.3g

## Simple Heart Shape Chaffles

Servings: 4

Cooking Time: 5 Minutes

**Ingredients:**

2 large eggs

1 cup finely shredded mozzarella

2 tbsps. coconut flour

1 tsp. stevia

Coconut flour for topping

**Directions:**

1. Switch on your heart shape Belgian waffle maker.

2. Grease with cooking spray and let it preheat.

3. Mix together chaffle ingredients in a mixing bowl.

4. Pour chaffle mixture in heart shape Belgian makerand cook for about 5 minutes.

5. Once chaffles are cooked, carefully remove from the maker.

6. Sprinkle coconut flour on top.

7. Serve with warm keto BLT coffee.

8. Enjoy!

Nutrition value per Servings:

Calories 168  Fat 15.5g Carbohydrate 1.6g Protein 5.4g Sugars 0.6g

## Cauliflower Turkey Chaffle

Servings: 2

Cooking Time: 12 Minutes

**Ingredients:**

1 large egg (beaten)

½ cup cauliflower rice

¼ cup diced turkey

½ tsp coconut aminos or soy sauce

A pinch of ground black pepper

A pinch of white pepper

¼ tsp curry

¼ tsp oregano

1 tbsp butter (melted)

¾ cup shredded mozzarella cheese

1 garlic clove (crushed)

**Directions:**

1. Plug the waffle maker to preheat it and spray it with a non-stick spray.

2. In a mixing bowl, combine the cauliflower rice, white pepper, black pepper, curry and oregano.

3. In another mixing bowl, whisk together the eggs, butter, crushed garlic and coconut aminos.

4. Pour the egg mixture into the cheese mixture and mix until the ingredients are well combined.

5. Add the diced turkey and stir to combine.

6. Sprinkle 2 tbsp cheese over the waffle maker. Fill the waffle maker with an appropriate amount of the batter. Spread out the batter to the edges to cover all the holes on the waffle maker. Sprinkle another 2 tbsp cheese over the batter.

7. Close the waffle maker and cook for about 4 minutes or according to waffle maker's settings.

8. After the cooking cycle, use a plastic or silicone utensil to remove the chaffle from the waffle maker.

9. Repeat step 6 to 8 until you have cooked all the batter into chaffles.

10. Serve warm and enjoy.

Nutrition value per Servings:

Calories 168  Fat 5.5g Carbohydrate 1.6g Protein 7.4g Sugars 0.6g

## Pork Chaffles On Pan

Servings: 4

Cooking Time: 5 minutes

**Ingredients:**

1 cup pork, minutesced

1 egg

½ cup chopped parsley

1 cup cheddar cheese

pinch of salt

1 tbsp. avocado oil

**Directions:**

1. Heat your nonstick pan over medium heat.

2. In a small bowl, mix together pork, parsley, egg, and cheese together

3. Grease pan with avocado oil.

4. Once the pan is hot, pour 2 tbsps. pork batter and cook for about 1-2 minutes.

5. Flip and cook for another 1-2 minutes.

6. Once chaffle is brown, remove from pan.

7. Serve BBQ sauce on top and enjoy!

Nutrition value per Servings:

Calories 178  Fat 15.5g  Carbohydrate 1.9g  Protein 5.4g  Sugars 0.6g

## Oven-Baked Chaffles

Servings: 10

Cooking Time: 5 Minutes

**Ingredients:**

3 eggs

2 cups mozzarella cheese

¼ cup coconut flour

1 tsp. baking powder

1 tbsp. coconut oil

1 tsp stevia

1 tbsp. coconut cream

**Directions:**

1. Preheat oven on 4000 F.

2. Mix together all ingredients in a bowl.

3. Pour batter in silicon waffle mold and set it on a baking tray.

4. Bake chaffles in an oven for about 10-15 minutes.

5. Once cooked, remove from oven

6. Serve hot with coffee and enjoy!

Nutrition value per Servings:

Calories 188  Fat 17.5g  Carbohydrate 2.6g  Protein 8.4g  Sugars 0.6g

## Pumpkin Pecan Chaffle

Servings: 2

Cooking Time: 10 Minutes

**Ingredients:**

2 tbsp toasted pecans (chopped)

2 tbsp almond flour

1 tbsp pumpkin puree

½ tsp pumpkin spice

½ cup grated mozzarella cheese

1 tsp granulated swerve sweetener

1 egg

½ tsp nutmeg

½ tsp vanilla extract

½ tsp baking powder

**Directions:**

1. Plug the waffle maker to preheat it and spray it with a non-stick spray.

2. In a mixing bowl, combine the almond flour, baking powder, pumpkin spice, swerve, cheese and nutmeg.

3. In another mixing bowl, whisk together the pumpkin puree egg and vanilla extract.

4. Pour the egg mixture into the flour mixture and mix until the ingredients are well combined.

5. Pour an appropriate amount of the batter into the waffle maker and spread out the batter to the edges to cover all the holes on the waffle maker.

6. Close the waffle maker and cook for about 5 minutes or according to your waffle maker's settings.

7. After the cooking cycle, use a silicone or plastic utensil to remove the chaffle from the waffle maker.

8. Repeat step 5 to 7 until you have cooked all the batter into chaffles.

9. Serve warm and top with whipped cream. Enjoy!!!

Nutrition value per Servings:

Calories 178  Fat 5.5g  Carbohydrate 0.6g  Protein 6.4g  Sugars 0.6g

## Sloppy Joe Chaffle

Servings: 2

Cooking Time: 20 Minutes

**Ingredients:**

Chaffle:

1 large egg (beaten)

1/8 tsp onion powder

1 tbsp almond flour

½ cup shredded mozzarella cheese

1 tsp nutmeg

¼ tsp baking powder

Sloppy Joe Filling:

2 tsp olive oil

1 pounds ground beef

1 celery stalk (chopped)

2 tbsp ketch up

2 tsp Worcestershire sauce

1 small onions (chopped)

1 green bell pepper (chopped)

1 tbsp sugar free maple syrup

1 cup tomato sauce (7.9 ounce)

2 garlic cloves (minced)

½ tsp salt or to taste

½ tsp ground black pepper or to taste

**Directions:**

1. For the chaffle:
2. Plug the waffle maker and preheat it. Spray it with non-stick spray.
3. Combine the baking powder, nutmeg, flour and onion powder in a mixing bowl. Add the eggs and mix.
4. Add the cheese and mix until the ingredients are well combined and you have formed a smooth batter.
5. Pour the batter into the waffle maker and spread it out to the edges of the waffle maker to cover all the holes on it.
6. Close the waffle lid and cook for about 5 minutes or according to waffle maker's settings.
7. After the cooking cycle, remove the chaffle from the waffle maker with a plastic or silicone utensil. Transfer the chaffle to a wire rack to cool.
8. For the sloppy joe filling:
9. Heat up a large skillet over medium to high heat.
10. Add the ground beef and saute until the beef is browned.
11. Use a slotted spoon to transfer the ground beef to a paper towel lined plate to drain. Drain all the grease in the skillet.
12. Add the olive oil to the skillet and heat it up.
13. Add the onions, green pepper, celery and garlic. Saute until the veggies are tender, stirring often to prevent burning.
14. Stir in the tomato sauce, Worcestershire sauce, ketchup, maple syrup, salt and pepper.
15. Add the browned beef and bring the mixture to a boil. Reduce the heat and simmer for about 10 minutes.
16. Remove the skillet from heat.
17. Scoop the sloppy joe into the chaffles and enjoy.

Nutrition value per Servings:

Calories 168  Fat 15.5g  Carbohydrate 1.6g  Protein 5.4g  Sugars 0.6g

## Choco Peanut Butter Chaffle

Servings: 2

Cooking Time: 10 Minutes

**Ingredients:**

Filling:

3 tbsp all-natural peanut butter

2 tsp swerve sweetener

1 tsp vanilla extract

2 tbsp heavy cream

Chaffle:

¼ tsp baking powder

1 tbsp unsweetened cocoa powder

4 tsp almond flour

½ tsp vanilla extract

1 tbsp granulated swerve sweetener

1 large egg (beaten)

1 tbsp heavy cream

**Directions:**

1. For the chaffle:

2. Plug the waffle maker and preheat it. Spray it with a non-stick spray.

3. In a large mixing bowl, combine the almond flour, cocoa powder, baking powder and swerve.

4. Add the egg, vanilla extract and heavy cream. Mix until the ingredients are well combined and you form a smooth batter.

5. Pour some of the batter into the preheated waffle maker. Spread out the batter to the edges of the waffle maker to cover all the holes on the waffle iron.

6. Close the lid of the waffle iron and bake for about 5 minutes or according to waffle maker's settings.

7. After the baking cycle, use a plastic or silicone utensil to remove the chaffle from the waffle maker.

8. Repeat step 4 to 6 until you have cooked all the batter into chaffles.

9. Transfer the chaffles to a wire rack and let the chaffles cool completely.

10. For the filling:

11. Combine the vanilla, swerve, heavy cream and peanut butter in a bowl. Mix until the ingredients are well combined.

12. Spread the peanut butter frosting over the chaffles and serve.

13. Enjoy.

Nutrition value per Servings:

Calories 158  Fat 18.5g Carbohydrate 2.6g Protein 7.4g Sugars 0.6g

## Lobster Chaffle

Servings: 2

Cooking Time: 8 Minutes

**Ingredients:**

1 egg (beaten)

½ cup shredded mozzarella cheese ¼ tsp garlic powder

¼ tsp onion powder

1/8 tsp Italian seasoning Lobster Filling:

½ cup lobster tails (defrosted)

1 tbsp mayonnaise

1 tsp dried basil

1 tsp lemon juice

1 tbsp chopped green onion

**Directions:**

1. Plug the waffle maker to preheat it and spray it with a non-stick cooking spray.

2. In a mixing bowl, combine the mozzarella, Italian seasoning, garlic and onion powder. Add the egg and mix until the ingredients are well combined.

3. Pour an appropriate amount of the batter into the waffle maker and spread out the batter to cover all the holes on the waffle maker.

4. Close the waffle maker and cook for about minutes or according to your waffle maker's settings.

5. After the cooking cycle, use a plastic or silicone utensil to remove and transfer the chaffle to a wire rack to cool.

6. Repeat step 3 to 5 until you have cooked all the batter into chaffles.

7. For the filling, put the lobster tail in a mixing bowl and add the mayonnaise, basil and lemon juice.

Toss until the ingredients are well combine.

8. Fill the chaffles with the lobster mixture and garnish with chopped green onion.

9. Serve and enjoy.

Nutrition value per Servings:

Calories 168  Fat 15.5g Carbohydrate 1.6g Protein 5.4g Sugars 0.6g

## Simple Chaffles Without Maker

Servings:2

Cooking Time:5minutes

**Ingredients:**

1 tbsp. chia seeds

1 egg

1/2 cup cheddar cheese

pinch of salt

1 tbsp. avocado oil

**Directions:**

1. Heat your nonstick pan over medium heat

2. In a small bowl, mix together chia seeds, salt, egg, and cheese together

3. Grease pan with avocado oil.

4. Once the pan is hot, pour 2 tbsps. chaffle batter and cook for about 1-2 minutes.

5. Flip and cook for another 1-2 minutes.

6. Once chaffle is brown remove from pan.

7. Serve with berries on top and enjoy.

Nutrition value per Servings:

Calories 132  Fat 5.5g Carbohydrate 1.6g Protein 6.4g Sugars 0.6g

## Heart Shape Chaffles

Servings:2

Cooking Time:5 Minutes

**Ingredients:**

1 egg

1 cup mozzarella cheese

1 tsp baking powder

¼ cup almond flour

1 tbsp. coconut oil

**Directions:**

1. Heat your nonstick pan over medium heat.

2. Mix together all ingredients in a bowl.

3. Grease pan with avocado oil and place a heart shape cookie cutter over the pan.

4. Once the pan is hot, pour the batter equally in 2 cutters.

5. Cook for another 1-2 minutes.

6. Once chaffle is set, remove the cutter, flip and cook for another 1-2 minutes.

7. Once chaffles are brown, remove from the pan.

8. Serve hot and enjoy!

Nutrition value per Servings:

Calories 128  Fat 10.5g Carbohydrate 1.6g Protein 7.4g Sugars 0.6g

## Bacon Chaffles With Herb Dip

Servings: 2

Cooking Time: 10 Minutes

**Ingredients:**

Chaffles

1 organic egg, beaten

½ cup Swiss/Gruyere cheese blend, shredded

2 tablespoons cooked bacon pieces

1 tablespoon jalapeño pepper, chopped

Dip

¼ cup heavy cream

¼ teaspoon fresh dill, minced

Pinch of ground black pepper

**Directions:**

1. Preheat a mini waffle iron and then grease it.

2. For chaffles: In a medium bowl, put all ingredients and mix well.

3. Place half of the mixture into preheated waffle iron and cook for about 5 minutes.

4. Repeat with the remaining mixture.

5. Meanwhile, for dip: in a bowl, mix together the cream and stevia.

6. Serve warm chaffles alongside the dip.

Nutrition value:

Calories 210 Fat 13 g  Carbs 2.3 g  Fiber 0.1 g Sugar 0.7 g  Protein 11.9 g

## Broccoli Chaffles On Pan

Servings:4

Cooking Time:5 Minutes

**Ingredients:**

1 egg

1 cup cheddar cheese

½ cup broccoli chopped

1 tsp baking powder

1 pinch garlic powder

1 pinch salt

1 pinch black pepper

1 tbsp. coconut oil

**Directions:**

1. Heat your nonstick pan over medium heat.

2. Mix together all ingredients in a bowl.

3. Grease pan with oil.

4. Once the pan is hot, pour broccoli and cheese batter on greased pan

5. Cook for 1-2 minutes.

6. Flip and cook for another 1-2 minutes.

7. Once chaffles are brown, remove from the pan.

8. Serve with raspberries and melted coconut oil on top.

9. Enjoy!

Nutrition value per Servings:

Calories 198  Fat 16.5g Carbohydrate 1.6g Protein 5.4g Sugars 0.6g

## Chicken Chaffles With Tzatziki

Servings: 2

Cooking Time: 12 Minutes

**Ingredients:**

Chaffles

1 organic egg, beaten

1/3 cup grass-fed cooked chicken, chopped 1/3 cup mozzarella cheese, shredded

¼ teaspoon garlic, minced

¼ teaspoon dried basil, crushed

Tzatziki

¼ cup plain Greek yogurt

½ of small cucumber, peeled, seeded, and chopped

1 teaspoon olive oil

½ teaspoon fresh lemon juice

Pinch of ground black pepper

¼ tablespoon fresh dill, chopped

½ of garlic clove, peeled

**Directions:**

1. Preheat a mini waffle iron and then grease it.

2. For chaffles: In a medium bowl, put all ingredients and with your hands, mix until well combined. Place half of the mixture into preheated waffle iron and cook for about 4-6 minutes.

3. Repeat with the remaining mixture.

4. Meanwhile, for tzatziki: in a food processor, place all the ingredients and pulse until well combined.

5. Serve warm chaffles alongside the tzatziki.

Nutrition value:

Calories 131 Fat 5 g Carbs 4.7 g Fiber 0.3 g Protein 13 g

## Cereal And Walnut Chaffle

Servings: 2

Cooking Time: 6 Minutes

**Ingredients:**

1 milliliter of cereal flavoring ¼ tsp baking powder

1 tsp granulated swerve

1/8 tsp xanthan gum

1 tbsp butter (melted)

½ tsp coconut flour

2 tbsp toasted walnut (chopped)

1 tbsp cream cheese

2 tbsp almond flour

1 large egg (beaten)

¼ tsp cinnamon

1/8 tsp nutmeg

**Directions:**

1. Plug the waffle maker to preheat it and spray it with a non-stick spray.

2. In a mixing bowl, whisk together the egg, cereal flavoring, cream cheese and butter.

3. In another mixing bowl, combine the coconut flour, almond flour, cinnamon, nutmeg, swerve, xanthan gum and baking powder.

4. Pour the egg mixture into the flour mixture and mix until you form a smooth batter. 5. Fold in the chopped walnuts.

6. Pour in an appropriate amount of the batter into the waffle maker and spread out the batter to the edges to cover all the holes on the waffle maker.

7. Close the waffle maker and cook for

about 3 minutes or according to your waffle maker's settings.

8. After the cooking cycle, use a plastic or silicone utensil to remove the chaffle from the waffle maker.

9. Repeat step 6 to 8 until you have cooked all the batter into chaffles.

10. Serve and top with sour cream or heavy cream.

Nutrition value per Servings:

Calories 158  Fat 18.5g Carbohydrate 1.6g Protein 4.4g Sugars 0.6g

## Cornbread Chaffle

Servings: 3

Cooking Time: 12 Minutes

**Ingredients:**

1 ½ tbsp melted butter

3 tbsp almond flour

1 milliliter cornbread flavoring

2 tbsp Mexican blend cheese

2 tbsp shredded parmesan cheese

1 small jalapeno (seeded and sliced)

2 tsp swerve sweetener

1 large egg (beaten)

½ tsp all spice

**Directions:**

1. Plug the waffle maker to preheat it and spray it with a non-stick cooking spray.

2. In a mixing bowl, combine almond flour, jalapeno, all spice, baking powder and swerve.

3. In another mixing bowl, whisk together the egg, butter and cornbread flavoring.

4. Pour the egg mixture into the flour mixture and mix until you form a smooth batter. Stir in the cheese.

5. Sprinkle some parmesan cheese over the waffle maker. Pour an appropriate amount of the batter into the waffle maker and spread out the batter to the edges to cover all the holes on the waffle maker. Sprinkle some parmesan over the batter

6. Close the waffle maker and bake for about 5 minutes or according to you waffle maker's settings.

7. After the baking cycle, remove the chaffle from the waffle maker with a plastic or silicone utensil.

8. Repeat step 5 to 7 until you have cooked all the batter into chaffles.

9. Serve warm with your desired topping and enjoy.

Nutrition value per Servings:

Calories 198  Fat 18.5g Carbohydrate 1.6g Protein 7.4g Sugars 0.6g

## Midday Chaffle Snacks

Servings: 4

Cooking Time: 5 Minutes

**Ingredients:**

4 minutesi Chaffles

2 oz. coconut flakes

2 oz. kiwi slice

2 oz. raspberry

2 oz. almonds chopped

<u>Chaffle ingredients:</u>

1 egg

1/2 cup mozzarella cheese

1 tsp stevia

1 tsp vanilla

2 tbsps. almond flour

**Directions:**

1. Make 4 minutesi chaffles with the chaffle ingredients.

2. Arrange coconut flakes, raspberries, almonds and raspberries on each chaffle.

3. Serve and enjoy keto snacks

Nutrition value per Servings:

Calories 168  Fat 15.5g Carbohydrate 1.6g Protein 5.4g Sugars 0.6g

## Spinach Chaffle

Servings: 2

Cooking Time: 10 Minutes

**Ingredients:**

1 egg (beaten)

¼ tsp pepper or to taste

½ tsp Italian seasoning

1/8 tsp thyme

½ cup finely chopped spinach

½ cup shredded cheddar cheese

¼ cup parmesan cheese for sprinkling

**Directions:**

1. Plug the waffle maker to preheat it and spray it with a non-stick cooking spray.

2. In a mixing bowl, combine the cheddar, spinach, Italian seasoning, thyme and pepper. Add the egg and mix until the ingredients are well combined.

3. Sprinkle some parmesan cheese over the waffle maker. Pour ½ of the batter into the waffle maker and spread out the batter to cover all the holes on the waffle maker. Sprinkle some cheese over the batter.

4. Close the waffle maker and cook for 5 minutes or according to your waffle maker's settings.

5. After the cooking cycle, use a silicone or plastic utensil to remove the chaffle from the waffle maker.

6. Repeat step 3 to 5 to make the second chaffle.

7. Serve chaffle and top with sour cream or use the chaffles for sandwich.

Nutrition value per Servings:

Calories 218  Fat 19.5g Carbohydrate 0.6g Protein 7.4g Sugars 0.6g

## Bbq Chicken Chaffle

Servings: 2

Cooking Time: 8 Minutes

**Ingredients:**

1 tbsp sugar free BBQ sauce

1/3 cup cooked chicken (diced)

1 egg (beaten)

1 tbsp almond flour

1 red bell pepper (chopped)

½ cup shredded mozzarella cheese ¼ tsp garlic powder

1/4 tsp oregano

**Directions:**

1. Plug the waffle maker to preheat it and spray it with a non-stick cooking spray.

2. In a mixing bowl, whisk together the egg and BBQ sauce. Add the almond flour, mozzarella cheese, pepper, garlic and oregano. Mix until the well combined.

3. Add the diced chicken and mix.

4. Pour and appropriate amount of the batter

into the waffle maker and spread the batter to the edges to cover all the holes on the waffle maker.

5. Close the waffle and cook for about 4 minutes.

6. After the cooking cycle, use a silicone or plastic utensil to remove and transfer the chaffle to a wire rack to cool.

7. Repeat step 4 to 6 until you have cooked all the batter into chaffles.

8. Serve warm and enjoy.

Nutrition value per Servings:

Calories 168  Fat 15.5g Carbohydrate 1.6g Protein 5.4g Sugars 0.6g

## Shirataki Rice Chaffle

Servings: 4

Cooking Time: 20 Minutes

**Ingredients:**

2 tbsp almond flour

½ tsp oregano

1 bag of shirataki rice

1 tsp baking powder

1 cup shredded cheddar cheese

2 eggs (beaten)

**Directions:**

1. Rinse the shirataki rice with warm water for about 30 seconds and rinse it.

2. Plug the waffle maker to preheat it and spray it with a non-stick cooking spray.

3. In a mixing bowl, combine the rinsed rice, almond flour, baking powder, oregano and shredded cheese. Add the eggs and mix until the ingredients are well combined.

4. Fill the waffle maker with an appropriate

amount of the batter and spread out the batter to the edges to cover all the holes on the waffle maker.

5. Close the waffle make and cook for about minutes or according to you waffle maker's settings.

6. After the cooking cycle, use a silicone or plastic utensil to remove the chaffles from the waffle maker.

7. Repeat step 4 to 6 until you have cooked all the batter into chaffles.

8. Serve and enjoy.

Nutrition value per Servings:

Calories 208  Fat 13.5g Carbohydrate 0.7g Protein 8.2g Sugars 0.6g

## Ham Chaffle

Servings: 1

Cooking Time: 5 Minutes

**Ingredients:**

1 large egg

4 tbsp chopped ham steak

1 scallion (chopped)

½ cup shredded mozzarella cheese ¼ tsp garlic salt

1/8 tsp Italian seasoning

½ jalapeno pepper (chopped)

**Directions:**

1. Plug the waffle maker to preheat it and spray it with a non-stick spray.

2. In a mixing bowl, combine the cheese, Italian seasoning, jalapeno, scallion, ham and garlic salt. Add the egg and mix until the ingredients are well combined.

3. Fill the waffle maker with an appropriate amount of the batter. Spread the batter to the

edges of the waffle maker to cover all the holes on it.

4. Close the waffle maker and cook for about minutes or according to waffle maker's settings.

5. After the cooking cycle, remove the chaffle from the waffle maker with plastic or silicone utensil.

6. Serve and enjoy.

Nutrition value per Servings:

Calories 208  Fat 13.5g Carbohydrate 0.7g Protein 8.2g Sugars 0.6g

# Zucchini Bacon Chaffles

Servings: 2

Cooking Time: 12 Minutes

**Ingredients:**

1 cup grated zucchini

1 tbsp bacon bits (finely chopped)

¼ cup shredded mozzarella cheese

½ cup shredded parmesan

½ tsp salt or to taste

½ tsp ground black pepper or to taste ½ tsp onion powder

¼ tsp nutmeg

2 eggs

**Directions:**

1. Add ¼ tsp salt to the grated zucchini and let it sit for about 5 minutes.

2. Put the grated zucchini in a clean towel and squeeze out excess water.

3. Plug the waffle maker and preheat it. Spray it with non-stick spray.

4. Break the eggs into a mixing bowl and beat.

5. Add the grated zucchini, bacon bit, nutmeg, onion powder, pepper, salt and mozzarella.

6. Add ¾ of the parmesan cheese. You have to set aside some parmesan cheese.

7. Mix until the ingredients are well combined.

8. Fill the preheated waffle maker with the batter and spread out the batter to the edge to cover all the holes on the waffle maker.

9. Close the waffle maker lid and cook until the chaffle is golden brown and crispy. The zucchini chaffle may take longer than other chaffles to get crispy.

10. After the baking cycle, use a plastic or silicone utensil to remove the chaffle from the waffle maker.

11. Repeat step 8 to 10 until you have cooked all the batter into chaffles.

12. Serve and enjoy.

Nutrition value per Servings:

Calories 208  Fat 13.5g Carbohydrate 0.7g Protein 8.2g Sugars 0.6g

# Spinach Artichoke Chaffle With Bacon

Servings: 2

Cooking Time: 8 Minutes

**Ingredients:**

4 slices of bacon

½ cup chopped spinach

1/3 cup marinated artichoke (chopped)

1 egg

¼ tsp garlic powder

¼ tsp smoked paprika

2 tbsp cream cheese (softened)

1/3 cup shredded mozzarella

**Directions:**

1. Heat up a frying pan and add the bacon slices. Sear until both sides of the bacon slices are browned. Use a slotted spoon to transfer the bacon to a paper towel line plate to drain.

2. Once the bacon slices are cool, chop them into bits and set aside.

3. Plug the waffle maker to preheat it and spray it with a non-stick cooking spray.

4. In a mixing bowl, combine mozzarella, garlic, paprika, cream cheese and egg. Mix until the ingredients are well combined.

5. Add the spinach, artichoke and bacon bit. Mix until they are well incorporated.

6. Pour an appropriate amount of the batter into the waffle maker and spread the batter to the edges to cover all the holes on the waffle maker.

7. Close the waffle maker and cook 4 minutes or more, according to your waffle maker's settings.

8. After the cooking cycle, use a silicone or plastic utensil to remove the chaffle from the waffle maker.

9. Repeat step 6 to 8 until you have cooked all the batter into chaffles.

10. Serve and top with sour cream as desired.

Nutrition value per Servings:

Calories 258  Fat 16.5g Carbohydrate 1.7g Protein 8.2g Sugars 0.6g

## Chocolate Cannoli Chaffle

Servings: 4

Cooking Time: 10 Minutes

**Ingredients:**

Cannoli Topping:

2 tbsp granulated swerve

4 tbsp cream cheese

¼ tsp vanilla extract

¼ tsp cinnamon

6 tbsp ricotta cheese

1 tsp lemon juice

Chaffle:

3 tbsp almond flour

1 tbsp swerve

1 egg

1/8 tsp baking powder

3/4 tbsp butter (melted)

½ tsp nutmeg

1 tbsp sugar free chocolate chips 1/8 tsp vanilla extract

**Directions:**

1. Plug the waffle maker to preheat it and spray it with a non-stick spray.

2. In a mixing bowl, whisk together the egg, butter and vanilla extract.

3. In another mixing bowl, combine the almond flour, baking powder, nutmeg, chocolate chips and swerve.

4. Pour the egg mixture into the flour mixture and mix until the ingredients are well combined and you have formed a smooth batter.

5. Fill your waffle maker with an appropriate amount of the batter and spread out the batter to the edged to cover all the holes on the waffle maker.

6. Close the waffle maker and cook for about 4 minutes or according to waffle maker's settings.

7. After the baking cycle, remove the chaffle from the waffle maker with a plastic or silicone utensil.

8. Repeat step 5 to 7 until you have cooked all the batter into waffles.

9. For the topping, pour the cream cheese into a blender and add the ricotta, lemon juice, cinnamon, vanilla and swerve sweetener. Blend until smooth and fluffy.

10. Spread the cream over the chaffles and enjoy.

Nutrition value per Servings:

Calories 208  Fat 18.5g Carbohydrate 1.7g Protein 4.2g Sugars 0.9g

## Broccoli And Cheese Chaffle

Servings: 1

Cooking Time: 15 Minutes

**Ingredients:**

1/3 cup broccoli (finely chopped) ½ tsp oregano

1/8 tsp salt or to taste

1/8 tsp ground black pepper or to taste' ½ tsp garlic powder

½ tsp onion powder

1 egg (beaten)

4 tbsp shredded cheddar cheese

**Directions:**

1. Plug the waffle maker to preheat it and spray it with a non-stick cooking spray.

2. In a mixing bowl, combine the cheese, oregano, pepper, garlic, salt and onion. Add the egg and mix until the ingredients are well combined.

3. Fold in the chopped broccoli.

4. Pour an appropriate amount of the batter into your waffle maker and spread out the batter to the edges to cover all the holes on the waffle maker.

5. Close the waffle maker and cook for about 6-8 until the chaffle is browned. Cook time may vary in some waffle makers.

6. After the cooking cycle, use a silicone or plastic utensil to remove the chaffle from the waffle maker.

7. Repeat step 4 to 6 until you have cooked all the batter into chaffles.

8. Serve and top with sour cream as desired.

Nutrition value per Servings:

Calories 108  Fat 12.5g Carbohydrate 2.1g Protein 5.3g Sugars 1.1g

## Eggnog Chaffle

Servings: 2

Cooking Time: 5 Minutes

**Ingredients:**

2 tbsp coconut flour

½ tsp baking powder

1 tsp cinnamon

2 tbsp cream cheese

2 tsp swerve

1/8 tsp salt

1/8 tsp nutmeg

1 egg (beaten)

4 tbsp keto eggnog

Eggnog Filling:

4 tbsp keto eggnog

¼ tsp vanilla extract

¼ cup heavy cream

2 tsp granulated swerve 1/8 tsp nutmeg

**Directions:**

1. Plug the waffle maker to preheat it and spray it with a non-stick cooking spray.

2. Combine the coconut flour, baking powder,

swerve, salt, cinnamon and nutmeg in a mixing bowl.

3. In another mixing bowl, whisk together the eggnog, cream cheese and egg.

4. Pour in the egg mixture into the flour mixture and mix until the ingredients are well combined.

5. Fill the waffle maker with an appropriate amount of the batter. Spread out the batter to cover all the holes on the waffle maker.

6. Close the waffle maker and cook for about 5 minutes or according to your waffle maker's settings.

7. After the baking cycle, remove the chaffle from the waffle maker with a plastic or silicone utensil.

8. Repeat step 5 to 7 until you have cooked all the batter into chaffles.

9. For the eggnog cream, whisk together the cream cheese, heavy cream, vanilla and eggnog. Add the swerve and nutmeg; mix until the ingredients are well combined.

10. Top the chaffles with the eggnog cream and enjoy

Nutrition value per Servings:

Calories 208  Fat 13.5g Carbohydrate 0.7g Protein 8.2g Sugars 0.6g

## Double Cheese Chaffles With Mayonnaise Dip

Servings: 2

Cooking Time: 8 Minutes

**Ingredients:**

Chaffles

½ cup mozzarella cheese, shredded

1 tablespoon Parmesan cheese, shredded

1 organic egg

¾ teaspoon coconut flour

¼ teaspoon organic baking powder

1/8 teaspoon Italian seasoning

Pinch of salt

Dip

¼ cup mayonnaise

Pinch of garlic powder

Pinch of ground black pepper

**Directions:**

1. Preheat a mini waffle iron and then grease it.

2. For chaffles: In a medium bowl, put all ingredients and with a fork, mix until well combined. Place half of the mixture into preheated waffle iron and cook for about 3-4 minutes.

3. Repeat with the remaining mixture.

4. Meanwhile, for dip: in a bowl, mix together the cream and stevia.

5. Serve warm chaffles alongside the dip.

Nutrition value:

Calories 248   Fat 24.3 g Carbs 1.g  Fiber 0.4 g Sugar 0.2 g  Protein 5.9 g

## Carrot Cake Chaffle

Servings: 10

Cooking Time: 18 Minutes

**Ingredients:**

1 tbsp toasted pecans (chopped)

2 tbsp granulated swerve

1 tsp pumpkin spice

1 tsp baking powder

½ shredded carrots

2 tbsp butter (melted)

1 tsp cinnamon

1 tsp vanilla extract (optional)

2 tbsp heavy whipping cream ¾ cup almond flour

1 egg (beaten)

Butter cream cheese frosting:

½ cup cream cheese (softened)

¼ cup butter (softened)

½ tsp vanilla extract

¼ cup granulated swerve

**Directions:**

1. Plug the chaffle maker to preheat it and spray it with a non-stick cooking spray.

2. In a mixing bowl, combine the almond flour, cinnamon, carrot, pumpkin spice and swerve.

3. In another mixing bowl, whisk together the eggs, butter, heavy whipping cream and vanilla extract.

4. Pour the flour mixture into the egg mixture and mix until you form a smooth batter.

5. Fold in the chopped pecans.

6. Pour in an appropriate amount of the batter into your waffle maker and spread out the batter to the edges to cover all the holes on the waffle maker.

7. Close the waffle maker and cook for about 3 minutes or according to your waffle maker's settings.

8. After the cooking cycle, use a plastic or silicone utensil to remove the chaffle from the waffle maker.

9. Repeat step 6 to 8 until you have cooked all the batter into chaffles.

10. For the frosting, combine the cream cheese and cutter int a mixer and mix until well combined.

11. Add the swerve and vanilla extract and slowly until the sweetener is well incorporated.

Mix on high

until the frosting is fluffy.

12. Place one chaffle on a flat surface and spread some cream frosting over it. Layer another chaffle over the first one a spread some cream over it too.

13. Repeat step 12 until you have assembled all the chaffles into a cake.

14. Cut and serve.

Nutrition value per Servings:

Calories 208  Fat 13.5g  Carbohydrate 0.7g  Protein 8.2g  Sugars 0.6g

## Chaffles With Chocolate Balls

Servings: 2

Cooking Time: 5 Minutes

**Ingredients:**

1/4 cup heavy cream

½ cup unsweetened cocoa powder 1/4 cup coconut meat

Chaffle ingredients:

1 egg

½ cup mozzarella cheese

**Directions:**

1. Make 2 chaffles with chaffle ingredients.

2. Meanwhile, mix together all ingredients in a mixing bowl.

3. Make two balls from the mixture and freeze in the freezer for about 2 hours until set.

4. Serve with keto chaffles and enjoy!

Nutrition value per Servings:

Calories 178  Fat 10.5g  Carbohydrate 1.7g  Protein 8.6g  Sugars 1.6g

## Bacon Jalapeno Popper Chaffle

Servings: 3

Cooking Time: 10 Minutes

**Ingredients:**

4 slices bacon (diced)

3 eggs

3 tbsp coconut flour

1 tsp baking powder

¼ tsp salt

½ tsp oregano

A pinch of onion powder

A pinch of garlic powder

½ cup cream cheese

1 cup shredded cheddar cheese

2 jalapeno pepper (deseeded and chopped) ½ cup sour cream

**Directions:**

1. Plug the waffle maker to preheat it and spray it with a non-stick cooking spray.

2. Heat up a frying pan over medium to high heat. Add the bacon and saute until the bacon is brown and crispy.

3. Use a slotted spoon to transfer the bacon to a paper towel lined plate to drain.

4. In a mixing bowl, combine the coconut flour, baking powder, salt, oregano, onion and garlic.

5. In another mixing bowl, whisk together the egg and cream cheese until well combined.

6. Add the cheddar cheese and mix. Pour in the flour mixture and mix until you form a smooth batter.

7. Pour an appropriate amount of the batter into the waffle maker and spread the batter to the edges to cover all the holes on the waffle maker.

8. Close the waffle maker and cook for about 5 minutes or according to waffle maker's settings.

9. After the cooking cycle, use a plastic or silicone utensil to remove the chaffle from the waffle maker.

10. Repeat step 7 to 9 until you have cooked all the batter into chaffles.

11. Serve warm and top with sour cream, crispy bacon and jalapeno slices.

Nutrition value per Servings:

Calories 208  Fat 13.5g Carbohydrate 0.7g Protein 8.2g Sugars 0.6g

## Apple Pie Chaffle

Servings: 2

Cooking Time: 6 Minutes

**Ingredients:**

1 egg (beaten)

1 tbsp almond flour

1 big apple (finely chopped)

1 tbsp heavy whipping cream

1 tsp cinnamon

1 tbsp granulated swerve

½ tsp vanilla extract

1/3 cup mozzarella cheese

Topping:

¼ tbsp sugar free maple syrup

**Directions:**

1. Plug the waffle maker and preheat it. Spray it with non-stick spray.

2. In a large mixing bowl, combine the swerve, almond flour, mozzarella, cinnamon

and chopped apple.

3. Add the eggs, vanilla extract and heavy whipping cream. Mix until all the ingredients are well combined.

4. Fill the waffle maker with the batter and spread out the batter to the edges of the waffle maker to all the holes on it.

5. Close the lid of the waffle maker and cook for about 4 minute or according to waffle maker's settings.

6. After the cooking cycle, remove the chaffle from the waffle maker with a plastic or silicone utensil.

7. Repeat step 4 to 6 until you have cooked all the batter into chaffles.

8. Serve and top with maple syrup.

Nutrition value per Servings:

Calories 228 Fat 17.5g Carbohydrate 2.7g Protein 5.2g Sugars 2g

## French Toast Chaffle Sticks

Servings: 8

Cooking Time: 40 Minutes

**Ingredients:**

6 organic eggs

2 cups mozzarella cheese, shredded ¼ cup coconut flour

2 tablespoons powdered erythritol

1 teaspoon ground cinnamon

1 tablespoon butter, melted

**Directions:**

1. Preheat your oven to 350°F and line a large baking sheet with a greased piece of foil.

2. Preheat a waffle iron and then grease it.

3. In a bowl, add 4 eggs and beat well.

4. Add the cheese, coconut flour, erythritol and ½ teaspoon of cinnamon and mix until well combined.

5. Place ¼ of the mixture into preheated waffle iron and cook for about 6-8 minutes.

6. Repeat with the remaining mixture.

7. Set the chaffles aside to cool.

8. Cut each chaffle into 4 strips.

9. In a large bowl, add the remaining eggs and cinnamon and beat until well combined.

10. Dip the chaffle sticks in the egg mixture evenly.

11. Arrange the chaffle sticks onto the prepared baking sheet in a single layer.

12. Bake for about 10 minutes.

13. Remove the baking sheet from oven and brush the top of each stick with the melted butter.

14. Flip the stick and bake for about 6-8 minutes.

15. Serve immediately.

Nutrition value:

Calories 96 Fat 6.3 g Carbs 3.2 g Fiber 1.7 g Sugar 0.3 g Protein 6.7 g

## Sweet Brownie Chaffle

Servings: 2

Cooking Time: 14 Minutes

**Ingredients:**

1 large egg

¼ tsp baking powder

½ tsp vanilla extract

½ tsp ginger

2 tbsp cream cheese (melted)

1 ½ tsp cocoa powder

1 tbsp swerve

Topping:

½ tsp vanilla extract.

½ tsp cinnamon

¼ tsp liquid stevia

2 tbsp heavy cream

6 tbsp cream cheese (melted)

**Directions:**

1. Plug the waffle maker to preheat it and spray it with a non-stick cooking spray.

2. In a mixing bowl, combine the swerve, cocoa powder, ginger and baking powder.

3. In another mixing bowl, whisk together the cream cheese, egg and vanilla.

4. Pour the cocoa powder mixture into the egg mixture and mix until the ingredients are well combined.

5. Fill the waffle maker with an appropriate amount of batter and spread the batter to the edges to cover all the holes on the waffle maker.

6. Close the waffle maker and cook for about 7 minutes or according to your waffle maker's settings.

7. After the cooking cycle, use a silicone or plastic utensil to remove the chaffle from the waffle maker. Set aside to cool completely

8. Repeat step 5 to 7 until all the batter has been cooked into chaffles.

9. For the filling, combine the vanilla, cream cheese, stevia, cinnamon and heavy cream in a mixing bowl. Mix until well combined.

10. Spread the cream frosting over the surface of one chaffle and cover with another chaffle.

11. Place the filled chaffles in a refrigerator and chill for about 15 minutes.

12. Serve and enjoy.

Nutrition value per Servings:

Calories 238  Fat 16.5g Carbohydrate 1.7g Protein 8.2g Sugars 0.6g

## Savory Chaffle Stick

Servings: 16

Cooking Time: 25 Minutes

**Ingredients:**

6 eggs

2 cups shredded mozzarella cheese A pinch of salt

½ tsp ground black pepper or to taste ½ tsp baking powder

4 tbsp coconut flour

1 tsp onion powder

1 tsp garlic powder

1 tsp oregano

¼ tsp Italian seasoning

1 tbsp olive oil

1 tbsp melted butter

**Directions:**

1. Plug the waffle maker to preheat it and spray it with a non-stick cooking spray.

2. Break 4 of the eggs into a mixing bowl and beat. Add the coconut flour, baking powder, salt, cheese and Italian seasoning. Combine until the ingredients are well combined. Add more flour if the mixture is too thick.

3. Pour an appropriate amount of the batter into the waffle maker and spread out the batter to cover all the holes on the waffle maker.

4. Cover the waffle maker and cook for about 7 minutes or according to your waffle maker's settings. Make sure the chaffle is browned.

5. After the cooking cycle, use a plastic or silicone utensil to remove the chaffle form the waffle maker.

6. Repeat step 3 to 5 until you have cooked all the batter into chaffles.

7. Cut the chaffles into sticks. Each mini chaffle should make about 4 sticks.

8. Preheat the oven to 350°F. Line a baking sheet with parchment paper and grease it with the melted butter.

9. Break the remaining two eggs into another mixing bowl and beat.

10. In another mixing bowl, combine the oregano, pepper, garlic and onion.

11. Dip one chaffle stick into the egg. Bring it out and hold it for a few seconds to allow excess liquid to drip off.

12. Dip the wet chaffle stick into the seasoning mixture and make sure it is coated with seasoning. Drop it on the baking sheet.

13. Repeat step 11 and 12 until all the chaffle sticks are coated.

14. Arrange the chaffle sticks into the baking sheet in a single layer.

15. Place the baking sheet in the oven and bake for 10 minutes.

16. Remove the baking sheet from the oven, brush the oil over the sticks and flip them.

17. Return it to the oven and bake for an additional 6 minutes or until the stick are golden brown.

18. Remove the sticks from the oven and let them cool for a few minutes.

19. Serve and enjoy.

Nutrition value per Servings:

Calories 208  Fat 13.5g Carbohydrate 0.7g Protein 8.2g Sugars 0.6g

## Keto Avocado Chaffle Toast

Servings: 1

Cooking Time: 8 Minutes

**Ingredients:**

Avocado Topping:

1 tbsp butter

1 green bell pepper (finely chopped) ½ cup feta cheese

½ avocado

1 tsp lemon juice

¼ tsp nutmeg

¼ tsp onion powder

½ tsp ground black pepper or to taste

Chaffle:

½ mozzarella cheese

1 egg (beaten)

1 tbsp Almond flour

1 tsp cinnamon

½ tsp baking soda

**Directions:**

1. Plug the waffle maker tom preheat it and spray it with a non-stick spray.

2. In a mixing bowl, combine the mozzarella, almond flour, baking soda and cinnamon. Add the egg and mix until the ingredients are well combined and you form a smooth batter.

3. Fill the waffle maker with appropriate amount of the batter and spread the batter to the edges of the waffle maker to cover all the holes on the waffle iron.

4. Close the lid of the waffle maker and cook for about 3 to minutes or according to waffle maker's settings.

5. Meanwhile, dice the avocado into a bowl and mash until smooth. Add the bell pepper, nutmeg, onion powder, ground pepper and lemon juice. Mix until well combined.

6. After the baking cycle, remove the chaffle the waffle maker with a silicone or plastic utensil. 7. Repeat step 3, 4 and 6 until you have cooked all the batter into chaffles.

8. Brush the butter over the chaffles. Spread the avocado mixture over the chaffles. Top with shredded feta cheese.

9. Serve and enjoy.

Nutrition value per Servings:

Calories 208  Fat 15.5g  Carbohydrate 1.7g  Protein 8.2g  Sugars 0.6g

## Okonomiyaki Chaffle

Servings: 1

Cooking Time: 8 Minutes

**Ingredients:**

4 tbsp finely shredded cabbage

2 eggs (beaten)

1/3 cup shredded mozzarella cheese

1 slice of bacon (finely chopped) A pinch of salt

1 tsp tamari sauce

1 tbsp chopped green onion

1/8 tsp ground black pepper or to taste

Topping:

1 tbsp kewpie mayonnaise or American mayonnaise

2 tbsp bonito flakes

2 tsp Worcestershire sauce

**Directions:**

1. Heat up a frying pan over medium to high heat and add the chopped bacon.

2. Sear until the bacon is brown and crispy. Use a slotted spoon to transfer the bacon to a paper towel lined plate to drain.

3. Plug the waffle maker to preheat it and spray it with a non-stick spray.

4. In a mixing bowl, combine the crispy bacon, cabbage, cheese, onion, pepper and salt. Add the egg and tamari. Mix until the ingredients are well combined.

5. Pour an appropriate amount of the batter into the waffle maker and spread out the batter to cover all the holes on the waffle maker.

6. Close the waffle maker and cook for about 4 minutes or according to your waffle maker's settings.

7. After the cooking cycle, use a silicone or plastic utensil to remove the chaffle from the waffle maker.

8. Repeat step 5 to 7 until you have cooked all the batter into chaffles.

9. Top the chaffles with sauce, mayonnaise and bonito flakes.

10. Serve warm and enjoy.

Nutrition value per Servings:

Calories 248  Fat 10.5g  Carbohydrate 0.6g  Protein 7.6g  Sugars 1.2g

## Blt Chaffle Sandwich

Servings: 1

Cooking Time: 10 Minutes

**Ingredients:**

Sandwich Filling:

2 strips of bacon

A pinch of salt

2 slices tomato

1 tbsp mayonnaise

3 pieces lettuce

Chaffle:

1 egg (beaten)

½ cup shredded mozzarella cheese ¼ tsp onion powder

¼ tsp garlic powder

½ tsp curry powder

**Directions:**

1. Plug the waffle maker and preheat it. Spray it with a non-stick spray.

2. In a mixing bowl, combine the cheese, onion powder, garlic and curry powder. Add the egg and mix until the ingredients are well combined.

3. Fill the waffle maker with the batter and spread the batter to the edges of the waffle maker to cover all the holes on the waffle iron.

4. Close the lid of the waffle maker and cook for about minutes or according to waffle maker's settings.

5. After the cooking cycle, remove the chaffle from the waffle maker using a silicone or plastic utensil.

6. Repeat step 3 to 5 until you have cooked all the batter into chaffles. Set the chaffles aside to cool.

7. Heat up a skillet over medium heat. Add the bacon strips and sear until all sides of the bacon is browned, turning and pressing the bacon while searing.

8. Use a slotted spoon to transfer the bacon to a paper towel lined plate to drain.

9. Place the chaffles on a flat surface and spread mayonnaise over the face of the chaffles.

10. Divide the lettuce into two and layer it on one portion on both chaffles.

11. Layer the tomatoes on one of the chaffles and sprinkle with salt. Layer the bacon over the tomatoes and place the other chaffle over the one containing the bacon.

12. Press and serve immediately. Enjoy!!!

Nutrition value per Servings:

Calories 208  Fat 13.5g  Carbohydrate 0.7g  Protein 8.2g  Sugars 0.6g

# METRIC CONVERSION

## Weights

| IMPERIAL | METRIC | IMPERIAL | METRIC |
|---|---|---|---|
| ½ oz | 15g | 7oz | 200g |
| ¾ oz | 20g | 8oz (½lb) | 230g |
| 1oz | 30g | 9oz | 255g |
| 2oz | 60g | 10oz | 285g |
| 3oz | 85g | 11oz | 310g |
| 4oz (¼lb) | 115g | 12oz (¾lb) | 340g |
| 5oz | 140g | 13oz | 370g |
| 6oz | 170g | 14oz | 400g |

| IMPERIAL | METRIC |
|---|---|
| 15oz | 425g |
| 16oz (1lb) | 450g |
| 24oz | 680g |
| 32oz (2lb) | 0.9kg |
| 48oz (3lb) | 1.4kg |
| 64oz (4lb) | 1.8kg |

1kg = 35oz/2.2lbs

**g** · **oz**

1oz = 28.35g   1g = 0.035oz

## OVEN TEMPS

| Gas | °F | °C | |
|---|---|---|---|
| ½ | 250 | 120 | VERY SLOW |
| 1 | 275 | 140 | |
| 2 | 300 | 150 | SLOW |
| 3 | 325 | 170 | |
| 4 | 350 | 180 | MODERATE |
| 5 | 375 | 190 | |
| 6 | 400 | 200 | MOD. HOT |
| 7 | 425 | 220 | |
| 8 | 450 | 230 | HOT |
| 9 | 475 | 240 | VERY HOT |

°C × 1.8 + 32 = °F
°F − 32 ÷ 1.8 = °C

## LIQUIDS

| PNT | METRIC | CUP | VOL |
|---|---|---|---|
| | 100ml | | 3½ |
| | 125ml | ½ | 4½ |
| ¼ | 150ml | | 5 |
| | 200ml | | 7 |
| | 250ml | 1 | 9 |
| ½ | 275ml | | 10 |
| | 300ml | | 11 |
| | 400ml | | 14 |
| | 500ml | 2 | 18 |
| 1 | 570ml | | 20 |
| | 750ml | 3 | 26 |
| 1¾ | 1.0L | 4 | 35 |
| 2 | 1.1L | | 40 |
| | 1.3L | 5 | 46 |
| 3 | 1.7L | | 60 |
| | 2.0L | 8 | 70 |

## CUPS

| | IMP. | METRIC |
|---|---|---|
| Flour | 5oz | 140g |
| Caster Sugar | 8oz | 225g |
| Brown Sugar | 6oz | 170g |
| Butter | 8oz | 225g |
| Sultanas/Raisins | 7oz | 200g |
| Currants | 5oz | 140g |
| Golden Syrup | 12oz | 340g |
| Uncooked Rice | 7oz | 200g |
| Grated Cheese | 4oz | 110g |

**Water**
Boils at: 100°C  212°F
Freezes at: 0°C  32°F

**1 Litre** = 1.76 Pints
**1 Pint** UK = 568 ml
**1 Pint** US = 16 fl oz

**1 fl oz** = 28.41 ml
**1 ml** = 0.035 fl oz
**1 Cup** US = 250 ml